About Island Press

Island Press, a nonprofit organization, publishes, markets, and distributes the most advanced thinking on the conservation of our natural resources—books about soil, land, water, forests, wildlife, and hazardous and toxic wastes. These books are practical tools used by public officials, business and industry leaders, natural resource managers, and concerned citizens working to solve both local and global resource problems.

Founded in 1978, Island Press reorganized in 1984 to meet the increasing demand for substantive books on all resource-related issues. Island Press publishes and distributes under its own imprint and offers these services to other nonprofit organizations.

Support for Island Press is provided by Apple Computers, Inc., The Mary Reynolds Babcock Foundation, The Educational Foundation of America, The Charles Engelhard Foundation, The Ford Foundation, The George Gund Foundation, The William and Flora Hewlett Foundation, The Joyce Foundation, The J. M. Kaplan Fund, The John D. and Catherine T. MacArthur Foundation, The Andrew W. Mellon Foundation, The Joyce Mertz-Gilmore Foundation, The New-Land Foundation, Northwest Area Foundation, The Jessie Smith Noyes Foundation, The J. N. Pew, Jr. Charitable Trust, The Rockefeller Brothers Fund, The Florence and John Schumann Foundation, The Tides Foundation, and individual donors.

About The Conservation Foundation

A nonprofit organization founded in 1948, The Conservation Foundation is dedicated to improving the quality of the environment through wise use of the earth's resources. Its long-standing interest and involvement in land conservation and development issues emphasize a comprehensive approach: through public advocacy characterized by reason and balance, cooperative problem solving, and the development of new ideas, it seeks effective solutions to current and emerging environmental problems.

Creating Successful Communities

Creating Successful Communities

A GUIDEBOOK TO GROWTH MANAGEMENT STRATEGIES

Michael A. Mantell
Stephen F. Harper · Luther Propst

The Conservation Foundation

ISLAND PRESS

Washington, D.C. □ Covelo, California

Grateful acknowledgment is made for permission to reprint the following:

Illustrations by Roger K. Lewis, four of which were previously published by
the American Institute of Architecture in *Shaping the City*, © 1987.

"Gifts of Land," from *Connecticut Woodlands* magazine,
volume 53, number 1, 1988.

LIBRARY OF CONGRESS CATALOGING-IN-PUBLICATION DATA

Mantell, Michael A.
    Creating successful communities : a guidebook to growth management
strategies / by Michael A. Mantell, Stephen F. Harper, Luther Propst.
        p.   cm.
    "The Conservation Foundation."
    Includes index.
    ISBN 1-55963-014-0 (pbk.)
    1. Community development, Urban—United States.   2. City planning—
Environmental aspects—United States.   3. Land use, Urban—United
States.   I. Harper, Stephen F.   II. Propst, Luther.
III. Conservation Foundation.   IV. Title.
HN90.C6M36   1989
307.1'216'0973—dc20   89-15473
                                                               CIP

Printed on recycled, acid-free paper
Manufactured in the United States of America

10   9   8   7   6   5   4   3   2   1

Contents

Preface

IN growing communities across the United States, citizens, developers, and local governments are working together to foster creative development and protect sensitive land resources. *Creating Successful Communities: A Guidebook to Growth Management Strategies* looks at some of the techniques they are using and the results they are achieving. It points the way toward actions and strategies that can help create the successful communities of the twenty-first century.

The Successful Communities Guidebook

Creating Successful Communities: A Guidebook to Growth Management Strategies has been prepared in response to the need in many communities for practical assistance in preserving important natural and cultural resources and community distinctiveness while anticipating, planning for, and managing growth. The emphasis is on protecting and enhancing key community assets and fostering quality development in appropriate sites.

Growth management objectives vary according to the unique circumstances and characteristics of each community.* Because there is so much variation among communities, this *Guidebook* does not attempt to prescribe a single strategy or set of techniques as most appropriate. Rather, it introduces growth management techniques, provides illustrative examples of how specific communities have successfully used these techniques, and directs the reader to more detailed sources of information.

The materials that follow focus both on tools for protecting distinctive resources and on strategies for more effective participation in growth management decision-making. The first five chapters provide guidance on how to employ growth management strategies to protect and enhance specific resources, including farmland; rivers and wetlands; historic and culturally significant properties and districts; aesthetic resources; and open space. Community profiles summarizing the growth management strategies that specific communities have used to protect these resources follow each chapter. References to more detailed sources of information are also provided at the end of each chapter.

The final two chapters focus on organizing a nonprofit organization and participating effectively in growth management decisions to make a difference. Chapter 6 examines the steps necessary to build and maintain an effective nonprofit organization devoted to managing growth and protecting key community assets and resources. Chapter 7 outlines some basic rules of the road for citizens seeking to create and enhance successful communities.

These chapters are supplemented by a companion volume, *Resource Guide for Creating Successful Communities*, that contains a variety of rich material on corresponding subjects. Included in the companion volume are representative ordinances, easements, and articles of incorporation that provide examples of how various communities and organizations have implemented the concepts discussed throughout this book.

A collection of diverse materials on selected topics, these books are written principally for involved citizens. They are both products of The Conservation Foundation's Successful Communities Program. Initiated in 1988, Successful Communities seeks to protect and improve the quality of the environment in localities, regions, and states where rapid growth threatens distinctive natural and cultural assets and character. To this end, the program supports the efforts

---

* "Growth management" is defined very broadly in this book to include many specific techniques—used singly or, more typically, in combination—to influence or guide the amount, pace, type, density, location, costs, impacts, and quality of local development. See Appendix A for an explanation of growth management terms and techniques.

of governments and nongovernmental organizations to enhance the quality of development. It builds upon The Conservation Foundation's 40-year history of fashioning innovative approaches to the wise use of land resources.

Successful Communities offers practical ideas and technical know-how to states and localities throughout the country to help them accommodate growth while retaining the open spaces, historic buildings, scenic views, farmlands, natural features, and other qualities that make each community distinctive. With overall guidance provided by a distinguished Advisory Committee chaired by Anne T. Bass of Fort Worth, Texas, the program has four principal components:

- Direct technical assistance to states, nonprofit organizations, and designated "leadership communities" around the country;
- Research and education, including this *Guidebook*, a quarterly newsletter, conferences and workshops, and actions at the state and federal levels to improve growth management policies;
- Innovation grants to catalyze and foster creative growth management actions at the local level; and
- A land trust—the Successful Communities Trust— to intervene in the real estate market to protect critical natural and historic resources.

Many people both inside and outside The Conservation Foundation worked on these materials and provided valuable insights about critical issues and places covered in them. Foremost among them are Doug Wheeler, Jack Noble, Bob McCoy, David Brower, Chris Duerksen, and Mary Means, who were key to helping conceptualize and review these materials. Many others thoughtfully reviewed individual chapters or sections and provided important insights and information along the way, including John Banta, Constance Beaumont, David Doheny, Jean Hocker, Jon Kusler, Ed McMahon, Tim Mealey, Phyllis Myers, Richard Roddewig, Tom Smith, and Ed Thompson. Each of the profiles was compiled through interviews with and reviews of drafts by relevant government officials, citizen leaders, developers, and heads of growth management organizations. All of the re-

viewers, who bear no responsibility for the finishe product, deserve much thanks and credit for the i spiring work they are doing around the country managing growth.

Appreciation is extended, as well, to Roger Lew for the use of his wonderful drawings and to Russe Brenneman, the California Coastal Conservancy, N tional Trust for Historic Preservation, Regional Pla Association, and the Trust for Public Land for permi sion to reprint various articles and portions of thei publications.

At The Conservation Foundation, two former sta members—Lisa Fernandez and Abby Goldsmith—a well as current research fellow Richard Russell did th lion's share of the work in compiling the profiles groups and communities. *Creating Successful Com munities* benefited tremendously from their stron skills and enthusiasm.

Solid administrative support was provided through out the effort by Bonita Franklin, Jo Halfant, Rosemar O'Neill, Joy Patterson, and Marsha White. It ha also been a pleasure to work with our colleagues a Island Press, particularly Karen Berger and Nanc Seidule.

A final word of gratitude is due The Andrew W Mellon Foundation, which has supported the researc component of Successful Communities from its in ception, including the preparation of this book. It leadership and insistence upon solid analysis have helped this program immeasurably.

Because of the rapid changes occurring in the growth management field and the ability to draw on relevant experiences from work in various commu nities, this *Guidebook* will be periodically updated Through supplements, readers will be kept abreast o changing tools, examples, and insights, and provided additional material on various subjects not exten sively covered here.

Your comments and suggestions are encouraged. So, too, is your continued involvement, interest, and lead ership in helping to achieve genuinely successful communities.

Successful Communities Program
The Conservation Foundation
September 1989

Introduction

WE can all point to places or communities that seem uniquely special—that stand out in terms of their distinctive character, charm, and resources, the quality of the services they provide, the way they function. Whether we think of these places because of nostalgic associations, frequent travel, or current everyday living, they seem to be ideal, or at least very successful, in the way they have created and retained significant character and resources as they have changed and grown over time.

For every one of these places, however, most of us could also name communities that once had a special quality about them or the potential to achieve it, but which have since become just another unrecognizable part of a larger, sprawling metropolis. All too many of our most favored communities and landscapes have or are about to become paved over for strips of highway, franchise architecture, and the like, trading in a sense of place and authenticity for a feeling of sameness and homogenization. Steadily, perceptibly, too many American communities are losing the distinctive qualities that trigger people's desires to live there, work there, or visit there.

The enormous pressures for growth and development and the resulting effects on the landscape have seemed especially overwhelming in the last decade or so. The need for jobs, tax revenues, diversified local economies, and mixes of housing opportunities, and the public's desire for detached homes and yards, are real and legitimate. Yet we urgently need to find more effective strategies that will enable our communities to grow in ways that enhance, not degrade, the qualities that lend them distinction and character.

Creating Successful Communities

The past two decades have brought significant improvements in this nation's environmental quality. Major strides have been made, for example, in protecting air and water quality and in adding to the country's reserves of protected lands. Land planning systems and environmental review requirements have been installed and strengthened in states and localities throughout the country.

Yet, after decades of environmental action by federal, state, and local governments, and by citizens' groups across the country, serious degradation of the American landscape continues. Distinctive buildings are being destroyed. Wetlands, free-flowing rivers, and other natural systems are being disrupted. Opportunities for solitude, for adventure, for quiet enjoyment of natural surroundings are fast disappearing.

"Despite all our efforts," then Conservation Foundation president (and current administrator of the U.S. Environmental Protection Agency) William K. Reilly testified before the President's Commission on Americans Outdoors, "there is a steady, perceptible degradation of the countryside—an erosion of the distinctive qualities that differentiate one place from another. As they confront piecemeal urbanization, people all over the country are asking, 'How can we save our special places?' "

There is an urgent need to refocus our efforts in seeking to achieve "successful communities," which build upon and create distinctive assets and character. Fortunately, there are developers, citizens, and government officials who are working to protect critical natural and historic resources and to foster development that enhances local qualities. But much more needs to be done to create and maintain what is distinctive and special about our communities.

Admittedly, what makes a community successful rests largely in the eye of the beholder. It is more a subjective judgment and a feeling than quantifiable factors and data. Is it a good place to work, to live, to raise a family, to enjoy leisure time? These are commonly the needs fulfilled by communities considered successful.

Successful communities incorporate many elements—commercial vitality, for example, jobs, good

ROGER K. LEWIS

schools, a mix of housing types, adequate transportation systems—that go beyond environmental and aesthetic concerns. They are places that allow for and foster racial, cultural, and economic diversity. Nevertheless, how a place looks and feels, how it treats its heritage, says much about whether there is, in fact, a sense of community, a sense of caring by its citizenry about its future.

The Need for Local Action

Preserving special places requires local action, for it is principally at this level that most special places are known and valued. It is this dependence on local action, even more than the power of pressures for growth and change, that makes heritage protection unique among conservation needs. To be sure, supportive action outside the locality is crucial: federal and state governments exert influence through tax and regulatory policies; the ownership of public land; grants-in-aid to farmers and other landowners; the construction

of public works; and in many other ways. Most recently, there has been a resurgence in state growth management programs—for example, in Florida, Georgia, New Jersey, Rhode Island, Vermont, and Maine—that offers much promise for addressing these issues more effectively.

Yet, as the President's Commission on Americans Outdoors put it, "Wise development cannot be dictated from a national plan, but must happen due to the actions of thousands of local governments. Local coalitions, community by community, are our best way to address the widely varying wants and needs of Americans across the country."

The key ingredient in helping to bring about a successful community is forging a vision of what the place can be. Concerned citizens must go beyond specific parcels and projects to developing an inspiring yet realistic vision, one that incorporates development and change as well as the protection of community resources and character. With a vision, the San Antonio River, which was slated to be buried under concrete, becomes the site of a famed river walk lined by trees, a flagstone walkway, shops, and art galleries and he focal point for the city's prosperous tourist and convention trade.

Obviously, not every community has a scenic river or breathtaking view of a mountain range. Nearly all, however, have some asset—often unnoticed—that can serve to make the community distinctive. Near Boston, for example, the Massachusetts town of Lowell used the unlikely asset of abandoned factory buildings to spur a renaissance.

As the material in chapter 7 discusses, people need a vision of what they want their community to be, one that builds on its distinctive character and assets, if efforts are to be successful. The vision needs to go beyond the commonplace, beyond simply "managing growth" to a far-reaching, positive ideal of what a community, at its best, can become.

To be workable, the vision needs to incorporate change and development as well as preservation. Development will continue to occur. Citizen action may be able to move it from one community to another or to shape its density, character, and cost. But such action cannot ultimately prevent change. The failure to accept this is what causes many people to regard all development as the enemy and makes it impossible to achieve successful communities in light of the polarization and poorly designed sprawl that often ensues.

Developing and implementing a vision for a place are by no means easy tasks. It takes a compelling idea, persistence, consensus, influence, and many other difficult attributes. Every planning process starts out by attempting to set forth goals and objectives. But we are all too familiar with where many well-intended planning processes have ended up. As Victoria Tschienkel, former secretary of Florida's Department of Environmental Regulation, has said:

> I think that we can probably take care of pollution-related problems in the state but it's going to be tough. . . . [E]ven if we do that I'm not sure that this is going to be a very nice place to live, because of the densities of the population and lack of sense of community. Florida could end up as just one convenience store after another. If we can't come up with an image of what this state should be we can protect the environment, but will we still be glad to live here?

Several forces militate against such broad thinking and action. Many people simply do not care: landowners may focus their efforts only on the lots they own, developers only on the parcels they can develop, and neighborhood residents only on their immediate area. Other people who do care may want no development or as little as possible; this works to define development as pollution and often leads to polarization and little creativity in the way a community evolves. In some communities, citizens often have to be negative or extreme to be heard and given a seat at the decision-making tables; as a result, they and developers get into a habit of confrontation that becomes difficult to break. These are serious obstacles for even the most enlightened residents and communities to overcome.

There are, however, some key ways to make a compelling vision come to life. Especially critical factors for successful initiatives are "hometown heroes"—persistent local individuals—and effective quality-of-life lobbies, who spearhead land use conservation and planning efforts.* Whether they are government officials, neighborhood activists, or business leaders, people with vision and tenacity are critical to successful communities. Individuals do make a difference. Alongside "hometown heroes," effective quality-of-life lobbies provide needed continuity in leadership and can help ensure continuing positive government responses.

Widespread interest in a land use issue is aroused typically in response to a particular controversial development proposal—and then it may evaporate as quickly as it was formed. Effective involvement in local growth management decision-making requires more. No matter what methods a single individual or local organization chooses in efforts to promote a conservation or quality-of-life agenda, effective action—whether through advocacy, land acquisition, education, fund-raising, or other strategies—requires a sustained presence. Without persistence, flexibility, vision, and some good humor, even the most sophisticated plans and innovative tools and techniques will fall short of the mark.

Successful communities are not static. A place cannot be frozen in time. Thus, as communities continue to evolve, so, too, should efforts to ensure their success. Similarly, observations on what ingredients make for successful communities continually change in response to changing needs, opportunities, and circumstances. Indeed, successful communities constantly experiment with a broad array of growth management techniques to retain distinctiveness and protect key natural and cultural assets. Whether at the local, regional, or state level, growth management advocates must act quickly to ensure that plans, programs, and strategies adjust in response to new pressures and evolving objectives.

By focusing on key assets and by building strong constituencies for protection and sensitive development, successful communities can be created and sustained.

---

* Christopher J. Duerksen's work for The Conservation Foundation in the mid-1980s identified "hometown heroes" and several other "success factors" that enabled some communities to be more successful than others; these are discussed in the *Conservation Foundation Letter*, 1987, No. 6.

Creating Successful Communities

CHAPTER 1

Agricultural Land

SUBURBS-IN-WAITING: THE THREATS TO
AGRICULTURAL LAND RESOURCES

THE POLITICS OF AGRICULTURAL LAND
PRESERVATION

PLANNING FOR AGRICULTURAL LAND PRESERVATION
Determine Objectives
Build Consensus for Action: Form an Advisory Committee
Gather Information

LOCAL AGRICULTURAL PRESERVATION TECHNIQUES
Agricultural Zoning
Purchase of Development Rights
Transfer of Development Rights

THE ROLE OF PRIVATE LAND TRUSTS

STATE AGRICULTURAL LAND PRESERVATION
PROGRAMS
Differential Property Taxation
Agricultural Districting
Right-to-Farm Legislation
Purchase of Development Rights

LEGAL CONSIDERATIONS IN PROTECTING FARMLAND

SUGGESTIONS FOR DEVELOPING AN EFFECTIVE
LOCAL PROGRAM

PROFILES
Black Hawk County, Iowa
Hardin County, Kentucky
King County, Washington
Lancaster County, Pennsylvania
Montgomery County, Maryland

INFORMATION RESOURCES

ORGANIZATIONAL RESOURCES

3

*I think our government will remain virtuous for many
centuries, as long as they remain chiefly agricultural.*
—THOMAS JEFFERSON

Suburbs-in-Waiting: The Threats to Agricultural Land Resources

America's agricultural land, with skilled farmers and a temperate climate, has made this country the "breadbasket of the world." The perceived abundance of farmland means that agricultural land protection is not often high on the agenda of decision-makers. Many local officials, who often favor growth in tax revenue more than agricultural preservation, picture prime farmland as shopping centers and suburbs-in-waiting:

> The idea that agricultural zoning would be permanent is new to most planning commissions. Previously most planners and most zoning ordinances treated the agricultural zones as if their sole purpose was to await the salvation of urban development.[1]

This picture is reinforced by the fact that the best agricultural land (because it is unwooded, relatively flat, and has well-drained soils) often is well suited for development.

The process by which agricultural land becomes suburban and urban land tends to be incremental and characterized by subtle changes. The actual breaking of ground is only the conclusion of this conversion process. The principal factors that drive this farmland conversion process include:

- The local economic viability of agriculture;[2]
- The loss of the critical mass of agricultural land within an area necessary to support agricultural services and markets, such as farm supply and implement businesses;
- Local annexation policy and public investment decisions, especially for road improvements, and sewer or water system construction;
- The strength of local growth pressures and the resulting difference in land values for agricultural use and for development;
- The difference in land values of rural and urban land;
- The circumstances, lifestyle preferences, and life cycles of individual farm families;

The adequacy of local growth management on the urban fringe (many cities have effective growth management in established neighborhoods where neighborhood associations are strong, and a laissez-faire attitude in urban fringe areas).

Urban residents increasingly are drawn to the attractions of pastoral landscapes and rural lifestyles. While the first such immigrants often settle on "ranchettes" or "farmettes"—parcels of perhaps 5 to 20 acres serviced by country roads, private wells, and septic systems—their growing numbers begin to require extension of public services and better roads. Denser development and commercial uses soon follow, often with little or no land use controls. In effect, the advent of newcomers serves to replicate the suburbs from which they recently fled.

Intrusion of low-density, scattered development into agricultural districts on just a few parcels casts the shadow of inevitable development over a much larger area. The encroachment of development sets an example for other farmers and creates conflicts between farmers and the new residents over the smells, noise, pesticides, and other attributes of agriculture. The suburban residents bring problems such as trespassing by children attracted to potentially hazardous farm ponds and barns. It may also bring vandalism and theft. Continuing subdivision development leads to commercial development and drives land prices higher, making it more difficult and expensive to assemble or maintain enough land to support viable agricultural operations. Long-established land tenure patterns change as smaller parcels begin to predominate and landowner-farmers become tenant-farmers. Many parcels held by speculators or developers simply may be left idle.

These changes create an "impermanence syndrome," causing remaining farmers to doubt the future viability of agriculture in the area and encouraging these farmers to move or abandon their farming operations. As these farmers reduce their capital investment, and agricultural support services close or convert to lawn and garden operations, the syndrome is reinforced.

4

The Politics of Agricultural Land Preservation

Rural areas in this country generally have little tradition of land use planning or control; planning and growth management, in fact, is often quite controversial among rural landowners. Some farmers support and even initiate efforts to prevent suburban intrusion into agricultural districts. Other farmers see these efforts as wrongfully reducing land values and strongly object to such efforts. These farmers often point out that, when development pressures are great, efforts to preserve farmland may only induce the remaining farmers to sell out immediately to avoid potential future controls.

Local agricultural land preservation efforts—and the climate in which they arise—can be divided roughly into two types:

- Those in farm communities where little or no suburban intrusion has occurred and land values have not appreciated due to development pressure; and
- Those in communities where land values have substantially appreciated due to development pressure and local land uses include a mix of both suburban and agricultural uses.

Successful farmland preservation programs must carefully and realistically assess local conditions and tailor the program to these conditions. The tools appropriate for protecting a viable agricultural district differ from those appropriate for preserving remnant farm parcels within a mixed agricultural and suburban area. In essentially suburban areas, effective farmland protection programs often focus on preserving remnant farms, in part for their cultural and recreational value as a place where suburban residents can ride horses and learn about farm operations and lifestyles, as well as for their traditional agricultural values. These programs rely more upon incentives and acquisition of development rights than upon agricultural zoning and regulations.

With this distinction in mind, this chapter includes the following sections:

- Approaches to planning for farmland preservation;
- Specific farmland preservation techniques; and
- Legal considerations in farmland preservation.

Planning for Agricultural Land Preservation

DETERMINE OBJECTIVES

The first step in protecting local agricultural land is to assess realistically the objectives of a local agricultural preservation program. There are diverse and numerous reasons for local agricultural preservation, including:

- Permanently preserving sources of food and fiber and protecting the viability of the local agricultural economy by preventing suburban encroachment;
- Preserving rural lifestyles and pastoral landscapes to the extent feasible as suburban development encroaches into agricultural areas;
- Preserving remnant farms in an essentially suburban landscape to provide landscape diversity, a rural local image, and for recreational, educational, and cultural benefits.

The appropriate approach and tools to consider depend largely upon which of these objectives are viable and are most important.

BUILD CONSENSUS FOR ACTION: FORM AN ADVISORY COMMITTEE

Widespread community involvement and a level of community consensus are crucial. "Community" necessarily means owners of agricultural land, feed and implement dealers, agricultural lenders, the county agricultural extension agent, a soil conservation district representative, and others who have a stake in the future of local agriculture. Unanimous support from the agricultural community is not necessary, but effective farmland preservation action rarely takes place over the objection of the agricultural community.

Formation of an agricultural advisory committee or agricultural representation on a broader community advisory group will serve to strengthen the program and add credibility to the process by helping to avoid the accusation that a program has been "shoved down the throats" of local farmers by new suburban residents.

GATHER INFORMATION

After realistically determining the program's objectives and developing a broad community coalition for effective action, a work program should be developed. The first step is to gather as much relevant information as possible about the characteristics of local agricultural operations and resources and the threats to those operations and resources. The information necessary to mount a credible case for preservation can also help to build community support for agricultural preservation. This information should document the following factors:

- *Economic and cultural contributions.* To build the case that agriculture is an important part of the local economic base, or that local remnant agricultural operations make an important contribution to local distinctiveness, image, and quality of life.

• *Land identification.* To identify districts that should be preserved in order to protect and enhance the local agricultural economy, or to identify farms that should be preserved for their unique economic, recreational, cultural, and aesthetic assets.

• *Land use patterns.* To document trends in the use of agricultural land, particularly its conversion to suburban and urban uses.

Table 1

Sources of Important Land Use Data

Information Needed	*Potential Information Sources*

Land already developed	Local planning office
	  Aerial photographs
	  Current land use maps

Land projected for urbanization	Local planning office
	  Water and sewer plans
	  Capital budget plans
	  Comprehensive plans

Land already subdivided	Local planning or recorder's office
	  Plat maps
	Local assessor's office
	  Tax parcel maps

Land owned by developers/speculators	Local assessor's office
	  Tax parcel map
	  Tax rolls
	Local recorder's office
	Real estate agents and lenders

Land with poor soil	U.S. Soil Conservation Service
	  County soil survey
	  Soil capabilities map

"Sensitive" lands
(e.g., wetlands, steep slopes)
	U.S. Soil Conservation Service
	  Soil Surveys
	Local planning office
	  Aerial photographs
	  USGS topographic maps

Small and odd lots	Local planning office
	  Aerial photographs
	Local assessor's office
	  Tax parcel maps

Public open space	Local planning office

• *Costs of sprawl.* To document the local fiscal, economic, and environmental costs of suburban sprawl relative to a compact form of development. The costs to consider include the increased public costs of providing public facilities and services, the economic impacts on agricultural operations resulting from suburban intrusions, and the environmental degradation associated with low-density "leapfrog" development.

There are a variety of sources for information on these areas of research. For example, in documenting the local economic importance of agriculture, the U.S. Census of Agriculture, conducted by the Census Bureau, provides data on the number of farms, farm size, value of farm equipment and other inputs, and level of farm sales. The county agricultural extension agent, a federal employee who provides technical assistance to local farmers, can also help in the use of census documents as well as provide additional information on locally grown crops, the profitability of local agricultural operations, and the overall contribution of agriculture to the local economy.*

Opinion Surveys

A community survey, questionnaire, or canvass is often an effective way to document the noneconomic or cultural benefits of preserving agricultural land. These tools can document how agriculture affects the community's self-image and quality of life. A local newspaper or television station, the journalism department of a nearby university, or a local or regional planning agency probably will be glad to manage or assist with the undertaking. Surveys in many rural and urbanizing communities have shown that the loss of farmland is a widespread local concern, and that residents are willing to support regulations, bond issues, and incentive programs for farmland preservation. The results of polls and surveys often differ significantly from the impression left from public hearings, which tend to attract vocal people with strongly held opinions that may not represent the majority viewpoint.

Identifying Lands

Identifying that part of the local agricultural landscape to preserve is a critical concern. One farmland preservation authority has developed a conceptual formula that describes a method for determining how to identify potential agricultural districts. In this for-

mula, the location of potential agricultural districts is determined by subtracting the following types of land from all land in the community:

• Land already urbanized;
• Land officially projected for urbanization;
• Land already subdivided;
• Land owned by developers or speculators;
• Land with poor soil;
• "Sensitive" land (e.g., wetlands);
• Small and oddly shaped parcels; and
• Publicly owned open space.[3]

Once the data necessary to fill in these variables have been gathered, the location and total acreage of potential agricultural districts can be roughly calculated. This information can be presented effectively in a series of transparent maps using a common scale. By overlaying these maps, one can identify the potential agricultural districts. Table 1 summarizes where the data necessary to perform this type of evaluation can be found in most communities.

Identifying Soils

Identification of potential agricultural districts is the beginning, rather than the end, of the evaluation process. A more detailed analysis of such land can isolate the best agricultural land within these areas. The local office of the Soil Conservation Service (SCS) (an agency of the U.S. Department of Agriculture), the county agricultural extension agent, or the local soil conservation district each has several sources of information available that can assist in identifying local soils best suited for agriculture. These agencies also can help in interpreting soils maps and soils surveys.

These sources of information include the SCS soil classification system, surveys of important agricultural soils, and the Land Evaluation and Site Assessment (LESA) System:

• The Soil Conservation Service's soil classification system divides soils into eight "soil capability classes," based on their capacity for supporting crops. The highest producing agricultural soils are called "prime farmland soils." These are soils "that have the best combination of physical and chemical characteristics for producing food, feed, forage, fiber, and oil seed crops, and is also available for these uses." They produce the most food or fiber with the least inputs of fertilizer and labor. In addition, the SCS identifies "unique" farmland. These are lands that, due to a combination of good soil, location, moisture, and other beneficial characteris-

---

* The State Department of Agriculture may be able to assist with similar information and expertise. The agricultural school of a state university may also be helpful on these issues, especially in undertaking discrete research projects. Faculty members or graduate students may lend their expertise.

ROGER K. LEWIS

tics, are well suited to producing specialty crops such as fruits and vegetables.

- Based upon soil surveys, the SCS has prepared "Important Farmland Surveys," showing the location of both prime and unique farmlands for many counties.

- The Land Evaluation and Site Assessment (LESA) System is a computerized information system managed by the SCS that can be used by local governments to determine which lands are best suited for agriculture; rate a district for the viability of continued agricultural use; choose a minimum residential parcel size in agricultural areas; and determine where public infrastructure projects should be located to minimize conversion pressure on farmland.

Local Agricultural Preservation Techniques

The most promising approaches to local farmland preservation can be classified as follows:

- Agricultural zoning;
- Purchase of development rights to agricultural land; and
- Transfer of development rights.

AGRICULTURAL ZONING

Agricultural zoning is a widely used farmland preservation technique; however, agricultural zoning appears in many forms and varies widely in effectiveness. Whatever approach is taken, agricultural zoning needs to ensure that suburban and urban development do not intrude into viable agricultural districts. The ultimate success of agricultural zoning is determined largely by how strong the community consensus is for farmland preservation, so that local authorities can resist the temptation to grant rezoning and variance requests that are inconsistent with preserving farmland.

Agricultural zoning techniques can be grouped as follows:

1. Large lot residential zoning;
2. Exclusive agricultural zoning;
3. Cluster zoning; and
4. Performance-based zoning.

Large Lot Residential Zoning

Early agricultural zoning ordinances typically were ineffective in protecting agricultural areas from suburban intrusion. Relatively small minimum lot sizes for nonfarm residences (e.g., 120,000 square feet or less) are a common feature of such ordinances.

These minimum lot size regulations reduce the density of residential development, often resulting in residential lots that are "too small to plow and too big to mow." If used judiciously, they may temporarily discourage subdivision development, but when relied upon too widely, only exacerbate urban sprawl. Rather than encouraging agricultural land preservation, the result is often inefficient subdivision tracts that unnecessarily consume agricultural land and rural landscapes. These large minimum lot size regulations have not prevented suburban intrusion into agricultural districts and are an ineffective approach for preserving agricultural lands.

An innovative approach to determining minimum lot sizes based upon agricultural characteristics is the use of density-based allocations. Two examples are fixed area-based allocation and quarter/quarter zoning.

Fixed area-based allocation ordinances base the minimum lot size on the minimum acreage necessary to support an economic farm operation. Minimum lot sizes are thus large enough to retain agricultural operations rather than to encourage large lot residential subdivisions. The minimum acreage necessary to support a farm operation will vary according to local agricultural and real estate economics.

Another example of density-based zoning is called "quarter/quarter" zoning. This technique allows one nonfarm lot for every 40 acres (one quarter of a quarter section of land). Some quarter/quarter zoning ordinances also require that development occur on the least productive part of a parcel, and establish building site and other standards that effectively reduce densities. Blue Earth County, Minnesota, for example, includes within its quarter/quarter ordinance a density transfer option and a bonus for siting development on less-productive soils.

Exclusive Agricultural Zoning

Regulations in exclusive agricultural zoning districts strictly control or prohibit uses that are unrelated to agricultural operations. Exclusive agricultural use ordinances prohibit nonfarm dwellings, with "farm" defined in economic or other performance terms. Boone County, Illinois, for example, defines "farm" as "any parcel of land used solely for the growing, harvesting and management of crops and livestock." In addition, the county requires a $10,000 minimum annual gross agricultural income threshold.[4]

Cluster Zoning

Cluster zoning (described in Appendix A) can be used to serve agricultural land while allowing residential development on the same parcel. Cluster regulations may require or encourage (principally through density bonuses and reduced dimensional standards) the clustering of development on the least productive portions of a farm parcel. Local regulations may require clustered or attached housing, rather than large lot subdivisions, and may require this housing to be placed on the portions of a parcel least suited for agricultural production. Special permit criteria can ensure that the undeveloped portion of the site is permanently dedicated for agricultural purposes, and that the preserved land has access, dimension, character, and location that promotes the viable use of the land for agricultural purposes.

Boulder County, Colorado, has implemented an effective cluster zoning ordinance. Much of the county is included in agricultural districts, permitting development at a density of one unit per 35 acres. The owner of a 35-acre parcel can add an additional unit if the two units are clustered on 25 percent or less of the total acreage of the parcel and the owner places a conservation easement on the balance of the parcel, ensuring its preservation for agricultural uses. (Cluster zoning is further explained in Appendix A.)

Performance-Based Zoning

Land use controls based upon performance standards are a potentially useful approach that is widely used to protect agricultural land. This technique is particularly useful in rural communities facing relatively intense development pressures and lacking sophisticated planning and administrative capabilities. By shifting much of the data-gathering burden to applicants, these ordinances provide site-specific land use control without requiring expensive and time-consuming data-gathering and analysis.

Rural Hardin County, Kentucky, has adopted effective performance-based controls to protect agricultural lands. The county's Development Guidance System is based on land use compatibility and soil quality. Using a point system and directing growth to areas adjacent to a federal highway, the program avoids the political problems that previous zoning proposals had faced in this conservative jurisdiction. (See the profile on Hardin County's program at the end of this chapter.)

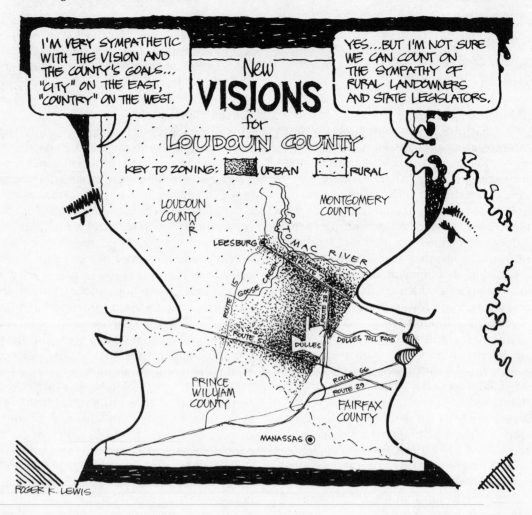

Black Hawk County, Iowa, has implemented innovative performance-based agricultural zoning. The county protects its rich farmland resource by basing its zoning directly on soil productivity. The SCS Soil Survey ratings for the county were used to develop "corn suitability ratings." The higher the rating for a given parcel, the tighter the land use restrictions that apply. (See the profile on Black Hawk County at the end of this chapter.)

Despite their attractiveness, several words of caution about performance standards are in order. Their effectiveness depends primarily on the quality and thoroughness of the standards themselves and how well they are tailored to local conditions. While performance standards are attractive to many rural communities lacking sophisticated planning capabilities, a community must have or contract for the site plan review and administrative capability to evaluate the adequacy and accuracy of developers' documentation.

Conditional use zoning is widely used to implement performance standards for agricultural land preservation. A conditional use zoning system may allow only agriculture-related uses "as of right." Nonfarm residential and commercial uses are allowed by special permit and are subject to criteria designed to minimize the impacts on agricultural operations and resources. Sherman County, Oregon, for example, conditions approval of nonfarm residential units on a showing that such development is not detrimental to agricultural uses and will not alter the stability of the agricultural land pattern.

One planner has sketched the steps involved in a performance standards approach:

Step 1. Set out the public objectives of the program;

Step 2. Identify enough buildable land to accommodate anticipated near-term needs;

Step 3. Isolate and contain existing urban land uses within designated areas;

Step 4. Select a specific zoning approach—e.g., large lot zoning or exclusive agricultural zoning;

Step 5. Establish a performance standard or conditional use process that accounts for a lack of thorough planning data by providing case-by-case review of nonfarm development according to specific performance criteria;

Step 6.   Adopt the ordinance; and

Step 7.   Go back and, based on experience with the performance standards, undertake more thorough planning studies.[5]

PURCHASE OF DEVELOPMENT RIGHTS

Paralleling the state farmland acquisition programs discussed below, a number of communities, particularly in the East, have instituted programs to purchase the development rights to selected farm parcels. Many urban fringe communities that wish to retain a mixed suburban-agricultural landscape find purchase of development rights (PDR) programs are effective in lieu of or in addition to agricultural zoning programs, and more politically feasible than a purely regulatory program. The acquisition of development rights to farmland provides permanent protection, while zoning is subject to political pressures for change. Unlike regulatory programs in these communities, purchase of development rights is most often enthusiastically supported by most local farmers. These programs typ-

ically rely upon local bond issues or real estate transfer taxes for funding.

After acquisition of development rights, farms remain in private ownership, but the landowner has sold the right to develop the property. By acquiring only the development rights, rather than the full fee interest, the local government ensures that the parcel will remain in agricultural use, with the following additional benefits:

- Acquisition of development rights to agricultural land is often considerably less expensive than full fee acquisition. Rather than paying market value for the parcel, the community only pays the difference in the market value of the parcel and its value for agricultural use.

- The community avoids maintenance and management responsibilities. Agricultural operations remain in private ownership, so the community does not have to maintain the land or assume potential personal injury liability.

- The land remains on the tax roles, albeit at a re-

duced valuation to reflect the land's market value in light of the development restrictions on the land.

- The local agricultural economy is often bolstered by the funds used to acquire agricultural development rights when farmers invest the funds in farm equipment or supplies.

The first PDR program was implemented on Long Island in Suffolk County, New York, in 1974. By 1988, the county had acquired development rights on over 6,000 acres.[6] Several other communities have followed, including Howard County, Maryland, and Burlington County, New Jersey.

King County, Washington, in metropolitan Seattle, has implemented one of the nation's leading local PDR programs. The county's farmland had declined from 165,000 acres in 1945 to 55,000 30 years later. In 1979, King County voters overwhelmingly approved a $50 million bond issue to acquire development rights for selected parcels of the county's remaining farmland. (See the profile at the end of this chapter on the King County program.)

TRANSFER OF DEVELOPMENT RIGHTS

A few communities have implemented effective transfer of development rights (TDR) programs designed to preserve agricultural land. (TDR, or "TDC" where "credits" are used instead of "rights" is explained in Appendix A.) TDR programs can achieve the same farmland preservation results as the purchase of development rights, while avoiding the large public acquisition costs. TDR requires considerable planning and administrative sophistication, especially when used for preserving large agricultural districts rather than individual buildings. TDR, however, can be politically palatable because, in effect, new development (rather than farmers or the general public) absorbs the cost of protecting agricultural land.

Despite this tool's tremendous potential, it has not been widely used due to the complexity of setting up and administering a TDR program. With the few pioneering communities that adopted TDR several years ago beginning to demonstrate that the programs can effectively preserve large amounts of farmland, an increasing number of communities have recently implemented TDR programs.

The Pinelands Commission in New Jersey has implemented an ambitious transfer of development rights program for agricultural and resource preservation within the Pinelands Reserve. In order to protect the environmental quality of the Pinelands region, the commission has divided the region into seven management districts. These districts include regional growth areas (the "receiving areas," where development is encouraged) and preservation and agricultural areas (the "sending areas," where development is strictly limited). The Pinelands Development Credit Program provides a mechanism for landowners in preservation and agricultural districts to share in increased development values in the regional growth areas. Credits are allocated by a rather complex formula to owners of vacant land within the sending areas and sold in an open market for use in the receiving areas. Purchasers of each credit are allowed to build four additional residential units per acre above normal density limits in the receiving areas in accordance with local zoning regulations.[7]

Montgomery County, Maryland, has developed a TDR program in which land in "sending areas" (generally speaking, the county's best remaining farmland) was substantially downzoned from a 5-acre minimum lot size to a 25-acre minimum lot size. While landowners in these sending areas can only build one house per every 25 acres, they can realize the former permitted level of development by selling development rights to developers who are building in designated "receiving areas." (The receiving areas are generally the urban parts of the county closer to Washington, D.C.)

Briefly, the program works as follows: An owner of 25 acres in the "sending area" is allocated five development rights, only one of which may be used to develop the parcel. All five may be transferred to receiving areas. The 25-acre minimum lot size is based on a study of local agriculture and the minimum acreage deemed necessary to sustain a farming operation in the county.

The Montgomery County TDR program—which has saved over 20,000 acres of agricultural land in the county—is a mature TDR program that demonstrates the tool's potential effectiveness in an area facing severe development pressure. The program also demonstrates that opposition can arise to increased density in the receiving areas. (See the end of this chapter for a profile of the program.)

When considering a local TDR program, the following points should be kept in mind:

- The program must be structured so that it is easy for agricultural landowners, developers, title lawyers, real estate agents, and bankers to understand it and work with it.
- The program must give strong incentives for agricultural landowners to sell TDRs, rather than develop at the permitted density (e.g., by substantial downzoning in the sending areas).

Merely passing an ordinance that permits TDR is insufficient. A TDR program changes the way real estate agents, bankers, developers, and real estate lawyers do business. They must support the program, and, more importantly, they must understand its intricacies. Neighboring landowners in the receiving area must also tolerate the increased densities in these areas. A "blue ribbon committee" with representatives from these interest groups may be necessary to create an effective TDR program.

The program must provide adequate incentives for developers to buy TDRs. At least four conditions are necessary to provide this incentive:

1. There must be a substantial density bonus in the receiving area that is available only by purchasing development rights.

2. There must be a market demand in the receiving area for this density bonus. The density permitted without purchasing additional development rights in the receiving area must be substantially below market demand. Likewise, there must be enough desirable land designated in the receiving area to encourage development to concentrate in these areas.

3. Developers must understand clearly that purchasing development rights is the only way to obtain an increased density in the receiving areas. The locality must not undermine the program by granting variances or rezonings.

4. The municipality must ensure that developers can obtain increased density after purchasing development rights without prolonged delays. The local government must not undermine the program by denying increased density due to opposition from neighboring landowners.

The Role of Private Land Trusts

Private, nonprofit land trusts have often improved the effectiveness of local farmland acquisition programs. These land-saving organizations can bring flexibility and responsiveness to the often cumbersome process by which public agencies acquire land. Local land trusts play numerous roles in agricultural land conservation: they negotiate for the purchase or donation of farmland conservation easements; they undertake challenging "limited development" projects that use the profits generated by well-sited limited development to fund the protection of the agriculturally productive balance of a farm or ranch; they work closely with government agencies to acquire selected land for later resale to the agency; and they provide technical assistance to local landowners on farmland conservation, estate and income tax planning, and other related topics.

At the national level, the American Farmland Trust (AFT), with headquarters in Washington, D.C., and regional offices throughout the country, helps spearhead efforts for more effective agricultural land policies and assists local and state efforts, often acquiring easements and other interests in farmland.

Perhaps the first agricultural land trust formed under the leadership of the local farm community is the Marin Agricultural Land Trust (MALT). Joining with local environmentalists concerned about the encroachment of Bay Area development into the county, Marin's dairy farmers incorporated MALT as a means of protecting the hillside grazing and hay lands that are the resource base for their industry. The Peninsula Open Space Trust (POST), also in the San Francisco Bay Area, has formed a for-profit subsidiary, Conservation Partners, which is in the "conservation brokerage" business. Among other activities, it works in the real estate market to find conservation-oriented buyers for important farms and other resource properties. (POST is profiled in chapter 5.)

State Agricultural Land Preservation Programs

States have been more active in protecting agricultural land than in protecting many other resources. Local planners and activists should familiarize themselves with applicable state programs and ensure that local efforts complement state programs. State farmland preservation programs typically fall into one of four categories:

- Differential property taxation;
- Agricultural districting;
- Right-to-farm legislation; and
- Purchase of development rights.

DIFFERENTIAL PROPERTY TAXATION

At least 47 states have implemented differential property taxation programs benefiting agriculture, according to a recent study.[8] All differential taxation programs are voluntary, only applying to farmers who volunteer. Generally speaking, there are four types of differential taxation programs:

1. Straight preferential or use-value assessment, which, as the name implies, assesses farmland (and frequently other open lands) based upon the value of the property in its current use rather than upon market value;

2. Deferred taxation programs that combine use-value assessment with a "rollback tax" or recapture provision to recoup some or all of the tax benefits in the event that the farmland is developed;

3. Restrictive agreement programs that work similarly to a preferential assessment program with a recapture provision, but involve contractual agreements between the state and the landowner; and

4. Circuit-breaker programs that relieve property taxes once they reach a certain threshold level.

California's Williamson Act[9] is a leading restrictive agreement program. It entails ten-year agreements between owners of agricultural land and the state. The agreement binds the farmland owner not to develop the land in exchange for use-value assessment. Unless the farmer or state gives notice, the agreement continues to be extended each year. Once notice is given it takes ten years for the land to be released; in the meantime, however, the property tax assessment begins to increase so that, theoretically, the assessment will be for the land's full market value at the end of the ten-year period. As of 1981, 44 percent of the state's farmland was under a Williamson Act contract.[10]

Wisconsin's circuit-breaker program[11] provides a credit against state income tax liability. The benefits are contingent upon whether the local government has adopted agricultural preservation plans and zoning ordinances. In this way, the state provides an incentive for farmers to work within their local governments to develop an effective agricultural preservation program.

Overall, differential property taxation programs have been only marginally effective. They provide a significant tax benefit only when the market value of a farm parcel is significantly greater than the use value of the land in agriculture—i.e., in areas under heavy

ROGER K. LEWIS

development pressure. In such areas, however, the financial attractions of selling out for development are so great that even tax benefits and the threat of a recapture provision frequently do not prevent land conversion. Unless there is a substantial recapture penalty, these programs may simply provide a windfall to owners of agricultural land. If development pressures are insignificant, differential taxation benefits are an inefficient or ineffective approach to preventing conversion of agricultural lands. According to one estimate, 85 percent of farmland transfers are to buyers who intend to continue the agricultural use of the land.[12] Providing tax benefits to these landowners, when there is little or no pressure to develop the land, reduces the local tax base with little protective effect.

AGRICULTURAL DISTRICTING

A number of states have created agricultural districting programs, in which agricultural districts can be formed at the initiative of local agricultural landowners. In these districts, agricultural landowners are granted a variety of benefits to encourage and protect agricultural operations, in exchange for undertaking certain obligations not to develop for a period of years. In essence, agricultural districts directly address the "impermanence syndrome" by officially designating and protecting agriculture as the preeminent land use in a designated district. In exchange for agreeing to some form of agricultural districting or signing restrictive agreements, farmers in a district receive some combination of the following benefits:

Use-value assessment;

- Protection against nuisance suits;

- Protection against extensions of public facilities and services that would encourage urban development and taxes and assessments for urban services;

- Protection against the use of eminent domain;

- Protection against annexation; and

- Eligibility for or priority in state purchase of development rights programs.

Formation of an agricultural district must be approved by the state or, in some cases, local government based on specified criteria, which might include district size, contiguity of the parcels, and the productive characteristics of the land. This idea has been popular with farmers in most states that have implemented agricultural districting, leading to significant participation rates. New York and Virginia have two of the leading state agricultural districting programs.[13]

RIGHT-TO-FARM LEGISLATION

The concept of state "right-to-farm" programs is similar to that of agricultural districting. Both combat the "impermanence syndrome" by protecting agricultural operations. Right-to-farm statutes are a much more modest approach. Many states have enacted right-to-farm laws, which vary considerably from state to state, but generally they declare that properly managed agricultural operations are not a nuisance, and they limit local power to restrict conventional agricultural practices. The intention is to prevent the nuisance suits and regulations that often arise as suburban residential development exposes nonfarm residents to the normal odors and noises of agricultural operations.

PURCHASE OF DEVELOPMENT RIGHTS

An increasing number of states have adopted and funded purchase of development rights (PDR) programs. These programs basically entail state acquisition of the right to develop selected agricultural lands. Selection criteria include soil quality; contiguity with other farmland; the size of the parcel; inclusion in a viable agricultural district; the severity of development pressures; the price of the development rights; and geographic location. State PDR programs typically are found in states with strong suburban development pressures, where the total acreage of prime agricultural land is such that limited state acquisition can make a difference in the future of the resource. These states include Maryland, New Jersey, Massachusetts, Connecticut, Vermont, and Pennsylvania, among others.

These programs may be funded through bonds or through revenues raised by an earmarked tax. In 1987, for example, Pennsylvania voters approved a $100 million bond issue to fund acquisition of farmland development rights. Maryland, which funds its program through real estate transfer taxes, adds the wrinkle of matching county funding on a 60/40 basis.

Legal Considerations in Protecting Farmland

Local farmland preservation programs present a full range of legal issues. As with any resource protection program, consideration of the legal defensibility of a proposed program starts with an examination of state enabling legislation or a community's home rule charter. Most forms of agricultural zoning, for example, fall easily within general state grants of authority. In some states (Oregon and Wisconsin, for example) agricultural zoning is *required* under specified conditions. TDR programs require a close examination of state law, especially since they may not be considered authorized under general zoning enabling legislation.

The "taking" issue may arise whenever farmland preservation regulations greatly reduce the development potential and value of agricultural land. Exclusive agricultural zoning regulations generally are upheld so long as agriculture is an economically viable use of the land.

The legal defensibility of agricultural preservation controls will be improved by the following actions:

- Documenting clearly in a comprehensive plan or planning studies the need for (and benefits of) agricultural preservation controls;

- Applying agricultural preservation controls to an entire district or a relatively large number of farm parcels, rather than a small number of remnant farm parcels in an essentially suburbanized landscape; and

- Providing a density transfer mechanism (e.g., on-site clustering or transfer of development rights).

Suggestions for Developing an Effective Local Program

The following general suggestions can improve local agricultural protection programs.

- *Clearly define objectives.* Agricultural land preservation programs must be based upon explicit and clear objectives. Before taking action, determine exactly what is desired (preserving an economically viable agricultural district, preserving selected remnant farm parcels, encouraging compact urban growth) and tailor efforts to meet these objectives.

- *Take action early.* The earlier farmland conversion is spotted and addressed, the more effective the program and the lower the economic costs and political divisiveness of effective action.

- *Provide adequate room for growth.* Housing and job opportunities should be available in the community in order to accommodate local needs and prevent development pressures from overwhelming an otherwise effective farmland protection program.

- *Provide a safety valve.* Consider mechanisms such as on-site clustering or off-site density transfer to prevent hardships and to spread the economic burden of preserving farmland.

- *Build coalitions.* Obtain support for agricultural preservation from members of the farm community as well as from other local constituencies.

- *Eternal vigilance is the price of farmland protection.* Even the most effective land use controls can be eviscerated through poor implementation. Once adopted, rezonings, variances, and individual permitting decisions should be monitored closely to prevent backsliding.

PROFILE

BLACK HAWK COUNTY, IOWA

Agricultural Zoning Based on Soil Productivity

Community Characteristics

Black Hawk County covers 570 square miles of land 90 miles west of the Mississippi River and 80 miles south of the Minnesota border.

Seventy percent of Black Hawk is covered with prime soils (U.S. Soil Conservation Service classes I and II) consisting of glacial till and wind-carried loess from further west. A 160-day growing season and regular early summer rains provide ideal conditions for the production of grain crops, principally corn and soybeans.

In the late 1970s, 83 percent of the residents inhabited the urban area at the center of the county—the adjacent cities of Waterloo and Cedar Falls, which together occupy about 10 percent of the land in the county. About 12,000 county residents lived in unincorporated or rural areas.

At that time, John Deere and Company employed 8,000 in the metropolitan area. A nationwide pork distributor and two major educational institutions also contributed significantly to the economy.

More recently, even before the 1988 drought, times have been hard. During the 1980–82 recession, the pork distributor folded. As the farm crisis worsened and agricultural markets declined, the farm equipment business bottomed out and John Deere, the principal employer in the area, let go almost half its workforce. The population of the county has been in decline since 1980.

Growth Patterns

After 1890, more than 50 percent of the county's population was urban, with agriculture still the major industry but involving fewer people. The urbanizing trend continued until after World War II, when industrial and commercial workers, encouraged by cheap cars and cheap fuel, began to settle away from Waterloo and Cedar Falls, where they worked.

By the 1950s, inner suburbs and bedroom communities were well established, and scattered piecemeal development patterns took hold in rural areas. In the 1960s, roads to these outer areas brought strip commercial developments and office corridors.

Resources Threatened

By the early 1970s, the county realized that effective planning and land use control mechanisms were needed in order to preserve the county's best lands for farming in the face of continuing steady growth. Zoning laws at the time allowed rural residential development in virtually all unincorporated areas of the county. Rural growth was on the rise, and more and more prime agricultural soil lay useless beneath people's newly built homes.

Measures Taken

The county had to solve two problems in order to guide future growth and guarantee future agricultural use of its prime land. The first problem was that agricultural land was exempt from regulation under the current zoning ordinance. The second problem arose from the abundance of Class I and II soils, which precluded using SCS soil classification as a criterion to limit development.

The county solved the first problem by defining a farm as containing a minimum of 35 acres. Basically, this meant that if you wanted to build in the countryside on prime soils, you needed to own more than

35 acres. Nonfarm parcels were regulated by the zoning ordinance, which requires a minimum one-and-one-half-acre lot size in rural areas, except in subdivisions, where the minimum lot size is 15,000 square feet.

The U.S. Department of Agriculture's Soil Conservation Service assisted with the second problem by assigning a "corn suitability rating" (CSR) to every mapping unit of the existing county soil survey. The CSR took into account more than soil quality. It also included fertility characteristics and predicted yields for commonly grown crops. The CSR numbers range from 5 to 100—the higher the number, the more productive the soil.

Almost 70 percent of Black Hawk county soil had a CSR rating of 70 or higher, and the Planning Commission used this threshold in evaluating development requests, defining soils with a rating of 70 or more as "prime" agricultural soils. Under the zoning ordinance, such soils are protected from development and are to be preserved for agricultural use. Soils with productivity ratings below the county-designated cutoff are not regulated from development. When the ordinance was first adopted in 1973, a threshold CSR rating of 85 or above identified protected soils, but this definition did not sufficiently restrict development of important farmland.

Experience

Between 1979 and 1981, the county evaluated requests for rezoning of more than 680 acres of mostly prime farmland. The county only approved 72 acres for rezoning. Of these, 42 acres contained a majority of prime soil.

Until the early 1980s, residential development went unabated in unincorporated areas, but development no longer occurred on prime soils, which remained in agricultural production.

Four of the six counties bordering Black Hawk have adopted similar zoning ordinances, largely through the efforts of the area's Regional Council of Governments, which provided staff for the development and application of Black Hawk's policies.

County citizens have criticized the adoption of a single criterion—soil productivity—for guiding growth. They point out that the mere failure of a piece of land to meet productivity standards should not

mean it will be open to unguided development. The objections prompted a new comprehensive plan th encourages development in incorporated areas and a dresses protecting natural areas that may not conta productive soil.

The original CSR-based zoning ordinance w amended in 1982 to include a section identifying oth significant lands for protection. These included we lands, forests, and open prairies. In the 1982 revision the CSR rating above which soils receive protecte status was lowered to 50. The Planning Commissio reasoned that most parts of the country would beg f such productive soil, and that therefore it was wor evaluating the need for development upon it.

Black Hawk County exemplifies the depressed agr cultural economy plaguing Iowa and other centr states. It is essentially a one-industry communit where a large portion of the population is depende on agriculture and the farm equipment industry f livelihood. The region has lost tremendous amounts population. A county planner estimates the 1988 po ulation as 129,000, down from a 1980 population 137,000.

Building activity has been slight throughout th mid-1980s because of poor economic conditions i the county. The lethargy of the real estate market ha weakened the incentive to protect farmland. In 198 five out of six zoning requests on first-rate county so were approved, and the other request was withdraw before evaluation. Nevertheless, the county remai committed to the CSR program.

An original goal of the new ordinance was to guic growth into incorporated portions of the county. On of the ways it did this was by requiring developers t supply sewage and water treatment plants in the proposed subdivisions. The cost of these facilitie shifted developers' sights away from rural areas whe no infrastructure existed to incorporated parts of th county where land is more expensive but public se vices are in place.

CONTACT

Zoning Administrator
Black Hawk County
209 Fifth Street
Waterloo, IA 50701
(319) 235-0311

PROFILE

HARDIN COUNTY, KENTUCKY

Development Guidance System

Community Characteristics

Hardin County is located 45 miles southwest of Louisville, Kentucky's largest city. Bound on the north by the Ohio River, Hardin County soil is rich cropland thanks to minerals deposited over the centuries by the river.

Prior to the establishment of the Fort Knox military reservation in the late forties, Hardin depended almost exclusively on cultivating tobacco and corn for its livelihood. Thirty-six percent of the labor force still works in agriculture, out of an estimated 1988 county population of 98,300. Hardin has remained rural over the majority of its 616 square miles, but now Fort Knox contributes more to the local economy than all other industry and agriculture combined.

Growth Patterns

Ninety-six percent of the county is unincorporated, and most of the development has occurred in areas of prime farmland and most lacking in established infrastructure.

Adjacent to Fort Knox, Radcliff has become Hardin's largest city, with over 20,000 residents, even though the town was only incorporated in 1956. Radcliff's population doubled between 1970 and 1980, causing rapid unplanned development in the area, now viewed as an unsightly strip by surrounding towns.

Elizabethtown, the county seat, is 13 miles south of Radcliff and is almost the same size. The town became Kentucky's major transportation hub when several major highway junctions sprouted there in the early sixties. Much of the strip development outside Radcliff occurred along the highway corridor between the towns.

Resources Threatened

Farmland covers about 60 percent of the land in the county, and over 80 percent of that contains Class I, II, and III soils (as classified by the Soil Conservation Service). Prime soils and agricultural production were threatened by the proliferation of development in the agricultural areas of the county.

Measures Taken

In 1973, the county failed on its first attempt to form an effective planning commission, largely because citizens strongly opposed the imposition of land use controls, which they felt threatened their autonomy. After a hiatus, the county commission hired a full-time planner, who worked on developing a basic planning philosophy for the county, as well as on plans for land use, community facilities, and transportation. These measures were adopted in pieces during the early 1980s as public animosity to planning lessened.

In 1984, the county legislative body enacted the Development Guidance System (DGS), which steers growth away from valuable farmland into areas where capital investment in infrastructure has already occurred.

Through the DGS, all previously unzoned areas (most of the county) were designated as one district. Here, few uses are unequivocally prohibited or automatically allowed. Almost all development proposals require a conditional use permit to proceed. The DGS evaluates the proposal's suitability for a permit through three steps. In each, the proposal gains points. Out of a total possible 325 points, 150 are required for automatic approval, and less than 90 lead to automatic rejection. Proposals falling in between are reviewed by the county planning commission. The steps are:

- Evaluation of development potential on the proposed site, based on (a) soil productivity and (b) existence of nearby services. High-quality agricultural soil and the lack of nearby infrastructure would lead to a low score.

- Public assessment of the proposal's compatibility with existing uses in the surrounding area. The planning commission organizes local meetings between the developer and local landowners, in which the goal is to achieve a consensus on addressing the proposal's neighborhood impacts.

- Review of the proposal by county officials. If the proposal receives enough points based on the first two steps, affected agencies review the proposal to ensure conformity with existing standards and regulations. If it meets approval, a permit is issued.

Planning commission review staff are given short deadlines in which to examine submitted information. The approval process is often as little as six weeks.

Experience

The DGS rewards proposals located near existing development. As areas grow, more proposals will be found to be compatible. Review under the DGS does not address goals for the future or long-range growth management issues. Theoretically, under this planning system, the entire county could become intensely developed.

So far, the DGS has been an effective planning tool for a rural area that wants to keep good farmland in production, but also wants to encourage developme where it fits well with surrounding uses.

During its first four years, the DGS processed 139 a plications for development approval on undevelope sites. Sixty-four percent, or 89, of these were approve In total, development was approved on almost 2,00 acres over the first four years of the DGS program.

More applications were denied on top-quality soi than on middle soil groups. In addition to soil produ tivity, the criterion of compatibility with surroundi development proved decisive in many cases. Sevent nine percent of the applications for development ou side growth corridors were denied approval, and on 29 percent of approved proposals were outside growt corridors. Approved sites had an average of 35 perce of the surrounding area developed; denied sites ha about 20 percent developed.

The DGS has helped bring about greater objectivi in development approvals, which are largely remove from the legislative agenda, except in the case of pe mit appeals, which have been few so far. In this sens the DGS has perhaps reduced political pressure o land use planning. The DGS is so low-profile that th planning commission has had to make special effor to educate the public about it and the importance citizen participation. This has been accomplishe through an ad campaign in newspapers, a videotap presentation explaining the ordinance, and work shops for local organizations.

CONTACT

Hardin County Planning and Development Commission
14 Public Square
Elizabethtown, KY 42701
(502) 769-5479

PROFILE

KING COUNTY, WASHINGTON

Purchase of Development Rights (PDR) Program

Community Characteristics

...ound on the east by the Cascades, and on the west by ...get Sound, King County is a study in landscape ...versity. In addition to containing one of the nations ...ost scenic mountain ranges and a major West Coast ...aterway, King County also embraces several fertile ...ver valleys and metropolitan Seattle. One-fourth of ...e county's 2,125 square miles is within the Sno-...ualmie National Forest in the county's eastern ...aches. The county is also bisected east-west by the ...xtreme western reach of U.S. Route 90, which meets ...e largest West Coast interstate, I-5, on the outskirts ...f Seattle.

Sixty percent of the county's population of 1.25 mil-...on (a third of all of Washington State) lives in Seattle ...r smaller cities. The county's population density is ...n times the state average.

Between 1945 and 1975, urban growth consumed ...wo-thirds of the county's farmland. Lands with prime ...oils decreased from 165,000 acres to 55,000 acres. ...More recently, the rate of loss has averaged 2,000 acres ... year. Active farm operations have declined even ...nore steeply—from 6,500 at the end of World War II to ...,200 in 1975. Almost a fourth of those remaining are ...ommercial farms that earn 90 percent of the gross ...arm income in the county. The majority of farmers ...eap most of their income from nonfarm jobs. Agricul-...ure accounts for only 1 percent of all jobs in the ...ounty.

Orchards, berry, and vegetable farms dominate the ...andscape in the fertile valleys close to Seattle. These ...alleys contain 33,000 acres of the remaining farm-...and in the county. However, dairy farms account for ...0 percent of the agricultural land use countywide.

At the outskirts of the metropolitan area, farmers' ...narkets, roadside stands, and "u-pick" operations still ...ccount for a large part of farm product sales. Fruit ...nd vegetable markets have deteriorated recently, and production drop-offs have been reinforced by harvest labor shortages.

Growth Patterns

Superior access to Seattle, Washington's largest and most important metropolitan area, has made the prime farming lands in the river valleys—tradition-ally farmland strongholds—vulnerable to rapid ur-banization.

Most dairy operations take place on the plateaus at a greater distance from the metropolis than fruit and vegetable farming. Recently, a large amount of plateau farmland has been converted to large lot residential developments, hobby farms, and ranchettes.

Measures Taken

Despite a farmland protection policy dating back to 1964, urban growth continued to absorb agricultural areas. In 1976, the county placed an 18-month mor-atorium on development of lands that it determined to be severely threatened. During this time, advisory com-mittees of farmers formed to examine farmland reten-tion options. They recommended a program to acquire development rights through voluntary offerings.

In 1979, county voters passed a $50 million prop-erty tax bond issue for the Purchase of Development Rights (PDR) Program proposition with 63 percent voter support.

The program is authorized by an ordinance that divides eligible farmlands into three priority catego-ries based on the extent to which the land is threat-ened by development. The county acquires the devel-opment rights through a series of purchase rounds, in which only Priority 1 lands can participate during the first two rounds. In the third round, Priorities 1 and 2 lands may be considered, and after the third round all lands are eligible. The rounds continue until the $50 million is spent or six years have passed.

Legally, the program involves purchase of conservation easements rather than purchase of development rights. The manager of the agricultural program points out that "King County actually acquires an easement in gross which extinguishes certain of the landowner's bundle of rights. King County does not acquire the right to develop the property and thus, owns nothing that can be resold, traded or transferred."

The value of the development right is the difference between the land's value as farmland and its value for the "highest and best use." The value is determined by appraisals done separately by two independent appraisers selected through competitive bidding procedures. Their work is reviewed by a third appraiser. A citizen committee recommends which lands to purchase out of all the properties that have been voluntarily offered and meet the ordinance criteria.

Experience

The County Office of Agriculture began to implement the PDR program by notifying Priority 1 property owners of their eligibility. Almost half responded, indicating interest in receiving an appraisal of their property, both for agricultural value and market value. The average appraised value of development rights on eligible lands was $5,000 per acre.

The last acquisition financed by the 1979 bond is-sue was finalized in 1987. The county purchased development rights on a total of 12,658 acres of farmland from 187 different properties, for a total cost to the county of $53.8 million. The original goal had been to acquire between 10,000 and 15,000 acres, so the program's administrator calls it "immensely successful."

The program is now being monitored through preexisting county activities like building permits. The county has performed aerial surveys of program properties to ensure that owners are in conformity with the restrictive covenants recorded in their deeds, which ordain that no more than 5 percent of the property be covered by nontillable surface.

The ordinance authorizing the farmland preservation program designated seven eligible acquisition areas in the county. Some of these areas were only 1,500 acres, and development rights were acquired on only perhaps 1,000 of these. The parcels acquired in each area varied in size from 4 acres to 389 acres.

The county is not considering another farmland preservation bond issue at this time. First, county officials wish to determine whether this fragmented and geographically discontinuous PDR program effectively reduces overall development pressure on farm lands in the county.

CONTACT

Capital Improvement Section
Natural Resources and Parks Division
Parks, Planning and Resources Department
2040 84th Avenue Southeast
Mercer Island, WA 98040
(206) 296-4221

PROFILE

LANCASTER COUNTY, PENNSYLVANIA

Conservation Easement Program

Community Characteristics _____

wo distinct corridors, one man-made, the other deter-
ined by ancient natural forces, wind their way
cross Lancaster's landscape and characterize the con-
asting elements currently shaping the county. The
ennsylvania Turnpike stretches across the length of
e county just short of its northern edge, and the
usquehanna River forms its long southwestern bor-
er. The same forces that carved the river also depos-
ed rich soils.

Lancaster is the most productive agricultural
ounty east of the Mississippi, and the value of its
arm production exceeds that of any nonirrigated
ounty in the country. Farmland covers 65 percent of
ancaster County's 942 square miles, and accounts for
ne-sixth of the state's entire agricultural production.
oultry, hog, and dairy husbandry have grown in the
ast 20 years, and the county leads the state in corn,
ay, and tobacco production.

Dutch Mennonite farmers have tilled the land for
00 years. Their stewardship of the land, and the
ich soils contained in the county's limestone valleys
nd rolling schist hills, distinguish Lancaster from
imilar agricultural landscapes. Many farmers use
ineteenth-century methods of animal husbandry
nd raising of crops, and many parts of the county
ook and feel like something out of a bygone era.

Today, 4,900 farms are active in the county, run
ostly by families, and their average size is only 84
cres, which is very small compared with state and
ational averages. About 10 percent of Lancaster's
opulace is involved in agricultural activities, com-
ared with the national average of 1 percent.

Even so, in Lancaster County, as in the country na-
ionally, the portion of the population involved in
arming has declined. Some consolidation of production, along with urban development, are causing the
number of active farms to fall. Receipts from agriculture have stabilized during the mid-1980s, but farming is no longer a growing industry in Lancaster.

Growth Patterns _____

The county is wedged between two of the state's largest metropolitan areas. The city of Lancaster, the
county's hub, lies 37 miles east of Harrisburg and 66
miles west of Philadelphia. The Turnpike, carrying
growing numbers of travelers between the cities, has
also brought industry, commerce, and tourism to the
area. As a result, Lancaster has a diverse economic
base and a very low unemployment rate.

The county itself is now defined as "metropolitan."
Since 1950, population has soared by over 50 percent.
In 1988, Lancaster was home to 400,000 people. Development has raised land values, making it difficult to
buy land for agriculture, and attractive for farmers to
sell for nonfarm uses.

Resources Threatened _____

Since 1965, annual farmland loss has been as much as
8,000 acres. In the last five years (1983–88), between
3,000 and 5,000 acres a year have been lost. Much of
the development has occurred in a scattered, fragmented fashion away from dense population centers,
often in the midst of rural farming operations.

This type of development requires new infrastructure. Moreover, newcomers tend to be intolerant of
"nuisances" caused by farming operations. Such unplanned growth severely threatens prime farmland.

23

Measures Taken

Lancaster County commissioners adopted an Agricultural Land Preservation Conservation Easement Program in 1980. A nine-member Agricultural Preserve Board was appointed to administer the program. The program has several facets.

- Agricultural security areas are identified as areas at least 500 acres in size that contain mostly prime agricultural soil, are actively used for farming, and do not contain public sewerage facilities. Conservation easements are pursued principally on land located inside designated security areas, and the designation is necessary on lands requiring expenditure of public funds for preservation.

- Conservation easement donations are received by the county from landowners who volunteer to restrict their property deeds to agricultural use, without receiving compensation except in the form of possible tax benefits. Easements are donated for 25 years or in perpetuity.

- Conservation easement sales originally offered an incentive payment to landowners of $250 per acre. Due to lack of interest in this program among landowners, this portion of the program has been turned into a purchase of development rights program. The county offers up to appraised value for conservation easements. In 1988, the county acquired four easements and paid up to $3,200 per acre. The county makes offers only on land in the agricultural security areas.

- Right of first refusal agreements are contracts between the landowner and the county giving the county the first right to purchase the owner's property if it's to be sold. This guarantees the county an opportunity to buy the property, impose conservation easements, and then resell it.

- Purchase and resale allows the county to acquire a farm in the open market. This procedure is limited to properties where development pressure is high and whose continued capacity as farmland is crucial to maintain the quality of an agricultural security area.

A Lancaster County Agricultural Land Preservation Fund pays for purchasing conservation easements and other costs of the preservation program. Federal revenue sharing was terminated by Congress in 1987, so the $300,000 budget in that year came entirely from the county. In 1988, the budget was $330,000; it was $406,000 in 1989.

In addition, the Lancaster Farmland Trust is a private nonprofit preservation support group. It has raised funds for acquiring conservation easements, performed property surveys and appraisals, paid for legal expenses of IRS rulings, and encouraged landowners considering easement donations. It is a crucial public constituency for farmland preservation in the county.

Experience

Little prospect for countywide zoning exists in Lancaster County. Each of 60 municipalities has autonomous land use powers. The county conservation easement program has worked effectively in the context of decentralized local authority to preserve regional character. The success of the program is illustrated by the fact that:

- Seventy percent of new development has taken place in planned growth areas with existing infrastructure.

- Each of the county's 41 townships has some kind of land use plan and zoning ordinances. Thirty-two have agricultural zoning protecting farmland from conversion and promoting farm use.

- At the end of 1988, five agricultural security areas containing about 500 farms with over 35,000 acres had been established.

- The county is a national leader in the number of farms preserved by conservation easement donation. Over 5,600 acres on 64 farms are now protected through voluntary conservation easements. The majority of these were donated in perpetuity, the balance for 25 years.

- In 1987, the county implemented the purchase and resale option for the first time. The property was resold to a private party within 60 days. The county assumed the cost of development rights on the land and was surprised to find that this cost proved to be only about $500 an acre.

CONTACT

Lancaster County Agricultural Preserve Board
50 North Duke Street
P.O. Box 3480
Lancaster, PA 17603-1881
(717) 299-8300

PROFILE

MONTGOMERY COUNTY, MARYLAND

Transfer of Development Rights

Community Characteristics

This 500-square-mile county is part of the Washington, D.C., metropolitan area. Montgomery County is approximately two-thirds urban—its population of 665,000 means a density of 1,200 people per square mile. Suburban sprawl and office development, particularly along the Interstate 270 corridor, has created widespread traffic congestion.

Agriculture continues to be important to the county. The value of traditional commercial agricultural production is about $30 million a year, derived principally from corn, soybeans, hogs, and dairy cattle. Montgomery County planners also consider horticulture and associated services (lawn care and nurseries, for example) part of the agricultural industry. This industry brings in $130 million a year, and has grown over the past 20 years, whereas the value of farming in the county has declined. The waning value of commercial agriculture, and the rising economic contribution of a horticultural industry catering to a suburban lifestyle, illustrate the socioeconomic trends in Montgomery County.

Growth Pressures

Rapid development has strained the county's roads and public facilities and eliminated the agricultural economy in much of the county. Near Washington, older well-established single family neighborhoods clash with developers over proposals for large commercial complexes, office high-rises, and more parking garages.

Between 1979 and 1987, Montgomery County lost 19 percent of its agricultural land to urban development. However, the county still boasts 107,000 acres of active farmland curving around the area of dense urban development around Washington.

Measures Taken

A county-appointed task force concluded that Montgomery County needed more than a mere land preservation program: it needed a process that would maintain the viability of farming as a livelihood.

In order to protect farmland and maintain farming as a way of life at the "urban fringe," the county instituted a Transferable Development Rights (TDR) Program, and designated a "preferential agricultural zone," in which development was severely restricted.

This 89,000-acre district is officially called the "rural density transfer zone," or sending district, from which development rights may be purchased for use in undeveloped sites within the "growth centers," or receiving districts.

The sending district encompasses two-thirds of the active farmland in the county. The other farmland is generally located close to the developed areas and is zoned to make room for continued commercial and residential expansion.

The county previously had permitted two-acre and five-acre lots in the rural areas but, beginning in 1980, restricted development density in the sending district to one unit per 25 acres. In addition, the county encourages development in the rural zone to be clustered in one portion of the parcel.

Every five acres of land in the sending district generates one transferable development right which can then be sold for use in the receiving districts. This, in effect, compensates for the downzoning, and provides sending district landowners the incentive to sell their development rights. In the designated receiving districts, the purchase of a development right allows the buyer to build one additional residential unit per acre over the maximum permitted by zoning.

Farmers convinced the county to establish a bank to guarantee value for the development rights in case no market developed. Since the bank opened its doors in 1985, the private market for the TDRs has been strong, and the bank has never purchased TDRs or lent money based on TDR collateral.

Experience

Since 1983, when the first development rights were transferred, approximately 3,000 TDR transactions have taken place. Another 1,000 are being processed. Over 15,000 acres of active farmland are preserved by easements in perpetuity.

The county has identified more areas for the receiving districts, and expanded the preferential agricultural zone from its original 74,000 acres. This designation encourages agricultural and open space uses rather than residential development.

Usually a single development right sells for between $4,000 and $6,000. Real estate brokers list TDRs and collect a commission on their sale. Most sending district landowners have been contacted by firms seeking to list their rights.

Contact

Office of Economic Development
Suite 1500
101 Monroe Street
Rockville, MD 20850

Information Resources

Cook, Kenneth A. "American Agriculture at the Crossroads: A Conservation Assessment of the 1985 Food Security Act." Ankeny, Iowa: Soil and Water Conservation Society, undated.

This white paper discusses the conservation impacts of perhaps the most important land and water conservation initiative of the Reagan era.

National Agricultural Lands Study. *The Protection of Farmland: A Reference Guidebook for State and Local Governments*. Robert E. Coughlin and John C. Keene, Senior Authors and Editors, U.S. Government Printing Office, 1981.

An important volume produced by the National Agricultural Lands Study, the *Reference Guidebook* analyzes the effectiveness of the principal techniques for preserving farmland at the local level. Specific chapters focus on tax relief programs, agricultural districting, right-to-farm legislation, zoning, purchase of development rights, transfer of development rights, and legal and constitutional issues associated with agricultural land protection programs.

People for Open Space. *Endangered Harvest: The Future of Bay Area Farmland*. Summary Report of the Farmlands Conservation Project. San Francisco, CA: People for Open Space, 1985.

Examines development trends in the San Francisco Bay Area and their effects on the region's farmland. Documents the importance of that farmland to the regional economy and quality of life. Identifies ways in which action can be taken to preserve a permanent farm belt. An excellent publication by a local conservation organization which can serve as a model for other local organizations.

Steiner, Frederick R. *Ecological Planning for Farmlands Preservation*. Chicago: American Planning Association, 1984.

Summarizes the basic principles of ecological planning as they pertain to agland preservation. Describes means of organizing communities and various alternative preservation techniques.

Steiner, Frederick R., and John E. Theilacker. *Protecting Farmlands*. Westport, CT: AVI Publishing Company, 1984.

Provides an overview of farmland protection, specific state and local protection programs, the federal role in farmland protection, and international protection programs.

Toner, William. *Saving Farms and Farmland: A Community Guide*. Official Planning Advisory Service Report No. 333. Chicago, IL: American Society of Planning, 1978.

Introduces the reasons for farmland conservation, with specific tips on the process of saving farmland, and illustrative ordinance language.

Ward, Justin R. *Taxing the Rural Landscape: Improving State and Federal Policies for Prime Farmland*. Washington, D.C.: Natural Resources Defense Council, 1988.

Organizational Resources

American Farmland Trust

The American Farmland Trust undertakes a range of activities throughout the nation to protect agricultural land. It provides technical assistance to localities implementing agricultural land preservation strategies and directly protects farms by acquisition or similar techniques. 1920 N Street, N.W., Suite 400, Washington, D.C. 20036; (202) 659-5170.

National Association of Conservation Districts (NACD)

Conservation districts are the local agencies of state government concerned with conserving and developing water and land resources. The national association or the local Yellow Pages can provide information about contacting local conservation districts and their activities. 1012 Vermont Avenue, N.W., Suite 730, Washington, D.C. 20005; (202) 347-5995.

CHAPTER 2

Rivers and Wetlands

PROTECTING AND ENHANCING RIVERS
    Local Efforts to Protect Rivers
    Nonregulatory Techniques
    Private River Protection Initiatives
    State and Regional River Protection Programs
    Federal River Protection Programs

PROTECTING AND ENHANCING WETLANDS
    Local Wetlands Protection Programs
    Private Wetlands Protection Initiatives
    State Wetlands Protection Programs
    Federal Wetlands Protection Programs

SUGGESTIONS FOR BUILDING SUCCESSFUL LOCAL
  RIVER AND WETLANDS PROTECTION PROGRAMS

PROFILES
    Brandywine Conservancy
    Housatonic Valley Association
    Kissimmee River Basin
    Denver's Platte River Greenway
    Jackson, New Hampshire
    The Chesapeake Bay

INFORMATION RESOURCES

ORGANIZATIONAL RESOURCES

A river is more than an amenity, it is a treasure. It offers a necessity of life that must be rationed among those who have power over it.

—OLIVER WENDELL HOLMES

WATER is a basic necessity of life in both human and natural communities. Not only is a clean water supply critical to public and environmental health, but high-quality water resources contribute to economic well-being.

Activity on land has significant impacts on the quality and quantity of surface and groundwater. Sensitive land use strategies can protect and enhance the health of the hydrologic system, while, conversely, insensitive and poorly planned development can degrade and destroy entire water systems. Moreover, many communities have found that waterways can be the central feature around which to build local consensus for managing development to protect and enhance the area's distinctive resources and quality of life.

This chapter examines two interrelated types of water resources—rivers and wetlands. They are interrelated both geographically and hydrologically. Some of the most valuable inland wetlands, for example, occur on the fringe of rivers, spawning and sustaining many forms of river life. While the two are discussed separately, the information provided for each is similar, including:

- The public purposes served by protecting the resource;

- Local resource protection and enhancement programs;

- Complementary private initiatives;

- State and regional programs;

- Federal programs;

- Practical suggestions for building successful programs; and

- Profiles of communities and organizations that have implemented noteworthy resource protection efforts.

Protecting and Enhancing Rivers

Historically, rivers have been the birthplace of the world's great civilizations. The myths, folklore, and metaphors of both ancient and modern cultures reflect the central importance of rivers. Until railroads began to provide a cheaper form of transportation in the nineteenth century, the need to move people and goods on water dictated the location of major cities the world over. Even today, it is rare to find an American city of any size or economic distinction far from a river.

Where cities have not relied on rivers for transportation or hydropower, rivers have typically served other economic purposes. Denver, for example, grew along the confluence of the Platte River and Cherry Creek because gold was discovered there in the 1850s. Rivers also serve as a principal source of water supply for cities and farming, even where that water must be piped over long distances. Given the central importance of rivers to local development, they are a key

asset in many communities, and provide a good focus
around which to build local conservation and growth
management efforts.

Efforts to protect rivers and lands adjacent to rivers
typically serve multiple public objectives:

- Protection of people and property from flood damage;
- Protection of water quantity and quality for public drinking supplies;
- Protection of fish and wildlife habitat;
- Protection of ecological processes; and
- Promotion of scenic and recreational values.

The threats to river values are numerous:

- Construction of dams;
- Diversion of water for agricultural and urban uses;
- Contaminated runoff, such as oil and other toxic substances from impervious surfaces like roads, parking lots and industrial sites; animal wastes, chemical pesticides, and fertilizers from agricultural lands; hazardous wastes from landfills; and nutrients and contaminated wastewater from failing septic systems;
- Increased turbidity and sedimentation due to soil erosion from agricultural lands, disturbed hillsides, construction sites, mining sites, and logging sites;
- Impervious urban surfaces that increase runoff and flood hazards during wet periods, and prevent the recharge of the aquifers supplying much of the water flow during dry periods;
- Loss of public access due to inappropriate riverfront development;
- Channelization and shoreline engineering;
- Discharges from municipal sewage treatment plants and industrial facilities (called point source water pollution); and
- Litter from riparian landowners and recreational users.

Combating threats to river quality is made difficult by two related facts: (1) rivers typically cross many political jurisdictions; and (2) rivers are affected by what happens not just along their immediate shoreline but throughout their entire watershed as well. Thus, if the natural and human values of rivers are to be protected and restored, effective action must occur on a watershedwide basis, frequently in numerous jurisdictions.

LOCAL EFFORTS TO PROTECT RIVERS

The relationship between water quality and land use practices is clear. Successful river protection programs, therefore, tend to focus efforts both on critical lands immediately adjacent to the river as well as on lands throughout the entire watershed.

Many growth management techniques are relevant to river protection efforts, in part because of their usefulness in reducing soil erosion and stream sedimentation. For example, cluster zoning and related clustering techniques (discussed in Appendix A) can be used to preserve critical watersheds, to reduce the amount of impervious surfaces (which reduces the amount of pollution from storm-water runoff and road salt and sand), and to provide setbacks from rivers and wetlands. Hillside or slope protection programs (discussed in chapter 5) reduce land disturbance and impervious surfaces in steeply sloped areas, which reduces erosion, sedimentation, and water pollution from storm-water runoff. Programs to preserve woodlands or vegetation (chapter 5) also work to protect water quality.

The following discussion suggests some of the variety in local river protection programs.

Buffer Zones

River protection programs frequently establish some form of buffer zone or setback along the banks of a river. Buffer zones protect wildlife corridors, reduce exposure to flood hazards, ensure that vegetation along riverbanks will absorb and attenuate floodwaters, protect rivers from scenic degradation, and protect water quality by reducing and cleansing storm-water runoff. A buffer district requiring that development be set back from rivers and strictly regulating land-disturbing activity adjacent to a river is, in most cases, the most effective river protection regulation available to local governments. Sizable river setbacks are quite common. For example, Jackson, New Hampshire, has enacted a River Conservation District that requires a 75-foot minimum building setback from the town's major water courses. (See profile of Jackson at the end of this chapter.)

Delineating Buffer Zones. How to delineate the buffer zone is a key initial question. The width of the buffer should be based upon an evaluation of both the natural and the cultural characteristics of the river and the river corridor. Relevant natural factors include seasonal water levels, the nature and extent of adjacent wetlands and floodplains, the steepness of adjacent topography, the nature of riparian vegetation, and the wildlife values of adjacent lands. Relevant cultural factors include riverfront parcel size and depth, traditional use patterns of the river and its adjacent lands, and existing development along the river. Documenting the analyses of the factors can improve the legal defensibility of the buffer delineation and ensure that the buffer provides adequate protection.

Selecting the Type of Zone.   Based upon evaluation of the resource, permitted and existing uses, and current local land use programs, an approach to riverfront zoning should be selected. A riverfront buffer zone typically takes one of three forms: (1) a fixed setback standard that applies in existing riverfront zones; (2) a mapped zoning district that replaces the existing zoning districts along the river; or (3) a river conservation overlay zone.

A fixed river setback (which is much like a front or rear yard setback requirement) can be established in all zoning districts that border on a river. This setback can prohibit or strictly regulate the placement of structures or the disturbance of land within a minimum distance of the river. A minimum setback far in excess of a traditional front yard setback generally can be justified. For example, a setback requirement may apply landward for 150 feet from the midpoint or the mean high water mark of a river. The buffer should apply from a reference point on the river so that the zone will migrate as the river modifies its course.

A new zoning district can be created and mapped along the river corridor with new regulations for this district written into the zoning ordinance. This new district would replace the preexisting districts along the river. This approach may be preferred when a road, a railroad track, or similar boundary parallels the river and clearly delineates a strip of land between the river and the boundary.

An overlay zone can accommodate precisely various streamside characteristics, such as wetlands, riparian wildlife habitat, significant vegetation, and poorly drained soils. (Overlay zones are explained in Appendix A.) A river conservation overlay zone may or may not appear on the zoning map. For example, Brunswick, Maine, has a Shoreland Protection Zone that applies to all "land within 250 feet of the normal high water mark of any pond, river or salt water body." This area is delineated on the zoning map as one of the town's Natural Resource Protection Overlay Zones. In these zones, the permitted uses and special exception uses are the same as those in the underlying zoning districts, but subject to various performance standards.

While the geographic scope of a riverfront overlay district may not be mapped, it may be described in the text of the zoning ordinance. For example, the overlay zone may apply "within 500 feet of any portion of a wetland contiguous to" the river or "within 500 feet of Class I wildlife habitat." The precise location of the overlay district then depends upon the specific characteristics of an individual parcel and is determined on a case-by-case basis when development applications are filed. If the overlay zone is not mapped, the approximate location of the overlay district should appear in the community's natural heritage inventory, comprehensive plan, and perhaps on the zoning map—with the caveat that the mapped locations are only approximate and must be determined based upon a field survey.

Overlay zoning regulations may require that an applicant for development approval finance a field survey to determine the exact location of the various resource areas that define the overlay zone. This field survey is performed by a qualified professional biologist, soil scientist, or other appropriate scientist retained either by the developer or the community.

Placer County, California, delineates its waterfront overlay zone as follows:

A land strip on each side of the stream bed necessary to maintain existing water quality. The width of the stream environment zone shall be determined by investigation. Investigation shall consider:

(1) Soil type and how surface water filters into the ground;
(2) Types and amount of vegetative cover and how it stabilizes the soils;
(3) Slope of the land within the zone and how significant it is for retaining sediment from reaching the streams.

The intent of maintaining the Stream Environment Zone shall be to preserve the natural environment qualities and functions of the land to purify water before it reaches the streams.

Chapel Hill, North Carolina, takes a more objective approach in defining its Resource Conservation District:

A Resource Conservation District Elevation is hereby established, and defined to be that elevation two (2) feet above the 100-year floodplain elevation, as said 100-year elevation is delineated in the official Town floodplain maps.

The Resource Conservation District is hereby established as a district which overlays other zoning districts.... The Resource Conservation District shall consist of the area bounded by the Resource Conservation District Elevation and the areas within buffer zones established as follows:

a) Fifty (50) feet from the bank of a perennial stream draining less than one square mile, plus land with a slope greater than fifteen percent (15%), up to seventy-five (75) feet from such a bank, and

b) Fifty (50) feet from the bank of a perennial stream draining one square mile or more, plus land with a slope greater than fifteen percent (15%), up to one hundred (100) feet from such a bank.

These approaches demonstrate that there are numerous variations on performance-oriented overlay zones. A community may, for example, establish a fixed boundary, while providing landowners an opportunity to present documentation that the buffer should be narrower on their parcel. An ordinance that gives the landowner an opportunity to present such documentation improves both the legal defensibility and the political accountability of such regulations.

Choosing Permissible Land Uses.   In addition to determining the dimensions and specific type of buffer zone, a critical issue is what land uses will be allowed within this zone. Typically, only low-intensity uses such as recreation, grazing, or agriculture are permitted. Certain activities, such as altering streambanks, dredging, filling, and dumping of dredge spoils should be prohibited or strictly regulated. If a buffer zone is wide, low-density residential uses are often allowed outside the floodplain and the most sensitive portions of the buffer.

Agriculture can present special problems since farming often results in soil erosion and chemical runoff with the potential to severely degrade water quality. In its Shoreland Protection Zone, Brunswick, Maine, regulates agricultural uses by not only requiring that all structures be set back a minimum of 125 horizontal feet from the normal high-water mark of the river and be screened from the river by existing vegetation, but also prohibiting soil cultivation within 50 feet of the normal high-water mark of the river. The spreading or disposal of manure must be done in conformity with the state guidelines for manure and manure sludge disposal.

Overlay zoning districts are also widely used to provide performance standards throughout an entire watershed. The uses permitted in the preexisting zoning districts are still permitted, but all development within the watershed or critical portions of the watershed are subject to water quality protection performance standards.

NONREGULATORY TECHNIQUES

Effective land use regulations are essential for river protection. However, effective river protection programs typically cannot rely exclusively on regulatory elements, but must integrate regulatory elements with complementary nonregulatory approaches. A successful example of how complementary regulatory and nonregulatory approaches can be used to create an amenity along a river is the San Antonio Riverwalk. The Riverwalk has helped to transform downtown San Antonio into one of the leading tourist attractions in Texas and a prosperous downtown business district and convention center. (See the profile on San Antonio at the end of chapter 3.) The success of San Antonio's Riverwalk has also inspired similar efforts in other communities, including Denver (discussed below); the Bronx; Flint, Michigan; and Naperville, Illinois.[1]

Nonregulatory approaches have been especially effective in providing public access to rivers. While access easements generally can be required as a condition of granting a development permit,[2] land acquisition or agreements allowing access can provide access to lands that are not proposed for development.

Land acquisition is also an important tool for providing public access to rivers and protecting water resources. Land acquisition, of course, provides local government direct control over riparian land uses and their impacts. The drawbacks with acquisition are the frequently high cost of acquiring land, the local loss of tax revenues from removing land from the tax rolls, and the often high costs of managing and patrolling public land. Land acquisition has been an effective tool of land trusts and other privately inspired efforts.

PRIVATE RIVER PROTECTION INITIATIVES

Private, nonprofit citizen organizations often play an invaluable role in river protection and enhancement programs. Private initiatives have a solid track record of success in all aspects of river resource stewardship—from land protection and recreational development to resource enhancement.

A type of organization commonly formed to protect and enhance river resources is the watershed or river valley association. Organized to focus attention on and protect an entire watershed, these associations can help overcome the jurisdictional fragmentation that often hampers local efforts to manage a regional resource. (At the end of this chapter are discussions of three leading private nonprofit river protection organizations: the Housatonic Valley Association; the Brandywine Conservancy; and the Platte River Greenway Foundation.)

Although private river protection organizations are created and evolve under varying circumstances, a few central themes can be drawn from successful river protection programs:

- Early in life, river protection organizations generally focus exclusively on combating a direct threat to a river (the threat that catalyzes the organization). After establishing public visibility, identification with the river, and a track record of successful action, they often branch out to focus on activities throughout the entire watershed that affect the river's natural and cultural assets. These organizations evolve from a reactionary role to a creative role, in which they anticipate threats and enhance the status quo.

- As they mature, river protection organizations undertake a wide range of natural and cultural resource protection activities. These include traditional activities such as monitoring water quality; enhancing fisheries; acquiring critical parcels; promoting wild and scenic river designation; opposing dams, diversions, and illegal discharges; perfecting public access; as well as more innovative approaches such as drafting local river protection ordinances; assisting local governments with land use planning; planning and implementing greenways; sponsoring special events such as river celebrations, clean-up days, and canoe races; preserving historic and culturally significant buildings and sites connected with the river's history; publishing conservation handbooks and newsletters; conducting natural and cultural resource inventories; promoting soil protection and improved agricultural and forestry management practices; promoting recycling and proper disposal of household hazardous wastes; and addressing solid and hazardous waste transportation and disposal issues.

- Rivers are an ideal catalyst for public action on a host of issues. River protection groups have successfully used the protection and enhancement of rivers as a theme around which to build public involvement and consensus for more effective community land use and development programs throughout the region.

STATE AND REGIONAL RIVER PROTECTION PROGRAMS

Because of the regional scale of many watersheds, state and regional governments have been active in devising ways to protect rivers. At least 25 states have developed river protection programs. In many cases, state programs establish the policy or regulatory framework within which local programs operate.

Those concerned with river protection and revitalization should understand their state river protection programs and look for opportunities to build effective local programs as part of the state and regional framework.

Some examples of noteworthy state programs include:

The Massachusetts Scenic and Recreational Rivers Act was enacted in 1971 to classify and conserve the state's outstanding natural, cultural, and recreational rivers and streams. A comprehensive inventory of the state's rivers was undertaken.

Area legislators, local officials, landowners, and citizen advisory committees play an important role in the designation process. Before a river is designated, a protective order and management plan must be developed and adopted by the Department of Environmental Management. The protective orders regulate activities such as dredging and filling within 100 yards of a river's natural bank and are recorded on the deeds of riverfront land.

Because this state-level designation process was found to be both expensive and time-consuming, the original legislative authority has been deemphasized during recent years, and several innovative approaches to river conservation, which stress local initiative, have been developed. Rivers with state-approved but locally developed and supported conservation mechanisms or management plans can be officially recognized as "local scenic rivers" if those plans outline specific conservation strategies. The Scenic Rivers Program can offer technical assistance and, in some cases, funding to communities to help them develop these strategies. These river corridors receive priority for state grants and, if requested, additional state protection is available. Through 1988, eight rivers had been designated through local programs.

The Massachusetts Scenic Rivers Program is now recognized for its comprehensiveness and its local citizen participation. Reorienting the program to encourage local initiative and providing technical and financial assistance to responsive communities has created a growing state, local, and private partnership in river conservation.[3]

In 1981, the Oregon legislature established a two-pronged Riparian Tax Incentive Program to maintain or enhance streamside areas and improve instream fish habitat. The first prong of Oregon's program grants a complete property tax exemption for eligible lands. A participating landowner pays no property tax on a stream bed or forestry or agricultural lands within 100 feet of the stream's channel. The landowner must agree that only land use activities consistent with the protection or restoration of riparian habitat will be permitted along the stream corridor. This limits adverse land uses, such as grazing livestock down to the water's edge, in exchange for a property tax exemption for the affected area.

The second prong of Oregon's program provides an income tax credit for certified fish-habitat improvement projects. Up to 25 percent of the cost incurred in a project (for example, bank stabilization or fencing) can be deducted from one's personal or corporate state income tax. Both portions of the Oregon program are voluntary, relying on public-private cooperation.

The program does have its limitations. Participation does not result in public access. The state legislature has restricted both the number of miles of eligible streambank and the total tax credit allowed for the program in any given year. A property tax exemption for two miles of stream frontage, 100 feet deep, usually will not cover the cost of two miles of new fencing. It is not surprising, therefore, that applications have been slow to come in.

However, despite the monetary inducements, the basic thrust of the program is educational. The tax-relief approach does help to draw attention to the program and its other more long-term benefits for landowners, such as controlling soil erosion and maintaining the water-storage capacity of the riparian zone, which improves stream flow in the late summer. And because the program is voluntary, state officials now have a basis for working one-on-one with riparian landowners in a cooperative, constructive way.[4]

The Saco River Corridor Commission was created by the Maine legislature in 1973 as a steward of the Saco River, which flows from New Hampshire's White Mountains through fast-growing southern Maine to the Atlantic. The commission was created as a regional land use regulatory agency, consisting of one member from each of the 20 communities along the river. The commission has developed uniform zoning regulations adopted by all communities along the river corridor. Forty percent of the land in the river corridor is within a Resource Protection District, where all development other than farming and forestry is tightly controlled. In addition, approximately half of the land in the river corridor is designated a Limited Residential District, in which river frontage and setback requirements limit development along the river, and subdivision review discourages unsightly building location.

The Mississippi Headwaters Board in Minnesota, created in 1980, draws together eight counties. The board has prepared a comprehensive plan for the upper 40 miles of the river and a model land use ordinance, relying for advice and guidance on a formal citizens' advisory committee. When a county chooses not to adopt the provisions of the model ordinance or decides to withdraw from the board, the state (which helps fund the board) can assume management of the county's river segment.

The Kissimmee River Resource Planning and Management Committee (KRRPMC) has undertaken an ambitious regional program to protect and restore Florida's Kissimmee River. Channelized by the Army Corps of Engineers for flood control and other purposes, the Kissimmee lost over half of its original wetlands acreage. The KRRPMC's objectives include maintaining flood protection while enhancing the river's environmental quality. (The Kissimmee River effort is discussed in the profile at the end of this chapter.)

FEDERAL RIVER PROTECTION PROGRAMS

The National Wild and Scenic Rivers Act of 1968[5] establishes a system to protect free-flowing rivers with outstanding scenic, recreational, geologic, wildlife, historical, cultural, or similar values. Of the nearly 3.6 million miles of rivers and streams in the United States, 7,709 miles in 75 rivers or river segments have been designated as wild or scenic rivers through 1988.[6] Rivers are classified as "wild," "scenic," or "recreational," depending upon how close the river and its surrounding habitat are to a natural state. Rivers designated for protection are managed under plans approved by the secretary of the interior or, if the river flows through national forest land, by the secretary of agriculture.

The Wild and Scenic Rivers Act establishes a federal-state system of river conservation. The main protection tool is planning, although a designated river also can be protected through federal acquisition of surrounding land and prohibition of federal dam building. Designations are made by an act of Congress or by a state request and the approval of the secretary of the interior. Rivers may continue to be owned and managed by state or local governments or in partnership with the federal government.

The act also authorizes the National Park Service, through its River Conservation Technical Assistance Program, to help local and state agencies, private groups, and landowners to conduct statewide river assessments, river greenway plans, and conduct river conservation workshops. (See the Organizational Resources section at the end of this chapter.)

The National Flood Insurance Program (NFIP) provides a strong impetus for communities to enact floodplain zoning and to control construction practices within river and coastal floodplains. The National Flood Insurance Act of 1968, as amended by the Flood Disaster Protection Act of 1973, provides federally subsidized flood insurance for property in mapped flood-prone areas. In return, local and state governments must enact and enforce comprehensive floodplain management measures designed to reduce exposure to flood damage, including land use controls and building standards. The program supplements the traditional tools of local land use planning and development management in flood-prone areas.

The program has created flood insurance rate maps (FIRM), which delineate flood-prone areas. After a locality enters the program and complies with federal regulations, the local government must require that all development within the designated floodplain be designed and built to withstand a 100-year storm (that is the storm with a 1 percent chance of occurring in any given year.) Basically, new development, including substantial improvements to existing structures, within the 100-year floodplain must be elevated above the flood level.[7]

Protecting and Enhancing Wetlands

Wetlands (including areas such as coastal salt marshes, bottomland hardwood forests, bogs, prairie potholes, playa lakes, pocosins, and the wet tundra of Alaska), are (as this list implies) diverse ecosystems. But wetlands share a common denominator—they are covered with water all or part of the time due to tidal action, surface runoff, or groundwater. The characteristics of a wetland are determined by

> the depth of this water, its velocity, its periodicity and the length of inundation or saturation, its salinity, and the presence of dissolved or suspended substances. These factors also determine hydrologic functions and values, such as groundwater discharge and recharge, flood conveyance, and flood storage, as well as other wetland functions and values, e.g. habitat and recreational values.[8]

Wetlands—in their various forms—serve numerous critical ecologic, economic, and recreational functions:

- Wetlands provide critical breeding, nesting, and feeding habitats for many species of waterfowl, mammals, and reptiles. Although wetlands account for only 5 percent of the land surface in the 48 contiguous states, approximately one-third of the nation's endangered and threatened species live in or are dependent on wetland habitats.[9]
- Wetlands often protect and improve water quality by moderating surface runoff; recharging groundwater supplies; and trapping and removing sediment, nutrients, and chemical pollutants.

- Wetlands are the spawning and nursery grounds for many commercial fish and shellfish species. Coastal wetlands provide nursery and spawning grounds for 60 to 90 percent of U.S. commercial fisheries.[10]
- Wetlands reduce flood hazards by reducing the velocity of flowing water, absorbing and slowly releasing floodwaters, thereby lowering flood peaks.[11]
- Wetlands provide recreational opportunities for birders, hunters, canoeists, and others.
- As fish and shellfish breeding and spawning grounds, wetlands are critical to recreational fishing.
- Coastal wetlands and those inland wetlands adjoining larger lakes and rivers reduce the impact of storm tides and waves before they reach upland areas.

In spite of a growing appreciation of the value of wetlands and efforts to preserve them, wetland areas continue to be lost at a rapid rate, both from direct conversion and from degradation. According to one source, less than half of the original 215 million wetland acres found in the contiguous United States remain.[12]

LOCAL WETLANDS PROTECTION PROGRAMS

Pursuant both to general state police power enabling legislation and more specific legislative mandates, local governments have employed a variety of strategies to protect important local wetland resources. Many of the techniques used for river conservation also apply to wetlands. In addition to mapping wetland resources, specific types of local regulations include:

- Zoning;
- Subdivision regulations; and
- Mitigation requirements

Defining Wetlands
Effectively preserving wetlands requires evaluating the extent and variety of wetland resources in the applicable area. Determining the boundaries of a wetland, or "wetlands delineation," as planners and scientists call it, can be a difficult challenge. Not all wetlands are readily apparent as such to the untrained eye. Some inland wetlands, or "meadows," for example, may be mistaken for dry grassland. The extent of some wetlands varies seasonally, creating further difficulty in identifying wetlands. An expert is often needed to determine the scope of seasonal wetlands

during the dry season. From a policy standpoint, wetlands are characterized either as freshwater (also called inland) wetlands or as saltwater (also called coastal or tidal) wetlands.

The definition of wetlands in wetlands protection programs varies. Most wetlands regulatory programs, including the federal wetlands program, define wetlands based upon vegetation, soil type, and hydrology. Other programs define wetlands based only upon soil type.[13] In either case, a professional on-site evaluation is usually necessary to determine the precise extent of a wetland area.

The approximate scope of a wetland can be determined from evaluating wetlands inventories or soils maps. Technical assistance in using these resources or in mapping wetlands can generally be obtained from government sources, including state departments of environmental protection or geological surveys, the U.S. Soil Conservation Service, the local soil conservation districts, or the U.S. Fish and Wildlife Service, which maintains a National Wetland Inventory. Many of these agencies maintain wetland maps, generally based upon aerial photographs and/or U.S. Geological Survey topographic maps.

Given the nature of wetlands, however, many wetlands protection programs do not rely solely on mapping to delineate wetlands subject to regulation. As stated by a wetlands policy expert:

Detailed mapping may give rise to the erroneous belief that wetland boundaries can be located with mathematical precision. In fact, boundaries must be somewhat flexible since they reflect a natural transition from water to upland and fluctuating ground or surface water levels.[14]

As a result, wetlands regulatory programs often recognize that wetlands maps are appropriate for planning purposes, but not for determining actual regulatory boundaries. For regulatory purposes, most regulatory programs require an on-the-ground field investigation to locate precise wetland boundaries. Typically, this field investigation is undertaken by a soils scientist or wetlands biologist retained by the applicant and reviewed by the staff or a consultant of the regulatory agency.

Orono, Minnesota, for example, imposes wetland protection standards to manage wetlands delineated on USGS topographical maps, while allowing landowners to challenge that delineation through site-specific investigations.

Farmington, Connecticut's ordinance employs a similar approach:

To prove himself exempt from these regulations the applicant must present documentation by a soil scientist that the land in question, or a portion of it, does not have a soil type classified by the National Cooperative Soil Survey as poorly drained, very poorly drained, alluvial, or floodplain.[15]

Some jurisdictions, such as Concord, Massachusetts, have adopted detailed wetlands maps as an official zoning map, and adopted an overlay zone that applies to these mapped wetlands areas. The Concord Zoning Bylaws authorize a waiver from the district if the reviewing board determines that an area is, in fact, not a wetland.*

Zoning
Zoning is the most common form of local wetlands regulation. Wetlands zoning regulations are set forth either as an integral part of a comprehensive zoning ordinance or as a separate set of regulations. These regulations typically limit permissible uses to those that do not entail significant surface disturbance or runoff. Effective wetlands protection regulations address grazing and other agricultural uses, which may be apparently innocuous, but potentially destructive due to trampling of vegetation and runoff of nutrients and pesticides. (See page 38.)

The most common form of wetlands zoning identifies wetland areas and significantly restricts land-disturbing activities within these areas.

Wetlands zoning regulations often also establish a buffer zone with permissible uses within this buffer zone severely restricted. Protection provided by these buffer zones helps to insulate wetlands and water quality from impacts of surrounding land uses. For example, the town of Avon, Connecticut, has implemented inland wetlands and watercourses protection regulations that regulate activities within defined wetlands and watercourses and "within 40 feet of the boundary of such wetlands or 80 feet of the boundary of such watercourses." Likewise, Sharon, Connecticut, prohibits the placement of a waste disposal system within 50 feet of the boundary of any defined wetland.

METHODS OF ALTERING WETLANDS
Physical
1. Filling:
   —adding any material to change the bottom level of a wetland or to replace the wetland with dry land;

---

* The Concord, Massachusetts, Wetlands Conservancy District map, mapped at a scale of one inch equals 100 feet, consists of 122 separate sheets. This level of detail may be beyond the means of many communities.

WETLANDS CONVERSIONS
(mid-1950s to mid-1970s)

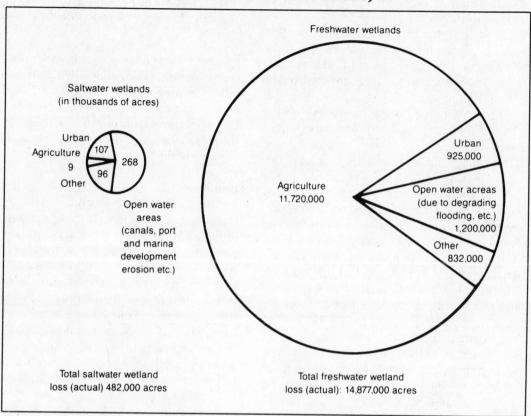

Freshwater wetlands

Saltwater wetlands
(in thousands of acres)

Urban
Agriculture
9
Other

107
96
268

Open water
areas
(canals, port
and marina
development
erosion etc.)

Urban
925,000

Open water acreas
(due to degrading
flooding, etc.)
1,200,000

Agriculture
11,720,000

Other
832,000

Total saltwater wetland
loss (actual) 482,000 acres

Total freshwater wetland
loss (actual): 14,877,000 acres

Source: U.S. Office of Technology Assessment and U.S. Fish and Wildlife Service National Wetland Trends Study, 1982

2. Draining:
—removing the water from a wetland by ditching, tiling, pumping, etc.;

3. Excavating:
—dredging and removing soil and vegetation from a wetland;

4. Diverting water away:
—preventing the flow of water into a wetland by removing water upstream, lowering lake levels, or lowering groundwater tables;

5. Clearing:
—removing vegetation by burning, digging, application of herbicide, scraping, mowing or otherwise cutting;

6. Flooding:
—raising water levels, either behind dams or by pumping or otherwise channeling water into a wetland;

7. Diverting or withholding sediment:
—trapping sediment, through construction of dams, channelization or other types of projects;

thereby inhibiting the regeneration of wetlands in natural areas of deposition, such as deltas;

8. Shading:
—placing pile-supported platforms or bridges over wetlands, causing vegetation to die;

9. Conducting activities in adjacent areas:
—disrupting the interactions between wetlands and adjacent land areas, or incidentally impacting wetlands through activities at adjoining sites;

Chemical

1. Changing nutrient levels:
—increasing or decreasing levels of nutrients within the local water and/or soil system, forcing changes in wetland plant community;

2. Introducing toxics:
—adding toxic compounds to a wetland either intentionally (e.g. herbicide treatment to reduce vegetation) or unintentionally, adversely affecting wetland plants and animals;

Biological

1. Grazing:
   —consumption and compaction of vegetation by either domestic or wild animals;
2. Disrupting natural populations:
   —reducing populations of existing species, introducing exotic species or otherwise disturbing resident organisms.

Subdivision Regulations

In addition to zoning, communities use subdivision regulations to protect wetlands resources. Many communities use subdivision regulations to protect wetland resources without creating an explicit wetlands protection program, by imposing limitations on the use of septic systems in or near poorly drained soils, and using open space dedications to buffer wetland areas.

Mitigation Requirements

When regulatory programs require an individual permit for development proposals that would affect wetlands, one of three outcomes is possible—denial, approval, or conditional approval. Many localities use conditional approvals in certain situations to require developers to minimize or compensate for the deleterious impacts of projects on wetlands resources.

The potentially broad scope of these actions is suggested by the definition of mitigation options summarized in the Council on Environmental Quality's National Environmental Policy Act guidelines. According to these guidelines, mitigation includes:

- Avoiding the impact altogether by not taking a certain action or parts of an action;
- Minimizing impacts by limiting the degree or magnitude of the action and its implementation;
- Rectifying the impact by repairing, rehabilitating, or restoring the affected environment;
- Reducing or eliminating the impact over time by preservation and maintenance operations during the life of the action; and
- Compensating for the impact by replacing or providing substitute resources or environments.[16]

The first two items might be better characterized as wetlands conservation rather than wetlands mitigation. Recently, the term "mitigation" has come to encompass actions taken on other sites to compensate for or replace wetlands disturbed by development projects (this is often termed "off-site mitigation"). Off-site mitigation is sometimes used to trade loss of wetlands on one site for restoration of degraded wetlands or creation of artificial wetlands at another site. However, wetland scientists have questioned the ability of man-made wetlands to replicate the functions of natural wetlands; for this reason, wetlands regulators generally oppose off-site mitigation, except to compensate for the unavoidable impacts of certain water-dependent uses.

A recent innovation in the evolution of mitigation requirements is the creation of "mitigation banks" as a means to facilitate off-site mitigation efforts. These programs create a revolving fund to finance restoration, replacement, acquisition, or improvement of wetland resources. Fees paid by developers or landowners proposing to destroy, disturb, or degrade wetlands finance a revolving fund in lieu of direct mitigation action. Although this controversial technique is still experimental, it addresses criticism that direct mitigation undertaken by developers often has not been successful. Local or state resource conservation agencies presumably are more likely to possess the expertise and sustained commitment necessary to ensure the success of a mitigation effort.

PRIVATE WETLANDS PROTECTION INITIATIVES

Private, nonprofit organizations have played a significant role in acquiring, preserving, and educating the public about wetlands. At the national level, the National Audubon Society has acquired approximately 500,000 acres of wetlands to preserve bird habitat. In 1983, the Nature Conservancy began a $55 million National Wetlands Conservation Project, which, as of 1986, had protected over 150,000 acres. These organizations and others acquire land both for their own management, and, in advance of the availability of public funds, for subsequent transfer to a federal, state, or local agency. Independent of the rigidities of the public appropriations process, and typically more adept at using easements, donations, and bargain sales, well-capitalized nonprofits often can make the difference between success and failure in wetlands acquisition projects.

Several Nature Conservancy projects illustrate the capabilities of nonprofits:

- The conservancy's largest purchase east of the Mississippi to date is some 70,000 acres of pristine tidal wetlands along Florida's Gulf Coast, in the Big Bend region. The conservancy acquired the property from Buckeye Cellulose, a division of Procter and Gamble, at a bargain sale. The state of Florida

ROGER K. LEWIS

later acquired the property with funds from its Save Our Coast land acquisition program.

- In the Cache River Basin in Arkansas, which attracts large concentrations of mallard ducks, the conservancy has acquired and transferred nearly 5,000 acres to the U.S. Fish and Wildlife Service, which has placed a priority on preserving the declining wetlands acreage in the basin.

- On Block Island, Rhode Island, the conservancy raised in excess of $1.5 million in donations as well as a $7 million low-interest loan to match federal and local funds. The conservancy has purchased critical wetlands at a bargain sale as a condition of receiving donations of other parcels from area landowners.

- Eighty-five hundred acres of wetlands owned by petrochemical companies at Peach Point, Texas, were acquired by the conservancy through donation and bargain sale and later sold to the Texas Parks and Wildlife Department for management as wildlife habitat.

Hunting and fishing groups also provide leadership in wetlands acquisition. Ducks Unlimited, for example, has acquired more than 3 million acres of wetlands in the United States and Canada and has spent major sums on habitat restoration. Ducks Unlimited and similar groups operating locally make rental payments to wetlands owners for conservation purposes, hunting, and fishing. Gun clubs in Southern California have donated over 25,000 acres of marshes, worth approximately $20 million, to the Nature Conservancy for subsequent transfer to the state.

Local conservancies and land trusts have also been instrumental in preserving and enhancing wetlands resources. These groups often use the same land protection techniques as national nonprofits such as the Nature Conservancy. Local land trusts often have an advantage in negotiating easement donations and bargain sales from neighboring landowners. (See chapter 6 for more detailed discussion of land trust management. Appendix B contains a discussion of land acquisition techniques.)

STATE WETLANDS PROTECTION PROGRAMS

States have been major factors in wetlands protection. State involvement is especially appropriate since wetlands often affect and are affected by developments and resources in a larger-than-local watershed. State programs include both regulatory and nonregulatory approaches.

Regulatory Programs

State regulatory efforts cover both coastal and inland wetlands, with the former generally receiving greater protection. Many coastal states regulate activities affecting coastal wetlands as part of comprehensive coastal programs approved under the federal Coastal Zone Management Act.[17]

Inland wetlands, which generally receive less protection than coastal wetlands, are managed through a variety of means, including floodplain management, shoreland protection statutes, and water quality control programs. Some 16 states administer specific wetland protection laws.[18] In most cases, states set standards for local development permitting and exercise review authority, rather than exercise direct state regulation.

New England states lead the nation in state regulation of inland wetlands, with noteworthy programs in Connecticut, Massachusetts, New Hampshire, and Rhode Island.[19] In each state, the scope of regulated wetlands is generally determined on a site-specific basis when a development application is made. General wetlands maps are used for planning purposes. In New Hampshire and Rhode Island, the state controls the program. In Connecticut and Massachusetts, the programs are delegated to the municipalities with state oversight. With minor statutory exceptions, each state requires a permit whenever any material is removed, deposited, or obstructs, alters, or pollutes a wetland.[20]

In 1987, New Jersey adopted a Freshwater Wetlands Protection Act, which establishes a comprehensive state wetlands regulation program. The program requires a permit from the state Department of Environmental Protection before undertaking activities in freshwater wetlands or adjacent to environmentally sensitive wetlands. (The act preempts any local wetlands regulations.) The act divides wetlands into three classes, and creates a buffer zone of 75 to 150 feet for wetlands of exceptional resource value, and a buffer zone of 25 to 50 feet for wetlands of intermediate resource value. Most activities regulated by the act are prohibited within these buffer zones. The act also creates a wetlands mitigation bank to finance off-site mitigation projects.

North Dakota also enacted a wetlands protection law in 1987. The North Dakota law requires that certain wetlands be replaced on an acre-for-acre basis when drained. This act also creates a state wetland bank and a revolving wetlands replacement fund.[21]

In addition, Wisconsin's Shoreline Zoning Act requires local governments to restrict development in shoreline wetlands. Also in the Midwest, Michigan's Goemaere-Anderson Wetland Protection Act combines permit requirements, strong penalties for noncompliance, and a well-developed education component in a successful state wetlands protection program.

Nonregulatory Programs

State-level nonregulatory programs are even more varied. Some states have very active wetlands acquisition programs: In Florida, for example, state water management districts have acquired hundreds of thousands of acres of inland wetlands and adjacent lands through the Save Our Rivers program. The program is funded by the state's 0.05 percent real estate conveyance tax, of which 10 percent is earmarked for acquisition of land for water management, supply, conservation, and protection.

New Jersey's "Green Acres" program funds both direct state wetlands acquisition, as well as low-interest loans to local governments for their own acquisition efforts. In the Pinelands National Reserve, over 25,200 acres have been purchased with federal and Green Acres funds since this planning area was designated in 1979.

States use a variety of mechanisms for funding these programs, including general obligation bonds, waterfowl stamps, income tax check-offs for nongame species, real estate transfer taxes, "vanity" license plate fees, and state sales tax revenues. The California Land Bank program is funded by landowners and developers paying money to settle title disputes on land claimed by the state pursuant to its public trust responsibilities.

States provide a variety of financial incentives for wetlands protection. Wyoming, for example, supplements federal incentives for rangeland improvements, including wetlands enhancement, on land leased from the Bureau of Land Management. The Reinvest in Minnesota program provides payments to owners of wetlands and adjacent lands in exchange for permanent conservation easements. South Dakota provides payments to landowners who retire wetlands and other areas from agriculture to provide wildlife habitat. More than half the states have programs providing one or more type of tax incentives for protection for wetlands and other open lands. These include property tax abatements or exemptions, property tax credits, and income tax deductions for easement donations.

FEDERAL WETLANDS PROTECTION PROGRAMS

The federal government is a major player in wetlands protection and management. The nation's principal wetlands protection program is found in Section 404 of the Clean Water Act, which prohibits the discharge of materials into "the waters of the United States," including their adjacent wetlands, without a valid permit.[22]

In essence, Section 404 of the act requires a permit from the U.S. Army Corps of Engineers (COE) before discharging dredged or fill materials into "the waters of the United States," including their adjacent wetlands.[23] The COE may issue a permit after adequate public notice and an opportunity for a public hearing. The COE evaluates 404 permit applications in accordance with its "public interest review" policy, the 404(b) (1) guidelines promulgated by EPA, the Fish and Wildlife Coordination Act, and the National Environmental Policy Act.

This federal program is an extraordinarily broad, complex, and potent tool to ensure that land development does not degrade wetlands and water resources. The program is not "user friendly." The Clean Water Act itself gives the reader no idea of the breadth or complexity of the program. Local officials and activists should understand the program so that local wetlands protection efforts complement the program to the extent possible.

As part of its oversight responsibilities for the Clean Water Act and under Section 404, the U.S. Environmental Protection Agency (EPA) recently announced a policy of "no net loss" for the nation's wetlands. This action follows the recommendations of the National Wetlands Policy Forum, convened by The Conservation Foundation and chaired by Governor Thomas H. Kean of New Jersey. Implementation of this goal and other recommendations of the Forum could have far-reaching ramifications for managing wetlands throughout the country.

The federal government also employs various non-regulatory tools for protecting and enhancing wetlands resources, including:

- Various wetlands acquisition programs undertaken by the Fish and Wildlife Service, National Park Service, the Bureau of Land Management, the For-est Service, and the National Oceanic and Atmospheric Administration;

- Funding programs to support state and local wetlands acquisition efforts, including the Migratory Bird Conservation Fund, the Land and Water Conservation Fund, and the matching grant programs of the Pittman-Robertson and the Dingell-Johnson acts;

- Various subsidy programs to encourage farmers not to cultivate wetlands, including the Water Bank Program, the "Swampbuster" provision of the 1985 Food Security Act, and the same act's Conservation Reserve Program;

- Income tax incentives for charitable contributions of wetlands and conservation easements to qualified nonprofits and government agencies; and

- Wetland restoration projects undertaken to improve wetlands values on federally owned land.

Suggestions for Building Successful Local River and Wetlands Protection Programs

The following suggestions can improve the effectiveness of local wetlands and river protection programs:

- Work with landowners and developers to identify mutual interests and ways of preserving critical watershed or buffer parcels before development plans reach an inflexible point.

- Think in terms of protecting critical lands throughout the entire watershed, not simply a river or wetland itself and its immediate environs.

- Manage rivers and wetlands from a hydrologic perspective. Successful programs are based upon an understanding and appreciation of hydrologic factors.

- Look for opportunities to restore degraded river segments or wetlands.

- Build regional programs that reflect the fact that rivers, wetlands, and their watersheds tend to overlap multiple jurisdictions.

- Build a broad constituency of interests supporting wetland or river protective actions, including birders, hikers, fishermen, hunters, canoeists, and others who enjoy and benefit from the resource involved.

- Combine multiple protection techniques, both regulatory and nonregulatory, to increase flexibility in preserving lands with varying characteristics.

- Reserve land acquisition for priority parcels under imminent threat of development.

- Understand and utilize federal and state wetlands protection programs. Build local programs to complement federal and state programs.

- Carefully draft regulations to ensure that they do not result in a regulatory "taking" by prohibiting all economically reasonable uses of a parcel.

PROFILE

BRANDYWINE CONSERVANCY

Full Service Environmental Management

Mission and Key Objectives ─────────────

The Brandywine Conservancy was formed in 1967 out of concern for the future of the natural and cultural resources of the rural Chadds Ford, Pennsylvania, area outside of Philadelphia. Soon thereafter, the conservancy took on the larger mission of preserving the scenic Brandywine River Valley. The conservancy preserves, protects, interprets, utilizes, and displays the resources of the Brandywine region through two operations—the Brandywine River Museum and the Environmental Management Center.

The Environmental Management Center advocates a comprehensive approach to resource preservation and environmental planning and management that strikes a balance between the preservation of important resources and the realities of environmental and economic change. It does this by providing landowners, local governments, and other organizations with technical consulting services, applied research, and the analysis of resources as well as economic and environmental issues affecting their protection. This is accomplished through the following programs:

- Land stewardship—assists private and public landowners in developing short- and long-range plans for protecting and improving, and (if consistent with the conservancy's mission and community goals) developing portions of their farmland, open space, waterways, or historic sites.

- Environmental management assistance—assists local and state agencies in developing plans and regulations to guide community growth and protect natural and cultural resources.

- Historic preservation—conducts historic site surveys, researches historic property records; prepares nominations to the National Register of Historic Places; develops concepts and plans for preservation, renovation, or conversion of historic structures or districts; and provides tax information and assistance to investors and owners of historic properties.

Geographic Scope ─────────────────

The activities of the Brandywine Conservancy Environmental Management Center focus on the Brandywine Valley of eastern Pennsylvania and northern Delaware, but consulting assistance is provided on specific issues on a much broader geographic basis.

Success Stories ──────────────────

The conservancy has preserved more than 16,000 acres of farmland, woodland, and stream valleys; listed more than 100 sites and historic districts on the National Register of Historic Places; and prepared innumerable local comprehensive plans and zoning and subdivision regulations for municipalities throughout Pennsylvania. Specific examples of successful conservancy projects include:

- In 1985, the conservancy initiated the Routes 202/1 Corridors Project to ensure adequate environmental and design controls in these fast-changing traffic corridors, to identify and eliminate safety hazards, and to stimulate long-term traffic planning. Since many streams originate along this road, zoning and land development codes must deal with sewage and storm-water management along the highway corridors. The conservancy was joined on this project by several state, regional, and local agencies,

44

which are now moving ahead to implement recommendations.

The Environmental Management Center has reviewed, revised, and helped draft local land use controls in more than 35 communities in six counties with an emphasis on zoning, subdivision, storm-water management, natural features protection, historic preservation, and transferable development rights.

In Chester County, the center organized conservation investors to purchase and protect 5,300 acres of prime farmland, woodland, and streams in its Buck and Doe Run Valley Farms acquisition project. The property was protected through the donation of conservation easements on 4,500 acres and a major nature preserve on 800 acres.

As part of its Environmental Management Assistance Program, the center maintains the *Environmental Management Handbook,* a reference of model ordinances, land use practices, and environmental law, which is updated annually. Subscribers have access to staff technical assistance, attend meetings and workshops, and receive the *Handbook,* updates, and *Environmental Currents,* the center's quarterly newsletter.

Organizational Structure

The Brandywine Conservancy is made up of the Brandywine River Museum and the Environmental Management Center. The latter has a professional staff of land use planners, landscape designers, natural resource managers, and specialists in historic preservation, horticulture, and environmental engineering.

Financial Characteristics

The Brandywine Conservancy receives its funding from individual, corporate, and foundation grants, and from membership dues. It also receives fees for technical assistance provided by the Environmental Management Center on an at-cost, hourly basis and charges admission to the Brandywine River Museum.

CONTACT

Brandywine Conservancy
Environmental Management Center
P.O. Box 141
Chadds Ford, PA 19317
(215) 388-7601

PROFILE

HOUSATONIC VALLEY ASSOCIATION

Planning to Protect Resources

Mission and Key Objectives

The Housatonic Valley Association (HVA) was formed to promote the conservation of the natural environment of Connecticut's Housatonic River Valley. It accomplishes this mission through public education, opposing projects that threaten the valley's natural resources, and offering professional conservation-minded land-planning services (see examples below). In recent years, the association has focused its efforts in four major areas—land planning in the river basin, fighting against a proposed natural gas pipeline, reviewing and commenting on river-related projects, and preparing testimony under the auspices of their Valley Watch program, and addressing groundwater protection issues through the Groundwater Action Program. In addition, the HVA has worked to protect public waterfront access.

The Housatonic Valley Association differs from many local conservation organizations in its extensive professional land-planning capabilities. Originally, its land-planning program focused on identifying and preserving farmlands and riverfront lands. Since 1981, HVA has expanded its scope to include protection of scenic landscapes, woodlands, wetlands, recreational open space, and historically significant lands. HVA works with landowners on management strategies that consider economic and environmental concerns to resolve potential land use conflicts and helps towns within the watershed to update their land use plans.

HVA targets its public education efforts at several levels. The association helped secondary schools develop environmental programs to stimulate appreciation of the natural resources of the river. For example, it has conducted projects testing the chemical, biological, and physical properties of adopted water bodies.

The HVA also publishes quarterly newsletters and periodic pamphlets on issues affecting the watershed.

Geographic Scope

The Housatonic Valley Association addresses environmental issues through the entire Housatonic Valley in Connecticut, from the Massachusetts border extending to its mouth in Long Island Sound. The river corridor in Connecticut is 80 miles long and includes 45 townships.

Success Stories

Since 1981, the HVA has protected approximately 7,000 acres of the watershed through the arrangement of partial or full-fee acquisition. Landowners in the valley request HVA's assistance, usually when selling land or planning an estate, if they want to protect certain natural resources on their property in the arrangement. The HVA will respond to a request for assistance if:

- The property is within the Housatonic Valley;
- It contains resources of high environmental value (i.e., farmland, wetlands, endangered species habitat, scenic vistas);
- The result will be a clear conservation advantage, such as a conservation easement, land donation to a land trust, sale of development rights, or more environmentally sound land use plans that meet local regulations.

46

The land-planning staff works with the landowner, civil engineers, attorneys, appraisers, accountants, and any other involved parties to devise a plan for "limited development" on the property. For example, they may coordinate an agreement to cluster development on subdivided lands or limit development to specific areas on large lots in order to preserve open space.

In some cases, the HVA acquires land or partial interest in land outright, then resells the land with restrictions. For example, HVA bought a 180-acre parcel of land in Bridgewater, Connecticut, valued at $700,000 for a bargain sale of $400,000. Subsequently, HVA prepared a conservation plan for the land that identified a small number of house sites where development would not infringe upon areas designated for protection. The land was resold with these restrictions on it. This arrangement resulted in the following benefits:

- An important stream belt was protected and development was limited to 6 units rather than the 25 that would have been allowed under unrestricted zoning;

- HVA received fees for its services out of the sale proceeds;

- The concerns of the town Planning and Zoning Commission were integrated into the plan.

HVA also conducted an acquisition–planning–resale strategy on the property where their office now stands. The association purchased 19 acres of the 27-acre tract and formulated an agreement with the landowner to subdivide the remainder into four plots. Two of these plots were resold with conservation easements, the proceeds from which were used to retire the debt for the entire property.

Other times, the HVA will participate in designing a plan that does not entail acquisition by the organization. For example, when a retiring couple moved permanently to their country home in Danbury, they decided to sell 110 of the 300 acres of the property. They were dismayed to find that local zoning laws would allow 40 to 45 houses on the 110 acres and feared intense development would destroy the character of the place they were intending to enjoy. Although the land was too far outside of the geographic scope for HVA to accept an easement, they assisted in developing a plan that resulted in a conservation easement agreement with the county Soil and Water Conservation District. This plan allows no development on the portions of the land where development would compromise agricultural use and only four houses on the remainder of the 110 acres. Any activities that might threaten water quality, soil, and livestock are prohibited in perpetuity.

Organizational Structure

The HVA is a membership organization with private nonprofit tax status and a paid staff of about seven full-time equivalents.

Financial Characteristics

Most of the HVA's funds come from two sources—donations, which include membership and corporate grants, and fees for professional planning services.

CONTACT

Housatonic Valley Association
P.O. Box 28
Cornwall Bridge, CT 06754
(203) 927-4649.

PROFILE

KISSIMMEE RIVER BASIN

Resource Planning and Management Committee

Community Characteristics

The lower Kissimmee River Basin covers nearly 500,000 acres in central Florida. Lake Kissimmee lies at the northern end of the basin, Lake Okeechobee at the southern end, and the Kissimmee River, channelized by the Corps of Engineers into the C-38 canal in the 1960s, flows the 56 miles between them. Originally, the Kissimmee River meandered 98 miles, nourishing 40,000 acres of wetlands, and extending up to one mile across. The channel is 200 to 350 feet wide and its construction drained all but about 13,000 acres of the floodplain. The basin is mainly in rural and agricultural use, primarily dairy and cattle farms, but urban development is increasing.

The Taylor Creek watershed includes about 128,000 acres along the northeastern shore of Lake Okeechobee. This basin is also largely in agricultural use, including improved pasture, dairy operations, and, to a lesser extent, cropland and citrus groves.

Growth Patterns

South Florida's population is one of the fastest growing in the country. Over the past several decades, millions of new residents and tourists have flocked to the sunny coasts of the Floridian peninsula. As development costs on the coast skyrocket and the amount of suitable land for development declines, new development presses inland, into the Kissimmee River Basin. Because the basin's growth rate has historically been slow, especially compared with coastal Florida, local government land development regulations have remained loose. Thus, they were ill equipped to deal with new growth pressures.

Resources Threatened

Uncontrolled development in the basin threatens a unique and productive ecosystem. The remaining 13,000 acres of floodplain provide prime wildlife habitat, recreation areas, and spawning ground for fisheries. Because of the region's subtropical climate, it is susceptible to flooding and water shortages, both of which could be exacerbated by unwise development practices. Finally, residential and commercial encroachment threatens the agricultural resources of the basin.

Water quality, and the economic and environmental benefits that clean water provides, may also be threatened by unplanned development. The Kissimmee River and Taylor Creek together contribute approximately 35 percent of the total inflow to Lake Okeechobee, a lake that supports a large recreational industry, and provides water to South Florida's urban areas, surrounding farms, and natural systems. Thus, any threat to water quality in the basin threatens this valuable water supply. Channelization of the Kissimmee River in the 1960s, and the subsequent agricultural and residential development in the drained wetlands, have substantially lowered water quality in the river and in Lake Okeechobee.

Measures Taken

Evolving scientific awareness and mounting development pressures created a need for more sensitively planned development. In 1984, in recognition of this need, then-governor Bob Graham established the Kissimmee River Resource Management and Planning Committee (KRRMPC), employing a strategy that had been used in several areas of the state. The committee was comprised of 35 people representing the major "stakeholders" in the future of the basin. They included:

Landowners in the basin;

Cattle and other agricultural interests;

Environmental interests;

The five counties in the lower Kissimmee River and Taylor Creek drainage basin and the city of Okeechobee; and

Regional and state departments having jurisdiction over the environmental and economic concerns of the area.

The committee was charged with recommending means by which local government could protect the lower Kissimmee River and Taylor Creek drainage basins from unregulated development. It identified the following five objectives for meeting this charge.

- To maintain or enhance water quality where possible or practical;
- To encourage development that does not interfere with the area's critical resources;
- To assure a reasonable level of flood control and water conservation;
- To maintain or enhance the Kissimmee's riverine system to assure environmental, recreational, and other benefits; and
- To protect cultural features as much as possible.

The committee's final report lays out final policy recommendations and "implementation actions" specifically stating which parties should carry out which actions and when. The recommendation and implementation actions are separated into four elements:

- Land acquisition strategy;
- Water quality protection;
- Land use management; and
- Economic development.

The recommendations regarding land use management emphasize local comprehensive plans and land use regulations. They state that there should be no new nonagricultural development in the lower Kissimmee River floodplain except on those lands identified for specific land uses by local government plans. These areas may be developed with regulations to ensure that there will be no significant adverse impact on the stated goal.

The recommendations regarding economic development are that economic development should be encouraged in the uplands but should be limited in the floodplain to low-intensity agriculture, compatible recreational opportunities, and lands identified for specific land uses by local government plans.

The report of the KRRMPC was transmitted to the governor, the cabinet, and the state land-planning agency in September 1985. The committee continues to meet both to monitor the progress of the plan's implementation and to recommend further action. It has already designed several model land-planning ordinances for localities in the basin.

The committee's recommendations are designed to give local governments some control over development. They are only one of a number of state and regional initiatives to protect and restore the Kissimmee River Basin. Restoration of the Kissimmee River is the first objective of the state's "Save Our Everglades" program. The Lake Okeechobee Technical Advisory Committee is studying ways to reduce the water quality problems in the lake; much of their work focuses on the Kissimmee River and Taylor Creek. The South Florida Water Management District has already diverted a section of the river back into historic oxbows. Dairy farmers in the basin are implementing best management practices to avoid further degradation of water quality.

Experience

The committee's recommendations were arrived at through negotiations with landowners and government officials in the basin. Thus, theoretically, all major stakeholders had a say in how the environmental and economic objectives would be met. As a result of this cooperative effort, localities are much more likely to implement the recommendations. Indeed, by September 1986, a year after the recommendations were transmitted to the governor, most of the initial recommendations of the Resource Management Plan had been implemented. The counties in the basin are in the process of developing ordinances that are based on the model ordinance produced by the committee.

CONTACT

South Florida Water Management District
P.O. Box V
West Palm Beach, FL 33402
(407) 686-8800

PROFILE

DENVER'S PLATTE RIVER GREENWAY*

Turning an Eyesore into an Asset

Community Characteristics

Denver is the capital and largest city in Colorado, with a metropolitan population of nearly 2 million. Known as the "Mile-High City," Denver rests on the eastern slope of the Rocky Mountains in the north-central part of the state. Located on the South Platte River, it is a commercial, government, oil, and transportation center.

Growth Pressures

Like many U.S. cities, Denver grew up along the banks of a river. Gold prospectors and miners settled at the confluence of the South Platte River and Cherry Creek, where gold was discovered in 1858. In addition to their promise of riches, the Platte River's waters were the lifeblood of the surrounding arid countryside and settlers gravitated to the river's banks. By 1867, this area was incorporated as the city of Denver.

Although the population of the metropolitan area as a whole increased nearly 30 percent in the 1960s and again in the 1970s, this growth has been uneven. Population growth in the core city slowed while growth in the suburban areas accelerated. The downtown area along the river is highly urbanized and industrialized and until recently, the river corridor had deteriorated, according to a local river activist, into "little more than a 10-mile sewer running through the heart of the city—all but lost amid aging industrial facades, piles of broken concrete, billboards, and viaducts."

Planning for the South Platte River in downtown

---

* Information for this profile is adapted from Robert M. Searns, "Denver Tames the Unruly Platte: A Ten-Mile River Greenway," *Landscape, Architecture* (July 1980): 382.

Denver is clearly an example of improving the river corridor rather than controlling new growth. The environmental and economic benefits of the river had diminished as a result of rampant urban and industrial development. The condition of the river was a safety concern as well. Two devastating floods, in 1965 and 1973, resulted in loss of life and of hundreds of millions of dollars of property damage.

Measures Taken

The Platte River in downtown Denver had become such an eyesore and threat to public health that in 1973, in response to public outcry, the city's mayor appointed a nine-member task force, the Platte River Development Committee (PRDC), to devise a strategy to do something about the river. He demanded that the project be one that could be planned and implemented quickly. To carry out this mandate, the mayor committed $1.9 million of city funds to the project and the City Council extended an additional $850,000 seed grant.

Within months, the PRDC assigned four local firms to design "pilot" projects along the city's ten-mile waterfront that would make the river accessible to the public, both on the shores and by boat. The overall plan was to connect a series of "pocket" parks by a trail system that would run the length of the Platte from city limit to city limit. The river would also be made accessible to boaters by removing some of the debris that had accumulated in the riverbed.

Three of the four projects were constructed within a year. The PRDC then sponsored a series of special events and celebrations to bring the public to the sites experience what the river could be. This strategy was a success. The stark contrast between the river environment in the "pocket" parks and the unrestored segments encouraged further funding from foundations and corporations for the creation of a continuous greenway along the river through the downtown. As an added incentive to donors, the committee created a nonprofit tax-exempt entity, the Platte River Greenway Foundation, to fund and coordinate execution of projects on behalf of the city.

The foundation raised $7 million from private and public sources. All funds were used to transform the industrial wasteland the Platte had become to an inviting recreational resource for city residents. The appendages of the urban environment—exposed concrete, utility outfalls, check dams—were modified to blend into, and even contribute to, the recreational objectives of the greenway. An eight-foot-wide, five-inch-thick biking and hiking trail was constructed along the bank, in places cantilevered over the river, constantly drawing users into intimate contact with the thread of nature running through their city. In 1974, the Platte was choked up with rubble and debris, turning away recreational boaters drawn by the possibilities of the river's lively current. Much of the menacing garbage was removed, and whitewater rapids were developed.

Experience

The downtown Denver greenway now consists of 15 miles of interconnected trails and 450 acres of open space. The project emphasizes a diversity of uses along the river. An estimated 150,000 people use it annually for activities such as hiking, biking, and boating. Although downtown Denver remains an urban and industrial center, facades and landscapes have been restored to be consistent with the greenway. The recreational corridor is separated from the sights and sounds of the city by steep banks and landscaping formed out of mounds of rubble.

Maintenance of the greenway initially proved to be a problem, not surprisingly, since the area had for years been used as a dumping ground. The foundation responded by committing $12,000 for a trial program to employ four rangers mounted on bicycles to promote the river's new image. This program was so successful that it became permanently funded through an endowment and in 1989 employed one full-time ranger and four seasonal rangers. Today, the downtown Denver portion of the greenway is maintained by a partnership of the foundation's trail rangers, the Denver Urban Drainage and Flood Control District, and the City of Denver Parks Department.

There are now 13 "pocket" parks along the ten-mile stretch of the Platte River. The greenway serves as the foundation of an educational program for elementary school students that emphasizes environmental education, history, and art. The foundation is working with the Federation of Garden Clubs and other agencies and organizations to develop the Overland Pond Educational Park. This five-acre park is landscaped with vegetation representing five of Colorado's ecological zones. The foundation is also working with the Boy Scouts and others to develop a former landfill site along the river as a Scout day camp.

In addition, this section of the greenway has served as a catalyst to neighboring communities. Both Adams County to the north and Arapahoe County to the south have developed trails along their segments of the Platte. By the end of 1988, these county trails will be connected to the downtown Denver section to create a continuous 45-mile stretch along the Platte. In addition, dozens of miles of trails have been constructed along major tributaries and gulches to connect surrounding neighborhoods and recreational areas to the greenway. Ultimately, the greenway system is expected to cover about 120 miles.

CONTACT

Platte River Greenway Foundation
1666 South University Boulevard
Denver, CO 80210
(303) 698-1322

PROFILE

JACKSON, NEW HAMPSHIRE

Protection Through Wild and Scenic River Designation

Community Characteristics

Jackson is located in the White Mountains of New Hampshire, ten miles from the Maine border. A town of 650 people with some 1,000 additional seasonal residents, it incorporates 68 square miles, approximately 70 percent of which is in the White Mountain National Forest. Four mountain ridges running north and south are divided by drainage courses that eventually flow into the Saco River. Through one of these drainages flows ten-mile-long Wildcat River, also known as Wildcat Brook, which forms a long series of cascading granite bedrock steps near the center of the town, forming Jackson Falls, the town's outstanding feature and main attraction. Wildcat River plummets from headwaters high in the National Forest down to its confluence with the Ellis River at the southern end of the town. Jackson is a mountain resort village, with Mount Washington, the highest peak in New England, dominating local views.

The local economy is based on outdoor recreational tourism. One of the earliest alpine ski resorts was established in Jackson over 50 years ago, and a prominent attraction of the area is a cross-country ski trail network of more than 125 kilometers. The town has been a resort and retirement community since the nineteenth century, and its character as such has been well preserved: some turn-of-the-century inns still welcome visitors today. Countywide, about 65 percent of the economy is based on retail trade and services, reflecting the importance of recreation and tourism to the region.

The landscape outside the village itself is mixed residential, forest, and open fields. In spite of new residential and resort complexes, open space and rural character have been retained, in part because of the National Forest.

The mountainous backdrop, the fields and wood-lands, and the historic village center are all connected by the free-flowing Wildcat River, which shapes the local landscape and contributes to its character.

Growth Pressures

Although Jackson has not grown significantly in permanent population during this century, the town's growing reputation as a vacation community has had a serious impact on second home development. The number of housing units in Jackson has increased 71 percent since 1970, to 829 in 1988. Recreational home development is concentrated in the village center and near the local ski areas. Between 1981 and 1987, the town planning board approved subdivisions for 334 lots on 980 acres.

In the summer months, about 200 people a day visit Jackson Falls, congregating above the first cascade, and exploring the washes and pools that run for about a quarter mile downstream. Although this entire segment of the river is intensively used, there is no official parking in the area, no signs directing visitors to specific spots, and no public amenities. Incidental parking spots have formed based on years of casual use, and along the river, a path has been cleared as a result of pedestrian use.

The riparian environment along Wildcat River and its tributaries was vulnerable to second home and condominium development. The rising pace of this sort of development in northern New Hampshire suggested that soon these fragile lands adjacent to nearly pristine free-flowing waters would be developed if no local action were taken. Based on inadequate septic design, the town had recently rejected a proposed condominium project that had received approval from the state Water Supply and Pollution Control Commision. The chairman of the Jackson Planning Board noted that the town could not rely on the state's judgment: local vigilance was crucial.

In 1983, a Massachusetts hydropower developer applied for a permit to study the feasibility of a hydropower installation at the site of Jackson Falls. The Federal Energy Regulatory Commission granted the permit in late July.

Measures Taken and Experience

Concern grew that the hydropower project would harm the aesthetic features of the river and the falls, and the local economy. Local officials, local and state conservation groups, and interested citizens pursued legal channels to rescind the permit—without success. With the support of the New Hampshire congressional delegation, legislation was signed into law in June 1984 that designated Wildcat Brook as a candidate for possible inclusion in the National Wild and Scenic River System. The bill imposed a six-year moratorium on federal activities that might affect the character of the river and surrounding lands. In August of the following year, the town of Jackson, the state of New Hampshire, the U.S. Forest Service, and the National Park Service (NPS) initiated a study to determine Wildcat Brook's eligibility for Wild and Scenic River status. The NPS provided the funds to perform the study.

The study stressed the objective of preparing a municipal action plan for conservation of Wildcat Brook and its tributaries. The Board of Selectmen of the town appointed a Wildcat Brook Advisory Committee (WBAC) to oversee development of the plan and coordinate public involvement in its preparation. The WBAC included local citizens, public officials, and U.S. Forest Service representatives. This composition responded to congressional intent that action be locally initiated and directed.

The WBAC served as a crucial link between the town's decision-makers and the community. Throughout the river study, the public was kept informed of progress through meetings, progress reports, workshops, surveys, and mailings. Thus, local support and direction for the plan were assured. Community involvement at the outset paid off when it came time to adopt elements of the conservation plan.

The WBAC developed a work plan highlighting three elements: (a) the elimination of the threat of hydropower development along the brook; (b) protection of the existing character of the river corridor; and (c) preservation of water quality and other natural and cultural resources. In addition, the WBAC developed

research agendas to serve as a foundation for the Wildcat Conservation Plan:

- The NPS conducted a resource eligibility assessment to determine whether the Wildcat qualified for addition to the Wild and Scenic River System, and found that it was eligible. The WBAC also considered alternatives to Wild and Scenic designation, such as state-level action or new local zoning policies, and found that Wild and Scenic designation offered the best guarantee against hydropower construction, and, additionally, offered the best incentives for the town to develop a strong river protection program.

- The WBAC performed a resident/landowner survey to find out whether local citizens would support such designation. Ninety-four percent of those surveyed believed that the town's rural character and scenic qualities were important to the local economy and worth protecting.

- A visitor use survey found that 80 percent of Wildcat Brook users are nonresidents and that recreational use of the river was concentrated around Jackson Falls. These findings helped focus part of the plan on a site-specific management strategy for the falls area.

- An evaluation of existing protection determined that the extensive National Forest lands in Jackson had helped to preserve open space. No further federal land acquisition was deemed necessary to protect the river.

Following the research and evaluation period, the WBAC developed a River Conservation Plan for Wildcat Brook. The plan includes acquisition of conservation easements, local land use controls, tax assessment policy, creation of a river management agency, and designation of the brook as a National Wild and Scenic River.

Conservation Easements

The WBAC evaluated the effectiveness of conservation easements on municipally and privately owned lands for protecting the Wildcat. Three hundred and forty-five acres of town-owned lands were already protected in perpetuity by conservation easements administered by the Jackson Conservation Commission and the Society for the Protection of New Hampshire Forests (SPNHF). The NPS entered into a five-year cooperative agreement with the town and SPNHF, facilitating the development of a full-fledged conservation easement program, as a component of the River Conservation Plan. The WBAC held workshops explaining land protection techniques and easement mechanics, and developed a map listing target properties of ten acres or more located along the brook. These owners were the subject of mail and telephone campaigns. In December, two easements totaling 86 acres were donated, bringing to 431 the number of acres protected by easement in the watershed.

New Land Use Regulations

Existing zoning and subdivision regulations were found to fall short of the goals of preserving the Wildcat River and the town's rural character. In March 1987, Jackson voters overwhelmingly approved two new ordinances to enhance natural resource protection within the watershed. A new floodplain law establishes a River Conservation District in the 100-year floodplain, prohibiting construction in a 75-foot setback zone, and limiting development to low-intensity uses.

The second measure proved significantly more controversial. Existing zoning in Jackson allowed minimum lot sizes of one acre in the commercial/village district and two acres in the rural/residential district. The new amendment introduced soil-based zoning, which bases minimum lot size on the soils' ability to handle wastewater effluent. Opponents of soil-based zoning identified the measure as an attempt to institute no-growth in Jackson. Calling the amendment "snob zoning," opponents suggested that young people might have trouble affording a new home if they needed four acres to build a house and predicted that their properties would be devalued. In the March 1987 vote, the ordinance achieved exactly the two-thirds majority it needed to pass. This measure helps preserve water quality, a stated priority of the WBAC, and an important criteria for Wild and Scenic designation.

Tax Assessments

New Hampshire has implemented a current use property tax assessment program for eligible undeveloped land. In 1986, about 32 percent of the town's total land outside the National Forest was enrolled in the program. Under Jackson's River Conservation Plan, the Board of Selectmen authorize participation by parcels that would otherwise be ineligible for the program.

Wild and Scenic River Designation

In October 1988, the Senate gave final congressional approval to a bill designating 14.5 miles of Wildcat River and its tributaries as a Federal Wild and Scenic River. Designation provides permanent protection from any federally approved dams or other water projects that would alter the river's free-flowing condition. Furthermore, the protection afforded the river under its new status requires no federal land acquisition. About half of the designated area is located in the National Forest, and will be administered by the Forest Service to protect its Wild and Scenic status. Outside of the National Forest, the river corridor will be managed in compliance with the local River Conservation Plan.

A Wildcat River Commission has been established, and is composed of local, state, and U.S. Forest Service officials and Jackson citizens, including at least two riparian property owners. The commission is responsible for overseeing management of the river, with responsibilities for: ensuring compliance with Wild and Scenic designation provisions; long-term implementation of the Conservation Plan; developing consistency agreements with state and federal agencies; education and training of the community; and implementing demonstration management plans for the Jackson Falls area and the commercial village area.

The federal designation provides local managers with an effective tool for protecting the river through a partnership between the local government and the federal government. Designation also protects against federal approval of dams.

CONTACTS

Jackson Conservation Commission
Box 158
Jackson, NH 03846
(603) 383-9546

Division of Planning and Design
National Park Service, North Atlantic Region
15 State Street
Boston, MA 02109
(617) 565-8807

PROFILE

THE CHESAPEAKE BAY

State and Local Action to Protect Wetlands and Water Resources

Community Characteristics

The Chesapeake Bay is the largest estuarine system in North America. The Bay is fed by over 50 tributary rivers, and drains some 64,000 square miles in six states and the District of Columbia. Its watershed extends from New York in the north to West Virginia in the west. Over 425,000 acres of marsh are adjacent to the Bay. Due to the circulation of freshwater and in-flowing ocean water within the estuary and the differing chemical composition of these waters, the Chesapeake Bay is among the most biologically productive ecosystems on earth.

Growth Pressures

The Bay has come under increasing pressure from upland agricultural activities and from development as suburban Washington and Baltimore expand. A significant report by the U.S. Environmental Protection Agency documenting the environmental decline of the Bay and recommending steps for its enhancement became a focal point for citizen and state government concern. A couple of major development projects along the Bay's shore, which destroyed edge habitat, created large impervious surfaces, dredged declining oyster bars, and served as aesthetic eyesores, also became catalysts for the passage of the Maryland Critical Areas Law.

Measures Taken—Maryland's Critical Areas Program

In response to evidence of widespread degradation, the U.S. Environmental Protection Agency and the four states bordering the Bay and containing its major tributaries committed to stem the decline of the Bay's environmental quality and productivity. Federal, state, and local pollution control, resource enhancement, and land management initiatives have been implemented to address the numerous threats. As part of this effort, Maryland and Virginia have enacted state land use programs to protect the Bay's water quality from the detrimental impacts of development.

In 1984, the Maryland legislature enacted the Chesapeake Bay Critical Area Act to protect the water quality and natural habitat of the Chesapeake Bay from the detrimental effects of development. The program recognizes that development activity immediately adjacent to the Bay has the greatest potential for degrading the water quality and fish and wildlife habitat in the Bay. The act defines the strip of land along the tidal shoreline of the Bay up to 1,000 feet from the water's edge, or from the landward boundary of adjacent wetlands, as a critical area. Localities can include other fragile or threatened areas within the critical area, and highly developed urban areas can be excluded from the critical area.

The state Critical Area Commission, consisting of 25 members, is responsible for developing criteria to guide future land use in the critical area. The criteria address development activities, resource utilization, and resource protection. The development activities criteria require local governments to divide critical areas into three development districts, and provide minimum standards for development within each district:

- In Intensely Developed Areas (IDA)—areas that are already intensely developed—local regulations must control storm-water runoff and conserve natural habitat.

- In Limited Development Areas (LDA)—areas that have a mix of developed and undeveloped land—local regulations must limit impervious surfaces to 15 percent of a site; include measures to preserve or replace forest cover; and encourage clustered development.
- In Resource Conservation Areas (RCA)—areas that are predominantly in wetlands, forestry, or agricultural uses—local regulations must limit residential density to one unit per 20 acres, and must encourage forestry and agricultural uses. New marinas are prohibited. The criteria allow designation of 5 percent of a locality's RCA land area as future IDA or LDA areas.

The resource utilization criteria require forest management plans for commercial tree harvesting; require setbacks from water bodies for harvesting; and restrict clear-cutting. They also require soil and water management plans for agricultural operations, and restrict the feeding or watering of livestock within 50 feet of the water's edge.

The resource protection criteria require identification and protection of critical habitat; 100-foot vegetated buffers along tidal waters and 25-foot buffers around nontidal wetlands.

Affected local governments must establish policies for land use and development within the critical areas. These local programs must map critical areas and implement local plans and regulations that comply with the commission's criteria. The commission reviews and approves or disapproves these local plans and is authorized to develop a plan for any locality that fails to submit an acceptable plan.

The Virginia Program

Four years after Maryland enacted the Chesapeake Bay Critical Area law, Virginia enacted a program that incorporates many of the same elements. In 1988, Virginia enacted the Chesapeake Bay Preservation Act to improve land use practices that directly affect the Chesapeake Bay. The act created the Chesapeake Bay Local Assistance Board, which is responsible for developing land use criteria for Tidewater localities. (The act affects cities and counties whose bordering waters are influenced by the tides.) The board is assisted by its staff agency, the Chesapeake Bay Local Assistance Department. The department provides technical and financial assistance to affected local governments and oversees implementation of the state criteria.

The board's criteria serve two purposes:

- To establish Chesapeake Bay Preservation Areas which include land areas such as wetlands, beaches, steep waterfront slopes, highly erodible soils, aquifer recharge areas, and floodplains; and
- To specify land use controls, such as performance standards, setbacks, density limitations, and storm water management, to apply within the Chesapeake Bay Preservation Areas.

By July 1, 1990, affected localities must establish preservation areas and implement land use controls in accordance with the board's criteria.

Experience

To date, the Maryland Critical Area Program has made some important progress, amidst concerns that its accomplishments have been mixed. Until recently, delays in the drafting and implementation of Critical Area Programs for each of the 60 Bay localities have slowed the planning process. With virtually all the counties and municipalities having fulfilled their planning requirements by the end of 1988, questions about grandfathering and growth allocations within the RCA still cloud the potential benefits of the program.

There is little doubt that this legislation has raised awareness in the communities around the Bay and forced serious consideration of vital environmental issues relating to development, which were once dismissed offhand. Whether the legislation, though, is capable of fulfilling its intention to preserve the Bay and prevent increased contamination of its waters and the loss of its vital shoreline buffer remains to be seen.

The Chesapeake Bay Foundation, a nonprofit citizens' organization, has played a critical role in developing a variety of governmental and private sector strategies to protect the Bay and in ensuring that adopted strategies are effectively implemented.

CONTACTS

Chesapeake Bay Critical Areas Commission
Tawes Office Building D-4
Taylor Avenue
Annapolis, MD 21401

Chesapeake Bay Foundation
162 Prince George Street
Annapolis, MD 21401

INFORMATION RESOURCES

The Conservation Foundation. *Protecting America's Wetlands: An Action Agenda—The Final Report of the National Wetlands Policy Forum*. Washington, D.C.: The Conservation Foundation, 1988.

The National Wetlands Policy Forum, chaired by Governor Thomas Kean of New Jersey, is a 25-member body comprised of senior officials of federal, state, and local government, industry, agriculture, and environmental groups. The report and its policy recommendations address a wide range of wetlands issues and represent the result of extensive consultation and discussion.

Diamant, Rolf, J. Glenn Eugster, and Christopher J. Duerksen. *A Citizen's Guide to River Conservation*. Washington, D.C.: The Conservation Foundation, 1984.

Provides an introduction to the protection of rivers and river corridors. Specific chapters focus on threats to rivers; strategies for organizing communities to protect rivers; tools for protecting rivers, such as zoning, easements, tax incentives; private nonprofit mechanisms for river conservation; and local, state, and federal programs for river conservation.

Kusler, Dr. Jon A. *Our National Wetland Heritage: A Protection Guidebook*. Washington, D.C.: Environmental Law Institute, 1983.

A comprehensive explanation of the importance of wetlands, wetland characteristics; federal, state, and local protection programs; legal issues; and public and private protection techniques.

Mitsch, William J. and James G. Gosselink. *Wetlands*. New York: Van Nostrand Reinhold Company, 1986.

This book is a detailed introduction to the wetlands ecosystems, functions, and management.

Rice, Barbara M., ed. *Conserving Our Wetland Resources: Avenues for Citizen Participation*. Annapolis, MD: Chesapeake Bay Foundation, 1987.

This handbook discusses wetlands values and threats, and how to participate in the Virginia and federal wetlands protection programs. It contains a particularly useful discussion of how citizens can participate effectively in the federal Section 404 program.

Thurow, Charles, William Toner, and Erley, Duncan. *Performance Controls for Sensitive Lands: A Practical Guide for Local Administrators*. Report Nos. 307, 308. Chicago, IL: American Society of Planning Officials, 1975.

Provides an introduction to performance standard controls as a means of protecting rivers and streams, wetlands, aquifers, hillsides, and woodlands. Includes numerous examples of local performance standard programs and ordinance language.

University of Wisconsin-Madison Arboretum: *Restoration and Management Notes*.

A semiannual journal of news and information about the restoration and management of landscapes, water resources, and ecosystems generally. Subscription costs $13/year. (Contact University of Wisconsin-Madison Arboretum, 1207 Seminole Highway, Madison, WI 53711.)

Wagner, Judith, et al. *Adopt-a-Stream Workbook: How to Protect Your Favorite River, Stream or Brook*. Boston: Massachusetts Department of Fisheries, Wildlife and Environmental Law Enforcement, Riverways Program, 1987.

A step-by-step guidebook for communities and organizations wishing to participate in the Massachusetts Adopt-a-Stream program. The material is also relevant to adopt-a-stream programs in other states.

ORGANIZATIONAL RESOURCES

American Rivers

American Rivers is the nation's principal river-saving organization and the only nonprofit charitable corporation devoted exclusively to preserving the nation's outstanding rivers and their landscapes. 801 Pennsylvania Avenue, S.E., Suite 303, Washington, D.C. 20003; (202) 547-6900.

Chesapeake Bay Foundation

The Chesapeake Bay Foundation is the single best source of information on the Chesapeake Bay and activities that affect the Bay. The foundation has offices in Maryland, Virginia, and Pennsylvania. It provides technical assistance and advice on issues concerning the Bay and its watershed. 162 Prince George Street, Annapolis MD 21401; (301) 268-8816.

Ducks Unlimited

Ducks Unlimited restores, preserves, and manages wetlands in prime waterfowl habitat. One Waterfowl Way, Long Grove, IL 60047; (312) 438-4300.

National Audubon Society

National Audubon is a national conservation organization with a particular emphasis on wetlands and with numerous regional and field offices, and local chapters. 950 Third Avenue, New York, NY 10022; (212) 832-3200.

National Park Service

The National Park Service's State and Local River Conservation Assistance Program is designed to assist state and local governments, private groups, and landowners in the development of river conservation and management plans. Projects range in scale from statewide river assessments to plans for a single stream or urban waterfront. Contact J. Glenn Eugster, Chief, Division of Park and Resource Planning, National Park Service, 143 South Third Street, Philadelphia, PA 19106; (215) 597-7386.

The Nature Conservancy

The Nature Conservancy acquires and manages critical wetlands and other lands that safeguard critical ecosystems or threatened species. 1815 North Lynn Street, Arlington, VA 22209; (703) 841-5300.

Trout Unlimited

Trout Unlimited is an international conservation organization established to protect streams and rivers in order to preserve and enhance the quality of trout and salmon fishing. 501 Church Street, NE, Vienna, VA 22180; (703) 281-1100.

Trust for Public Land

The Trust for Public Land is a nonprofit land acquisition organization that works with community groups, landowners, and public land management agencies to preserve land for public use. The trust helps community groups and local governments acquire urban, rural, recreational, scenic, and agricultural land. 420 C Street, N.E., Washington, D.C. 20002; (202) 543-7552.

The Waterfront Center

The Waterfront Center is a nonprofit information and consulting service that provides expertise in enhancing and revitalizing urban waterfronts. The center conducts an annual waterfront conference and provides advisory services to waterfront communities. 1536 44th Street, N.W., Washington, D.C. 20007; (202) 337-0356.

CHAPTER 3

Historic and Cultural Resources

We shape our buildings, and afterwards our buildings shape us.
—Winston Churchill

The Past in the Present _____

Many communities across the country are realizing what only a few jurisdictions long ago discovered: they have significant historical and cultural resources that, properly protected, can significantly enhance their livability and distinctiveness. Moreover, communities are learning that the preservation and enhancement of historic and cultural resources can provide substantial and direct economic benefits. Many communities have conquered the "no there there" syndrome by building growth management efforts around their historic and cultural resources, thereby, promoting quality economic development, appreciating property values, and a positive local image.

Historic and cultural resource preservation efforts in this country date back to the mid-1800s. In its early years, the historic preservation movement concentrated on saving specific historic landmarks, typically homes of historic figures (e.g., George Washington's Mount Vernon estate in Virginia) or places where great events occurred (e.g., Constitution Hall in Philadelphia). Such preservation efforts were generally mounted by private individuals or groups with the foresight to see the need to protect a young country's political heritage.

This focus broadened, however, in the early part of the twentieth century, as the preservation of historic districts, and of buildings significant for their architectural (rather than purely historical) features, became a concern. Recently, historic and cultural preservation efforts have broadened further to encompass protection of entire landscapes and the heritage of a rural area.

Among the most significant recent trends in local heritage preservation efforts is the emergence of programs to preserve local industrial or economic heritage and to use these assets as the basis for economic development. Lowell, Massachusetts, is perhaps the most renowned of such efforts.[1] Butte, Montana, and Beaumont, Texas, also illustrate how heritage preservation and economic revitalization can be integrated.[2] In addition, hundreds of communities have used the highly successful "Main Street" program to undertake local downtown preservation programs. These programs use historic preservation tools to implement

visionary planning efforts around the community's distinctive cultural features, turning apparent liabilities into assets.

Aside from profiling successful programs and private organizations, this chapter discusses the benefits and the methods of preserving and enhancing historical and cultural resources, including:

- Local historic and cultural preservation programs;
- Private preservation initiatives and opportunities;
- State historic preservation programs;
- Federal influences on local and state preservation efforts; and
- Legal considerations in developing local programs.

Local Historic and Cultural Preservation Programs _____

Many communities have learned that listing properties on the National Register of Historic Places, which provides some protection against federal actions that would have an adverse impact on registered property or property eligible for listing, has important benefits. Yet it does not go far enough; developing comprehensive local heritage preservation programs is necessary to help maintain and enhance cultural resources. Comprehensive heritage preservation programs help to build consensus and avoid divisive eleventh-hour battles to save important landmarks and resources. They also give the community more clout when dealing with state and federal agencies in regulatory decisions, in establishing funding priorities, in highway location decisions, and in environmental impact review.

In developing a local heritage protection program, a community should first consider the three "core" tools that serve as the foundation of most local heritage protection programs. Numerous other tools are also available. The three "core" techniques are:

- An historic resource inventory or survey;
- Comprehensive planning and zoning; and
- An historic preservation ordinance.

HISTORIC RESOURCE SURVEYS

The logical first step in developing an affirmative local preservation program is to inventory local historic and cultural properties and resources. An inventory determines or, as the case may be, confirms where to focus local efforts. Historic resource surveys often reveal that previously overlooked properties are worthy of preservation and perhaps eligible for National Register designation. A survey may also reveal landscapes or corridors worthy of historic district status. A thorough survey can also help avoid last-ditch, often futile preservation emergencies.

As a leading local preservation organization has written:

> Surveys . . . provide a basis for the public to protect endangered resources. Hastily conceived, last-minute attempts to save historic buildings are more easily avoided if their historical and architectural significance have been assessed previously in official surveys. If, for example, a proposed development threatens an old farmhouse, its inclusion in an official survey may lead to negotiations with the developer or to the exploration of options for preserving it. On the other hand, last-ditch efforts mounted to halt construction plans that have been developed over a period of months, or even years, often result in bitter, credibility-damaging battles. A community that has both surveyed and prioritized its resources is better equipped to make intelligent decisions about public expenditures to preserve those resources.[3]

The process of conducting the survey can be as important as the completed report. Surveys can be instrumental in building awareness of local heritage and in generating broader interest in comprehensive planning and growth management. Property owners may gain an increased understanding and sense of pride, reducing the prospects of destructive alterations.

In many rural communities, where there is little tradition of historic preservation or land use controls, the consensus-building effects of the survey process can be especially valuable. In Oley Township, Pennsylvania, for example, a survey identified 300 historic resources, predominantly farmsteads. This survey, conducted by the private Berks County Conservancy, with help from the state, resulted in National Register designation of the entire township in 1983 and a subsequent comprehensive planning effort focusing on both historic resources and farmland. This integration of an historic survey and local land use planning is necessary for a truly effective program.

Whether such integration proves feasible, a survey should be thorough, professional, and systematic. If possible, the survey should be conducted or directed by someone with appropriate professional training and experience, such as a local historian, an architectural historian, or a landscape architect. If volunteers are relied upon, they should obtain technical assistance from a professional, the State Historic Preservation Office (SHPO), a local university, or the National Trust for Historic Preservation (see Organizational Resources section below). The SHPOs may provide financial assistance to permit the community to hire an expert consultant. The National Trust may also be able to assist through its consultant services or financial assistance programs.

COMPREHENSIVE PLANNING AND ZONING

Lack of public appreciation of the value of preserving local historic and cultural resources, and the resulting low priority that preservation often receives in the local planning process, contribute to the threat of demolition or degradation of these resources. Before considering an historic preservation program, a community should ensure that the local comprehensive plan documents the numerous values to the community of its historic and cultural resources, and articulates priority for preserving these resources. This is important for a community with historic or cultural resources, whether or not the community contains any property listed on or eligible for the National Register of Historic Places.

In addition to planning for historic preservation, zoning for historic preservation is important. Zoning can either complement or undermine preservation efforts. To ensure that zoning complements historic and cultural preservation, the local comprehensive plan should give priority to coordinating or integrating preservation efforts with the town's zoning ordinance and other growth management programs.

Inappropriate zoning can compromise the integrity of historic property or districts in many ways. It can allow inappropriate uses or densities around historic properties or districts. Too much density can result in traffic congestion. Tall buildings can overshadow historic properties. Inadequate design standards in adjacent zones can detract from the integrity of the historic districts. Zoning that allows high-density development (in excess of the density of the existing structure) can also encourage market pressure for demolition because the vacant lot may be more valuable than the lot with the building.[4]

HISTORIC PRESERVATION ORDINANCES

Since Charleston, South Carolina, enacted America's first preservation ordinance in 1931, at least 1,200 communities have enacted such ordinances.[5] These ordinances typically establish a process for designating historic properties and districts, and for the review of alterations to and the demolition of designated historic properties. In designated districts, ordinances establish a procedure and standards to ensure that alterations, and in many districts new buildings, are compatible with the historic character of the district.

Drafting an Effective Preservation Ordinance

Because state historic preservation enabling legislation differs significantly from state to state, it is unwise to rely upon a single model historic preservation ordinance.[6] Model ordinances have been drafted for many states and are generally available from the state historic preservation officer.

The basic issues that must be addressed in drafting an effective local preservation ordinance include:

- Statement of purposes;
- Creation of an historic preservation commission;
- Delegation of powers and authorities;
- Criteria and procedures for designating historic districts and landmarks;
- Activities that require review by commission and a certificate of appropriateness;
- Criteria and procedures for review of applications for a certificate of appropriateness;
- Criteria and procedures for review of applications for a demolition permit and procedures to delay demolition;
- Jurisdiction over publicly owned property and governmental actions;
- Maintenance of historic properties;
- Appeals from commission decisions; and
- Enforcement and penalties.

There are several important and potentially controversial issues to be addressed in drafting and adopting a preservation ordinance.

Temporary Bans

Many communities have found it necessary to implement a temporary ban or moratorium on demolition and building permits while they conduct an historic resource inventory or discuss adopting an historic district ordinance. This measure prevents construction or demolition that may be incompatible with the preservation controls eventually enacted. A temporary ban will allow a public discussion without the pressures of pending applications and will ensure that a rush for demolition and building permits does not undermine the community's heritage protection efforts. The duration of a moratorium should be explicitly limited and related to the time and efforts necessary to conduct a survey or implement new measures.

Statement of Purposes

A statement of purposes should explain the numerous public benefits of the proposed historic preservation ordinance and the need for the proposed ordinance to secure these benefits. Historic preservation ordinances often promote economic development, tourism, downtown and community revitalization, real estate investment opportunities, an enhanced tax base with little expenditure for extensions of public facilities, educational benefits, community pride and sense of place, and aesthetic values. Moreover, effective historic preservation programs may make it easier for a community to attract new businesses and retain existing ones. Each of these public purposes should be evaluated and, if applicable, should be tailored to the community's specific circumstances. Where state court decisions have upheld local historic programs, these should be reviewed to determine which public purposes were persuasive. In addition to assisting in legal defense, a clear and thorough explanation of the public purposes helps build broad coalitions of public support.

Creation of an Historic Preservation Commission

Historic preservation ordinances typically create a local historic preservation commission or board, which is delegated primary responsibility for administering the ordinance. Generally comprised of five to nine members serving up to five-year terms, preservation commissions typically include a mix of professional and lay members. The National Historic Preservation Act Amendments of 1980 (discussed below) and, in many cases, state enabling acts require broad commission representation to qualify for certification. Inclusion of relevant professionals (e.g., historians, architects, planners) also helps in defending decisions against charges of arbitrariness.

Delegation of Powers and Authorities

One of the most important policy decisions a community faces when enacting an historic preservation ordinance is what powers to grant to the preservation commission. The potential scope of these powers may be broad or limited, depending upon state law. The powers commonly delegated to preservation commissions include:

- Survey and identify historically and architecturally significant structures and areas;
- Designate (or nominate for designation) and protect landmarks and their surroundings and landmark districts;
- Review applications for alteration, construction, or demolition of landmark buildings and all structures within a historic district;

ROGER K. LEWIS

- Require affirmative maintenance of historic structures;
- Make recommendations regarding local zoning amendments and comments on the local comprehensive plan;
- Undertake educational programs and activities;
- Establish standards and procedures for designation and development review;
- Accept funds from federal, state, and private sources;
- Buy, sell, or accept donations of properties; and
- Exercise the power of eminent domain.[7]

A preservation commission does not need to have all of these powers to function effectively:

> The key point is that the review body be given adequate power to protect landmarks, and this will almost certainly require that it have the power to forbid demolition or alteration, not just delay it, even though such power may be exercised infrequently. Experience throughout the country shows that landmarks commissions without ultimate authority to say "no" are not as effective as those that have such power.[8]

Certificates of Appropriateness

Among the most important functions of an historic preservation commission is to issue certificates of appropriateness for proposed demolitions, alterations, and new construction. Most communities with historic commissions limit the jurisdiction of the historic preservation commission to review of exterior changes to designated properties or buildings in designated districts.

In addition, some communities provide technical assistance to property owners on the details of the local preservation process and feasible means of adapting historic properties for new uses. In Merion Township, Pennsylvania, for example, the historical review board has published guidelines entitled, "Guide for Property Owners Within Their Historic Districts," to help owners understand what they can do with their property.

Delegation of Final Decision-Making Authority

A key issue related to the scope of the commission's authority concerns which governmental body has final authority to designate historic buildings and districts, to issue certificates of appropriateness, and to issue demolition permits. Three alternative approaches are common:

- The preservation commission exercises final decision-making authority;
- The preservation commission makes final decisions, but these decisions can be appealed to the local legislative body, which can overrule the preservation decision; or
- The preservation commission serves in an advisory capacity to the legislative body, which considers the commission's recommendations and makes all final decisions itself.

Preservationists usually prefer the first approach—with final decision-making authority vested in the preservation commission—because this approach provides the most insulation from political influences. The caveat is that a local legislative body is less likely to give a preservation commission both final decision-making authority and a strong array of preservation tools than it is to give one or the other. Preservationists may have to choose between a preservation commission with a powerful array of tools (such as the authority to prohibit a demolition) subject to close political control, or an independent commission with more circumscribed authority.[9] The second approach is common throughout the country, and is generally acceptable to preservationists because of the balance it strikes between preservation, property rights, and political control.[10] A preservation commission with only advisory authority generally has much less influence than a board whose decisions have some degree of finality.

The Process for Designating Historic Landmarks and Districts

State enabling legislation often establishes the framework for designating historic landmarks and districts. In most states, however, communities have considerable discretion to determine or refine these criteria and procedures. The criteria and procedures for designation are a critical, yet often overlooked, element of preservation programs. Appropriate designation standards are especially important in areas where historic or architectural significance is not immediately obvious.

Two important and potentially divisive issues concerning the designation process are who may nominate property or districts for designation and what is the appropriate role for the owner of nominated property or who has property in a nominated district.

Nomination.   In some communities, only preservation commission members or members of the legislative body can nominate a property or district. Other communities are more permissive. In Boulder, Colorado, for example, nominations can be made by any organization "with a recognized interest in historic preservation." Boston, Massachusetts, permits nomination by ten or more registered voters of the city. In drafting an ordinance, the advantages of a relatively open nominating process are that the process is more democratic and allows for a greater number of deserving properties and districts to come formally before the commission. The leading disadvantage of an open process is that poorly conceived or politically insensitive nominations—especially those actively opposed by the landowner—can create divisiveness and weaken the entire heritage preservation program.

Owner Consent.   Although there is no constitutional requirement of owner consent, enabling legislation in a few states requires consent of the owner prior to designation of individual properties. In addition, many communities require a petition or vote approved by a specified percentage of property owners in a proposed district. State enabling legislation and local ordinances may also require a "super-majority" of two-thirds or three-fourths of the owners in a proposed district.

Preservationists often resist such provisions for the following reason:

> For an ordinance intended to provide effective protection, these provisions make little sense; landmarks are landmarks no matter what an owner might think and should be designated and protected accordingly. It would be considered odd indeed if individual landowners could veto any zoning restrictions placed on their properties.[11]

The following provision can help to strike a balance between the interests of community and an affected property owner:

> The purpose of historic preservation is to protect the historic significance of a landmark or district for the benefit of the entire community. The wishes of the owner should be considered but should not be allowed to frustrate legitimate public purposes.[12]

Delineating Historic Districts and Determining Permitted Uses and Densities

The two usual methods of delineating an historic district and regulating the permitted land uses, densities, and development standards (in addition to the historic preservation standards) are: (1) to designate the historic district as a distinct zoning district and to include in the district regulations the permissible uses, densities, and development standards; and (2) to apply the historic district as an overlay zone.

An historic overlay zone may apply historic preservation standards to an historic district that crosses several different zoning districts. The historic standards do not replace the preexisting standards, but apply as additional requirements. This approach gives affected landowners the security of knowing that the historic preservation district will not change the permitted uses, densities, and criteria of the existing zone.

Many communities use historic overlay zoning, including Loudoun County, Virginia. (Loudoun County's program is profiled at the end of this chapter.) Many state enabling statutes authorize historic overlay districts, and courts have approved the approach.[13]

Demolition Permits
Historic landmarks and other designated historic properties are generally protected by "delay-of-demolition" provisions. Triggered by an application for a demolition permit, these provisions start the clock ticking on a limited cooling-off period, allowing time for alternatives to demolition to be explored by local officials and the property owner. As discussed earlier, historic preservation programs that authorize either the preservation commission or the legislative body to prohibit demolition under specified standards are more effective than programs that only authorize a delay in demolition.

Enforcement
One of the most difficult issues in historic preservation ordinances is how to adequately enforce its provisions. For some developers, paying a fine for illegally demolishing an historic building is simply treated as a small part of the cost of doing business. An innovative provision in the District of Columbia's ordinance grants the power to require parties that demolish property in violation of a preservation ordinance to rebuild it as it existed prior to demolition.[14]

BEYOND PLANS, SURVEYS, AND ORDINANCES

In addition to the "core" historic preservation tools—historic resource surveying, comprehensive planning and zoning, and historic preservation ordinances—many communities have adapted numerous other growth management techniques to preserve local heritage. Some of the more promising techniques that lend themselves to historic preservation objectives include acquisition, transfer of development rights, subdivision regulation, clustered development regulations, performance-based development permitting systems, building code revisions, and local tax policies.

Acquisition
Communities have purchased historic properties for a wide variety of municipal uses and for resale subject to preservation restrictions. Other communities have implemented programs for the acquisition of preservation easements.[15]

Most states authorize local preservation commissions to acquire historic sites; several states authorize the use of eminent domain to acquire historic buildings under limited circumstances. In many states, commissions may acquire not only full fee interests, but also preservation or facade easements. A preservation or facade easement is a formal agreement between the owner of an historic structure and a government agency or preservation organization giving the latter the right to approve changes to the building before they are undertaken.

Transfer of Development Rights (TDR)
This technique holds promise as an historic landmark preservation tool. Its use by New York City to preserve Grand Central Station has been approved by the United States Supreme Court.[16] A few states explicitly authorize its use as part of an historic preservation program; in many other states, localities have implemented TDR programs to preserve historic structures under the state's general enabling legislation, without specific enabling legislation.

Subdivision Regulation
Many communities have revised their subdivision regulations to encourage the preservation of historic districts and culturally significant landscapes. Communities have enacted waivers and special standards to encourage or require lot arrangement, street design and materials, sidewalk design and materials, and other development standards that are compatible with protection of local heritage.

Clustered Development Regulations
Clustered development regulations and other controls encouraging sensitive land development can be used to protect historically and culturally significant landscapes as well. (This technique is explained in Appendix A.)

Performance-Based Development Permitting Systems
Several communities, including Breckenridge, Colorado, have successfully used growth management permitting systems to protect historic properties. This technique authorizes a locality to evaluate the historic and cultural significance of each property as it is proposed for development or redevelopment. Breckenridge uses a performance-based control system to require developers to conduct a site-specific historic survey and, if important resources are identified, to

ROGER K. LEWIS

avoid or mitigate the negative impacts of the project on historic resources.

Building Code Revisions

Modern building codes often frustrate historic preservation efforts by requiring historic properties to modernize to new building standards that are difficult to meet in rehabilitated buildings. Landmark preservation efforts and building codes need to be coordinated. Both the Building Officials and Code Administrators International (BOCA) Basic Building Code and the Southern Building Code have been amended to include special provisions for rehabilitation of landmark buildings. Several states, including California, Hawaii, South Dakota, Idaho, Connecticut, and Massachusetts, as well as numerous cities, have adopted these or similar building code revisions.

Local preservation advocates can educate local leaders and building code officials to the approach to landmark preservation taken by BOCA and to the flexibility built into many state and local building codes.[17]

Local Tax Policies

Local property tax policies can have a significant effect on the fate of historic properties. Property taxes may be the largest single operating expense for owners of income-producing historic property. Property tax policies therefore may be a strong inducement for historic preservation. Property tax benefits can encourage historic preservation in numerous ways, for example, by reducing the incentive for a landowner to demolish in order to reduce the property tax burden of an empty or underutilized building; reducing property taxes to reflect decreased property value resulting from historic preservation regulations or preservation easements; and by encouraging renovation and reuse in return for tax concessions for renovated structures.

State property tax legislation determines the options available to a local government to influence historic preservation through property tax incentives. At least 14 states have legislation embodying one or more of these approaches.[18] In other situations, a community may consider approaching relevant state representatives for appropriate special or local enabling legislation. (Many state legislatures have little trouble enacting laws that may reduce someone's local taxes if supported by the affected local government.)

The variety of local approaches is illustrated by several examples:

- Austin, Texas, provides a property tax exemption of 50 percent of the assessed valuation of an historic structure and 25 percent of the associated land.

- San Antonio, Texas, affords a five-year full abatement of property taxes following rehabilitation of an historic structure, with a 50 percent abatement for a subsequent five-year period.

- In King County, Washington, historic properties can be assessed for local property taxes at their current use value rather than at market value.

Although local property tax incentives may be an important marginal inducement for historic preservation, the federal income tax credit available for historic rehabilitation is generally more important in making potential historic rehabilitation projects financially viable. These benefits are discussed in Appendix B.

Suggestions for the Development of Effective Local Programs

The following will improve the effectiveness of a local preservation program:

- Build community consensus about local historic and cultural resources that are distinctive and worthy of preservation. The successful industrial heritage program in Lowell, Massachusetts, demonstrates the importance of looking with an open mind at potential community assets.

- Undertake a thorough historic and cultural resource survey or inventory. This survey is the foundation of a comprehensive preservation program.

- Integrate historic and cultural preservation with the comprehensive plan and other land use controls to ensure that other planning objectives and growth management regulations, such as permitted densities and uses, do not undermine preservation objectives.

- Enact an ordinance allowing the local government to delay or prohibit demolition. Even if local land use controls effectively serve historic preservation objectives, an ordinance delaying demolition of significant structures can be valuable in allowing

the community time to mobilize to preserve resources. An ordinance prohibiting demolition of significant structures under certain circumstances is an even more powerful preservation tool.

- Protect the cultural and economic vitality of historic commercial districts. To ensure long-term success, local preservation programs must not only ensure the physical and aesthetic integrity of historic and cultural resources, but must also assist in ensuring that historic and culturally significant properties are economically viable. In many cases, this requires the community to take a hard look at the amount and nature of commercial development permitted outside of the community's traditional Main Street or downtown commercial district and encourage greater use of older, traditional core areas.

Private Preservation Options

While government's role in preservation has increased over time, there remains an essential role in all communities for effective private initiative and advocacy. Governments, and especially local governments, have often proven themselves fickle allies and fair-weather friends. For example, in 1986, Omaha, Nebraska, nominated a six-square-block area in the city's historic warehouse area for listing as an historic district in the National Register. Two years later, the city began demolition of the *entire* historic district as part of the city's riverfront development plan, largely to provide a "corporate campus" for a major agricultural corporation located in the city. It appears that the city and the corporation will be responsible for the largest single destruction ever of National Register properties.[19]

In addition to undertaking local research, conducting historic and cultural resource inventories, and advocating for effective preservation policies, local preservation organizations play an important role in directly preserving significant structures and parcels and in building a constituency for preservation.

DIRECT PRESERVATION

Private organizations can adapt a range of tools to preserve historic and culturally significant property. Illustrative projects include:

- Purchasing or accepting the donation of a "facade easement" on an historic building or a conservation easement on an historic parcel or site. In most states, easements are potentially quite potent and flexible tools for furthering preservation objectives. (The federal tax benefits of conservation and preservation donations are discussed in Appendix B.)

- Acquiring and undertaking "limited development" of historic or culturally significant parcels. (This increasingly popular technique is discussed in Appendix A.)

- Establishing a preservation "revolving fund," accumulated from fund-raising, charitable gifts, and project proceeds, that will fund preservation activity, especially short-term loans for preservation actions. Federal tax law allows nonprofit organizations to conduct business activities without federal income tax liability, so long as these activities are related to the purposes of the organization and the proceeds are used for approved charitable purposes. The Galveston Historical Foundation has successfully employed a revolving loan fund to preserve significant local property and has in the process become a major community force for preservation. (The foundation is profiled at the end of this chapter.)

- Restoring significant buildings and parcels, and reselling the property subject to appropriate easements or maintenance agreements.

CONSTITUENCY BUILDING

Local nonprofits play the important role of raising local appreciation of the value of preserving the community's heritage and building a local constituency for preservation. Two of the more promising tools for building a local preservation constituency include:

- Publicizing local resources:
- Educating owners of significant buildings

The Bucks County Conservancy in Pennsylvania, for example, started the Bucks County Register of Historic Places as a voluntary means of publicly recognizing local historic and architectural resources. Many groups have published books with photographs and descriptions of significant local buildings. These publications can build goodwill, increase local knowledge, build support for an historic district ordinance or other local political initiative, and can be used for raising funds. The content is derived from a local inventory of historic and cultural resources. Tours of significant houses are also popular and effective ways of publicizing local resources.

Recognizing that much damage to significant properties occurs due to owner indifference and ignorance, nonprofits work directly with property owners through voluntary programs. These programs can recognize significant property with a plaque or other sign of distinction, give annual awards to the exemplary stewards, and provide rehabilitation consulting or assistance.

State Historic Preservation Programs

Within the framework of the National Historic Preservation Act (NHPA), which is discussed below, all 50 states have designated a State Historic Preservation Office (SHPO) as the lead for their state preservation programs. In addition to participating in the federal programs, most states have established state-level historic preservation programs. The range of state program responsibilities duties include:

- Certifying local programs, thereby making local governments eligible for federal funding and giving them increased authority in the National Register nominating process;
- Conducting statewide surveys of historic resources;
- Coordinating development of statewide historic preservation plans and state registers;
- Managing the National Register nomination process;
- Acquiring and managing historic properties of statewide significance;
- Staffing state preservation commissions;
- Coordinating state involvement in "Section 106" reviews (discussed below);
- Administering federal grants for local programs;
- Promoting and enforcing historic preservation policies among other state agencies;
- Advising the U.S. Department of the Interior on applications for certification for federal tax benefits for rehabilitation of private properties; and
- Providing assistance (technical, educational, financial, and regulatory) to advance local preservation activities.

While some are stronger than others, these state programs often go beyond state preservation activities required by federal law. While there is considerable variety among state programs, some common features exist. These include creation of state registers of historic places; protection of historic resources through state environmental policy acts and statewide planning legislation; state Main Street programs; integration of historic preservation with tourism and economic development; the use of tax incentives to

promote historic preservation; and integration of historic preservation with statewide land use planning.

STATE REGISTERS OF HISTORIC PLACES

Many states, including California, Hawaii, Illinois, Kansas, and New York, have established state registers or lists of historic places, which provide varying degrees of protection to historic properties. This has proved on occasion to be an effective device for protecting designated properties from state-funded or state-permitted actions.

These programs typically provide that if a site is on, or eligible for, the state register, state agencies must consult with the SHPO, comply with preservation regulations, and, in some instances, demonstrate that no feasible alternative to a project exists or take steps to mitigate a project's adverse effects. Moreover, some states require that projects funded or permitted by local government must comply with state register requirements.

An important feature of state registration is that when a listed property is threatened, the program pro-

vides time for the SHPO, local officials, preservationists, and developers to identify ways to preserve it. In Hawaii, for example, owners of registered property must notify the state Historical Places Review Board of proposed construction. Notification triggers a 90-day period during which the landowner cannot begin or continue construction while the board's staff either approves the project, initiates condemnation, or commences salvage operations to preserve the structure.[20] Illinois has a similar requirement, but with a 210-day cooling-off period.[21]

Kansas legislation contains one of the strongest state protections for registered sites. A provision patterned after Section 4(f) of the federal Department of Transportation Act requires that any work by state or local government that threatens to encroach upon, damage, or destroy register property or its "environs" may not proceed until the governor or the local governing body finds that "there is no feasible and prudent alternative to the proposal and that it includes all possible planning to minimize harm."[22]

New Mexico provides for an emergency classification of property by temporarily listing it on the state register for up to one year. During this time, the SHPO determines the eligibility of the property for permanent registration.[23]

STATE ENVIRONMENTAL POLICY ACTS

About half the states have enacted state environmental policy acts (SEPA), which, in varying degrees, require comprehensive environmental review of state actions. In nearly every SEPA, historic resources and properties are included within the definition of environmental resources. Thus, permits to demolish or alter registered historic properties, and perhaps buildings within historic districts or eligible properties, may be subject to SEPA requirements.

As noted in *A Handbook on Historic Preservation Law:*

> [I]n some states, SEPAs have the potential to inject historic preservation concerns far deeper into state and local agency decision making than any of the more strictly preservation-related state laws. By imposing a duty on agencies to pursue less damaging alternatives where possible or at least to institute measures to reduce adverse efforts when approving a project, SEPAs have the potential to force more preservation-oriented decisions than many of the state registers.[24]

THE MAIN STREET PROGRAM

Perhaps the best example of what can be accomplished by a judicious melding of public and private initiative and funds is the highly successful Main Street program, created by the National Trust for Historic Preservation. The program has spurred economic development in many small towns and medium-sized communities while advancing preservation goals.

In brief, Main Street is an economic development program for small city downtowns and is based on the premise that one of the greatest assets those places have is their unique historic and architecturally significant structures. Building on these old buildings as assets instead of viewing them as stumbling blocks to new development, local Main Street managers are hired and paid for by the locality. The program was developed by the National Trust for Historic Preservation; however, several states have instituted their own programs. The National Trust Main Street Program maintains cooperative arrangements with many other states. For example, in Texas, the state provides technical assistance for a three-year period to five cities selected annually by the governor for the program. Areas of assistance include design and renovation, marketing, parking, and other areas where local expertise may not be available.[25] (Information on the Main Street Program is at the end of the chapter.)

INTEGRATION WITH ECONOMIC DEVELOPMENT AND TOURISM EFFORTS

An important trend is the increasing number of states that coordinate historic preservation policy with the missions of other agencies, particularly economic development and tourism. In Illinois, for example, a state historic preservation agency was recently carved out of the state department of natural resources and several other small independent agencies. The new agency has authority over all state-owned historic sites and is working closely with state tourism and economic development agencies to ensure that the areas around these sites realize their full economic potential. Where sites are located in rural areas, an effort is being made to provide visitors with easily accessible accommodations and restaurants whose business can contribute to the local economy.[26]

Similarly, in California, the legislature created a state heritage task force, to study future needs and document the important links between preservation, historic sites, and the state's largest industry, tourism.[27] The work of the task force resulted in some important changes in state law and policy.[28]

TAX POLICIES

Many states have used state tax legislation to encourage preservation. One widely used approach is preferential tax treatment. For example, North Carolina provides the owners of locally designated properties with a 50 percent reduction in assessed valuation. In the event that such designation is lost or there is a destruction of the property's key historic features, the state recoups the tax benefits with interest.[29] In Oregon, owners of properties listed on the National Register are eligible for a 15-year freeze on assessed valuation. In addition, properties must be opened to the public once a year and maintained according to specified standards.[30]

Other states employ various other property tax incentives, including total or partial abatements and tax credits based on percentage of renovation or restoration costs.

INTEGRATION WITH STATEWIDE LAND USE PLANNING

A final promising state approach to historic preservation exists in states that have statewide land use planning or state land use controls. New Jersey, for example, sets state historic preservation standards that guide local planning efforts. The State Planning Act of 1986 calls for preparation of a state development and redevelopment plan that includes a broad range of goals to protect and enhance the quality of life in the state. Municipalities are to prepare local plans that are consistent with the state plan. The state plan provides for preservation of historic resources and requires localities to do likewise in the local planning and land use control process. Local plans must indicate the location, significance, proposed use, and means of preserving identified sites and districts, as well as formal standards for making designations.

Local preservation activists should get involved early in these planning processes to ensure that protection of significant historic resources is not overlooked.

Federal Influences on Historic Preservation

The federal government exerts a powerful influence over state and local historic preservation efforts. Important federal laws and programs include the:

- National Register of Historic Places;
- Department of Transportation Act of 1966;
- The review process created in Section 106 of the National Historic Preservation Act;
- Income tax credits for historic rehabilitation;
- National Park Service grant assistance for local preservation programs;
- Grant assistance under the Housing and Community Development Act of 1974; and
- National Environmental Policy Act.

The National Historic Preservation Act of 1966 (NHPA),[31] substantially amended in 1980, is the principal federal historic preservation statute. The NHPA institutionalized the National Register of Historic Places and created the Section 106 review process and the Advisory Council on Historic Preservation. The NHPA effectively provides the impetus for government historic preservation activity at all levels through the designation of State Historic Preservation Offices (SHPOs), who review and certify local preservation ordinances.

The National Register has been termed the "national record of cultural resources worthy of preservation."[32] Administered by the National Park Service within the U.S. Department of the Interior, the National Register includes five resource categories:

- Districts;
- Sites (e.g., locations of significant events);
- Buildings;
- Structures (e.g., large-scale engineering structures);
- Objects (e.g., trains and ships).

Within these categories, resources can be nominated individually, thematically, in groups, or as part of districts. Two separate designations exist—the National Register and National Historic Landmarks (NHL). NHL status is reserved for properties of exceptional national significance. Properties designated as National Historic Landmarks typically are on the Register; but most National Register properties are not NHLs.

The National Register designation process, which entails local nomination through SHPOs, is rigorous. To be designated, nominated properties must possess authenticity of historic identity. Although designation per se does not automatically restrict what private owners can do with their properties, it does provide a substantial foundation for local regulatory actions. The nominating process can be a powerful catalyst for motivating local preservation action, such as creation of historic district zoning and acquisition of significant properties. Listing on the National Register is not required for implementation of local historic district zoning.*

Section 4(f) of the Department of Transportation Act of 1966[33] strongly discourages the use of federal funds for highway construction projects that would have an adverse impact on historic resources (whether designated in the National Register or by state or local action), public parks, recreation areas, and wildlife refuges. The act prohibits the secretary of transportation from approving any federal spending or program that would require the "use" of land determined to be historically significant. The word "use" has been defined to include not only physical construction, but also noise and increased congestion from property proximate to such sites. The provision allows "use" of these sites only if there is no feasible and prudent alternative, in which case "all possible planning to minimize harm" must be undertaken.

Section 106 of the NHPA requires that all federal agency actions having an "adverse impact" on property listed on the National Register and all property *eligible* for designation must be reviewed by the Advisory Council on Historic Preservation, an independent federal agency charged with advising the president and Congress on historic preservation matters. The Advisory Council—consisting of 19 members appointed by the president including the secretaries of interior, transportation, housing and urban develop-

---

* A Department of Interior publication, *How to Complete National Register Forms*, and other information cited at the end of this chapter describe the designation process and the criteria used.

ment, and agriculture—is given an opportunity to comment on the proposed action. Such actions include not only direct federal agency undertakings, but also projects receiving federal funding, approvals, or licenses. Section 106 in essence establishes a consultation process: the sponsoring agency must consider the Advisory Council's comments, but the process is entirely procedural. An agency is *not* required to take any substantive action in response to the Advisory Council's comments.

The federal income tax code provides tax benefits for certain private historic rehabilitation expenditures. (These federal tax benefits are explained in Appendix B.)

Federal funding for local preservation activities is available both from the National Park Service (NPS) and the Department of Housing and Urban Development. Through the SHPOs, the NPS makes funds available for surveys, planning, acquisition, and appropriate development of National Register properties. Federal funds for preservation are available under the Housing and Community Development Act of 1974. In

addition, under Title I of the National Housing Act,[34] the Federal Housing Administration has the authority to insure property rehabilitation loans provided by private lenders.

The National Environmental Policy Act (NEPA)[35] requires environmental review of "major federal actions," including private actions requiring a federal permit. NEPA applies to federal actions that affect historic resources, but unlike Section 106 (discussed earlier), NEPA reviews are not limited to property listed on or eligible for the National Register.

Legal Considerations in Local Preservation Programs

The Supreme Court decision that established historic preservation objectives as a sufficient basis for local regulatory efforts was *Penn Central Transportation Co. v. New York City*, 438 U.S. 104 (1978), in which the Court upheld the constitutionality of using New York

City's landmarks ordinance to preserve Grand Central Station. The following general guidelines have evolved from numerous decisions and statutes since *Penn Central*:

- Carefully review state statutes and cases interpreting them before undertaking preservation efforts to determine the scope of local authority and the required procedures. State historic preservation enabling and other state preservation statutes vary widely from state to state.

- Clearly and thoroughly state and document the public benefits of historic and cultural preservation. These benefits should be documented in the public record and should be summarized in the text of the ordinance. Potential benefits include aesthetics, contribution to the community's ability to retain existing businesses and attract new ones, tourism development, positive impacts on the tax base and property values from rehabilitation and reuse of old buildings, and the fiscal savings in providing old buildings, rather than new construction, with public service and facilities.

- Provide for fair procedures. Local preservation ordinances should establish procedures to ensure that affected landowners receive adequate notice, that hearings and deliberations are fair and open, and that all other requirements of procedural due process are met.

- Provide procedures in local ordinances to ensure that preservation ordinances apply fairly. Procedures should be written into local ordinances to allow equitable relief for a landowner who demonstrates through professional appraisals or market analyses that an ordinance would deny all economically reasonable use of his property.

PROFILE

GALVESTON HISTORICAL FOUNDATION

Preserving and Creating a Community

Mission _____

The Galveston Historical Foundation (GHF) initiates and supports historic preservation throughout the city and promotes broad-based community participation in local revitalization projects. A key way that GHF supports historic preservation in Galveston is by financing the purchase and resale of properties, subject to deed restrictions and rehabilitation requirements.

Geographic Scope _____

A city of 70,000 residents, Galveston is on a barrier island by the same name, located one mile off the Texas coast, 50 miles southeast of Houston. Galveston's economy depends on its deep-water port, large medical institutions, and 4 million tourists a year.

Galveston was the most important Gulf Coast commercial trade center from the middle of the nineteenth century until around 1910, when a dredged ship channel was completed to Houston, and commerce moved inland. The channel has spurred development of oil refineries and petrochemical facilities on the mainland that provide an economic base for the cities there. The bay between Galveston Island and the mainland is precariously balanced between the demands of commercial fishing and recreation on the one hand, and industrial uses on the other. Unlike many of its neighbors, Galveston retains a distinctiveness based on preservation of its historic ambiance and its unique island setting.

Population growth is not a significant cause of development pressure in Galveston. The 1970 census counted about 70,000 residents, and during the remainder of the decade the population actually declined. By the late 1980s, it regained its 1970 level. Threats to Galveston's historic distinctiveness have

instead been caused by real estate developments in the downtown area and deterioration in some residential districts.

Success Stories _____

By the mid-1950s, real estate developers and others were haphazardly demolishing structures, including ones dating from the nineteenth-century. In 1954, the Galveston Historical Society, then a literary group, incorporated as a foundation and began raising funds to preserve local historic buildings and residences. Yet it was not until the 1970s that the city as a whole recognized the need to protect its more than 1,500 historic structures.

Around 1970, the Junior League of Galveston County focused attention on the Strand, a deteriorated, ten-block nineteenth-century commercial area badly in need of preservation and economic revitalization. In 1973, two locally based foundations provided GHF with seed money to establish the Strand Revolving Fund to initiate preservation and revitalization throughout the area.

The fund enabled GHF to revitalize the Strand by purchasing buildings and reselling them for active use, subject to deed restrictions and restoration requirements. GHF assisted purchasers of the historic buildings by gaining agreement from a group of local lenders to provide long-term financing. Six local financial institutions thus made available $1 million in financing, which they later increased to $1.6 million.

In 1975, GHF attracted a grant from the National Endowment for the Arts (NEA), which funded the development of an overall plan for the Strand. GHF and the local arts council also organized public events and festivals which drew visitors to witness the Strand's potential. For example, GHF's annual festival in December, "Dickens on the Strand," now contributes nearly $10 million to the local economy and attracts over 100,000 visitors each year.

GHF efforts have paid off. The Strand is the only commercial district in Texas that has been designated a National Historic Landmark. The project has attracted $60 million in private investment for rehabilitation and active use of the area, which is now heavily frequented by visitors and residents. The success has also triggered renovation of surrounding areas once slated for demolition.

In addition to efforts to revitalize the Strand, GHF also created a Residential Program to preserve and support historic residential neighborhoods in Galveston. This program also includes a revolving fund, which to date has purchased eight endangered houses and resold them with deed restrictions. Other accomplishments of the Residential Program include a neighborhood field-worker liaison between GHF and neighborhood organizations and the Paint Partnership Program, which has provided free paint for the exteriors of more than 400 older houses throughout the city. The Residential Program has catalyzed the formation of three neighborhood associations in historic areas of the City, and was instrumental in expanding an existing residential historic district.

During the past 15 years, GHF has helped to ensure a unique local identity. For example, GHF decided, early on, to attract individual buyers and investors for the Strand project, rather than turn it over to one large developer. What the result lacks in cohesion, it more than makes up for in individuality and variety. This feeling of diversity is one of the city's greatest assets.

Organizational Structure

GHF is a nonprofit corporation. Its board consists of more than 25 volunteer members, including local corporate professionals, Strand merchants, entrepreneurs, teachers, homemakers and architects.

The corporation employs some 30 professional and support staff. About nine are responsible for overall operations, including the director's office, accounting, public relations, and development. The remaining staff run GHF programs, which include the Residential Program, events, two historic house museums, the historic Tall Ship ELISSA, the county museum, the Strand Visitors Center, tour service and education.

GHF has a total of 2,700 individual and corporate members. The membership is fee-based, and has many different membership categories, which vary with financial commitment levels.

Financial Characteristics

GHF had a $2 million budget in fiscal year 1988/1989, and, as of 1988, an endowment of $350,000. In 1988, GHF covered 83 percent of its budget with earned income (admissions, public events, membership dues, the county museum management contract, and a portion of the city's hotel/motel tax). The remaining 17 percent was raised from fund-raising events and small donations, and from foundation, corporate, and individual gifts.

Contact

Galveston Historical Foundation
2016 Strand
Galveston Island, TX 77550

PROFILE

ILLINOIS AND MICHIGAN CANAL NATIONAL HERITAGE CORRIDOR

A Broad-based Approach to Revitalizing Historic and Economic Assets

Regional Characteristics

The Illinois and Michigan canal, constructed from 1836 to 1848 to link the Great Lakes and the Mississippi River systems, stretches 120 miles from Lake Michigan at Chicago through northeastern Illinois to the towns of LaSalle and Peru in the north-central part of the state. Forty-one communities, many suffering from industrial emigration and high unemployment, lie in the region.

The canal corridor has had a diverse and illustrious history in the century and a half since its creation. For 30 years, as a result of the canal, northeastern Illinois flourished as one of the most industrialized regions in the nation. However, with the coming of the railroad and a more technically advanced waterway, the canal fell into disuse and was eventually closed in 1933.

During the years preceding World War II, local civilian Conservation Corps members transformed the canal corridor into a linear park. State and local parks were developed on adjacent lands, and portions of the canal were rehabilitated. Despite these efforts, a lack of funding during the 1940s and 1950s contributed to the deterioration of many of these improvements.

Growth Patterns

Many of the communities along the canal corridor have experienced both population and economic decline in the past few decades. Although many industries have contracted or left the region in recent years, the area remains a viable transportation and industrial corridor, with a growing number of companies, illustrating that the objective of the canal corridor is not an effort to limit growth, but rather to stimulate the regional economy with tourism and heritage activities,

to provide recreational opportunities, and to revitalize existing business and industry.

Resources Threatened

The Illinois and Michigan canal corridor was threatened both by continued degradation due to lack of maintenance, and by the state's intention to sell canal land to generate revenue. Both of these possibilities threatened numerous historically and culturally significant structures as well as forests and parks that had been established on public lands.

Measures Taken

Local action to protect the canal and surrounding lands began in the late 1950s and early 1960s, when the easternmost section of the canal right-of-way was paved over during construction of an expressway. The state, viewing the abandoned canal primarily as surplus property and a source of income, initiated plans to sell portions of the canal and surrounding lands. These actions triggered an unanticipated grass-roots response that forced the state to reconsider its original plans.

In 1974, local citizens, aided by the Open Lands Project, a private nonprofit conservation group, succeeded in having the entire canal transferred to the jurisdiction of the Illinois Department of Conservation. The state legislature also designated the southernmost 61.5 miles of the canal as a state park.

The Open Lands Project has been an important regional actor in catalyzing action on the canal since the 1960s. Open Lands, which is dedicated to preserving public open space in northeastern Illinois, first directed its efforts to the southern portion of the corridor because of the private ownership of land surrounding the canal further north. Citizens along the northern portion of the canal soon began to urge the organization to work to preserve the northern portion.

The Open Lands Project, in cooperation with several other organizations, saw an opportunity for the Illinois and Michigan Canal in the National Park Service's new initiative to establish "urban cultural parks." In 1980, it initiated the Des Plaines River Valley Program, a project that focused on the canal area excluded from state park designation.

A coalition of local officials, industry, and the Upper Illinois Valley Association, a nonprofit organization borne from Open Lands Project, lobbied members of Congress to sponsor a bill authorizing the National Park Service to develop a corridor plan and to explore alternatives for implementation. The Park Service provided staff who collaborated with local officials in articulating a vision of what people wanted to see happen along the canal. The plan identifies 39 significant natural areas and over 200 historic sites and districts, as well as areas with significant potential for tourism promotion.

In 1984, Congress designated the Illinois and Michigan Canal National Heritage Corridor, which gives new direction to the future of the region by creating a partnership between the federal government, the state, local governments, and private organizations. The legislation establishes a 19-member corridor commission to provide technical assistance and coordination in maintaining a sensitive balance between nature and industry. Significantly, the designation of the corridor does not impose any new regulations on development in the region. As the private sector leader, the Upper Illinois Valley Association has taken responsibility for public education and coordination of public-private partnerships for local renewal and preservation efforts.

Experience

An integrated approach to conservation has been successful, involving reclamation, revitalization of local economies, and protection of natural resources. Historic preservation has provided an anchor for tourism development and has successfully transformed symbols of decline into public attractions and economic assets. For example, in 1983, the Upper Illinois Valley Association identified an abandoned Lockport warehouse originally constructed to store canal construction equipment as a potential tourism anchor. Today, the building houses a private restaurant, a gallery of the Illinois State Museum, and a visitor center.

Other rehabilitation efforts have taken completely different, innovative tacks. Where decades of tailings from a now-abandoned mine lay adjacent to the canal, artists have reshaped the mounds of dirt into huge "earth art" installations. One such sculpture is in the shape of a huge water bug. Visitors can explore and play on and around these gargantuan sculptures, effectively transforming an eyesore into a recreational park.

Much of the funding for these projects is provided by private/public partnerships. For example, U.S. Steel Realty Development, the Upper Illinois Valley Association, and the National Trust for Historic Preservation have developed final plans for "Heritage Business Park" at the site of a partially abandoned U.S. Steel mill. The conversion of the 170-acre site in Joliet will include offices, light industry, an open-air museum, and a recreational and archeological park along the banks of the canal. This project was motivated by the determination of local citizens, community groups, business and industry leaders, historians and redevelopment specialists to revitalize the steel mill site.

CONTACT

Open Lands Project
53 W. Jackson Boulevard
Chicago, IL 60604

PROFILE

LOUDOUN COUNTY, VIRGINIA

Overlay Zoning

Community Characteristics

The Loudoun County seat, Leesburg, is only a 20-mile drive from Washington, D.C. Two primary highways carry traffic westward from the nation's capital, through intensely developed Fairfax County into the heart of Loudoun. An additional toll road from the highly developed Dulles Airport corridor is planned.

The landscape consists of a series of undulating valleys punctuated in a north-south direction by low ridges announcing the Blue Ridge mountains, which begin at the county's western edge. The Potomac River flows along the county's northern border, and the two biggest creeks running into it have been designated as scenic under Virginia state law.

In the early eighteenth century, English settlers established large plantations in the southern part of the county, while smaller farms were settled by German and Quaker immigrants to the west. This mix of plantations and small farms with accompanying villages forms the historic heritage of Loudoun.

About 90 percent of Loudoun's 521 square miles lies in open space, of which over half is occupied by crops or pasture. The value of agricultural production in the late 1970s neared $30 million, while tourism accounted for almost $20 million.

Growth Pressures

The population of Loudoun County settled around 20,000 by the early nineteenth century, and did not start to grow again until after World War II. Between 1970 and 1980, the population grew by more than half, to almost 60,000. In early 1988, county planners estimate the population at 81,000 based on building permits.

The rapid growth of suburban Washington has

brought a recent tide of development into Loudoun County that threatens to destroy the county's open space, historic sites, rural character, and traditional development patterns. Development pressure is particularly intense close to the eastern border of the county, where some local officials feel they are finally reaping the economic benefits they have watched neighboring Fairfax County enjoy for some time. Large subdivisions and office developments in this area have contributed to much of the population growth in Loudoun over the past 20 years.

Loudoun County's distinctive character depends on retaining a sense of the relationship between the land and the buildings upon it. Thus, historic preservation is inextricably tied to protection of open space and agriculture, the context in which the buildings function.

The Virginia Historic Landmarks Commission has identified more than 1,000 historic sites and buildings in Loudoun County. Twenty-one sites and nine historic districts rank on the National Register of Historic Places and the Virginia Landmarks Register. Four are National Historic Landmarks. The Waterford National Historic District includes an entire early-nineteenth-century village and surrounding farms in a remarkable state of preservation.

Measures Taken

In 1972, Loudoun County adopted local legislation allowing the creation of historic districts. This comprehensive ordinance was enabled by state legislation that facilitated designation of historic districts and provided for greater control over proposed changes to buildings in areas designated as historic.

In Loudoun County, the historic district ordinance applies to nine districts, three of which are parts of incorporated towns in the county. Some districts were established by the county's overall rezoning in 1972. Since then, new districts have been designated through application by landowners for the Historic and Cultural Conservation Overlay District.

The ordinance establishes a committee to review and approve proposed changes to buildings in the districts and requires compatibility with existing farm operations and the scenic qualities of the rural or village landscape. Another unusual provision allows an historic building to be sold apart from the land on which it stands, and moved. This eliminates the necessity of subdividing the land in order to save historic buildings. Divorced from their context, however, such buildings are no longer eligible for Historic Landmark designation.

The districts are administered as overlays to existing zoning. This overlay zoning regulates neither how historic structures are used nor the density of new development.

In 1987, a 100-page document addressing criteria for construction in historic districts was incorporated into the ordinance by reference. These criteria describe how to compatibly integrate new construction in an historic district. The document describes, among other things, materials to be used, and height and sign limitations for each historic district in the county.

Experience

Efforts to obtain designation as an historic district have been initiated by private citizens and supported by county and town governments. The Goose Creek Historic and Cultural Conservation District illustrates the process by which historic district designation was approved in one case. As development continued in the eastern reaches of the county, where growth spilled over from Fairfax, a local employee of the Virginia Historic Landmarks Commission joined forces with representatives of two local environmental groups to identify areas worthy of historic preservation and natural resource protection.

These three local citizens proposed a 10,000-acre area for historic district designation. They undertook a public education campaign to garner support for the designation and persuaded a local organization to support them and submit the application to the County Planning Commission in 1975. The application included letters of support from state and local groups, the petition of property owners in the area proposed for designation, and a description of the area and its significance. Two years later, the County Board of Supervisors approved historic designation for the

district. It was the first time the county applied the historic district ordinance to a large rural area.

A different kind of example is Waterford, an unincorporated town with National Historic Landmark status, which had long sought to protect its historic character. The town took advantage of county historic district designation to establish an open-space easement program, which has protected over 200 acres from development. The easement program, however, has not adequately protected the 1,400-acre district, given the strong development pressure in the area. Residents have weathered a proposal to subdivide a 77-acre parcel within the district. After much controversy, an agreement was reached that would allow the construction of 14 new houses and the refurbishing of 3 old ones on 27 acres. A conservation easement on the remaining 50 acres was acquired for $200,000, of which half came from local donations and half from the state. Other farm parcels within and around the district may come on the market, creating a serious ongoing threat to the integrity of the federal landmark.

The new construction guidelines add persuasive power to the ordinance because they provide the review committee with a straightforward tool by which to judge proposals for construction or modification. Applicants are more likely to respond to modifications the committee might suggest, given a tangible set of guidelines against which to judge their proposal.

A weakness of the ordinance is its cumbersome enforcement provisions. Under Virginia law, the county does not have the power to levy civil penalties, such as fines. Rather, the county must rely upon enforcement in criminal court, which it tries to avoid. In addition, the county building inspector will not issue an occupancy permit to a building in violation of the code.

Loudoun County's ordinance provides designated districts with control over the design and placement of new development. This control will help retain the distinctive character of designated historic districts. But it is a fragmented kind of control with dispersed applicability. Considering the intensity of development pressures advancing from the Washington, D.C., metropolitan area, Loudoun County will need more effective protection mechanisms than those currently in place to accommodate new development without diminishing the county's historic and distinctive assets.

CONTACT

Department of Planning, Zoning and Community Development
39 Catoctin Circle, S.E.
Leesburg, VA 22075

PROFILE

SAN ANTONIO, TEXAS

Protecting and Revitalizing Significant Resources

Community Characteristics _____

The tenth largest city in the country, San Antonio has a population of 1.4 million, of which over 50 percent is Hispanic. San Antonio gets its distinctive historical character from Indian–Spanish–Mexican settlement of the area before the era of British western expansion.

In 1718, a Spanish military expedition traveling north from Mexico chose the site for the abundance of water emanating from a spring. Franciscan friars traveling with the expedition put to work local Coahuiltecan Indians, who first irrigated the land for cultivation. The friars established a number of Catholic missions along the banks of the river close to its source.

The city grew up around the spring, the headwaters of the San Antonio River, which flows south into the Gulf of Mexico, and provides the city with a "spine," around which commerce and recreation mingle.

San Antonio has long maintained a link to its past and an appreciation for its river. As the river flows through downtown, it makes a one-and-one-half-mile horseshoe bend called the Paseo del Rio. Lying 16 to 18 feet below-grade, the downtown river and the walkways along it are sheltered from the noise and the heat of the city streets. Although the city owns the river proper, adjacent lands are a patchwork of publicly and privately owned parcels.

The Hispanic and military presence continue to determine the flavor of San Antonio. The city is only 150 miles from the Mexican border and is an important center for trade with Mexico. Five U.S. military bases surrounding San Antonio employ almost 80,000 people and contribute $2.4 billion to San Antonio's economy. San Antonio also relies heavily on tourism, but the military is the largest payroll.

Growth Pressures _____

Despite the failure of economic growth to meet expectations in the early 1980s, San Antonio's population has been one of the fastest growing in the country, with a metropolitan area growth rate of 19 percent between 1980 and 1986. However, economic growth has been distributed unevenly in the city. According to the founder of an organization of San Antonio inner-city churches with an influential citywide political voice, San Antonio is actually two cities. One is poor, largely Hispanic, and suffers from unemployment and illiteracy. For example, only 20 to 50 single-family units have been built on the poor west side per year since 1980, compared with 10,000 per year countywide.

In the middle-class, largely white north side of town, per capita income is well above the city average of $7,600. Here, some housing stock has doubled since 1980. Corporate development has found its roots along highway corridors almost exclusively in this northern section of the city. The imbalance of physical growth in the city illustrates the lack of an overall growth management plan.

San Antonio's aggressive efforts to promote economic development have been most successful in the downtown area, where the public and private sectors have recently invested an estimated $1 billion. Downtown development has centered around San Antonio's Riverwalk, a promenade of hotels, restaurants, and shops catering to tourists and convention-goers.

The Alamo, the original eighteenth-century Franciscan mission in the heart of the city, was threatened in 1903 by hotel developers. The mission was saved by the Daughters of the Republic of Texas. Historic Landmark designation has since been given to ten districts and 150 structures and sites. But development pressure in the densely settled downtown area continued to threaten buildings that were part of the original settlement of the city. The San Antonio River itself was first highlighted as a potential centerpiece for the city in 1924, when the San Antonio Conservation Society opposed covering over the river's headwaters for a flood control project.

In 1939, San Antonio adopted a Historic Preservation Ordinance, the third U.S. city to do so, but the law did not effectively prevent demolition of historic structures after a mandatory waiting period had elapsed.

Measures Taken

HISTORIC PRESERVATION

By the late 1970s, the city felt it needed more effective protection and incentives for historic preservation. Over five years, 1,400 historical, archaeological, natural, scenic, and architectural resources were inventoried, mostly in the downtown area. A new ordinance was written to reinforce and strengthen protection of these special resources, most of which fall inside the boundaries of the overlay historic districts that the previous ordinance had created.

Each inventoried resource is labeled "exceptional" or "significant." The categories determine the burden of proof an applicant is required to overcome in order to receive a permit to destroy the structure or site. Permits are approved for "exceptional resources" only if the applicant meets a lengthy list of criteria showing unreasonable economic hardship. "Significant resources" applicants may qualify for a permit if they satisfy economic hardship criteria or criteria for "unusual and compelling circumstances."

The ordinance created a review board, or preservation commission, with advisory powers only. The city council alone has the power to designate historic sites and approve permit applications.

The ordinance requires the City Department of Building Inspections to adhere to the same set of building criteria the preservation commission uses in issuing recommendations to the City Council. The criteria cover new construction or any other type of alteration, including repair and maintenance, and signs.

In addition, the ordinance:

- Submits publicly owned utilities and other city-owned properties to the same review and approval procedures required of other properties.
- Authorizes the city to review and approve replacement plans before issuing a permit for demolition.

This clause ensures that suitable new construction will occur on the site.

- Allows the city a six-month period prior to formal hearings on the proposed demolition to seek alternatives. The ordinance requires notification of the preservation commission by city officials entertaining demolition applications to ensure that plans exist for suitable rehabilitation or replacement.
- Removes the incentive for potential applicants to purposely neglect their buildings in the interests of more easily obtaining demolition approval. One section enlists the cooperation of the city building inspector to require repairs to existing historic structures. If the city is forced to demolish a neglected building for public safety reasons, the preservation commission is prohibited from considering new construction applications on that site for a period of two years. The city may not even grant a permit for surface parking on the lot.

RIVERWALK

For over half a century, efforts to protect the San Antonio River as it passes through the city have been spurred by citizen action. In the 1920s, Emily Edwards, under the auspices of the San Antonio Conservation Society, led a successful battle against paving over the Paseo del Rio for flood control. Soon thereafter, Robert Hugman, a San Antonian architect, designed the first pedestrian walkway along the river. His plans were carried out in the 1930s under the Works Progress Administration. Individual artists and craftspeople landscaped the walk by designing arches, bridges, and benches for it, lending a unique quality to the Riverwalk that remains today.

After the heyday of the thirties, the Riverwalk was neglected and deteriorated for 15 years until, again, citizen initiative revitalized it. Two San Antonians, an architect and a businessman, envisioned the commercial potential of the downtown river and lobbied local businessmen to galvanize support for their vision. In 1964, the voters of San Antonio showed their support for the Riverwalk project by approving a $30 million municipal bond with more than $300,000 earmarked for improvements to the Riverwalk. Riverwalk has since been extended from its original reaches to the site of the World's Fair, now a convention center, and recently, to an up-scale shopping mall that was built to incorporate Riverwalk.

Throughout the revitalization of the last two decades, Riverwalk development standards have become increasingly stringent. Since 1962, an 11-member Riverwalk Advisory Commission has guided development in the Riverwalk District. As part of San Antonio's ongoing comprehensive planning process, the commission created a unified set of planning and development criteria to guide development and activities within the San Antonio Riverwalk Overlay District.

These guidelines were developed to protect:

- The heritage and character of the environment;
- The city's economy;
- The tourism/convention trade; and
- Property values.

The Riverwalk Overlay District establishes four different districts along the river. Criteria that address a host of parameters—such as gradient, sign regulation, building design, drainage, and refuse disposal—are determined for each parcel of land within the districts. Before building, remodeling, or erecting a sign, one must apply for a permit and meet the criteria for that district. The Riverwalk Commission meets monthly to review these permits and must approve the plans for the proposed project before a building permit is issued.

Experience

HISTORIC PRESERVATION

The new ordinance places a heavy burden of proof on applicants. This challenge, plus the fact that the review board considers applications on a case-by-case basis, makes it difficult to receive approval for tearing down significant sites in the city.

So far, the provision countering the incentive to neglect historic buildings and the provision requiring replacement plans have effectively stopped almost all demolition of historic sites in the downtown area. The Review Board has more than once rejected replacement plans. The new ordinance adds specificity to preservation review. The San Antonio Historic Preservation office recognizes that the ordinance is only as effective as the people implementing it, including not only the agents of the city, but property owners, developers, and the San Antonio public as well. The ordinance works well because it contains flexibility: those who wrote it and those who use it understand that protection is in no way absolute.

In San Antonio, there are many private groups with long-standing commitment to historic preservation. These groups serve a crucial private sector role. They reinforce governmental preservation efforts by educating the public and serving as role models who support protection of the city's distinctive character. These private sector entrepreneurs are particularly important

where some property owners still contest the concept of zoning as a legitimate planning tool.

RIVERWALK

The Riverwalk project has succeeded in turning a dilapidated downtown shopping district into a thriving pedestrian commercial center. The promenade is lined with restaurants, hotels, and shops. Tourists commute between downtown, the mall, and the convention center on a network of water taxis. Lush native and exotic plants border the walkways and terraces. And a busy schedule of special events lures residents and tourists to the area. According to one estimate, tourism added $1 billion to the San Antonio economy in 1987. One of the few drawbacks is that increased activity and number of people in the area have led to environmental degradation of the river and water quality.

CONTACT

Historic Preservation Office
City of San Antonio
San Antonio, TX 78285

INFORMATION RESOURCES

Brandywine Conservancy. *Protecting Historic Properties: A Guide to Research and Preservation.* Chadds Ford, PA: Brandywine Conservancy, 1984.

Practical guidance for local historic preservation efforts. Chapters focus on researching historic buildings and the process of nominating a building for the National Register of Historic Places, and specific means of preserving sites—with special discussion of easements.

Duerksen, Christopher J. *Aesthetics and Land Use Controls: Beyond Ecology and Economics.* Planning Advisory Service Report No. 399. Chicago, IL: American Planning Association, 1986.

An introduction to the use of land use regulations to improve urban design in historic areas, protect scenic views, preserve trees, and limit signs. Focuses both on legal issues and general principles as well as specific examples of controls drawn from communities. Sample ordinances are also provided.

Duerksen, Christopher J., ed. *A Handbook on Historic Preservation Law*. Washington, D.C.: The Conservation Foundation and The National Center for Preservation Law, 1983.

Covers all legal aspects of historic preservation at the local, state, and federal levels. Includes discussion of key constitutional concerns affecting local preservation programs and provides guidance on winning preservation cases before judicial and administrative bodies. Includes model preservation ordinance and easement provisions.

Maddex, Diane, ed. *The Brown Book: A Directory of Preservation Information*. 2d ed. Washington, D.C.: National Trust for Historic Preservation, The Preservation Press, 1988.

Catalogs a variety of historic preservation-related information, including federal and state program contacts, information sources, local organizations, and court cases.

National Center for Preservation Law. *Preservation Law Updates*. Washington, D.C.: National Center for Preservation Law.

Issued frequently throughout the year, and available on subscription basis, the *Updates* summarize important court decisions or analyze issues of concern to local historic preservationists.

National Trust for Historic Preservation. *Preservation Law Reporter*, Washington, D.C.

A quarterly publication, edited by the general counsel's office of the National Trust, which includes current reports and articles on preservation-related court cases, federal legislation, tax rulings, state and local laws, conferences and recent publications.

Preservation Action. *Blueprint for Lobbying: A Citizen's Guide to the Politics of Preservation*. Washington, D.C.: Preservation Action, 1984.

A brief handbook on how to lobby Congress on legislation related to historic preservation issues. Although the focus is on national-level lobbying activity, many of the ideas provided in this book are applicable to lobbying at the state and local level as well.

Roddewig, Richard J. *Preparing a Historic Preservation Ordinance*. Planning Advisory Service Report No. 374. Chicago, IL: American Planning Association, 1983.

Provides an introduction to historic preservation ordinances as well as specific guidance on how to tailor the various standard or typical ordinance provisions to suit local circumstances. Includes sample excerpts of ordinances, plans, and design guidelines from several communities.

ORGANIZATIONAL RESOURCES

Advisory Council on Historic Preservation, 1100 Pennsylvania Avenue, N.W., Suite 809, Washington, D.C. 20004, (202) 786-0503.

The Advisory Council on Historic Preservation advises the president and Congress on historic preservation matters. The council comments upon federal actions that having an adverse impact upon historic property.

National Center for Preservation Law, 1015 31st Street, N.W., Suite 100, Washington, D.C. 20007; (202) 338-0392.

This organization monitors judicial decisions and legislative action involving preservation law and publishes *Preservation Law Updates*, a newsletter.

National Main Street Center. National Trust for Historic Preservation, 1785 Massachusetts Avenue, N.W., Washington, D.C. 20036; (202) 673-4219.

The National Main Street Center is a program of the National Trust for Historic Preservation. Through cooperative agreements with state governments, the program assists localities with downtown historic preservation and economic revitalization.

National Trust for Historic Preservation, 1785 Massachusetts Avenue, N.W., Washington, D.C. 20036; (202) 673-4000.

The National Trust for Historic Preservation is the leading nonprofit organization concerned with historic preservation. The National Trust provides technical assistance and financial aid to local nonprofit groups and citizens for historic preservation. The trust operates numerous programs to promote and demonstrate historic preservation techniques and practices. In addition to its Washington, D.C., headquarters, it operates several regional and field offices.

Preservation Action, 1350 Connecticut Avenue, N.W., Washington, D.C. 20036; (202) 659-0915.

Preservation Action is a national grass-roots lobby for historic preservation.

CHAPTER 4

Aesthetic Resources

The concept of the public welfare is broad and inclusive. The values it represents are spiritual as well as physical, aesthetic as well as monetary. It is within the power of the legislature to determine that the community should be beautiful as well as healthy, spacious as well as clean, well-balanced as well as carefully patrolled.

—WILLIAM O. DOUGLAS

THE use of growth management strategies to preserve and enhance tangible natural and cultural resources—such as open space, wetlands, farmland, and historic districts—is essential to successful communities. An increasing number of communities, however, recognize that they must go beyond economic, ecological, and historic preservation objectives to protect the less-tangible aesthetic resources that often define what can or does make them distinctive. In many communities, public awareness over degradation of pastoral landscapes and the physical decline of downtowns has galvanized consensus that something must be done, often much more effectively than warnings against "inefficient urban sprawl" and "loss of environmentally sensitive resources." Although aesthetic objectives will vary, they typically include controlling clutter from billboards and signs, preserving scenic views, and improving the physical appearance of existing and new development.

Widespread local efforts to protect or improve aesthetic assets are not an entirely new phenomenon. Early examples of community action include building-height limitations imposed in New York City in 1888 and in Baltimore in 1904. Perhaps the most notable characteristic of these and other early aesthetic controls is the imputation of such nonaesthetic purposes as a legal justification. When reviewing these ordinances, Courts, in the words of one authority, ". . . generally clothed such enactments in terms of fire protection, safety, and economics. Aesthetics were considered to be a matter of luxury and taste; courts generally struck down laws if they were based solely on aesthetic considerations."[1]

Attitudes toward purely aesthetic objectives began to change in the 1950s. The United States Supreme Court's holding in *Berman v. Parker,*[2] an urban renewal case, was an important milestone. By the late 1970s, judicial thought had evolved to the point that in *Penn Central Transportation Company v. New York City,* the U.S. Supreme Court declared: "We emphasize what is not in dispute. . . . This court has recognized . . . that states and cities may enact land-use regulations or controls to enhance the quality of life by preserving the character and the desirable aesthetic features of a city. . . ."[3] Many federal and state decisions have since reinforced this precedent. In so doing, courts have created a clear trend of permitting the "increasingly widespread efforts by local governments to go beyond ecology and economics to protect what is special about their communities."[4]

Recent business research also shows that a community's aesthetic qualities, its livability, and its quality of life are far from merely a matter of luxury and taste, but are important factors in retaining existing businesses and attracting new ones, particularly in the most dynamic sectors of the economy, such as health care, electronics, and professional services. Factors vary widely from industry to industry, but a 1981 report revealed that the third most important location factor (after labor climate and proximity to markets) was an area's attractiveness to managers and skilled workers.[5]

This chapter discusses local and state programs designed to protect and enhance local aesthetic assets. The discussion is divided into four categories:

- Billboard and sign controls;
- View protection;
- Design review;[6] and
- Legal considerations in protecting aesthetic resources.

Billboard and Sign Control ─────────────

I think that I shall never see
A billboard lovely as a tree.
Indeed, unless the billboards fall
I'll never see a tree at all.
— OGDEN NASH

While it may take years and large sums of money for poorly planned development to clutter the landscape, a few billboards can accomplish the same result overnight. Citing a statistic that there are now more than twice as many billboards along American roadsides as there were when the federal Highway Beautification Act[7] passed in 1965, one sign control enthusiast has written wistfully of "a jurisdiction whose citizens treat their roadsides as something more than advertising space to rent."[8]

Although the sign control issue is broader than just billboards, the latter, by virtue of their sheer size and number, have generated the lion's share of attention. Most local regulations distinguish between signs and billboards. For regulatory purposes, signs are generally divided into two categories: on-premise signs and off-premise signs. The terms "off-premises sign" and "billboard" are frequently used interchangeably.[9] Most local zoning regulations distinguish on- and off-premise signs either by definition or in the actual regulations. "Sign" is usually defined broadly. Boulder County, Colorado, for example, defines "sign" as:

Any structure or wall or other object, or part thereof, which is used for display of any message or which attracts or is designed to attract attention to a specific product, service, activity, event, person, institution or business.

Springfield, Massachusetts, also uses a broad definition:

Any name, identification, description, display, illustration or device which is affixed to or represented directly or indirectly upon a building, structure or land in view of the general public, and which directs attention to a product, place, activity, person, institution or business.

"Billboard" and "off-premise sign" are less broadly defined. Bar Harbor, Maine, for example, defines "billboard" as:

Anything designed, intended or used for advertising a product, property, business, entertainment, service, amusement or the like, and not located where the matter advertised is available or occurs.

Similarly, East Lyme, Connecticut, defines "off-premise sign" as:

A sign which directs attention to a business, product, activity or service which is generally conducted, sold or offered elsewhere than upon the premises where such sign is located.

LOCAL BILLBOARD CONTROL

Many communities have determined that billboards significantly degrade the landscape, create risks to traffic safety, hinder beneficial economic development and tourism, and lack the redeeming business identification purposes of on-premise signs. They have, therefore, worked for the elimination of outdoor off-premise commercial signs.

The federal Highway Beautification Act (HBA) was enacted in 1965 as the foundation for state and local billboard control efforts. Because all states have responded to the federal HBA by enacting some type of billboard control legislation, a local program must carefully evaluate the extent of local billboard control authority under both the federal act and state law.

Controlling Billboards Outside of Federal Highway Corridors

Operating within the constraints of federal and state law, hundreds of communities nationwide have enacted a wide variety of effective billboard control regulations.

Billboard Bans

Communities are free to ban all *new* billboards (even along federal highways) and, depending upon state law, to require the removal of *existing* billboards after a reasonable grace period. Existing billboards protected by the federal Highway Beautification Act may not be removed except in conformance with the act.

Complete bans on all billboards are increasingly commonplace:

- A growing number of the nation's largest cities— including Houston, San Diego, St. Louis, Honolulu, and Denver—have banned billboards.

- Many fast-growing Sunbelt communities have banned or strictly restricted billboards. These cities and counties include Austin, Texas; Fairfax County, Virginia; Scottsdale, Arizona; Jacksonville, Florida; Henrico County (Richmond), Virginia; and Raleigh, North Carolina.

- Major tourist destinations have banned billboards, including Virginia Beach, Virginia; Conway and Concord, New Hampshire; Sun Valley, Idaho; Hilton Head, South Carolina; Nags Heads, North Carolina; Miami Beach and Boca Raton, Florida; Gatlinburg, Tennessee; Ocean City, Maryland; and Provincetown and Martha's Vineyard, Massachusetts.

- Numerous areas known for their high quality of life and ability to attract desirable, clean, and high-paying employers ban billboards. These include Boulder and Aspen, Colorado; Santa Monica, Marin County, and Santa Barbara, California; Stamford, Connecticut; Santa Fe, New Mexico; Oak Ridge, Tennessee; Portland, Maine; Burlington, Vermont; Chapel Hill, North Carolina; and Cambridge, Massachusetts.

- Many economically and demographically mainstream communities have banned billboards. These include: Little Rock, Arkansas; Dover, Delaware; Evanston, Illinois; Anchorage, Alaska; and Olympia, Washington. In fact, 117 cities and towns in Connecticut, 178 cities and towns in Massachusetts, and over 100 jurisdictions in California have banned billboards.[10]

Billboard Moratoria*

Numerous communities have found it necessary and legally defensible to impose a temporary ban on the erection of billboards while the community studies permanent billboard controls. Tucson, Arizona; Raleigh, North Carolina; Denver and Colorado Springs, Colorado; Charleston, South Carolina; Little Rock, Arkansas; and Stockton, California are among the communities nationwide that have imposed billboard moratoria to allow time for evaluation of existing regulations and implementation of appropriate revisions.

A moratorium on the erection of new billboards is often essential in implementing effective billboard controls. York County, South Carolina, officials learned this lesson when they began discussing a comprehensive zoning revision without imposing a moratorium on new billboards. In the eight months that the county studied and drafted new regulations,

---

* Moratoria or temporary bans on construction are discussed in Appendix A.

the county experienced a billboard boom. During this period, the county issued 150 permits for new billboards, many for massive double-decked, four-sided monopoles reaching above the treeline.

Amortization of Nonconforming Billboards. Many communities require removal of nonconforming billboards and signs through a process known as amortization. Rather than paying a landowner cash for removing potentially nuisancelike uses such as billboards and junkyards, or allowing them to continue indefinitely, many communities allow these uses to remain in existence for a number of years after enactment of a new regulation. During this period, the owner may both depreciate a billboard and earn a reasonable return on the investment. At the end of the amortization period, the billboard must be removed or brought into conformity. Some states, such as Indiana, New Hampshire, Ohio, Connecticut, and Tennessee, prohibit amortization; however, the majority of states allow it.

Amortization periods for billboards ranging from three to ten years have been approved in many recent cases.[11] These amortization periods appear reasonable in light of the fact that most signs are depreciated for federal tax purposes in five years or less.[12]

Controlling Billboards Along Federal Highways

The federal Highway Beautification Act preempts local control of billboards located within 660 feet of interstate highways or federal primary highways and visible from the highway. Most important, this law effectively prohibits amortization of billboards within federal highway corridors by requiring that owners of nonconforming billboards receive cash payments for removal, even if amortization of nonconforming billboards is permitted by state law.

In a series of memoranda from the Department of Transportation,[13] the department has interpreted the HBA as follows:

- Communities may ban the erection of *new* billboards along federal highways;

- Communities may limit the size, height, placement, and spacing between new billboards along federal highways;

- Communities may impose reasonable regulations reducing the size and height of *existing* billboards without triggering the cash compensation requirement, if the size and height can be reduced without forcing removal of the billboard. The cash compensation requirement is "not violated if the sign's owner can do something which is not unreasonably burdensome to avoid removal of the sign." Cash

ROGER K. LEWIS

compensation is not required even if the billboard company decides to remove a sign rather than comply with a new regulation.

- Communities may remove billboards without paying cash compensation if the billboard company refuses after a reasonable time to comply with regulations reducing the size and height of billboards.

- Communities may charge permit fees, and remove billboards without cash payment for failure to obtain a permit.

The act does not appreciably interfere with local governments that want to allow unrestricted billboards. The act permits local authorities to zone land along federal highways as commercial development, and to allow billboards within these commercial districts. The act established no federal standards for what constitutes a *bona fide* roadside commercial district. The absence of standards has led to widespread commercial zoning along rural highway corridors—even where commercial activity is unrealistic—to ac-

commodate billboards in circumvention of the purposes of the act. States are free to determine what constitutes a commercial district and, in some cases, have designated all road corridors commercial.[14] Although court decisions have invalidated such "phony zoning," the practice receives little policing by the Federal Highway Administration.[15] The Southern Environmental Law Center has characterized the HBA commercial zoning provisions as the "exception that has swallowed the rule."*

Suggestions for Local Billboard Control Programs

Based upon review of local programs, and recommendations of the Coalition for Scenic Beauty and the

---

* Initially supported by a wide variety of public interests, the HBA has been a major disappointment for scenic protection advocates and has been targeted for repeal by scenic protection groups. The reasons for this turnabout have been summarized as follows: "The act has been almost totally transformed into a sign industry dominated program that is actually enriching and subsidizing the industry it was meant to regulate, and is serving as a protective umbrella to shield the industry from state and local governments that desire to effectively control billboard blight."[17]

Southern Environmental Law Center (two active billboard control advocates),[16] communities considering local billboard controls should evaluate the following options:

- *Temporary ban during review.* Before reviewing billboard control policy, a moratorium on new billboard permits allows public discussion of billboard regulations without a rush for new permits, and prohibits new billboards that may conflict with the purpose of new regulations. A temporary ban must be reasonable in duration and no longer than the time necessary for planning and drafting an ordinance. Generally an 18- to 24-month period is considered acceptable.

- *Ban on all new billboards.* The Highway Beautification Act and most state billboard control legislation allow local prohibition of the erection of new billboards. Although this measure does not address existing landscape degradation, it ensures that the status quo does not deteriorate, and that new roads or road segments will not suffer billboard clutter.

- *Amortization of nonconforming billboards.* In most states, localities can require the removal of nonconforming billboards after a reasonable amortization or grace period. A provision compelling the removal of billboards that do not conform to existing zoning regulations and are not situated in federal highway corridors is common.

Aside from a total ban, the following options are also available:

- *Billboard cap.* Many communities have implemented a cap on the current number of billboards, with new construction allowed only when one or more existing billboards are removed, so long as the new billboard is no larger than the one removed. For example, Chattanooga, Tennessee, and Mobile, Alabama, require removal of an existing billboard for every new billboard erected. San Antonio, Texas, requires removal of two existing billboards for every new billboard erected.

- *Special permit criteria.* Many communities permit new billboards only by conditional or special use permit and only in industrial districts. This allows a public hearing for each billboard application to ensure compatibility with surrounding uses.

- *Billboard-free districts.* Communities prohibit billboards in or near (e.g., within 1,500 feet of) any historic district, residential area, downtown commercial district, neighborhood commercial district, park, scenic vista, community gateway, or similar community resource and along scenic corridors and highways. For example, Tucson, Arizona,

limits billboards to 72 square feet and prohibits them completely in historic districts, along scenic streets, gateways, roads, airport approaches, and certain business districts.

- *Site-specific height limits.* Communities prohibit billboards that rise above the treeline or which are on or over the roofs of buildings.

- *Annual permit fees.* Communities charge fees to cover the expenses (including staff and office space costs) of processing permit applications, ensuring compliance, and maintaining a sign inventory. The Coalition for Scenic Beauty recommends a fee of at least $200 per sign structure.

- *Size, height, and spacing requirements.* Communities implement size, height, and spacing limits, such as limiting billboards to 25 to 35 feet in height, and 300 to 350 square feet in size, and with spacing requirements of 1,500 to 2,000 feet between billboards on primary roads, and 1,000 to 1,500 feet between billboards on secondary roads.

- *Taxation.* Communities impose special road-view taxes on billboards. The revenues from the tax may be used to finance the acquisition and removal of nonconforming billboards, to acquire scenic easements, or for other public purposes. For example, Baldwin County, Alabama, has enacted a 10 percent gross receipts tax on billboards.

STATE BILLBOARD CONTROLS

The earliest state-level response to the visual threat of billboard clutter came in Hawaii, where billboards were completely banned in 1927.[18] Alaska banned billboards upon becoming a state in 1958; Vermont in 1968; and Maine in 1984. Several other states have taken effective steps short of a complete ban to control billboard proliferation.

Vermont's program, created by the Tourist Information Act of 1967,[19] prohibits off-premises outdoor advertising. To accommodate business concerns about providing tourist information, the act established a statewide information network, including business directional signs, sign plazas, tourist information centers, and tourist guidebooks.[20] The Maine Traveler Information Services Act creates a similar program.

The state of Washington enacted the Scenic Vistas Act in 1971,[21] which establishes a state scenic highway system and bans all signs visible from designated roads and from interstate highways or primary roads. Existing billboards on these roads were given a three-year period before removal was required.[22]

Oregon also has implemented effective statewide billboard controls. The Oregon Motorist Information Act of 1971[23] prohibited new billboards after June

1975, and requires renewable, one-year permits for preexisting billboards. The act allows directional signs for certain attractions and creates a system of information centers, logo signs, sign plazas, and a reservation system.[24]

Suggestions for State Billboard Control Programs

The Southern Environmental Law Center has recommended the following improvements to state sign control programs:[25]

- Prohibit new construction of billboards on all state highways, including interstate and federally funded primary highways, and all other portions of state roads not regulated by municipalities.

- Establish a system of designated scenic roads where existing billboards would be removed.

- Prohibit all off-premise signs and displays that are within 2,000 feet of any state or national park, wildlife refuge, recreation area, scenic area, wild and scenic river, any historic site or district listed in the National Register of Historic Places, or adjacent to any road designated as scenic.

- Revise the definition of commercial and industrial zone in the state billboard control legislation to require three actively operated and visibly commercial establishments within 800 feet of each other on the same side of the road and visible from the highway in order for an area to qualify as a commercial district along a federal highway where billboards are permitted.

- Prohibit by statute the cutting of trees and vegetation on public rights-of-way.

- Establish a system of logo signs and visitor information centers to inform traveling motorists of businesses and services in the state, commensurate with an automatic freeze on any new sign permits on the portion of the highway with such logo signs.

ON-PREMISE SIGN CONTROL

Many communities have determined that, without appropriate regulation, on-premise advertising becomes a competition to attract attention in which the largest and most garish sign wins and the community, including its business community, loses. Communities have responded to on-premise advertising with innovative and widely varying approaches. An increasing number of communities—going beyond merely imposing dimensional standards for signs—have implemented regulations to ensure that signs meet the needs of businesses and the public without degrading community appearance. Communities have found that attractive or thematic signage is good both for business and community appearance.

While localities generally cannot regulate the *content* of signs, reasonable restrictions on the size, placement, and appearance of on-premise advertising signs are routinely upheld.[26]

Lake Wales, Florida, has enacted and successfully defended a comprehensive and well-written sign control ordinance.[27]

Lubbock, Texas, has integrated its sign ordinance with its urban design and historic preservation regulations. Sign standards vary among several districts. (This program is profiled at the end of this chapter.)

Chula Vista, California, has created optional planned sign districts, in which commercial and industrial developers provide coordinated design, materials, and placement in exchange for flexibility in the size and number of permitted signs.[28]

Scottsdale, Arizona, requires individual sign permits and imposes an absolute five-foot height limit on all free-standing signs. The city also reviews the location, color, lettering, style, proportion, illumination, design, and number of signs. Only one free-standing sign for each multitenant development project is permitted.[29]

Ann Arbor, Michigan, limits the size of signs by allowing each business two square feet of sign area for each foot of street frontage. In addition, the city uses a "message unit" rule to limit the number of signs: Each business is limited to ten message units, defined as a word, symbol, or number over four inches in height. A two-unit bonus is available for signs under 15 feet in height.[30]

Suggestions for Local On-Premise Sign Control Programs

Based upon review of local programs, and recommendations of the Coalition for Scenic Beauty, communities considering local on-premise sign controls should evaluate the following options:

- Limit free-standing signs to one per business with a maximum height of no more than 20 feet.

- Prohibit or strictly regulate "problem" signs such as portable signs, pennants, banners, streamers, and flashing or intermittent lights.

- Limit shopping centers, malls, office parks, and similar large developments to one group identity sign with no free-standing separate sign for individual businesses.

- Allow a size bonus for ground signs relative to free-standing pole signs.

- Impose special controls in historic districts, downtown commercial districts, and pedestrian-oriented districts.

- Regulate the color, lettering, style, proportion, illumination, and design to ensure compatibility with local character.

View Protection ────────────────

An increasing number of communities—from central cities to rural towns—have come to realize that scenic vistas, scenic roadways, and similar intangible aesthetic features contribute immeasurably to a community's image and sense of place. Realizing the fragility of these aesthetic resources, many communities have created comprehensive programs to protect and enhance these assets. This section focuses on two types of programs: designation and protection of scenic roadways and protection of scenic vistas.

PROTECTING SCENIC ROADWAYS

Efforts to create and protect scenic parkways date back to the movement in the 1930s to create the Blue Ridge Parkway in Virginia and North Carolina, and the Sky-

line Drive in Virginia, both of which are now administered by the National Park Service. The importance of scenic roads is made clear by the 1987 report of the President's Commission on Americans Outdoors:

> Americans are at home on the road. Pleasure driving to view the historic, natural, and pastoral qualities offered by many of our nation's secondary roads is an important part of recreation for a majority of our population, comprising some 15 percent of all vehicle miles driven. Nearly half (43%) of American adults drive for pleasure.[31]

The aesthetic quality of scenic roadways is easily compromised. Billboards, garish signs, poorly designed residential development, strip commercial development, and incompatible uses such as unbuffered gravel pits, junkyards, mines, and industrial facilities can irreparably mar an otherwise attractive landscape. On the other hand, a program that ensures appropriate signage and design for commercial development and encourages creative residential siting can improve property values and increase tourism. Such efforts can be particularly complex because scenic roadways typically cross several political boundaries, often requiring a regional approach.

Numerous tools are available to implement a scenic road protection program. These can be helpful when used alone, but generally are more effective when used in combination with other tools as part of a comprehensive scenic road program. Six promising tools for scenic road protection are:

1. Designation of scenic roads;
2. Parkway design standards;
3. Land and easement acquisition;
4. Zoning and land use controls;
5. Traveler information programs; and
6. Transfer of development rights.

Designation of Scenic Roads

The President's Commission on Americans Outdoors recommends that local and state governments create and protect a network of scenic roads. Many states have scenic roadway programs with widely varying criteria and degrees of effectiveness, so the significance of state designation depends on state law.

Some state scenic roadway programs provide potent tools to protect designated scenic roads.[32] For example, the Connecticut Scenic Roadway Act[33] authorizes local governments to designate scenic roads. To be eligible for scenic designation a road segment

must be free of intensive commercial development and intensive vehicular traffic and must meet at least one of the following criteria: (1) It is unpaved; (2) it is bordered by mature trees or stone walls; (3) the traveled portion is no more than twenty feet in width; (4) it offers scenic views; (5) it blends naturally into the surrounding terrain; or (6) it parallels or crosses over brooks, streams, lakes or ponds.

Under this program, the owners of a majority of the lot frontage on the road must agree to designation. A designated road is maintained by the town, which may regulate future alterations and improvements to the road corridor, including the removal of stone walls and mature trees.

In states that do not have effective scenic road programs, or if a state program fails to meet local needs, local or regional governments can develop their own criteria for designating scenic roads. Even without state funding or official state recognition, designation of a scenic road in a local comprehensive plan should be the first step in developing a comprehensive scenic road program. This designation can guide public and private decisions that affect the character of the road corridor. Using the plan, the community may be able to encourage, if not require, state road improvements to be consistent with the designation. Designation in a local plan will also help justify land use regulations

and special permit criteria that preserve scenic corridors.

According to the President's Commission on Americans Outdoors, these criteria could include:

- Examples of the area's historic, pastoral, and natural heritage;
- Scenic views from either side of the designated byway;
- The presence of accessible recreation facilities and opportunities—trails, parks, picnic sites, boat ramps;
- Signs of minimum size to inform travelers about the area's recreational and natural attractions, services, and history; and
- Minimal visual blight, such as billboards and junkyards.[34]

Parkway Design Standards and Complementary Facilities

The Federal Highway Administration and the National Park Service can provide technical assistance for designing scenic roads and complementary facilities such as rest areas, picnic areas, campgrounds, bikeways, and cultural landmarks. A request from a congressman to these agencies may be helpful.

Land and Easement Acquisition

Acquisition of conservation or scenic easements can be used to protect scenic roads. The potential uses of this tool vary from purchasing at great cost the development rights for a large suburban farm, to purchasing at very little cost a scenic easement protecting an historic stone wall or prohibiting the erection of a billboard. The National Park Service has used conservation easements extensively to protect land along the Blue Ridge Parkway and Skyline Drive.[35]

Zoning and Land Use Controls

Many land use control techniques discussed in Appendix A, the Primer Glossary of Growth Management Tools, can be adapted to preserve and enhance the aesthetic and recreational values of scenic road corridors. Perhaps the most valuable tool is to require clustered residential development with housing sited to preserve the pastoral landscape along the road, rather than conventional subdivisions.[36] Other potentially valuable techniques include setback requirements with vegetation protection standards within the setback, design and landscaping review, and sign control.

Many communities have created scenic highway districts. For example, Charleston County, South Carolina, has enacted an overlay Scenic Highway District. In designated districts, outdoor advertising is prohibited, residential development must preserve open landscapes and views, buffering is required, and trees of more than six inches in diameter or shrubs must be preserved.

Hilton Head, South Carolina, has enacted a road corridor overlay zone to protect the town's main highways. The district requires regulated setbacks for buildings or parking areas that vary depending upon the density of vegetation within the setback.[37]

A noted authority has described the innovative scenic road protection program in Austin, Texas, as follows:

> Austin has created special controls on land located within 200 feet of designated "scenic" and "principal" roadways. It has also enacted special protective regulations for land within 1,000 feet of Route 360, the Capital of Texas Highway. The following special restrictions apply:
>
> 1. *Scenic Roadways.* No off-premises signs are allowed within a 200-foot zone on either side of road. On-premises signs are restricted to one small monument-style sign integrated into the landscaping plan. Special size and height limits apply as does a prohibition on flashing signs.
> 2. *Principal Roadways.* Only one freestanding commercial sign is permitted on each parcel; a 1,000 foot spacing requirement exists for off-premises signs.
> 3. *Capital of Texas Highway.* Only monument-style signs with a maximum of two colors are allowed. Signs must be of natural color, and materials must be compatible with surrounding environment. No flashing or neon signs or internal lighting are permitted.[38]

Traveler Information Programs

Interpretive signs and markers enhance the traveler's appreciation of the natural or cultural heritage of the landscape. Scenic turnouts, perhaps in conjunction with identification signs, help create the best viewing opportunities. A uniform system of symbols and signs enhances the visitor's experience.

Transfer of Development Rights

Transfer of development rights (TDR) programs have been used for many purposes, including the protection of scenic road corridors.* For example, Monterey County, California, has implemented a local coastal plan that preserves the "viewshed" of Highway 1 along the spectacular Big Sur coast. Under a transferable development credits (TDC) program, new development must be sited in such a way that it cannot be seen from the highway.[39]

---

* TDR is explained in Appendix A, A Primer on Growth Management Tools and Techniques.

PROTECTING SCENIC VISTAS

An increasing number of communities realize that scenic views are an important strand in the tapestry of community distinctiveness and image. Difficult to define, scenic views include views of many types of natural and cultural features, such as mountains, bluffs, farmland, state capitols, historic buildings and landmarks, city halls, monuments, urban skylines, and any variety of surface water. These views are in many cases easy to map.

Denver, Colorado, Austin, Texas, and King County, Washington, are among the leaders in implementing effective, innovative, and legally sound programs to preserve scenic views. Both Denver and Austin have implemented programs to protect views of their state's capitols, and Denver and King County have acted to protect their mountain views.

Austin, Texas, uses overlay zones to establish building height limits within numerous view corridors designed to protect views of the state capitol from various points and corridors around the city. Height limits are determined by a complex formula based upon sightline elevation from the viewpoint to the base of the capitol dome. Austin's program also includes transferable development rights as a means for shifting previously permitted densities to designated receiving zones that are not within a capitol sight line.[40] (Austin's program is profiled at the end of this chapter.)

Denver, Colorado's view protection ordinance is designed to protect views of the state capitol and views from specified parks of the mountain ranges west of the city. Like Austin, Denver uses overlay zoning to restrict building heights to preserve views from specified reference points. (The Denver program is profiled at the end of this chapter.)

King County, Washington, where Seattle is located, has prohibited billboards that block views of Mount Ranier, Mount Baker, the Olympic Mountains, Puget Sound, lakes, and rivers. The county also prohibits billboards around county landmarks, historic sites, state or county parks, and other scenic lands.

Many other communities have implemented traditional height limitations to protect scenic vistas.

- Philadelphia long maintained an unofficial policy of discouraging downtown development that would block views of the statue of William Penn atop City Hall. More recently, the city's development code has been amended to permit taller structures in designated zones as long as City Hall sight lines are not blocked.

- The relatively low profile of Washington, D.C., and the spectacular views from throughout the region of many federal buildings and monuments, is due to a

District-wide 110-foot height ceiling enacted by Congress in 1910.

- San Francisco, Pittsburgh, and Seattle each use height limits to protect views of rivers and bays. One element of San Francisco's new comprehensive downtown regulations imposes height limits designed to allow sunshine to reach public parks and plazas.

Other communities use special permit criteria to protect scenic vistas. For example, Wilmington, Delaware, has taken steps to preserve scenic views of the Christina River and Brandywine Creek. The city has enacted waterfront development review standards, which it applies when reviewing special exception applications in the waterfront districts. These review standards provide that:

> The maintenance of and improvement in views from and to the river is encouraged; specifically encouraged are scenic vistas, especially those designated on the Waterfront Development District Map A (Sites of Visual Merit) and working/commercial views.

The development standards then incorporate a map of the waterfront district that identifies significant views, as well as historic and architecturally significant buildings. This process provides precise guidance to developers about which sites the city expects to be protected. Since the designated significant views are clearly delineated and part of a comprehensive view protection program, this, in turn, strengthens the city's legal position.

Design Review

An important manifestation of increased concern for community appearance is the large number of communities that have adopted design review programs. The motivations for these programs are the desire to enhance the community's appearance, to protect its character and distinctiveness, and to secure the economic benefits of appropriate design. A recent National League of Cities publication summarizes the connection between community appearance and eco-

nomic development by noting that "building high quality urban environments and building healthy local economies go hand in hand. . . . City officials are finding attention to design to be an invaluable asset with many economic, social, and environmental benefits."[41]

Quality design is particularly important in communities lacking obvious natural or cultural features that mark some places as inherently distinctive (whether a mountain range, a bay, pastoral rolling farmland, or an historic district). This fact was captured by a committee of the Lubbock, Texas, Chamber of Commerce, which spearheaded a comprehensive revision of Lubbock's master plan and urban design controls:

> An area such as Lubbock without great natural interest or beauty must create its own. Its citizens must aggressively begin to control, direct, and plan with imagination, taste and selflessness if they are to have a city which is designed for beauty.[42]

Design review began in this country as a means of preserving the integrity of historic districts. Many communities also use design review to improve the quality and appearance of development in nonhistoric districts. Design review standards focus on such attributes of development as visual "harmony" and "character." In some cases, design "distinctiveness," rather than compatibility, is the principal objective.

The subjectivity inherent in such standards has generated much controversy among architects and developers. Some architects have charged design review stifles design creativity. While formal review may prevent the worst new development, these critics argue, it often prevents the best as well. The opposing view, in the words of one architecture critic, is that "constraints stimulate creativity. It's like a sonnet or a fugue—the rules give you a net and court to play on."[43] Nevertheless, successful design review programs create standards and procedures that encourage design creativity within a framework of minimum community standards.

THE FOCUS OF DESIGN REVIEW

The focus of local design review programs varies widely according to the geographic, development, and political circumstances of each community. Within this variety, there is a basic set of elements commonly covered by design review ordinances:

- Mass, which is the height of a building, its bulk, and the nature of its roof line;
- The proportion between the height of a building and its width (is its appearance predominantly horizontal or predominantly vertical?);

- The nature of open spaces around buildings, including the extent of setbacks, the existence of any side yards (with an occasional view to the rear) and their size, and the continuity of such spaces along the street;
- The existence of trees and other landscaping, and the extent of paving;
- The nature of the openings in the facade, primarily doors and windows—their location, size, and proportions;
- The type of roof—flat, gabled, hip, gambrel, mansard, etc.;
- The nature of projections from the buildings, particularly porches;
- The nature of the materials;
- Color;
- Texture;
- The details of ornamentation; and
- Signs.[44]

ADMINISTERING DESIGN REVIEW

Design review ordinances typically create special review boards or commissions; however, design review is sometimes administered directly by a local planning and zoning commission or the legislative body. Enabling legislation in many states directs the composition and procedures of design review boards. In other states, communities have wide discretion in administering a design review program.

Design review boards are either advisory or have direct regulatory authority. If design review boards have decision-making authority, applicants frequently have a right of appeal to the local legislative body.

The composition of design review boards varies, although many ordinances mandate a mix of design professionals (such as architects, landscape architects, and engineers) and lay people. Professional representation requirements can present problems in small communities lacking a large pool of local practitioners.

The following examples illustrate the different approaches taken by local design review programs:

- Numerous suburban Chicago communities, including Libertyville (see profile at end of chapter), have established "appearance commissions" that administer "appearance codes" regulating exterior design features of commercial, industrial, and multifamily development.[45]
- In San Francisco, stringent downtown development controls include a competitive "beauty contest"

process for allocating the limited amount of office development allowed each year. A three-member architecture review panel advises the city planning commission, which exercises decision-making authority.

- In Dallas, Texas, under a "conservation district" ordinance, local property owners can petition the city to establish a district requiring special design and other controls in areas that do not qualify as historic districts. Once city officials determine that the area contains "distinctive architectural or cultural attributes" and has a "distinctive atmosphere or character that can be conserved by protecting those attributes," a district is designated. The city planning department then prepares a plan for the area that identifies features and assets worthy of protection. After approval of the plan, an ordinance is drafted to place appropriate controls on building height, setbacks, landscaping, signs, and other attributes of development necessary to conserve the distinctive character of the area.[46]

In many communities, design review has emphasized tree protection. Individual trees within urban and suburban areas contribute much to the environment and aesthetics. Street trees moderate many ill effects of urban life: they moderate the microclimate by shading the street and reducing winds; buffer street noises; provide habitat for birds and small animals, and are pleasing to the eye. Street trees are also important because the street and street frontages are a city's principal public space and ordering device. Trees along a street can tie a neighborhood or development together. For this reason, Southern Living magazine says that "for the South's relatively low density cities, trees and landscape will do more than buildings to make a great urban presence."[47]

Many jurisdictions therefore protect specimen trees on private property, both in the review of new development and in the review of applications to remove trees. For instance, Alexandria, Virginia, designates historic or specimen trees, and requires permission from the planning commission for removing certain trees and permission from the city arborist for removal of other trees.[48]

SUGGESTIONS FOR SUCCESSFUL DESIGN REVIEW PROGRAMS

The following recommendations will improve the effectiveness of a design review program:

- Build community consensus about assets that are distinctive, desirable, and worthy of conserving.

These assets should be the basis for design review standards. In addition to protecting distinctive local architectural traditions, communities often focus on factors such as pedestrian orientation; public access to water or linear parks; absence of blank street-level walls; retail services on pedestrian streets; continuity of facades; building materials; and landscaping.

- Integrate design review with local comprehensive plans and other land use controls to ensure that other planning objectives and growth management regulations, such as permitted density and uses, do not undermine design objectives.

- Focus design standards and review on important aspects of design, rather than minute details, in order to avoid stifling creativity and a "nitpicking" image. One way to avoid fixating on minor details is to publish preapproved designs for signs, ornamentation, street furniture, lighting standards, and other accessories.

- Include specific design standards or guidelines. Provide as much detail and direction as possible. Supplement written standards with sketches, photographs, and guidebooks that illustrate acceptable and unacceptable design characteristics. This improves both political and legal acceptability.

- Include both design professionals and lay people on review boards. Professionals lend expertise to the exercise of aesthetic judgments, ensure that board decisions and recommendations are technically sound, and provide credibility with development consultants; while nonprofessionals avoid the fact and appearance of elitism, and ensure that the process is accessible to lay people. If the board is all lay people, the importance of a professional consultant is greater.

- Provide an early opportunity for developers to consult with the board or its staff in order to resolve questions and ambiguities early in the development process.

- Document the review process to demonstrate the fair exercise of design judgment.

- Provide specific reasons for denials. Indicate what revisions could be made to make the proposal acceptable.

Legal Considerations in Scenic Protection Programs

Two of the most common legal challenges to scenic protection programs are: (1) the aesthetic objective of the program does not promote a legitimate public pur-

ROGER K. LEWIS

pose; and (2) regulation of signs violates constitutionally protected freedom of speech.

By the 1970s, nearly all states had endorsed aesthetic regulations, to the point that commentators found that "no trend is more clearly defined in planning law than that of courts upholding regulations whose primary purpose is aesthetics."[49] The current state of the law has been summarized as follows:

> Court decisions in at least 19 states have held that the aesthetic interest in community appearance and quality of life considerations may constitute the basis for land use regulation . . . in virtually all other states, courts are likely to uphold regulations based on the aesthetic interest in community appearance when they are linked to other non-aesthetic public purposes such as traffic safety, protection of property values or tourism.[50]

Well-planned and well-drafted scenic protection measures generally withstand legal challenges unless an ordinance, as applied, has the effect of denying all economically reasonable use of parcel. A scenic pro-

tection ordinance, however, should carefully spell out the importance of the program, not only to the community's appearance and image, but also to tourism development, to the community's ability to retain existing, and attract new, business, and to conserving and enhancing overall property values.

A recent Colorado Supreme Court decision upholding Denver's view protection ordinance gives strong support to the validity of scenic protection measures.[51] The court upheld denial of an application to construct a 21-story office building based upon the view protection ordinance. The court held that the ordinance protects Denver's "unique environmental heritage" and does not constitute a taking, despite the substantial diminution in property value resulting from the ordinance. This program demonstrates the type of thorough analysis that improves the legal defensibility and effectiveness of aesthetic-based land use controls. (This program is profiled at the end of the chapter.)

Standards such as "harmony," "visual integrity,"

"character," have been upheld in some states, but should be defined by more specific and predictable standards to the extent feasible.[52]

LEGAL CONSIDERATIONS IN SIGN CONTROL

A recent United States Supreme Court decision has clarified and expanded the ability of local governments to control signs. Although it is now possible to draft legally defensible on- and off-premise sign controls, communities should be particularly careful in implementing these programs for three reasons:

- Sign regulation raises First Amendment freedom of speech limitations. These limits do not prevent effective local regulation, but they influence *how* a community goes about it. Proper draftsmanship can avoid these limitations.

- The Highway Beautification Act imposes federal restrictions on local billboard controls. Local regulations must accommodate these federal requirements.

- A community must be cautious when implementing billboard controls because the outdoor advertising industry is an aggressive and sophisticated opponent of billboard regulation. The industry freely exercises its prerogative to litigate against billboard controls.

For these reasons, communities should ensure that their municipal attorneys are familiar with recent trends in sign control law, so that their legal advice is not unduly restrictive or out-of-date.

Public Benefits of Sign Control

In addition to community appearance concerns, traffic safety, the promotion of local economic development and tourism, and the protection of property values are acceptable reasons to regulate signs. These concerns should be explicitly stated and documented.

Traffic safety is a valid nonaesthetic justification for billboard controls. A federal court recently noted that:

No empirical studies are necessary for reasonable people to conclude that billboards pose a traffic hazard, since by their very nature they are designed to distract drivers and their passengers from maintaining their view of the road.[53]

In addition, the limited empirical research on the subject indicates that billboards may constitute a highway traffic safety hazard. In 1980, the Federal Highway Administration reviewed the research on the effect of billboards on highway safety and concluded both that "there is a positive correlation between the existence of signs and accident rates" and that more research needed to be done.[54]

The promotion of local economic development and tourism are important community benefits of sign control. Many successful local billboard control campaigns have been led by local chambers of commerce and tourist boards concerned about the impact of landscape degradation on local business and tourism. For example, the Houston Chamber of Commerce has made billboard control a top priority and spearheaded efforts in that city to ban billboards.[55] In Columbia, South Carolina, the Greater Columbia Chamber of Commerce has prepared a model sign control ordinance and called upon local governments to enact tighter controls on the number, size, and height of signs in central South Carolina.[56]

Freedom of Speech

While it is well settled that local governments have the authority to control signs, this authority is subject to the freedom of speech guarantee of the First Amendment to the U.S. Constitution. The First Amendment provides in part that Congress shall make no law "abridging the freedom of speech." (The Fourteenth Amendment applies this prohibition to state and local action.) Over the years, courts have developed a fairly permissive standard when reviewing laws and regulations that do not control the *content* of speech, but merely the time, place, and manner of delivery of the message. Courts generally allow such regulation unless it unduly impedes the normal flow of expression. On the other hand, courts almost always invalidate regulations that influence the content of speech.

In 1984, the U.S. Supreme Court decided an important sign control case upholding the city of Los Angeles's prohibition on the placement of signs on sidewalks, utility poles, lampposts, trees, or other types of public property:[57]

The problem addressed by this ordinance—the visual assault on the citizens of Los Angeles presented by an accumulation of signs posted on the public property— constitutes a significant substantive evil within the City's power to prohibit. "[T]he city's interest in attempting to preserve [or improve] the quality of urban life is one that must be accorded high respect."[58]

The following general principles establish the legal parameters of sign control:

- A total ban on all signs on public property is constitutional.[59]

- Regulations can distinguish between on-premises and off-premises advertising. Off-premises commercial advertising can be entirely prohibited.[60]

- Regulations must carefully avoid content-based distinctions and should be wary of regulating noncommercial speech (i.e., a message that is political or ideological in nature and is afforded greater protection under the First Amendment). A provision in the city of Raleigh billboard ordinance reads: "Any sign authorized in this chapter is allowed to contain non-commercial copy in lieu of any other copy." This ordinance was approved by the U.S. Court of Appeals for the Fourth Circuit and therefore provides a tested safe harbor for complying with this requirement.[61] For further protection, the Southern Environmental Law Center recommends limiting official discretion in determining what constitutes noncommercial speech by defining "noncommercial speech" as speech that "does not direct attention to a business operated for profit, or to a commodity or service for sale."[62]

- Comprehensive time, place, and manner restrictions on signs are permissible, including controls on size, height, location, spacing, shape, lighting, motion, design, and appearance.

- Most courts recognize the validity of aesthetics alone as the basis for sign control; however, traffic safety, protection of property values, and promotion of economic development and tourism should be considered as additional reasons for implementing sign controls. If these are factors in a community's decision to control signs, the ordinance should clearly state these purposes.[63]

- A prohibition on political or ideological lawn signs or a prohibition of such signs throughout the community is unconstitutional.[64]

PROFILE

AUSTIN, TEXAS

Capitol View Protection Overlay Zones and Land Use Controls on Principal Roadways

Community Characteristics

Austin, capital of Texas, lies in a valley near the center of the state. Surrounded by low hills and valleys, the city, first settled in the mid-1800s, developed around a meandering curve of the Colorado River. Today, Congress Avenue, a major central-city transportation corridor, bisects the city north-south, dips into the valley by the river, crosses it, and ascends to the pink granite capitol building on the north slope.

Interstate Route 35 parallels Congress Avenue as it proceeds north towards Dallas/Fort Worth, almost 200 miles away. Divided highway spurs off the interstate nearly encircle Austin.

Hydroelectric power dams built by the Lower Colorado River Authority form a chain of lakes cascading down into the city from 60 miles northwest. These reservoirs form a spectacular recreational resource for the city.

Austin is the principal seat of the University of Texas. Five other higher-education establishments are located in Austin as well. Several other state institutions and Bergstrom Air Force Base, in addition to government, constitute the bulk of large employers in the city. As high-technology industries and service enterprises take over more of the traditional government sector employment, Austin's economy and employment patterns continue to diversify.

A cultural hub, Austin offers art galleries, an orchestra, a theater, a museum, and a ballet company. The city also has nurtured several artists and writers who made their careers there, including O. Henry and the sculptress Elizabeth Ney. In the early 1980s, the city adopted an ordinance requiring public buildings to include art in their construction budgets.

Austin boasts several prime examples of southern colonial architecture dating from the era of the Republic of Texas, when diplomats resided in the town. The most dramatic residence is the governor's mansion, which overlooks the capitol building. In the early 1850s, slaves hauled pine logs 30 miles to the site, where the logs were then fashioned into fluted Greek pillars with Ionic capitals and erected along the mansion's east facade.

Strong community and citizen involvement is a tradition in the Texas capital. In 1986, 266 neighborhood organizations were registered with the city. Thirteen of these have established plans for their jurisdictions, and several provide services such as tours for visitors and newsletters for local residents.

Growth Patterns

The Austin metropolitan area has grown 20 percent since 1980. The region now holds about 650,000 residents, almost 400,000 of whom live within the city limits. Austin's population has more than tripled since the early 1960s.

Nonresidential space nearly doubled between 1980 and 1985, straining public infrastructure and services. In 1985 alone, the city approved for development 16 million square feet of office and retail space. To accommodate the city's burgeoning population and employment base, developers increasingly have relied on erecting high-rises within the city limits, where a large part of the new growth occurred. However, employment growth continues a boom-and-bust pattern. From 1980 to 1985, employment growth grew at a 6.8 percent annual rate; in 1985 and 1986, employment growth slowed to 1 percent per year, and remained stagnant or declined in 1987.

At the same time, physical development is dispersing. The city's steering committee predicts that "the greatest concentrations of new residential development will be located in the Municipal Utility Districts (MUDs) scattered around the periphery of the city."

These growing suburban enclaves have encroached on sensitive environmental areas northwest and southwest of the city. Water pollution, and loss of wildlife habitat and native vegetation, are rising.

Resources Threatened

The Texas capitol building is the largest of U.S. state capitols. It is higher than the United States Capitol building by one foot. The capitol is an important symbolic landmark in Austin and the whole of Texas. Increasing heights of buildings in the downtown area threatened to obscure the building and diminish its distinctiveness.

Roadsides grew more cluttered as billboard companies and advertisers recognized the advantage of targeting the rising population traveling increasing numbers of miles along roads in and around the city.

Measures Taken

CAPITOL VIEW PROTECTION

In August 1984, Austin adopted an ordinance protecting public views of the state capitol from designated points in the city including major roads, bridges, and parks.

In concept and application, Austin's capitol view protection ordinance mirrors Denver's (see profile in this section). But much more rigorous and investigative work preceded enactment of Austin's ordinance. The city examined the historical significance of the capitol building and the Austin skyline. The study took into account the policies of the city's comprehensive plan, which stresses preserving the unique character of the city. Sixty significant view corridors were identified and divided into four categories: stationary (parks), threshold (at entryways to the city), sustained (across bridges), and dramatic glimpses. Land uses within each corridor were analyzed, as was the view itself (from a reference point at the outer edge of the corridor). The economic impacts of imposing height controls were analyzed for each corridor and for the entire city.

The background investigations and analyses were important in establishing a strong basis in fact for the ordinance. The economic impact analysis was particularly important in allaying fears that adverse impacts would be excessive and uneconomical.

A complex formula governs the calculation of height limitations in each corridor. Although the calculations are more complex than in Denver's ordinance, the basic determination is the line of sight from the reference point to the protected view, in this case the capitol dome (from the base up).

An innovative component of Austin's view protection ordinance was the transfer of development rights (TDR) provision that enables landowners subject to restrictions to apply their unused density to other sites outside the view corridors. Twenty-two properties within the view corridors were certified for TDRs, enabling transfer to two designated downtown zoning districts. The TDR privilege, if unused, expired three years after the ordinance was enacted.

SCENIC ROADWAYS

Austin also enacted special regulations for roadside land within 200 feet of designated "scenic" or "principal" roadways, and within 1,000 feet of "Hill Country roadways," which are located on the western fringe of the city, on the edge of Texas Hill Country.

On designated scenic roadways, no off-premise signs are allowed within a 200-foot zone on either side of the road. Each property is limited to one "monument-style" on-premise sign integrated into the landscape plan. Flashing signs are prohibited, and the signs are restricted in height and size.

On designated principal roadways, only one freestanding commercial sign is allowed per parcel. Off-premise billboards are prohibited.

Roads designated as Hill Country roadways are classified into high-, medium- and low-intensity zones, with density restrictions that vary accordingly. Some of the following provisions apply to the other classes of protected roadways (as described above) in less restrictive forms.

- Height restrictions change with the distance from the right-of-way, between not less than 28 feet to not more than 65 feet in high-intensity areas farthest from the road.

- Site design must preserve scenic vistas, and mirrored glass is prohibited everywhere.

- Landscaping requirements include preserving 40 percent of a site "in a natural state," and planting native tree species to compensate for removal during construction.

- Each tract is limited to one or two access points to a Hill Country roadway, depending on traffic volume, and driveways must be at least 400 feet apart.

- One provision provides incentives for property owners and developers to incorporate joint-use driveways in their projects by allowing the site a greater amount of impervious cover if joint-use access is integral to the site plan.

The ordinance provides waivers from density, height, setback, and landscaping provisions as performance bonuses for innovative site designs that further the goals of the ordinance by preserving the environmental and scenic qualities of the area.

Experience

CAPITOL VIEW PROTECTION

Austin commissioned a study completed in 1986 that predicted continued rapid growth in and around the city. However, since that time, the pace of development has subsided, and by mid-1988, planning staff remarked that "the downtown boom is over." For example, since the ordinance was enacted, no TDRs have been transferred for lack of demand. For that reason, planning staff speculate that the legislature will probably extend the time limitations of such transfers.

Some of the originally designated view corridors were reduced after the ordinance was adopted, when the city discovered that permits had already been issued for buildings that, when built, would block views.

Since Austin is the state capital, much of the land belongs to the state. The view protection ordinance would not have functioned effectively without state enforcement. At the time of Austin's adoption of the regulations, the state adopted an almost identical ordinance.

The principal challenge so far to the ordinance has been the construction of a parking garage (owned by the state) that a local citizen noticed would obstruct the view of the capitol if built to its full height. The city planning staff consequently lobbied the state legislature heavily for height restriction on the building. Eventually, the top level was lopped off the construction plans, and the view has been preserved.

SCENIC ROADWAYS

The land use controls on designated roadways do not change zoning and apply to current and future site plans only. Mid-century, most of Austin's roadways were zoned commercial and have remained so. This zoning designation has limited the impact of the new "scenic roadway" controls. New development usually extends existing strip development patterns, but modifies traditional design elements so as to comply with the new regulations. For the most part, the regulations only affect signs and access.

The zoning board receives at least 200 site plan permit applications a year. Most applicants easily comply with sign requirements, but frequently request variances to increase their development's access to the road. The city has occasionally used its police power to close what the ordinance has defined as "excess driveways." In some instances, access has become a local issue, pitting the city against commercial development.

CONTACT

Land Development Department
Office of Land Development Services
1700 South Lamar Boulevard
Austin, TX 78704

PROFILE

DENVER, COLORADO

Protection of Mountain Views

Community Characteristics

The Denver metropolitan area, which includes the central city and suburbs, contains almost 1.9 million people. Behind Phoenix, Arizona, Denver is the largest North American metropolitan region between the Missouri River and the Pacific states. Between 1980 and 1986, the Denver area population grew by more than 14 percent.

Denver is distinguished by its altitude ("the Mile-High City") and its location at the western edge of the Great Plains. True to its nickname, "Gateway to the Rockies," Denver is the hub of commerce, services, finance, and transportation for the western plains and the southern half of the Rocky Mountain region. Denver's civic identity depends to a great extent on its sense of connection to the mountains. Much of Denver's visual impact derives from a jagged 150-mile long panorama of 14,000-foot peaks visible from the city.

Over 200 parks comprising more than 4,000 acres lie within the city limits. Residents also rely on nearby mountain parks for local recreation.

Growth Patterns

By the mid-1980s, the spate of largely oil-related growth Denver experienced through the 1960s and 1970s had mainly abated. The downtown is now for the most part built up; there is little construction occurring in the center of the city. Much of the new growth has shifted to the outlying areas of the city and the suburbs.

Resources Threatened

Denver's skyline is dominated by a prominent group of tall buildings downtown. More than 30 buildings are over 300 feet high. The tallest is the 715-foot Republic Building. The spread of tall buildings outside the downtown core threatened to block both the panoramic mountain views and the distinctive views of the urban skyline that inform Denver's pride of place.

Measures Taken

In 1968, Denver first enacted an ordinance to protect views of the mountains from key public places in the city. The ordinance recognizes the aesthetic importance of preserving the views that tie the rolling high plains to the mountains, and also cities the economic contribution those views make to the vitality of the city.

The mountain view protection ordinances create a series of overlay zones with restrictions tailored to the area to which each zone applies. Each zone resembles a triangle, formed by establishing a reference point at the triangle's eastern apex and projecting the zone westward like a fan. Maps incorporated into the ordinance illustrate the districts to which the restrictions apply. For each district, the ordinance establishes limits for building heights. Height restrictions are determined by drawing the line-of-sight plane from the reference point to the mountains. The sides of the triangle are based on the location of existing buildings that already obstruct views of the mountains and on the direction of distinctive views. Thus, the ordinance generally requires lower heights on buildings closer to the reference point than on buildings further away. (If the ground elevation rises substantially away from the reference point, then buildings farther away have a lower height limit than those nearby.)

The mountain view ordinances were enacted to prevent buildings outside the downtown core from interrupting important views. The downtown skyline is considered a part of these views, rather than a threat. For example, one of the protected views is about one and one-half miles east of downtown, making both the downtown skyline and the mountainous backdrop integral to the view. Recent amendments to the program protect "reverse" mountain views by protecting easterly views of the downtown skyline from the higher west side of the city.

The ordinance originally applied to eight districts, with three more incorporated by amendment since 1982. The original eight cover about 15 square miles, or about 10 percent of the city's 155 square miles. The largest view protection zone covers 3.5 square miles.

rado Supreme Court upheld the ordinance on appeal, stating that although property values were diminished by the restrictions, they were not completely wiped out, and stating further that "the protection of aesthetics is a legitimate function of a legislature," thus upholding the preservation of mountain views as a valid police power objective.

The city's policies of only applying the ordinance to protect views with "citywide" significance and ensuring that the height restrictions do not so severely restrict property values as to constitute a compensable "taking" have helped to ensure successful implementation and defense of the program.

The ordinance has been highly effective in preserving view corridors to the mountains. The city has wisely stressed both the aesthetic and the economic rationale for the restrictions. Both the public and elected officials recognize that the view protection program preserves something that makes the city distinctive, and by the same token supports the tourist and convention economy, and makes the city attractive to industry and commerce.

Experience

In 1982, developers wishing to construct a 21-story office building in one of the newly designated districts challenged the ordinance on the basis that it served no legitimate public purpose and constituted a "taking" of private property without compensation. The Colo-

CONTACT

City of Denver Planning Office
1445 Cleveland Place, Room 400
Denver, CO 80202

PROFILE

LIBERTYVILLE, ILLINOIS

Appearance Code with Special Criteria for Historic District

Community Characteristics

Libertyville is a town of about 18,000 people 46 miles north of Chicago. The "village," as it is officially called, is conveniently located just west of Interstate 94, the major north-south thoroughfare connecting Chicago and Milwaukee. The town sits astride an older highway that parallels I-94 and also brings traffic to the town.

Libertyville had its origins as a rural agricultural supply town about 150 years ago. For a century and a half, Libertyville was the only significant population center in the area, and Chicago seemed very far away. The town was uniquely situated to provide services to the surrounding farmlands, and to provide its inhabitants with shops and entertainment. For a long time, it was the only town in the region outside of Chicago to have its own theater. This distinctive historic heritage, well preserved in the downtown area, has augmented the town's appeal to prospective residents, businesses, and industry alike.

The village experienced steady growth through the 1960s, which accelerated through the 1970s. Held in check by the recession that ushered in the 1980s, development since mid-decade has been booming. As the building commissioner notes, Libertyville now has "snob appeal." Recently developed high-priced subdivisions have attracted an up-scale clientele to the area, and Libertyville is now considered a distinguished address in many circles.

Growth Pressures

The development in and around Libertyville is typical of the prevailing trend in which industry is moving away from the inner city to outer, formerly rural suburbs. The town's convenient location along primary thoroughfares that lead into the nation's third-largest city has concentrated development attention in the area.

Like growth rings on a tree, Libertyville has developed concentrically, spreading outward from the core downtown, which was built up between 1800 and about 1930. The next ring of development occurred between the end of World War II and the late 1960s, when middle-income families settled in split-levels and colonials. The outer ring of development is still being formed, and consists of large homes, many uniquely designed, built fairly close together on 10,000-square-foot minimum lots. (The "big house on little lot" syndrome illustrates well the squeeze dwellers at the urban fringe feel, as the population there grows, and land values soar. As the wide-open spaces diminish, new residents feel the pinch, both in their pocketbooks and in their lot sizes.)

By the early 1980s, the sheer pace of the building boom in Libertyville was beginning to undermine local efforts to retain the distinctive aesthetic qualities and quality-of-life that initially drew developers and new residents. The town agreed that in order to continue to attract development, it must institute controls to retain the intimate character of the "village" it once was, and at the same time encourage aesthetic integrity in new development.

Measures Taken

In 1982, the town enacted an ordinance establishing an Appearance Review Commission, and an accompanying ordinance that instituted design standards and criteria for new development.

Applicants seeking approval for signs, building construction (except one- and two-family houses), remodeling, additions, and landscaping must go through an Appearance Review Process to obtain a permit for their proposal. The Appearance Review Commission reviews application and holds meetings with applicants to discuss the proposal and bring it into compliance with the appearance code. Approval by the Appearance Review Commission is required for issuance of a building permit.

Applicants for building permits must submit site plans showing parking, location of trees, existing and proposed landscaping, exterior lighting, building elevations, section profiles, and samples of materials to be used in the development. Applicants for wall signs and outside lighting must also submit site plans showing elevation, size specifications, and relationship to surrounding buildings.

A chapter of the Libertyville Municipal Code constitutes an Appearance Code, which provides, according to the Purposes section, "overt and professionally appropriate standards for the evaluation of external design features in the Village." The code defines the vocabulary used therein, and then describes the criteria by which the Appearance Review Commission evaluates proposals. In general, the provisions in each criteria category promote harmony among buildings, streets, and parking areas; energy conservation; preservation of viewsheds; and accessibility for pedestrians. The criteria are neither very restrictive nor very specific.

A special section of the code addresses the historic core of Libertyville's downtown, and supplies additional appearance criteria to which applicants whose projects lie in this "Heritage Area" are subject. The intent of this section is to preserve and enhance the prevailing nineteenth- and early-twentieth-century architecture, without forcing "fake history" or "pseudo-period stylistic details." Some specifics include:

- The color, scale, form, and texture of new development in this area should retain continuity with adjacent buildings.

- The code encourages compatibility with existing historical styles of the district, and discourages the introduction of foreign stylistic details.

- Existing ratios of width to height should be maintained, as should the existing spacing between windows and doors.

- The provision of access through rear entrances is encouraged.

The last section of the Appearance Code addresses "continuing maintenance." Here, the code prohibits features approved by the Appearance Review Commission from modification through maintenance, and requires keeping plantings, landscapes, parking lots, and vacant lots in good repair, free of debris.

Experience

Libertyville's Appearance Code has been successful both in maintaining the historic character of the downtown "Heritage Area" and improving the appearance of development in other sections of town. Although local businesses—especially car lots—have been exceptionally innovative in finding loopholes, the program has worked well. Some businesses have anchored large garishly colored inflatables to their rooftops for weeks, and another building stationed a hot-air balloon in front of its entrance for days. Perhaps the most successful aspect of the program is that its existence has changed the way local design professionals and developers think and led to higher standards in initial development applications.

The local experience with protection of aesthetics has also led to adoption of a tree preservation ordinance. As of early 1989, the code was being rewritten to add greater specificity.

The growing number of high-income residents in the village is placing increasing pressure on local planners to add teeth and enforcement powers to the Appearance Review Commission. As a result, additional personnel have been hired to enforce the code.

CONTACT

Appearance Review Commission
City Hall
200 East Cook Avenue
Libertyville, IL 60048

PROFILE

LUBBOCK, TEXAS

Sign Controls Integrated with Urban Design Standards

Community Characteristics

Lubbock is the industrial and commercial hub of the south plains of western Texas, just below the Panhandle. Ranchers settled there in 1870, and the town was incorporated in 1909. Regional agriculture is rooted in cotton, wheat, and grain crops, which form an important part of a diverse local economy. Lubbock is a leading inland cotton and cottonseed oil market. The city is also home of Texas Tech University, the region's main medical facilities, and regional government offices. Reese Air Force Base, Texas Instruments Corporation, and the headquarters of the country's largest cafeteria chain are other major contributors to the local economy.

Lubbock is encircled by a freeway, and three major highways intersect in Lubbock, creating an excellent highway system.

Two tributaries of the Double Mountain Fork of the Brazos River meet in Lubbock. But the flow of the Yellow House and the Blackwater are so sparse that agriculture depends heavily on groundwater irrigation.

Lubbock grew rapidly after World War II: between 1940 and 1960, the population increased fourfold, to 130,000. Between 1970 and 1980, the city grew another 16 percent, to around 190,000 by the mid-1980s.

Growth Pressures

For many years, Lubbock incorporated 90 square miles, but recently it annexed another 22 square miles, which gave the city undeveloped land to accommodate growth. A newly annexed railroad and highway spur to the west of town has shifted 300 acres of wholesale food and farm equipment warehouse

business to this area. Building permits peaked about three years ago; recent growth has been mostly residential and in the southwestern section of the town. This residential growth pattern in a southwesterly direction is typical in the high plains, where cities tend to "grow into the wind" to avoid odors and air pollution.

Since the 1950s, industrial and commercial development has concentrated around dense traffic corridors, but this growth pattern has not been borne out recently in Lubbock. Large tracts of land around the loop were originally zoned commercial with the expectation that large shopping malls would be built there. A declining economy has led to subdivision of these large tracts for smaller businesses and office buildings. This type of development is not spread out in shallow lots along highway corridors, but rather is developed in deep lots and multiple layers. (See below under Experience for how this new development pattern has influenced the city's sign ordinance.)

Rapid growth over the past four decades took its toll on Lubbock. Commercial strip development and increasing numbers of businesses trying to outdo each other in identifying and advertising themselves contributed to overall visual clutter. The eclectic and desultory clutter eclipsed views of the surrounding open plains and destroyed any sense of distinctiveness the town possessed. Original Spanish-style architecture still existed, but was increasingly hard to find.

Measures Taken

In May 1970, a tornado struck Lubbock, killing 26 people and decimating the center of the city. The dramatic three-mile stretch of rubble catapulted Lubbock's leaders into a rehabilitation campaign to initiate a new Comprehensive Plan for the entire city that would include an urban design component.

The Planning Commission developed design standards for a new Civic Center to be erected in the middle of the ruins, based on a design theme set by the city's Urban Renewal Agency. The city then realized that certain allowable land uses, notably signs and billboards, would clash on the periphery of the proposed development. The city appointed a five-member Zoning Revision Committee to revise the Zoning Ordinance. In 1975, 60 percent of those voting favored an advisory referendum proposing strict sign regulations. The vote encouraged several citizens' groups to begin lobbying the city to make Lubbock more attractive.

A month later, the urban design component of the new Comprehensive Plan was completed, which included an inventory of distinctive sites in the city. The Planning Commission put together and widely showed a slide presentation about the inventory. In July 1975, the City Council enacted the new Zoning Ordinance, which included a provision controlling signs.

The new ordinance requires signs to conform to city-wide performance standards that consider compatibility with lot size, wall area, and building setback. Previously, sign permits were tied to zoning classifications and were not subject to independent review.

Billboards are treated as a land use in and of themselves, not as an accessory use of a given lot. As such, billboards must conform to land use regulations of each zone, and very few areas in the city permit billboards. The ordinance set a six-and-one-half-year amortization period during which all nonconforming signs were to be brought into compliance or be removed.

Several supplements have been added to the Comprehensive Plan since 1975, including a survey of architecturally significant structures in the city and an "urban image analysis" of pictorial and historical considerations to include in the plan. In 1978, three years after the issue was initially addressed in the new Zoning Ordinance, a Design-Historic District Ordinance amendment was added. Shortly after that, the first Urban Design Commission was appointed as an advisory group to the City Council.

To obtain historic district designation, a landowner must petition the commission to note his property as subject to specific design regulations identified in the ordinance. The designation applies to individual properties, not whole blocks. It encourages preservation in a fragmented, somewhat haphazard way since it relies exclusively on a petition by the landowner.

Portions of the Lubbock Zoning Ordinance appear in the companion to this book.

Experience

When the sign ordinance first went into effect, it was challenged by the billboard industry; the Texas Supreme Court, however, upheld the regulations. By the time the amortization period was up, about 60 percent of the signs in the city were in compliance. During the amortization period, the zoning office performed an inventory of nonconforming signs, and when the time was up, contacted all owners of signs in violation individually. These meetings explained to violators how to bring themselves in compliance or request a variance. In general, zoning staff were able to convince people that compliance was in their benefit, that a smaller sign could be attractive and competitive and cost less than a large one. (Some oil companies now compete with each other for the most aesthetic service station sign.)

Since the inception of the ordinance, zoning staff removed 200 billboards. A few years ago, state enabling legislation for billboard regulation changed, requiring compensation for amortization, depending on the circumstances. Lubbock's amortization period was long enough to avoid payment to billboard owners. Under the new legislation, Lubbock has removed another 70 billboards, and expects to remove 50 more in the next few years. A zoning official estimates that about 100 billboards will remain in compliance with the ordinance.

Although the billboard industry has been less active locally, apparently no business has failed because of the sign ordinance. In fact, the ordinance has stimulated private initiative. The local sign industry has introduced new designs and materials to ensure continuing business with clients responding to the new regulations. Sign companies have admitted that their business generally has increased in the past ten years as owners complying with the ordinance require new signs. A new sign company has recently settled in town.

The zoning administrator responsible for enforcing the sign controls points out that the ordinance has been extremely effective in eliminating portable signs and signs with flashing lights close to streets. Both of these types of signs are prohibited.

Since its inception, the sign regulations have been revised. Zoning administrators wrote the original ordinance with the expectation of corridor-style development, and prohibited business identification signs in areas that were not along thoroughfares or expressways. Businesses conforming to the new development pattern (see Growth Pressures, above) convinced the city to change the ordinance so that they could erect signs identifying themselves on their lots even though they were located away from highways.

The ordinance has been well supported by the public. City Council candidates running against the Zoning Ordinance have been defeated since 1976, and council members who support the urban design program receive endorsement from citizen groups like Citizens for Good Signs.

CONTACT

Zoning Specialist
P.O. Box 2000
Lubbock, TX 79457

INFORMATION RESOURCES

Coalition for Scenic Beauty, Center for Sign Control. *Sign Control News*.

Periodic newsletter published by the Coalition for Scenic Beauty. Covers recent legal and regulatory events involving sign control at all levels. Available to Coalition members for membership fee.

Duerksen, Christopher J. *Aesthetics and Land Use Controls: Beyond Ecology and Economics*. Planning Advisory Service Report Number 399. Chicago, IL: American Planning Association, 1986.

Provides an introduction to the use of land use regulations to improve urban design in historic areas, protect scenic views, preserve trees, and limit signs and outdoor communications. Focuses both on legal issues and general principles as well as specific examples of controls drawn from communities. Sample ordinances are also provided.

Federal Highway Administration, U.S. Department of Transportation. *Scenic Byways '88* (April 1988). Publication Number FHWA-DF-88-002.

This handbook provides an overview of federal, state, and local scenic road programs. In addition, it contains important addresses, sources of federal assistance, and a bibliography.

Glassford, Peggy. *Appearance Codes for Small Communities*. Planning Advisory Service Report No. 379. Chicago, IL: American Planning Association, 1983.

Provides an introduction to design review and regulations in small communities. Includes illustrative sample ordinance provisions from several communities.

Lu, Weming. "Preservation Criteria: Defining and Protecting Design Relationships." In *Old and New Architecture: Design Relationships*. Washington, D.C.: Preservation Press, 1980.

Provides a good discussion of preservation criteria, including the use of sketches incorporated by reference into design review ordinances.

Mandelker, Daniel R., and William R. Ewald. *Street Graphics and the Law*. Chicago: American Planning Association Planners Press, 1988.

The most useful single source available on sign regulation. Explains the administrative and legal aspects of sign control and includes a model sign control ordinance with commentary.

Ray, Genevieve H. *City Sampler: Catalogue of Urban Environmental Design Tools and Techniques in Local Government*. Washington, D.C.: Community Design Exchange, 1984.

Summarizes urban environmental design tools used to improve the quality of the urban environment. Emphasis is placed on design review, controls, and incentives. Specific programs are described and contacts listed. Available for $9 from Community Design Exchange, 1346 Connecticut Avenue, N.W., Suite 1009, Washington, D.C. 20036.

Southern Environmental Law Center. *Visual Pollution and Sign Control: A Legal Handbook on Billboard Reform*. Charlottesville, VA: Sign Control Project, Southern Environmental Law Center, 1987.

Provides an introduction to the key legal and organizational aspects of controlling billboards at the state and local level. Chapters focus on the Federal Highway Beautification Act, state regulatory programs, local programs, legal issues, and organizing to pass strong local controls. They have also published a companion volume called *Visual Pollution and Billboard Reform in Tennessee*.

Thomas, Ronald. *Cities by Design: An Introduction for Public Administrators*. Washington, D.C.: Community Design Exchange, 1984.

This illustrated booklet discusses urban environmental design. Available for $4.50 from Community Design Exchange, 1346 Connecticut Avenue, N.W., Suite 1009, Washington, D.C. 20036.

Whyte, William H. *The Social Life of Small Urban Spaces*. Washington, D.C.: The Conservation Foundation, 1980.

Describes why some small urban spaces work and others do not, and how to design attractive urban spaces.

ORGANIZATIONAL RESOURCES ——————

Scenic America (formerly Coalition for Scenic Beauty), 218 D Street, S.E., Washington, D.C. 20003; (202) 546-1100.

This organization is active in lobbying for scenic roads, sign control, and all aspects of scenic preservation. CSB is best known for its work for effective federal, state, and local sign and billboard controls. It is a national clearinghouse for billboard control information, publishes a newsletter, and provides assistance with information about billboard control efforts and other forms of aesthetic regulation.

Federal Highway Administration, 400 7th Street, S.W., Washington, D.C. 20590; (202) 366-2017.

The FHWA provides technical assistance for scenic road programs and published a useful handbook on scenic roads called *Scenic Byways 88*.

Southern Environmental Law Center, 201 West Main Street, Suite 14, Charlottesville, VA 22901-5003; (804) 977-4090.

This organization is a regional, nonprofit, environmental law firm, which provides free legal assistance to communities, interested citizens, and environmental organizations working to improve the southern environment. Its Sign Control Project works to strengthen highway beautification laws in the region and provides legal advice and litigation support to localities involved in billboard control litigation.

CHAPTER 5
Open Space Resources

OPEN SPACE RESOURCES FACE MANY THREATS

PROTECTING OPEN SPACE AND BUILDING
AFFORDABLE HOUSING

SPECIFIC OPEN SPACE RESOURCES AND PROTECTION
TOOLS
Greenbelts, Greenways, and Trails
Woodlands and Tree Protection
Wildlife Habitat and Areas Critical for Natural Diversity
Hillsides

LEGAL CONSIDERATIONS IN PROTECTING OPEN SPACE

SUGGESTIONS FOR BUILDING OPEN SPACE
PROTECTION PROGRAMS

PROFILES
Columbia, Missouri
Nantucket, Massachusetts
Boulder, Colorado
Peninsula Open Space Trust
Greenbelt Alliance

INFORMATION RESOURCES

ORGANIZATIONAL RESOURCES

Woe unto them that join house to house, that lay field to field,
'til there be no place, where they be alone in the midst of the
earth.

—Isaiah (5:8)

Open Space Resources Face Many Threats

The values provided by, and the means of protecting, the wide variety of lands encompassed by the term "open space" are very sweeping. The diversity of open space values is suggested by a report of the New York–area Regional Plan Association:

> It cleans the water we drink, and recycles the air we breathe. It is the trails we jog and walk and bicycle, the beaches we use on a hot summer day, and the scenery we see on the way. We all call it open space, but it is really land and water, from rural forest, fields, wetlands, lakes and streams, to vacant urban land.[1]

Open space lands serve numerous functions:

- *They provide economic resources.* Open lands are economically useful for agriculture, livestock grazing, and forestry. Undisturbed wetlands are vital to fisheries and water quality. The scenic beauty of open lands attracts tourists.
- *They provide direct health and safety benefits.* Open lands help recharge groundwater aquifers. Undeveloped watersheds protect the quality of public drinking water supplies. Conservation of unstable hillsides and floodplains prevents the loss of life and property damage. Forested lands cleanse the air and moderate temperatures.
- *They provide recreational opportunities.* Open lands serve as national, state, local, and private parks, preserves and recreation areas; archaeological preserves; and historic and cultural sites. They serve as urban greenbelts, greenways, and trails and provide public access to shores and rivers.
- *They preserve ecological resources.* Open lands protect animal and plant habitat, wilderness areas, scientific reserves, and unique and threatened species and ecosystems.
- *They promote aesthetic values and create community identity.* Pastoral and open landscapes create scenic vistas and parkways. They separate and maintain the distinct identity of communities and create "cultural landscapes."

Protecting Open Space and Building Affordable Housing

The scarcity of affordable housing—for first-time home-buyers, low-income and even middle-income people—in growing communities is an increasingly critical problem. Rising residential land values as well as housing prices are sometimes perceived to result from local growth management efforts. While many factors influence the cost of housing, and the relationship between land use controls and housing costs is difficult to determine, growth management opponents often allege that tighter local land use controls are responsible for increased housing prices. In many communities, open space protection is frequently pointed to as the primary culprit.

In debates over open space and resource protection issues, in fact, open space conservation and housing are often painted in "zero-sum" terms. Arguments are sometimes couched in "environment versus housing" or "trees versus people" terms. A recent publication of the San Francisco Bay Area's Greenbelt Alliance summarizes the typical result of this frequently hyperbolic debate:

> Throughout the Bay Area, the production of new housing and the protection of farmland and other essential open space are increasingly seen as conflicting claims on the region's land. In battles over these issues, developers, conservationists, neighborhood activists and local officials are frequently pitted against one another—and more often than not, the result is a stalemate where no one really wins.*

Several initiatives around the country demonstrate that effective strategies can work to stimulate both resource protection and affordable housing efforts. In fact, the recently adopted New Jersey State Plan recognizes that compact urban design with proper planning can result in an affirmative correlation between affordable housing and undeveloped countrysides. The executive summary of the preliminary state plan provides:

---

* Greenbelt Alliance (formerly People for Open Space), *Room Enough: Housing and Open Space in the Bay Area* (San Francisco, CA: People for Open Space, 1983), 4.

A sound State Plan would recognize that the *real* housing bill for a resident is the mortgage payment *plus taxes plus commuting costs*. Accordingly, it would promote policies which encourage housing where services can be provided most efficiently and where the commute to work is cost-effective. It would also encourage higher housing densities in appropriate areas to reduce the unit costs of construction.

To the extent that a community's growth management program has a significant deleterious impact on the affordability and availability of housing within the community, that program is not "comprehensive" and fails to provide for critical public needs. Such a program not only invites a backlash against growth management and resource protection and is not sustainable over the long-term, but also will not help to create a successful community.

Increasingly, open space and housing advocates are joining together to ensure an adequate supply of both. The Greenbelt Alliance, for example, has formed a Bay Area–wide coalition of environmental, open space, and housing interests to promote both more intensive development of already urbanized land and preservation of the open lands beyond. Five specific strategies form the land use planning core of this program:

- More effective use of vacant land;
- Construction of more housing along major streets;
- Construction of more housing downtown;
- Construction of second units on existing home sites; and
- Construction of housing on former industrial sites.

Housing and land conservation advocates joined forces in Vermont to establish the Vermont Housing and Conservation Trust Fund, a model program that addresses both concerns. Following extensive lobbying efforts by the Housing and Conservation Coalition, the Vermont legislature appropriated $3 million in 1987 to establish the trust fund to provide grants and low- and no-interest loans to innovative projects that conserve farmland, preserve natural areas, protect historic sites, acquire public recreation resources, and build affordable housing. In 1988, the legislature responded to strong public support for the program by appropriating an additional $22.4 million to the fund and by raising the state's real estate transfer tax to provide a permanent revenue base for this initiative.

Montgomery County, Maryland, has implemented innovative programs both to protect open space and to provide affordable housing.* To provide housing opportunities for low- and moderate-income residents,

Montgomery County's moderately priced dwelling unit law requires developers of most residential projects with 50 units or more to provide 15 percent of the total units as moderately priced dwelling units (MPDU). In exchange, developers are given a 20 percent density bonus so that, in effect, the MPDUs are produced free of land costs.

Typically, the MPDUs are similar in appearance to other units in the same development, but may lack certain amenities, such as a dishwasher, extra bedrooms, or a finished basement. The MPDUs may also differ in that a developer, in certain situations, may provide MPDUs as townhouses or clustered houses in a predominantly single-family detached subdivision.

Eligible low- and moderate-income applicants receive a certificate of participation that allows them to shop for MPDUs. Eligible applicants must qualify for financing and may have to pay a down payment and closing costs. Purchase, lease, and finance arrangements generally are negotiated between the applicant and the private developer. In most cases, demand has been so great that a lottery has been used.

The program requires developers to offer one-third of all MPDUs to the county's independent Housing Opportunities Commission (HOC). Since 1974, over 7,400 units have been sold or leased under the program, while the HOC itself has purchased close to 650 units scattered through 100 different developments. Funding comes from several local and state sources, including direct county funds, sale of tax exempt mortgage revenue bonds, and proceeds from the county's 4 percent condominium transfer tax, in addition to the traditional federal construction funds.

Protecting open space can be especially controversial in areas where housing costs are rising and potential home-buyers are getting pushed out of the market. Residents who cannot afford homes in areas where their families have lived for generations may be particularly hard-pressed to favor open space programs that are perceived to cost money and take land out of the housing market. Development interests in several areas across the country have pointed to "affordable housing" needs in opposing open space programs. There are growing attempts to reconcile these two needs. This chapter focuses on the variety of open space resources that have not been addressed in the preceding chapters. It discusses:

- Specific open space resources—including greenways, trails, and greenbelts; woodlands; wildlife habitat and natural areas; and hillsides—and protection programs and tools useful for protecting them;

---

* Montgomery County's farmland preservation program is discussed in a profile at the end of chapter 1.

- Legal considerations that are particularly relevant in open space protection programs; and
- Suggestions for building effective open space protection programs.

Critical issues in protecting open space and building affordable housing, such as ensuring that housing remains affordable for successive buyers and demonstrating the feasibility of both goals on a broader scale, should be addressed more thoroughly. More models need to be created. Yet programs and efforts such as these illustrate what is possible when housing and conservation interests are joined and governments respond with innovative approaches.

Specific Open Space Resources and Protection Tools

There are several specific but overlapping open space resources—greenways, trails, and greenbelts; woodlands; wildlife habitat and areas critical for natural diversity; and hillsides. Both regulatory and nonregulatory measures have proved effective in protecting these areas.

GREENBELTS, GREENWAYS, AND TRAILS

Noting that by the year 2000, 80 percent of Americans will live in metropolitan areas, the report of the President's Commission on Americans Outdoors stresses the growing need for convenient outdoor recreation lands and tracts of "green" in and near urban areas.[2] To meet this need, some communities have developed comprehensive strategies for protecting greenbelts, establishing greenways, and providing extensive trail systems.

A greenbelt is a contiguous, interrelated open space buffer surrounding an entire community or metropolitan area (a ring of green around a city). The resources protected in a greenbelt may include river and stream courses, wildlife refuges and migration corridors, scenic roads, hiking and bicycling trails created from utility easement corridors or abandoned rail lines, public parks, floodplains, farms, grazing lands, mountains and hillsides. These lands provide a correspondingly broad range of recreation, scenic, economic, and ecologic benefits. In addition to serving the functions typically served by open space lands, a successful urban greenbelt may help to contain the spread of suburban development (either from the community or toward the community from neighboring cities or metropolitan areas) and creates a green "gateway" to a community that enhances a community's individual character and distinctiveness.

The report of the President's Commission on Americans Outdoors recommends greenways as the most promising method for providing open spaces in urban areas and linking urban residents with suburban and rural recreational resources. The commission defines greenways as

local natural areas where recreation and conservation are among the primary values. They are fingers of green that come in many shapes and sizes. They may be in public or private ownership, and may serve many purposes. Greenways link people and resources. They can put recreation open space within a short walk from your home.[3]

There are many success stories involving local nonprofit organizations building coalitions to work with landowners and governmental agencies to develop a proposed trail or greenway. Ideally, such a coalition includes affected landowners who can work credibly with their neighbors to address common concerns about vandalism, litter, and other potential impacts of public access.

Given the regional expanse of greenbelts and greenways, an array of land protection techniques is necessary. With greenbelts, large-scale open space preservation is accomplished using public land acquisition in combination with land use regulations, tax incentives, and capital spending decisions. Exemplary programs in this country that combine public and private efforts include:

- The Bay Circuit Program in the Boston area, involving the state of Massachusetts's effort to link the north and south shores of Boston with a 100-mile arc of trails, protected farmland, and parks through a mixture of public and private means.
- Nantucket Island, Massachusetts, has implemented a land acquisition program with notable success. Funded through local real estate transfer taxes, the goal of the Nantucket program is the permanent preservation in open space of 15 percent of the island over a 20-year period. The quicker the pace of local real estate activity, the more funds are available to acquire land. (See the profile on the Nantucket program at the end of this chapter.)
- In the San Francisco Bay Area, the two-county East Bay Regional Park District, funded through property taxes, has acquired 200 miles of trails and waterways linking 65,000 acres of parkland with publicly owned waterfront lands. (The Bay Area also is home for the Greenbelt Alliance and the Peninsula Open Space Trust, two private nonprofit regional planning and land acquisition groups that

have built broad coalitions in support of a greenbelt. These groups are profiled at the end of this chapter.)

As the report of the President's Commission on Americans Outdoors makes clear, greenways can come in many forms. In addition to abandoned railroad corridors, many communities have created greenways and trail systems along rivers and streams, and in mountainous areas.* For example, the Delaware and Raritan Greenway Project in central New Jersey coordinates efforts of numerous area jurisdictions to preserve open space corridors linking the Delaware and Raritan Canal State Park to the surrounding communities. (Also, the City of Columbia, Missouri, has created a linear park out of an abandoned railroad line, which is discussed in the profile at the end of this chapter.)

Assembling the Land

Unless a ready-made corridor, such as an abandoned rail line or utility easement, is available, land assembly is the first hurdle in developing a greenway, greenbelt, or trail system. Several important steps should be taken:

- In developing a trail, one or several alternative trail alignments should first be plotted on a topographic map and "field checked" by walking the proposed route.

- Land ownership along the alignment should be identified to determine the owners with whom negotiations must be undertaken.

- Information about the landowners in the area—their attitudes toward the proposed trail, financial situations, estate planning objectives, and plans for the land, for example—will help determine which alternative alignment to select and how best to approach each landowner.

- Landowners who are likely to donate land should be approached first to develop momentum for the trail system. Landowners who are less sympathetic may be influenced by donations by their neighboring landowners.

Land Acquisition

The most direct approach for developing greenways, trails, and other forms of recreational access is land acquisition, which can be undertaken by both public agencies and nonprofit organizations. Full fee acquisition (buying all rights to private property) is particularly appropriate for parks and access points that require significant related development, such as a parking area. For most sections of a greenway system, however, acquisition of a full fee interest may be unnecessary or prohibitively expensive. In many situations, acquisition of public access easements and conservation easements can effectively complement fee simple acquisition.

Acquisition is often most successful as a joint public/private effort because some landowners may prefer to deal with a land trust or other group that has well-known community members or neighboring landowners on the board than with a municipal agency. Conversely, some landowners may only negotiate with a municipal agency that brings the power of eminent domain to the negotiating table.

Planning and Regulation

Local comprehensive plans can call for development of a greenway, and local land use regulations can then incorporate the greenway plans, so that, for example, dedication requirements and access easements become a requirement for approval of private development projects that increase recreational demand within the area.

Regulatory measures are widely used to require land dedication for recreational access as a condition of subdivision or development approval. For example, Currituck County, North Carolina, adopted a provision in 1971 requiring developers of more than 600 feet of waterfront property to provide a ten-foot public pedestrian accessway from a public roadway to the beach or sound. Under the California Coastal Act, both the California Coastal Commission and local governments require dedications of access easements for certain types of coastal development. These easements provide either "vertical" (from a road to the beach) or "horizontal" (along the beach above the high tide line) access.[4] Similarly, the Florida coastal construction regulation program requires an evaluation of interference with public beach access when reviewing new beachfront construction. Martin County, Florida, has implemented a well-documented and defensible Beach Impact Fee Ordinance, which requires developers to contribute to a fund, based upon the projected recreational demand resulting from a proposed development, to purchase and maintain public beachfront property.

Rails-to-Trails

Current trail development efforts illustrate the potential opportunities made available by abandoned railroad corridors. Under the sponsorship of the national Rails-to-Trails Conservancy, the Coalition for the Capital Crescent Trail has been formed in the Washington,

---

* Greenways and trails developed along rivers or streams are discussed in chapter 2, while the use of mountainous areas to create trail systems is discussed later in this chapter.

D.C., area to take advantage of the recent abandonment of a local rail spur to provide a continuous 20-mile trail from the Maryland suburbs to the Potomac River at Rock Creek Park. Support has been generated from Montgomery County, Maryland, and the National Park Service to pursue funding for corridor acquisition. A leading example of a rails-to-trails conversion that has been implemented is in Columbia, Missouri, where the city has turned a spur of the Missouri–Kansas–Texas railroad corridor into a linear park. (This effort is discussed in the profile at the end of this chapter.)

Opportunities for creating recreational and natural assets from abandoned railway rights-of-way exist throughout the country. In the early-twentieth-century heyday of railroading, there were more than 270,000 miles of railroad track—six times the present-day mileage of the interstate highway system. Postwar changes in freight and passenger transportation have eliminated over 125,000 miles of this original network, with the rail abandonment process continuing at least into the near future. Whatever this process means for the future of railroading, it presents a tremendous opportunity for developing trails and linear

parks. Abandoned rail corridors, with their gentle grades and right-of-way buffers, make ideal multipurpose trails. They often present a means of creating a greenway network by linking communities with outlying parks and rural lands. The Rails-to-Trails Conservancy* has documented 124 converted rail-trails in 25 states, totaling 1,900 miles of rail lines converted for trail use.[5]

WOODLANDS AND TREE PROTECTION

Woodlands provide wildlife habitat, recreational opportunities, aesthetic values, economic benefits from timber management, and ecological functions—such as watershed protection, climate moderation, air purification, and groundwater recharge. Wooded buffers along rivers and streams protect them from siltation and absorb flood waters.

However, heavily wooded land can present obsta-

* The Rails-to-Trails Conservancy, described in the Organizational Resources section below, specializes in assisting groups identify, build support for, and convert railroad corridors for use as trails.

cles to developers and, therefore, a common practice is to clear-cut wooded land before developing or marketing property. This practice leads to increased stream sedimentation and soil erosion, decreased groundwater recharge capacity, accelerated storm water runoff, and unnecessary habitat loss and aesthetic degradation. The practice frequently has a negative impact on neighboring property values. For these reasons, an increasing number of communities have begun to regulate such clear-cutting.

According to a recent report published by the American Planning Association, the basic types of local regulations protecting woodlands can be placed into three categories:[6]

- Tree protection ordinances preserving specific yard and street trees in the midst of development (discussed in chapter 4);
- Timber-harvesting ordinances regulating timber production practices in developing areas to prevent nuisances such as excessive noise as well as increased soil erosion and water quality damage; and
- Woodland protection ordinances identifying and preserving sensitive wooded areas.[7]

Timber-Harvesting Ordinances

An increasing number of communities regulate timber-harvesting practices, addressing noise, truck traffic, aesthetics, cutting practices, fire control, erosion control, and water quality. In Connecticut, at least 20 municipalities have enacted timber-harvesting regulations.[8] For example, the town of Haddam, Connecticut, requires a submission of a timber removal plan and a permit from the zoning enforcement officer for harvests exceeding 16 cords and requires plan approval by the planning commission for harvests exceeding 100 cords.

Woodland Protection Ordinances

Woodland protection ordinances have been adopted in numerous communities. The first step in any woodlands protection program is resource identification and evaluation. The basis for such a project is a woodland survey. Significant forested areas can be identified with a U.S. Geologic Survey topographic map or low-altitude aerial photographs. The state forester, the U.S. Soil Conservation Service, the county extension agency, or university forestry or botany departments may provide technical assistance in conducting a field survey to document species and stand quality. This information will help ensure that a protection program is targeted effectively.

Following an inventory, woodland protection programs can take many forms. One common approach involves performance standards. Development is not permitted unless the proposed project fulfills several criteria designed to ensure optimal protection of trees and natural ground cover.

Oakland County, Michigan, for example, has implemented an ordinance that applies a variety of specific standards, including:

- Residential units must blend into the natural landscape;
- Woodland preservation takes precedence over other uses where alternative locations exist for the other use; and
- Conservation of irreplaceable natural resources is the paramount land use review factor.

In addition, this ordinance controls the removal of trees with trunks more than three inches in diameter.[9]

Performance criteria to protect woodlands must be examined carefully to determine the appropriate level of woodland protection. If protecting water quality is a primary concern, a community, for instance, may regulate timber removal only within a buffer strip along a watercourse rather than throughout the entire town. Which uses to allow as-of-right (without a permit) needs to be carefully evaluated, as well. For example, "nonintensive" uses such as agriculture may be more destructive of forested lands than carefully sited residential development.

Many localities have implemented vegetation protection standards that are applied in site plan review for proposed residential or commercial development. These communities often learn that, unless similar provisions regulate land clearing and timber removal generally, some landowners will respond by simply clearing a parcel before submitting a development plan.

Cluster regulations or planned unit development (PUD) standards can also be used to protect woodlands. As in Appendix A, the PUD approach provides flexibility in the siting of development on large parcels. PUD regulations often allow or require the clustering of development on the portions of a parcel that are most suitable for development and the preservation of the balance of the parcel. The advantage of the technique is that a planned unit development can result in preservation of significant amounts of open land (frequently important stands of trees) without increasing the overall development density of the parcel.

WILDLIFE HABITAT AND AREAS CRITICAL FOR NATURAL DIVERSITY

The preservation of wildlife habitat and the natural diversity sustained by adequate wildlife habitat is a goal of many local, regional, and national citizens' organizations. National conservation organizations, such as the Nature Conservancy, and regional and local land trusts in all parts of the country buy land and conservation easements and enter into management agreements to preserve natural habitat.* Local programs to protect or enhance rivers, streams, and other open space resources also frequently protect important natural habitat. In addition, many local governments use their planning, regulatory, and land acquisition powers explicitly to protect or enhance wildlife habitat. These local actions are often necessary to complement habitat protection efforts undertaken by federal and state governments and nongovernmental conservation organizations.

An important first step in a local program to protect wildlife habitat and natural diversity is to inventory local natural resources. For example, Durham County, North Carolina, has undertaken a comprehensive inventory of its important natural and cultural areas and features. Maps identifying the county's significant natural and historic sites are now incorporated into the

---

* See Philip M. Hoose, *Building An Ark*, cited below in the Information Resources section, for more detail on these efforts.

county's land use plans and used by planning officials, developers, and landowners when making development decisions.[10]

Many states have established a natural heritage program, which can facilitate local natural heritage inventories. State natural heritage programs identify the state's most valuable and threatened natural features. Based upon a program created in the 1970s by the Nature Conservancy, these programs typically: (1) inventory plant and animal species and communities and rank them according to rarity; (2) identify lands where the highest-ranked species and communities occur; and (3) set land protection priorities based upon these rankings. The first step to undertaking a local natural heritage inventory is to consult a state's natural heritage program, which can serve as a baseline for local inventories and actions.

HILLSIDES

Hillsides are a particularly sensitive open space resource. In addition to their value as wildlife habitat, greenways, or woodlands, hillsides present the following specific development constraints:

- Increased soil erosion and stream siltation is a particular problem in the development of steeply sloped land.

- Landslides, mudslides, and erosion raise critical public safety concerns in many steeply sloped areas.

- Mountain ridges and hillsides visible from developed valleys are often important scenic resources that strongly influence the character of an entire region or community.

Identifying the Resource

The key first step in developing a hillside protection program is proper evaluation of hillside resources and threats. The starting point is a U.S. Geologic Survey topographic map. In addition, the USDA Soil Conservation Service publishes soil surveys that identify slopes and soil types inappropriate for development due to instability.

Regulatory Objectives

Designers for a hillside protection program also need to think through what they seek to accomplish. Walnut Creek, California, for example, has implemented a Hillside Planned Development District, which explicitly identifies the importance of open hillsides to the city's image and sense of identity. Its objectives include:

- Preserving hillsides in their natural state as part of a comprehensive open space system;

- Minimizing grading and resulting water runoff and soil erosion; and

- Preserving predominant views both of and from hillsides.[11]

Manitou Springs, Colorado, a rapidly growing city above Colorado Springs, has also adopted a comprehensive hillside protection ordinance. The ordinance—based principally upon the need to control erosion, storm-water drainage, and to assure emergency access—was recently upheld by the Colorado Supreme Court as a constitutional exercise of the city's police power.[12]

Regulatory Approaches

Three basic regulatory approaches to the control of hillside development are worthy of note:

- Slope-density formulas, varying the density of permitted development based upon the degree of hillside slope;

- Soil-based zoning districts, varying the density of

permitted development based upon the ability of on-site soils to withstand development; and

- Overall performance standards, varying the density of permitted development based upon factors such as slope stability and the levels of erosion and sedimentation that would result from a specific development proposal.[13]

Slope-density ordinances specify the percentage of a parcel that may be developed or the permitted density based upon the overall slope of the parcel. The minimum lot size may vary according to its average slope. This approach addresses the increased environmental and public safety risk of developing steep slopes.

The precise slope-to-density formula should include the following factors, as appropriate for local conditions:

- Geological and soils conditions, such as slope stability;

- The steepness of the slopes;

- The suitability of the site for on-site water supply and wastewater treatment, or the availability of public water and sewer;

- The amount and nature of roads required to provide access; and

- The type and amount of vegetative cover.

Soil-based zoning districts base development density on the capability of on-site soils to support development. This technique is increasingly popular in small towns that rely on individual septic systems and/or individual wells. The permitted density is derived from analysis of soils survey information available from the U.S. Soil Conservation Service. Density limits are based upon factors such as soil permeability, depth to bedrock or to the seasonal high water table, and gradient.

McHenry County, Illinois, has used soil survey information to develop "soils overlay regulations" that apply to areas with specific soil types and slopes exceeding a specified threshold. Its Steep Soils Overlay District applies in areas with slopes greater than 12 percent and with certain soil characteristics. In this overlay district, standards related to erosion control and sewage disposal apply.[14]

Soils-based zoning, with minimum lot sizes for residential development based upon the capacity of the soils for on-site sewage disposal, is also widely used in New England. Several Connecticut towns, for example, such as Canterbury, Washington, and Kent, base density on soil characteristics.[15]

Overall performance standards can be used to re-

quire permitted uses to comply with specific standards ensuring that slope and soil conditions can sustain the proposed use or density without threatening the public health, safety, or welfare. Performance standards can create an additional review either for uses permitted by right or uses that require a special permit. (Performance standards are discussed in more detail in the Primer in Appendix A.)

San Diego, California, has implemented and refined a leading hillside protection zoning district. Its Hillside Review Overlay Zone and Hillside Design and Development Guidelines apply as an overlay zone to areas with a natural gradient in excess of 25 percent and a minimum elevation differential of 50 feet. Within these areas, development must comply with several qualitative development guidelines and criteria designed to minimize disturbance of the natural terrain and conserve the aesthetic quality of the hillside area.

Grading controls apply in most towns and counties throughout the nation to control the negative impacts of hillside development. Most states mandate that localities adopt some type of grading or erosion and

sedimentation control program. While they often apply as a discrete regulation, rather than as part of a zoning ordinance, they can be adapted to provide specific controls as part of a hillside protection program.

Grading controls typically outline erosion control measures (such as the use of silt fences) that must be undertaken in conjunction with site grading, but can also specify the maximum percentage of a parcel that can be graded, limit the volume of earth that can be disturbed or removed from the site, and/or specify the times and manner in which grading is done. At a minimum, grading controls should require submission and approval of a grading plan before work begins.

Grading control programs often suffer from inadequate enforcement. No matter how a hillside protection program addresses development density, effective enforcement must be given high priority.

Acquisition Programs

In addition to regulatory programs to preserve hillsides, several communities have effectively used acquisition as a hillside protection strategy. Boulder,

Colorado, for example, has since 1967 earmarked part of the local sales tax to fund land acquisition in the city's scenic Flat Iron foothills. As of 1988, 17,000 acres of land had been preserved.[16] (Boulder's efforts are profiled at the end of this chapter.)

Legal Considerations in Protecting Open Space

Due to the diversity of resources encompassed by the term "open space," open space protection programs present a full range of legal issues. The following legal concerns deserve particular emphasis:

- *A locality often cannot regulate property so that only open space uses are permitted.*[17] Although a zoning revision can substantially—even dramatically—reduce the value of a parcel, the parcel generally must retain some economically feasible use. (This general rule often does not apply to wetlands or floodplains.) In proper circumstances, exclusive agricultural districts can provide an economically feasible use. Court decisions have upheld minimum lot sizes of as much as 40 acres or more in agricultural districts or particularly sensitive areas.
- *Public agencies should carefully identify and thoroughly document the need for community recreational lands and facilities; the recreational needs of proposed developments; and the linkage or connection between any land dedication or exaction requirements and the needs of proposed developments.* Courts generally uphold exaction or land dedication requirements for new development so long as they are reasonably related to the increased recreational demands resulting from new development. The recent United States Supreme Court opinion in *Nollan v. California Coastal Commission*[18] emphasizes the need to ensure that conditions imposed upon the issuance of development permits (particularly those that require public access) bear some reasonable relationship to a documented public need.
- *Open space preservation programs should clearly identify specific public functions served by open space preservation.* While courts generally recognize land use controls based upon purely aesthetic purposes as valid, documentation of the more traditional public health, safety, and economic objectives will improve the legal defensibility of the program in any constitutional or statutory challenge. The description of public purposes should, therefore, discuss the aesthetic benefits of open space preservation and should also emphasize tangible public health and safety benefits; benefits to local and regional tourism and economic development; and other fiscal benefits.
- *Open space programs should protect against the potential for personal injury claims against either private nonprofit organizations or public agencies,* which may increase when providing public access to open space. In some states (e.g., California), public agencies can enter into agreements with nonprofit organizations that transfer the state's partial immunity from personal injury claims to the nonprofit. Moreover, every state except Alaska has enacted recreational use statutes that protect private landowners who allow public recreational use of their property without charge from potential liability for injuries occurring to people using the land.[19] Before acquiring land, a nonprofit organization should consider liability issues. Most land trusts have found that, with proper risk management, the threat of liability can be reduced to an acceptable level.
- *Regulatory decisions must be clearly and completely independent of land acquisition policies.* Municipal officials should carefully avoid creating any appearance or inference that a purpose for rezoning property or for adopting any land use regulation—even a minor consideration in the decision—is to facilitate public acquisition.

Suggestions for Building Open Space Protection Programs

In addition to the requirements for a legally sound open space program, the following components are commonly found in successful open space preservation programs:

- *Develop open space protection programs around a clear vision of the future.* This vision of the community should be embodied in meaningful local land use plans and specific local policies directing growth in appropriate areas and discouraging growth in resource protection areas. This vision then guides local decision-making on specific capital improvements and development applications.
- *Combine regulatory and land acquisition measures.* Regulatory and land acquisition programs should be distinct but complementary. In turn, land acquisition efforts should be undertaken both by a public agency and by a local or regional nonprofit land trust. The public agency and the land trust

will likely find different niches and will excel in different circumstances.

- *Build strong community support outside of the local regulatory boards.* Open space protection efforts should be spearheaded or supported by local groups that can play at least two different roles: (1) advocate policies, monitor regulatory actions, and keep open space issues on the public agenda; (2) participate in land trust activities, such as negotiate acquisitions in land trust actions, manage land preservation agreements, and work quietly with benefactors for funding.

- *Document and publicize the diverse benefits of open space preservation.* Documentation should stress the tangible and economic benefits of open space protection. This documentation helps build broad coalitions for open space preservation and assists in legal defense if necessary.

- *Think, plan, and operate on a regional level.* Coordinated regionwide action is necessary to prevent development from "leapfrogging" narrow open space protection areas and to ensure that the plans and programs of neighboring communities do not conflict with one another.

PROFILE

COLUMBIA, MISSOURI

Acquisition of a Railroad Right-of-Way for a Greenway

Community Characteristics

Columbia lies halfway between St. Louis and Kansas City, about 10 miles north of the Missouri River. The University of Missouri, the state cancer hospital, and a major mental health clinic are located in Columbia. The population of about 70,000 enjoys abundant cultural and recreational opportunities afforded by a diverse array of educational institutions and an active Parks Department.

The development of the highway system in the 1920s placed Columbia at a major crossroads. Interstate Route 70 now traverses the northern section of the city. Beginning in the 1950s, Columbia committed large amounts of funding to public service projects—utilities and rehabilitation efforts. Around this time, the city also became the hub for a regional airport.

Growth Patterns

Columbia experienced the bulk of its growth during the 1960s; between 1970 and 1980 the city only grew 5.5 percent. Since then, the rate of growth in the central city has continued to decline, but development at the outskirts and in the surrounding county has more than made up for decline in the urban core. Outside the central city, growth was almost 12 percent between 1980 and 1984, while population growth in the city was only 2 percent. By mid-decade, the Columbia metropolitan area contained about 110,000 people, slightly more than half of whom live in the city itself.

Resources Threatened

The increased density of growth at the fringes of the city imperiled open space and recreational resources located there. The need to preserve pockets and corridors of green to break up and screen development at the edge of the city became a growing priority for the well-respected Parks Department. An abandoned spur line of the Missouri–Kansas–Texas (MKT) railway was viewed as an ideal corridor linking the city to the suburbs, easily convertible to public use.

Measures Taken

During the late 1970s, the city of Columbia sought to acquire the old 8.5-mile right-of-way and convert the 4.3-mile segment within the city limits to a linear park. Under the Railway Revitalization Act of 1977, the city was able to purchase outright from the railroad properties to which the MKT company owned title. However, there were 54 separately owned properties (constituting about 75 percent of the line) along the stretch, on which easements reverted back to individual landowners upon cessation of the railroad's use of the right-of-way. Many of these landowners were unwilling to donate their easements to the city: they argued that the proposed use was unacceptable for safety reasons and because their access might be restricted.

The U.S. Department of the Interior invited a mediator to help negotiate an acquisition process between landowners and the city. Over eight months, the mediator held meetings that resolved issues for property owners and initiated the transfer of title to the city.

Although resolution came relatively quickly, implementation was arduous. The acquisition process took ten years to complete, and in most cases (as is typical of such acquisition proceedings) required custom-made agreements tailored to the needs of each landowner. In some cases, the city paid for the value of the land and the cost to the landowner of installing a fence to separate his property from the right-of-way. In other cases, the city granted an easement to the owner for access across the former railroad, or the right to cut trees and bushes to control runoff received by abutting farmland. The superintendent called this ten-year process "arduous headbutting," in which the city sometimes had to condemn rights-of-way.

Experience

After tedious and expensive legal acquisition proceedings were finally completed, the city of Columbia began making improvements on the 4.3 miles of the old railway that lay inside city limits. The city converted 13 trestles (which cross a small tributary of the Missouri River that the railroad paralleled) to more solid bridges, and reinforced the treadway for running and biking.

All age groups now actively use the corridor, and the Parks Department maintains it to control erosion and ensure a smooth surface. The scenic trail provides a high-quality, natural environment that provides relief from and creates a buffer against impinging development. The city superintendent of parks observes that "[t]he trail is probably the most popularly regarded facility in our . . . parks system." Adjacent landowners who initially opposed the project have found their fears of vandalism unfounded.

The sole legal provision that applies only to the right-of-way and not to other recreation and nature facilities in the city is the requirement that dogs be held on a maximum four-foot leash at all times. This strict control is necessary for the security and safety of bikers and runners.

Contacts

City of Columbia
Parks Management Center
1507 Business Loop
70 West
Columbia, MO 65202

Rails-to-Trails Conservancy
1400 Sixteenth Street, N.W., Suite 300
Washington, D.C. 20036

PROFILE

NANTUCKET, MASSACHUSETTS

Land Bank

Community Characteristics

Nantucket, Massachusetts is a 50-square-mile island 22 miles off the coast of Cape Cod and also both a town and county of Massachusetts. It is a resort town of widespread repute to which vacationers from all along the northern Atlantic seaboard flock, swelling the permanent population of 6,000 sixfold during the summer months.

The island was first settled by fishermen and a few farm families. The fishing economy is still viable, although tourism replaced it long ago as the principal source of income for the town. Five wharves accommodate both pleasure and commercial fishing boats. A seaside mix of fishing industry, boutiques, and art galleries dominates the experience of many tourists to the island, especially the hundreds who come for the day from Cape Cod during the summer. Only three working farms remain, two of which sell fresh produce from the back of trucks on Nantucket's Main Street.

Growth Patterns

For many years, the Nantucket community had been trying to concentrate growth in existing village centers, away from open moors and beaches. However, every year more than 500 lots are subdivided on the island, and land prices jump about 20 percent. Off-island second-home owners buy about two-thirds of the real estate on the island.

Resources Threatened

Preserving original settlement patterns at village cores presented a challenge under traditional growth management strategies. A booming real estate business, which annually builds over 400 homes on the island and transferred $181 million worth of property in 1987 alone, threatens 88 miles of shoreline and other open space. The natural resources of the island, including inland ponds and open moors, are uniquely situated in a North Atlantic island environment. Their loss would be irreplaceable.

Measures Taken

In 1983, the Nantucket Planning Commission released a report of "goals and objectives for balanced growth," that introduced the idea of a land bank. The town filed special legislation with the state to establish a land bank program, with the target of preserving 15 percent of the island over 20 years, at an estimated cost of $160 million.

The bill passed the state legislature in late 1983, enabling the town to impose a special fee for a dedicated fund, which was voted into law by Nantucket voters the following February. The bill establishes a local land bank that finances acquisition of selected parcels through proceeds of a 2 percent real estate transfer fee.

A five-member locally elected commission administers the bank and uses the proceeds to acquire fee and less-than-fee interests in open space lands for perpetual public use and preservation in a largely natural state. The commission acts on its own authority; it requires no outside or higher approval to acquire property. The commission also has eminent domain powers, which require a two-thirds vote in support at town meeting, and the ability to borrow money to buy property.

The land bank also pays for debt service, staff, and other services in addition to land acquisition. The fund accepts tax-deductible cash contributions and other municipal appropriations and proceeds. With so many sources of revenue, the commission ably competes with private interests in the Nantucket real estate market.

Real estate buyers write a check to the land bank fund before recording their property deeds, which cannot be accepted without land bank certification. About 35 percent of transactions are exempt, including foreclosures, certain transfers to the government and nonprofit groups, and the first $100,000 for first-time home buyers.

Experience

As of December 1987, the bank had raised over $12.5 million from about 5,000 real estate transfers—about $80,000 a week. In 1985, the bank floated $11.5 million in tax-exempt municipal bonds backed by the tax as an income source.

The commission has acquired over 2.5 percent of the land area of the island—900 acres—for $18 million, including a golf course, ponds, moors, and ten acres of beachfront property. Most acquisitions were purchased at market value, although some were bargain sales that saved the commission about $3.5 million. Public donations totaling over $1 million have contributed to some purchases. In one case, neighbors chipped in two-thirds of the over half-a-million-dollar asking price, bringing the cost to the commission well within range. The parcel is now part of the land bank inventory.

Planners and conservationists question whether the land bank's ability to purchase land at market rates has eliminated the incentive for people to donate land for preservation. The temptingly high land prices might have discouraged such gifts, and, in any case, cash donations to the bank continue.

Other private and nonprofit efforts on the island, although without a direct role in the land bank, have preserved more than a third of the island over the past 25 years. The local land trust, the Nantucket Conservation Foundation, contributes enormously to preservation successes, and continues to demonstrate strong support. Recently, a 900-acre tract, equaling the acreage of all the lands acquired by the land bank, was donated to the Massachusetts Audubon Society in a will. The land bank program complements these private initiatives, and continued coordination with such efforts is important.

Other Massachusetts and Rhode Island towns have established land banks in the wake of Nantucket's positive experience, and five northeastern states are considering enabling legislation for land bank programs.

CONTACT

Director
Land Bank Commission
4 North Water Street
Nantucket, MA 02554

PROFILE

BOULDER, COLORADO

Open Space Preservation and Comprehensive Growth Management

Community Characteristics

Spreading eastward toward the Great Plains from the Continental Divide, Boulder County covers 742 square miles and extends over two plateaus abutting the flank of the Rocky Mountains north of Denver. The county has a population of over 210,000. The county seat, the city of Boulder, is home to the University of Colorado and its 23,000 students. The county is comprised of ten municipalities, the largest by far being Boulder, with almost a third of county residents.

The area was first settled by miners in the 1850s. Later, both precious metal mining in the foothills of the Rockies, and farming in the rich adjacent flatlands contributed to growth. Since the mid-twentieth century, Boulder county has attracted mostly white-collar economic development: government, industry, and research institutions.

The county is bisected by I-287. Another larger interstate, I-25, lies just east of the county and feeds arteries leading into the two largest cities of the county—Boulder and Longmont. Roosevelt National Forest spreads over much of the high western half of the county. Rocky Mountain National Park lies over the county's northwestern corner. One of the crown jewels of the national park system, Rocky Mountain brings millions of visitors through the city of Boulder on their way to the peaks—the county's dominant scenic resource.

The county provides easy access to recreational and scenic resources, proximity to Denver, and an attractive climate. These assets, and successful protection of them, have garnered Boulder a reputation for offering a very high quality of life. As the area's reputation grew and corporations and research institutions increased their numbers, hillsides to the west and flat agricultural lands to the east continued to disappear.

Growth Patterns

Between 1970 and 1980, the county grew by 44 percent. In the decade before that, the city of Boulder alone grew almost 80 percent. From 1980 to 1987, growth has subsided considerably, to about 12 percent. In the first half of the 1980s, the growth rate outside central cities of the county—Boulder and Longmont—was three times the city rate, suggesting a dispersal of development away from the urban core. Even so, the cities still contain more than half the county population.

Early in the settlement history of the region, citizens took steps to channel development away from the scenic amenities of the Front Range. Both the city of Boulder and the county, in fact, have been pioneers in preserving natural resources and implementing growth control measures.

City Measures

Voters began addressing the loss of open space in 1959, when they passed a referendum to establish the "Blue Line" along the western edge of the city to protect its scenic mountain vistas. The Blue Line indicated the limits of extension of city water service; however, it did not completely limit development outside the area it delineated. As a result, in 1964, Boulder purchased Enchanted Mesa—a scenic area in the foothills west of the city—for preservation as open space, in response to a proposed 155-acre resort there. Three years later, voters approved a 1 percent city sales tax, with 40 percent of the proceeds earmarked for acquisition of natural resources along the perimeter of the city in a swath called the "Greenbelt."

The City of Boulder Open Space Plan was adopted in 1974 with the goal of creating a solid ribbon of green around the city. The plan includes a detailed map designating all open space lands eventually to be acquired. The map helps to prevent the city from appearing to act arbitrarily and helps landowners located in these areas to plan effectively.

Existing and yet-to-be-acquired open lands typically follow drainage ways and tributaries. The Open Space staff reviews proposed annexations to the city to see if they overlap with areas designated for open space. At the very least, easements are obtained across properties developed in such areas, although usually the city purchases parcels outright.

The city's Open Space program is separate from the Boulder Parks Department, reflecting the distinct goals of the Open Space program. Such goals intend to provide passive visual amenities and environmental buffers to guide growth, not active recreation opportunities.

Financing for open space was enhanced in the early 1970s when voters supported issuing bonds backed by sales tax revenues. The last bond issue was in 1984 for $12 million. While the ability to float bonds has been a useful tool, sales tax revenues have consistently come up short of expectations, making it necessary to refinance the bonded indebtedness in 1986.

The Beginning of Joint City/County Growth Control

In 1970, the county joined the city of Boulder in adopting the Boulder Valley Comprehensive Plan, which is used to guide development, control of urban sprawl, and preserves open lands over a 58-square-mile area. The study for the area projected a population growth of 140,000 by the year 1990, which activated citizens to campaign for limits on growth.

PLACING AND REVISING CAPS ON GROWTH

In 1976, voters in the city approved the "Danish Plan," which limited the number of building permits issued in the city to an average of 450 a year for five years, bringing growth down to a rate of under 2 percent a year. Permits were approved according to a proposal's compliance with community objectives and other factors. This approval process, measured in points, was called the "merit system." A sunset clause caused the ordinance to expire in 1982.

Since then, the city has modified the growth cap several times, while maintaining the objective of keeping growth under 2 percent a year. In order to satisfy the slow growth goal, planners determined the number of building permits for dwelling units the city could issue on a yearly basis through 1990. This allocation by year is included in Boulder's land use regulations.

Since 1985, instead of awarding permits based on points, each applicant is issued a number of permits in proportion to the total pool of requests received. According to this method, called the Proportional Allocation System, if six permits are available in a given area that has met all land use and zoning requirements, and Developer A requests all six, and Developer B requests three, A will receive two-thirds of the permits, or four, and B will receive one-third, or two permits. Some exemptions to allocation restrictions include: low-income housing, student housing, and up to 30 discretionary exemptions a year for group housing and historic buildings.

PHASING GROWTH INTO URBAN SERVICE AREAS

Together, the county and the city ratified policies in the Boulder Valley Comprehensive Plan that govern physical expansion of the city and identify where future growth should occur. The policy directs new development into areas where adequate facilities and services exist. The plan also defines "adequate urban services," setting standards for availability, funding, operations, and conformance with public objectives. In the case of police protection, for example, patrol routes must be within two minutes' response time of development areas. These standards serve to identify areas suitable for further growth, and, significantly, help *limit* such development to those areas.

The plan divides the Boulder Valley into three zones along the growth continuum. Area I consists of the existing city, while Area III encompasses the remote lands, mostly unincorporated, where services are not expected to be established within the next 15 years. Area II includes those lands where services are expected to come on line, and where growth should occur. Annexation by the city and a city capital improvements program implement this growth policy, and encourage development upon annexation in Area II.

The city imposes a one-time-only development excise tax on developers that pays for providing services in the redevelopment or annexed area. This tax pays for services like police, streets, and park improvements.

FORMALIZING COLLABORATIVE CO-GOVERNMENT PLANNING

In 1978, the city and county entered into an intergovernmental agreement formalizing the coordination of planning activities between the jurisdictions. The agreement specifically requires the county to approve any changes to the Comprehensive Plan, annexations, and capital improvement programs proposed by the city. A mutual referral process allows each jurisdiction to review proposals put forth by the other.

The county reinforces the urban services area concept contained in the Comprehensive Plan by enforcing land use regulations that severely limit rural growth and by not providing urban services or facilities. Municipalities, not the county, are given responsibility for providing urban services, thereby preventing sprawl and fragmented "leapfrog remote development" that so often occur in unincorporated areas elsewhere.

County Measures

The county has its own farmland and open space protection program that complements that of the city of Boulder. County zoning and subdivision regulations severely hinder development outside urban service areas. In the forestry and agricultural districts covering much of the county, density is limited to one unit per 35 acres.

The county's nonurban planned-unit-development (NUPUD) program rewards clustered design and donation of open space easements with additional density. Under this program, the owner of a 35-acre parcel can obtain an additional unit in exchange for clustering on 25 percent of the space and maintaining the rest in agricultural or open space use. In mountainous areas, the regulations limit net density to one unit per 35 acres, and allows clustering on parcels of at least 70 acres.

Although on a smaller scale than the city of Boulder, the county has actively acquired open space, which it funds through a $1 million annual allocation from general revenues. In keeping with the county's principle of not providing urban services, it manages county open space for passive uses, rather than active recreational parks.

Experience

CITY OPEN SPACE PROGRAM

About 22,000 acres of open space have been acquired, most in fee simple, and some through the purchase of development rights. Future efforts are likely to focus to the east of the city, where municipally owned open space is thinnest. Friendly negotiations between owners and the city have dominated the acquisition process, although the threat of eminent domain has proved a useful tool at times.

ANNUAL PERMIT RESTRICTIONS

Over time, Boulder's 2 percent growth cap has rounded the peaks off the boom part of the city's boom-and-bust development cycle. In recent years, Boulder's growth has slowed so much that the annual caps on building permits have not been a real factor in regulating the issuance of building permits.

Critics claim that the program has driven up the local cost of housing. This claim has been disputed by longtime local planners, who point to the parallel rise of Denver housing costs. Downtown revitalization has been enhanced because a large portion of the annual permits has been set aside for construction in the core downtown area.

COUNTY NUPUD PROGRAM

About 50 different tracts of land have been approved for development under the NUPUD program, and the results appear to effectively preserve open space and active farmland. The clustered developments do not appear to obstruct farm operations.

Conclusion

Boulder's charm has attracted new businesses and residents for many years. Early on, citizens of the county, and particularly residents of the city of Boulder, have taken steps to ensure that this strong growth pressure does not overwhelm the county's distinctive character and open spaces. The process of managing the county's growth has been unending, and Boulder's unique success is in no small part due to the decisive collaboration between jurisdictions, and unrelenting commitment through the years to trying something new and then refining it over time.

CONTACTS

Office of Real Estate/Open Space
City of Boulder
1101 Arapahoe, Second Floor
P.O. Box 791
Boulder, CO 80306

Department of Community Planning and
Development
City of Boulder
1739 Broadway
Room 305
Boulder, CO 80302

PROFILE

PENINSULA OPEN SPACE TRUST

Effective Land Trust Action

Mission/Key Objectives

The mission of the Peninsula Open Space Trust (POST) is the preservation of the visual beauty of the San Francisco Peninsula landscape. The trust protects land for agriculture, recreation, wildlife habitat, and natural resource protection. POST accomplishes its objectives through:

- Acquisition (and subsequent resale with conservation restrictions);
- Consultation with private landowners on stewardship techniques and finances;
- Facilitation of negotiations to conserve parcels; and
- Recreational use development.

POST monitors land use legislation, but does not involve itself in zoning or other political issues related to land use. The organization maintains ties with land trusts throughout California and the nation, and communicates with its constituency through its quarterly newsletter, *Landscapes*.

Geographic Scope

POST's efforts encompass lands in San Mateo and Santa Clara counties on the San Francisco Peninsula. The organization concentrates on rural and undeveloped lands, especially visually important ridgelands. Priorities include:

- The Skyline Scenic Corridor;
- The San Francisco Baylands;
- The San Mateo Coast; and
- Rural lands adjacent to the high-growth areas of Santa Clara County.

Success Stories

Since 1977, POST has helped to preserve more than 20,000 acres of open land on the peninsula. POST has acquired approximately 4,900 of these acres and facilitated the conservation of the remainder. Here are descriptions of a few of POST's projects:

- A gift of 537 acres on Windy Hill in Portola Valley, in 1979, was the first major gift of land to POST. In 1981, POST collected $70,000 for construction of the eight-mile Windy Hill Trail on the property and supervised more than 100 volunteers who helped with the work. In 1987, a 430-acre addition to the preserve was made possible by POST's work with a landowner and the regional open space agency.
- In October 1987, POST purchased its largest and, arguably, most important acquisition, Cowell Ranch—1,270 acres of coastal property south of Half Moon Bay, which extends from the shore across the grassy ridges east of Highway 1. Conservation of the nearly two miles of beach and rolling hills is critical to avoid a continuous string of development similar to that on the San Francisco Bay side of the peninsula and to protect the coastal greenbelt, maintain agricultural operations, and provide public access. The price tag on the property is $6.7 million and POST's initial goal to raise $2 million in donations for a down payment was realized within six months. Of the remainder, $2.5 million was obtained by a matching challenge grant, and $2.2 million through a loan, both from the S. H. Cowell Foundation. POST hopes to sell conservation easements to the California State Coastal Conservancy and sell the protected land to farming interests.
- In 1987, POST received a gift of 112 acres in the La Honda watershed. This property offers a splendid

vantage point overlooking the mountains to the west. The protection of this area precludes development or logging that could degrade the upper watershed of La Honda Creek. Later the same year, POST sold the property at below market value to the Midpeninsula Regional Open Space District to add to their La Honda Creek Open Space Preserve.

Organizational Structure

POST is governed by a ten-member Board of Trustees, two of whom are appointed by officials of the Midpeninsula Regional Open Space District. The board meets monthly and has a Nominating Committee, a Fund Development Committee, and a Finance Committee. The board is assisted by an Advisory Council, with 30 members from such diverse backgrounds as law, real estate development, local government, finance, engineering, and environmental affairs.

The POST staff consists of four full-time employees (executive director, land counselor, fund development director, and administrative assistant) and two part-time employees (editor and bookkeeper).

Financial Characteristics

POST is funded by gifts from individuals, by grants from foundations, and by the sale of donated and purchased land. POST's annual operating budget is approximately $350,000 to $375,000. Since its founding in 1977, approximately 1,900 individuals have contributed to POST. About 700 donors give on an annual basis.

As of February 1988, POST's Revolving Land Acquisition Fund had net assets of more than $6 million, with the major portion in landholdings.

CONTACT

Executive Director
Peninsula Open Space Trust
3000 Sand Hill Road, Building 4, Suite 135
Menlo Park, CA 94025

PROFILE

GREENBELT ALLIANCE

Acting Regionally

Mission/Key Objectives

The Greenbelt Alliance (formerly called People for Open Space) is a 30-year-old nonprofit organization concerned with the regional planning and open space needs of the San Francisco Bay Area. Based on the premise that the region's health and economy and the well-being of its residents are directly linked to environmental quality, the Greenbelt Alliance pursues protection of the Bay Area's Greenbelt, that is, its system of farmland and other productive open space around the metropolitan area. As part of this effort, the organization is concerned with maintaining the quality of the urban environment, dealing with citizens' concerns about traffic, housing, and carelessly planned growth in the metropolitan area. The organization conducts research and education programs, works with local and regional civic and governmental leaders, and advocates policies that carry out its goals.

Geographic Scope

The activities of the Greenbelt Alliance cover nine counties in the San Francisco Bay Area. This area includes nearly 4 million acres of productive agricultural, watershed, recreational, and other critical lands.

The pattern of growth in the Bay Area has changed in recent years. Instead of concentrated population in a few compact central cities, development is sprawling far from previous development centers onto what were farm and pasturelands. At the current rate, the Greenbelt Alliance claims that most of the farmland will be lost within 40 years. As a regional organization, the Alliance is in a position to coordinate local decisions responsible for this trend, decisions that separately

may have little impact, but together, are changing the face of the Bay Area.

Success Stories

- The Greenbelt Alliance initiated and sponsored a referendum to approve a $225 million bond issue for regional open space acquisition. In November 1988, voters in the East Bay counties approved the bond issue for the East Bay Regional Parks District by a two-thirds majority.

- In 1986, the Greenbelt Alliance galvanized public support for the East Bay Regional Parks District's acquisition of Pleasanton Ridge, a 9,200-acre grassy hilltop that was also being eyed by a nearby town for annexation. Members wrote letters, lobbied, and brought citizens to hike on the ridge overlooking the Livermore Valley to see for themselves the resource at risk.

- In an effort to open up access for recreation to San Francisco watershed lands, the Alliance is in the process of creating the Bay Area Ridge Trail. This trail will eventually be several hundred miles long, circling the Bay Area's Greenbelt. The Greenbelt Alliance is sponsoring this effort, which is spearheaded by the Bay Areas Trail Council, a public-private partnership of nearly three dozen agencies and nonprofits.

- The organization publishes educational reports and videotapes on the resources of the Bay Area and citizens' guides to protecting them. For example, it recently produced *Treasures of the Greenbelt*, a 30-minute film on open space in the Bay Area, seen by over 400,000 people on regional public television. It also publishes a quarterly newsletter, *Greenbelt Action*, to keep members informed of relevant news and events in the Bay Area.

- The Greenbelt Alliance addresses housing and transportation issues. Its 1984 publication *Room Enough* pioneered a long-term view of reconciling regional housing and open space needs. This book proposed five strategies for meeting the region's housing needs without converting open space. As a follow-up, its "Future of the Metropolis" program is answering questions about the location of business centers, affordable and compact housing, and transit and road systems.

Organizational Structure

People for Open Space was formed in 1958 by a few concerned citizens to challenge a proposed sale of public watershed lands in Contra Costa County. The organization has since grown to 2,900 members.

Financial Characteristics

In 1988, Greenbelt Alliance had an annual budget of nearly $550,000. The majority of the organization's income came from grants, contributions, membership dues, and events.

CONTACT

Greenbelt Alliance
116 New Montgomery, Suite 640
San Francisco, CA 94105

INFORMATION RESOURCES

Hoose, Philip M. *Building An Ark: Tools for the Preservation of Natural Diversity Through Land Protection.* Covelo, CA: Island Press, 1981.

Provides an overview of means available to private organizations to preserve open space and important wildlife and plant resources. Includes chapters on inventorying natural heritage resources as well as specific management techniques.

Leedy, Daniel L., Robert M. Maestro, and Thomas M. Franklin. *Planning for Wildlife in Cities and Sub-*

urbs. Planning Advisory Service Report No. 331. Chicago, IL: American Society of Planning Officials, 1978.

Provides an introduction to the ways in which urban and suburban planners can incorporate wildlife considerations, drawn from accepted wildlife management principles, into the planning process.

Greenbelt Alliance (formerly People for Open Space). *Tools for the Greenbelt: A Citizen's Guide to Protecting Open Space.* San Francisco, CA: People for Open Space/Greenbelt Congress, 1985.

This is a handbook written for local open space activists. Provides an introduction to the land use planning process, techniques for preserving open space (including police power, public land acquisition, and private options), and provides case studies of two communities' efforts to preserve open space.

Rails-to-Trails Conservancy. *Converting Rails to Trails: A Citizens' Manual for Transforming Abandoned Rail Corridors into Multipurpose Public Paths.* Washington, D.C., 1987. (Available from Conservancy at 1325 Massachusetts Avenue, N.W., Washington, D.C. 20005.)

Provides grass-roots groups basic information and organizing techniques needed to convert abandoned railroad rights-of-way into trails.

Thurow, Charles, William Tones, and Duncan Erley. *Performance Controls for Sensitive Lands: A Practical Guide for Local Administrators.* Report Nos. 307, 308. Chicago, IL: American Society of Planning Officials, 1975.

Provides an introduction to performance standard controls as a means of protecting rivers and streams, wetlands, aquifers, hillsides, and woodlands. Includes numerous examples of local performance standard programs and ordinance language.

Housing

Myers, Phyllis. *Aging in Place: Strategies to Help the Elderly Stay in Revitalizing Neighborhoods.* Washington, D.C.: The Conservation Foundation, 1982.

Discusses several regulatory and nonregulatory techniques to retain and improve housing opportunities for the elderly.

NAHB National Research Center. *Affordable Housing, Challenge and Response.* Vol. 1, *Affordable Residential Land Development: A Guide for Local Government and Developers.* Washington, D.C.: U.S. Department of Housing and Urban Development, Innovating Technology and Special Projects Division (July 1987). Contact Affordable Housing Clearinghouse, c/o HUD USER, Box 280, Germantown, MD 20874.

This publication is a product of HUD's Joint Venture for Affordable Housing. It reports the results from housing demonstration projects undertaken in 27 cities to show how local governments and developers can cooperate to reduce the cost of housing. Separate illustrated sections discuss how local standards for site planning, streets, parking, sidewalks, curbs and gutters, storm drainage systems, sanitary sewers, and utilities can be modified to reduce the housing costs.

Nutt-Powell, Thomas E. *Manufactured Homes: Making Sense of a Housing Opportunity.* Chicago: American Planning Association, 1982.

Everything you always wanted to know about manufactured housing.

People for Open Space. *Room Enough: Housing and Open Space in the Bay Area.* The Report of the Housing/Greenbelt Program. San Francisco, CA: People for Open Space/Greenbelt Congress, 1983.

Examines growth and housing trends in the San Francisco Bay Area. Shows how traditional development patterns are destroying the region's functional open space greenbelt. Suggests strategies for accommodating housing and open space. An excellent local publication.

Sanders, Welford. *Regulating Manufactured Housing.* Planners Advisory Service Report No. 398. Chicago: American Planning Association, 1986.

Discusses development control options for manufactured housing. Explains considerations in drafting local regulations.

Sanders, Welford, et al. *Affordable Single-Family Housing: A Review of Development Standards.* Planners Advisory Service Report No. 385. Chicago: American Planning Association, 1984.

Discusses land use regulations to encourage affordable single-family houses. Includes case studies and sample ordinance language.

Weitz, Stevenson. *Affordable Housing: How Local Regulatory Improvements Can Help.* Washington, D.C.: U.S. Department of Housing and Urban De-velopment, 1982. Contact Affordable Housing Clearinghouse, c/o HUD USER, Box 280, Germantown, MD 20874.

Describes how local governments can reduce housing costs by updating land use regulations and streamlining procedures.

ORGANIZATIONAL RESOURCES

Land Trust Exchange

The Land Trust Exchange aids local land conservation groups to gain access to specialized land preservation expertise and serves as a clearinghouse on private land protection efforts and techniques. 1017 Duke Street, Alexandria, VA 22314; (703) 683-7778.

National Recreation and Parks Association

The National Recreation and Parks Association undertakes research and education in the fields related to parks management and improvement, recreation programs, and recreation facilities. Park Center Drive, Alexandria, VA 22302; (703) 820-4940.

The Nature Conservancy

The Nature Conservancy identifies, acquires, and manages lands critical to threatened and endangered ecosystems or plant or animal species. 1800 Kent Street, Suite 800, Arlington, VA 22209; (703) 841-5300.

Rails-to-Trails Conservancy

The Rails-to-Trails Conservancy is a national organization that aids local governments and organizations convert abandoned railroad rights-of-ways into public recreational trails. 1710 K Street, N.W., Suite 304, Washington, D.C. 20006; (202) 659-8520.

Trust for Public Land

The Trust for Public Land is a nonprofit land acquisition organization that works with community groups, landowners, and public land management agencies to preserve land for public use. The trust helps community groups and local governments acquire urban, rural, recreational, scenic, and agricultural land. 82 Second Street, San Francisco, CA 94105; (415) 495-4014.

CHAPTER 6

Starting and Managing a Nonprofit Corporation

🏠 🌲 🏛

WHAT DOES IT MEAN TO INCORPORATE?

WHAT DOES IT MEAN TO BE A NONPROFIT
CORPORATION?

STEPS FOR INCORPORATION

OBTAINING FEDERAL TAX-EXEMPT STATUS
Exempt from Which Taxes?
The Importance of Federal Tax Exemption
Filing for Tax-Exempt Status

QUALIFYING FOR TAX EXEMPTION

LIMITATIONS ON NONPROFIT POLITICAL ACTIVITY

THE SPECIAL ROLE OF LAND TRUSTS

EFFECTIVE SELECTION AND USE OF BOARDS OF
DIRECTORS
Choosing a Board
How Many Directors Are Needed?
Length of Terms
The Use of Committees
The Effective Use of Board Meetings

IDENTIFYING MISSIONS, OBJECTIVES, AND
STRATEGIES
The Statement of Mission
The Benefits of Planning

MAKING EFFECTIVE USE OF VOLUNTEERS
Recruiting Volunteers
Keeping Volunteers

Think globally, act locally.
— RENE DUBOIS

UNDERSTANDING the basic growth management framework and how growth management techniques can be used to protect and enhance specific community assets and resources is important. But determined action by concerned citizens—developing and building support for a vision of the future of the community, understanding the land development process, participating effectively in land use decisions, negotiating with local officials and developers, and creating a local organization to advocate and assist in implementing growth management strategies—often makes the critical difference in creating a successful community.

Coordinated action by a formal association, coalition of associations, or a nonprofit corporation generally is more effective than even the most accomplished individual action. Forming a nonprofit corporation helps to channel energy and expertise beyond the immediate crisis that often brings people together, attracts and retains interest among a diverse group, and provides the foundation for a long-term presence.

State and local quality-of-life organizations take many forms. They may be research and advocacy organizations that lobby for local growth management initiatives. The MSM Regional Council in New Jersey and the Greenbelt Alliance in California are noteworthy examples. They may be "watchdog" groups that participate regularly in local planning and regulatory decisions and strategically use litigation to further their objectives. Groups like 1,000 Friends of Oregon and the recently formed 1,000 Friends of Florida play this role effectively. They might also be foundations that focus public attention and funds on specific local assets, or land trusts that work with major landowners and benefactors to acquire and preserve key parcels. Over 800 land trusts exist throughout the country, several of which are discussed in this guidebook, including the Vermont Land Trust and the Brandywine Conservancy in Pennsylvania. (See profiles of some of the key groups that have made a difference at the end of chapter 7.)

How can a nonprofit organization—a quality-of-life lobby—organize to become an effective force for constructive change in a community? How can concerned citizens most effectively participate in the land use process?

There are some key advantages to and requirements for incorporating a nonprofit association and obtaining tax-exempt status for the new entity. There are also several issues to address in maintaining one over time. These are true whether a group of citizens seeks to form and maintain a nonprofit resource protection organization, a quality-of-life advocacy group, or a land trust.

What Does It Mean to Incorporate?

The term "corporation" simply denotes the existence of a separate legal entity or a "legal person" that can enter into contractual relationships, incur debt, and pay taxes. Incorporation is a convenient device for people pursuing a common objective, since it provides limited liability for corporate directors, officers, and employees. Limited liability means that, in most circumstances, the personal property of the corporation's directors, officers, and employees will not be reached to satisfy corporate debts. This protection is essential in persuading people to engage in potentially risky pursuits, such as bringing lawsuits or acquiring and managing real property. Incorporation also provides an effective and permanent operating structure, outlasting the individuals who formed it.

What Does It Mean to Be a Nonprofit Corporation?

Given the public and charitable purposes they serve, local quality-of-life lobbies, resource protection organizations, and land trusts are frequently incorporated as nonprofit (or in some states not-for-profit) organiza-

---

The information in this chapter is advisory in nature and does not satisfy the need for a citizen group seeking to establish a tax-exempt organization to obtain legal counsel. It is comprised, in part, of material reprinted by permission of the California State Coastal Conservancy from: Stephen F. Harper, *The Nonprofit Primer: A Guidebook for Land Trusts* (Oakland, Calif.: California State Coastal Conservancy, 1984).

139

tions. To be "nonprofit" does not mean a corporation cannot make money. Rather, it simply limits the uses to which corporate funds and property can be devoted. A nonprofit corporation can, in fact, realize a profit in the sense that its income may exceed its operating expenses. As distinct from for-profit corporations, however, nonprofits must devote all their revenues, including any "profit," to their charitable purpose; they may not distribute any excess revenues to their members.

Steps for Incorporation

State law governs the incorporation requirements for nonprofit corporations. The procedures and requirements vary considerably from state to state; but the basic steps are fairly uniform. Incorporation is a fairly straightforward process that can be undertaken by one or more persons, called the "incorporator(s)." The basic steps are as follows:

1. *Filing articles of incorporation.* Typically filed with the secretary of state's office, this document specifies the purposes for which the corporation is formed, the name of the prospective corporation, and other information about the corporation and the incorporators.

2. *Establishing a board of directors.* A board of directors is responsible for the overall management of the nonprofit corporation.

3. *Drafting corporate bylaws.* This is the instrument that governs the mechanics of operating a nonprofit corporation—such as dates and times for meetings; whether directors will be compensated and, if so, how much; provisions for hiring staff; and what kinds of transactions directors can carry out between themselves and the corporation.

Obtaining Federal Tax-Exempt Status

The operations of all corporations, both for-profit and not-for-profit, are subject to both state and federal laws, including federal tax laws. The federal income tax laws set forth requirements for nonprofit corporations to obtain tax-exempt status.

EXEMPT FROM WHICH TAXES?

Obtaining tax exemption is important since an organization's tax status can materially affect its real estate and fund-raising operations. State and local income and property tax exemptions often require federal tax exemption. There are three basic taxes from which a nonprofit corporation will want to obtain exemption:

1. Federal income tax;
2. State income tax; and
3. Local property tax.

THE IMPORTANCE OF FEDERAL TAX EXEMPTION

Section 501(c)(3) of the Internal Revenue Code (IRC) is the most common provision under which local nonprofit citizen organizations or land trusts seek federal income tax exemption. Obtaining tax exemption under IRC Section 501(c)(3) is critical, since it provides other benefits in addition to income tax exemption, including:

- Eligibility to receive tax-deductible charitable gifts under IRC Section 170;
- Exemption from federal employment taxes;
- Likelihood of similar exemption from state and local taxes; and
- Bulk postage rate privileges.

FILING FOR TAX-EXEMPT STATUS

To obtain tax-exempt status under IRC Section 501(c)(3), a nonprofit corporation should obtain copies of Form 1023 (the exemption application) and Publication 557 (instructions for filling it out) from a local IRS office. The completed application must be accompanied by a certified copy of the corporation's articles of incorporation and a copy of its bylaws adopted at the first directors' meeting. An attorney experienced in nonprofit incorporation should review the application before submission, to help prevent a negative determination by the IRS.

Qualifying for Tax Exemption

To qualify for tax-exempt status, a corporation must be organized and operated exclusively for "exempt purposes." Such purposes may include scientific, educational, and charitable endeavors. The corporation's net earnings may not be distributed to its directors, members, or any individual. The corporation must comply with restrictions placed upon lobbying and other political activities.

There are two types of tax-exempt organizations: public charities and private foundations. In filing for tax-exempt status, a corporation should avoid being classified by the IRS as a private foundation. While private foundations themselves are exempt from taxation, they do not offer the tax deductions to potential donors that public charities offer. To qualify as a public charity, a nonprofit corporation must meet the public support test in IRC Section 170(b)(1)(A)(vi). An organization is considered to be publicly supported if it normally receives a substantial portion of its total support from a variety of public or governmental contributions.

Another way for a nonprofit corporation to obtain tax-exempt status is for the corporation to be a satellite corporation under IRC Section 509(a)(3). To qualify as a satellite, the corporation must be operated, supervised, or controlled by one or more public charities or a governmental entity. An organization that operates as a satellite usually does so by having a majority of its board appointed by the governing body of another qualified charity or a unit of government.

Limitations on Nonprofit Political Activity

Although time and energy impose the only significant limits on individual lobbying activities, the Internal Revenue Code (IRC) imposes substantial limitations on the lobbying activities of nonprofit tax-exempt corporations. These limitations allow a nonprofit corporation to engage in limited political activity without placing its tax-exempt status in jeopardy.

The Internal Revenue Code distinguishes between two types of political activity: lobbying to influence legislation and intervening in political campaigns. Tax-exempt organizations are completely banned from participating in political campaigns. In contrast, a nonprofit corporation "may engage in insubstantial lobbying" activity attempting to influence legislation. The corporation will be denied tax-exempt status only if a "substantial part" of its activities consists of attempting to influence legislation.

Because this "substantial part" test does not create a clear, objective standard, many tax-exempt organizations elect to have their lobbying activities regulated by the objective standards of IRC Sections 501(h) and 4911. These sections set forth limits for lobbying expenditures and grass-roots expenditures. (See Information Resources on page 151–152.)

"Lobbying expenditures" (as defined in IRC section 4911) means "expenditures for the purpose of influencing legislation." An organization may spend a specified amount of its total expenditures (or its "exempt purpose expenditures," as the IRC phrases it) on direct lobbying without incurring penalty. This amount, called the "lobbying nontaxable amount," al-

lows a tax-exempt corporation whose total expenditures are not over $500,000 to spend up to 20 percent of its expenditures on non-candidate-related lobbying. This percentage decreases as total expenditures of the nonprofit organization exceed $500,000.*

"Grass roots expenditures" means "any attempt to influence any legislation through an attempt to affect the opinions of the general public or any segment thereof." The "Grass Roots Nontaxable Amount" (i.e., the amount an organization is permitted to spend on indirect efforts to influence legislation through grass roots lobbying) is 25 percent of that organization's lobbying nontaxable amount for a given taxable year.

If an organization elects to be governed by the provisions of Section 501(h) and 4911, and it exceeds the limitations imposed for lobbying or grass-roots expenditures, it does not lose tax-exempt status, but must pay an excise tax of 25 percent of the amount of excess lobbying or grass-roots expenditures for that taxable year. An organization will not lose its exempt status unless it "normally" makes lobbying or grass-roots expenditures in excess of 150 percent of the amount of lobbying nontaxable expenditures or of grass-roots nontaxable expenditures allowed that organization for each tax year.

The Special Role of Land Trusts

There are many varieties of nonprofit conservation and growth management organizations. However, for groups interested in acquiring and managing critical lands, the local land trust or conservancy provides one of the most effective organizational formats. Although not a substitute for governmental land use controls and land acquisition, private land trusts can be critical complements to governmental action. There are currently over 800 local land trusts nationwide; about half are entirely run by volunteers, with an annual budget of less than $10,000. As demonstrated by many success stories throughout the country, land trusts can provide the local leadership, commitment, and flexibility essential to local resource protection and growth management efforts.

Land trusts are private, tax-exempt, nonprofit corporations that basically seek to preserve land through real estate transactions such as land acquisition and other private means. They vary in geographic scope, degree of professionalism, and the types of land resources they seek to preserve.

As private organizations, land trusts have certain advantages over government agencies. They can:

_____
* See IRC Section 4911(c).

- Act quickly and efficiently to preserve land in a timely fashion;
- Enjoy a cooperative working relationship with private landowners who may be wary of dealing with a municipal agency;
- Provide continuity of management and concern for critical resources, often with less political influence than municipal agencies; and
- Acquire property at a lower cost by taking advantage of tax-deductible charitable contributions.

As tax-exempt nonprofit corporations, they:

- Can provide personal liability protection to their board members;
- Enjoy exemption from federal and state income tax (and perhaps from local property tax), and, when conveying property to public agencies, real estate transfer taxes; and
- Accord income, estate, and gift tax deductions to persons making qualified donations.

By acquiring land or interests in land, land trusts can:

- Preserve lands or provide public recreational access to lands;
- Provide responsible long-term stewardship of important resources; and
- Help public agencies acquire land on a time- and cost-effective basis through preacquisition and resale.

In addition, land trusts with a community orientation and focus:

- Provide local initiative for resource protection;
- Maintain the tradition of private land ownership through easements and other less than full fee acquisition techniques; and
- Help increase local awareness and support for resource stewardship.

Effective Selection and Use of Boards of Directors

The choice of a board of directors and the effective use of their time and talents are perhaps the most important tasks a new nonprofit corporation must face. This is especially true for land trusts, which must be active in fund-raising, land acquisition, land stewardship,

and other functions that require a high-level of board involvement.

The fundamental duties of a board of directors of a nonprofit corporation are to establish organizational objectives and policies, monitor progress toward meeting those objectives and policies, and, where resources permit, select an executive director to oversee day-to-day operations. As part of this process, nonprofit boards should engage in explicit long-term planning. Daily implementation of policy and objectives is the function of officers and staff, or members of the board if there is no permanent staff. Boards are also responsible for setting substantive strategies, fundraising, publicity, internal and external dispute resolution, legal affairs, and community relations.

Where staffing is possible, nonprofit corporations must carefully clarify the respective roles of board and staff. This will avoid confusion and potential morale problems. Directors should be active and involved and should set a firm course for the organization to follow. However, too much board involvement in daily decision-making can stifle creativity and leadership—two qualities most needed in a nonprofit's staff.

CHOOSING A BOARD

The principal attributes to seek in constituting a board of directors for a nonprofit organization have been distilled in the "three Ws":

Work;

Wisdom;

Wealth.

Potential directors should be evaluated in terms of these criteria. Everyone called to membership should offer at least one of these attributes. Even if wise and wealthy, however, a board prospect will be of little help unless he or she is willing and able to work.

In light of the varied responsibilities directors must undertake, it is important to marshal a diverse board. A board also should represent diverse elements of the community if the organization is to be seen as a community-based group. Look for businessmen, lawyers, community leaders, large landowners, representatives of other community groups, potential donors, civil engineers, public relations experts, and land development experts. Look also for problem-solvers able to work with people with different points of view.

HOW MANY DIRECTORS ARE NEEDED?

The size of a nonprofit's board is typically specified in the corporate bylaws. Choosing the right number is an important and delicate task. A minimum number of board members is necessary to assemble the diversity of skills and backgrounds, and to allow a fair distribution of responsibilities. The wider the geographic scope and the broader the substantive agenda, the larger the board should be.

On a spectrum from a very small board on one extreme to a very large one on the other, some general advantages and disadvantages of either direction are:

Small Board	Large Board
Advantages	*Advantages*
Efficient communications	Broadly representative
Efficient policy-making	Talent-rich
Sense of shared purpose	Division of labor
Disadvantages	*Disadvantages*
Underrepresentation	Inefficient action
Talent-poor	Unwieldy policy-making
Overworked	

Two potentially useful approaches are to establish a board with a minimum number of members and to augment this board by creating an advisory committee, or to establish a large board, with a small active executive committee to handle priority matters.

In composing a board for a new organization, not all available slots need to be filled immediately. Many nonprofits have started with directors whose abilities are most known, and let them—over a period of time—identify and enroll the additional directors necessary to fill out the board.

LENGTH OF TERMS

Experience and a track record of service are invaluable assets in a director. However, new blood can help an organization, bringing in new approaches, ideas, and energy. Each organization must balance these competing principles. Many have chosen to include in their bylaws a limitation of, for example, two consecutive terms of service. This permits regular addition of new board members and the subsequent reinvolvement of especially valuable former directors. Keeping the latter active on an advisory committee can be very helpful. Staggered terms also achieve continuity while bringing in new talent.

THE USE OF COMMITTEES

Two types of committees may be useful. First, it may be helpful to create standing committees within the board itself as a way of formally distributing responsibilities. These might include an executive commit-

tee, to act between board meetings on behalf of the larger board; a committee on fund-raising; a personnel committee (for organizations that have a staff); and a committee for each major substantive area of interest. These committees can be useful, but care should be taken to avoid fragmentation that can divide the board and affect its morale and sense of purpose. The *ad hoc* appointment of committees or task forces to handle specific issues may be more workable for small organizations.

Second, a local nonprofit corporation might augment its board by establishing an advisory committee. By doing so, it may draw upon a large fund of talent, without creating a cumbersome board. Although an advisory committee may play no formal governing role, it can improve the organization's decision-making, credibility, and stature. Such a committee can also serve as a training ground for prospective directors and a useful way to involve ex-directors.

THE EFFECTIVE USE OF BOARD MEETINGS

Board meetings can make or break an organization. The keys to any good meeting include:

- A good agenda;
- An efficient leader; and
- A meeting place conducive to productivity.

An agenda should be drafted and mailed to the board well before the meeting. Relevant staff members (if any) should attend, both to promote board familiarity with staff and to encourage staff leadership. Each staff person should present issues and accomplishments for which they have had responsibility.

The president or board chairperson should take responsibility for keeping discussion on track and avoiding unnecessary diversions.

Many nonprofit corporations find it effective to reserve one session each year, perhaps in a retreat format, solely for purposes of long-term planning and budget approval.

Identifying Missions, Objectives, and Strategies

All organizations operate upon a foundation of missions, objectives, and strategies. An organization's mission is the purpose an organization was founded to serve; the objectives are the more concrete accomplishments that the group seeks to achieve as part of promoting its mission; and strategies are the specific means chosen to realize those objectives.

THE STATEMENT OF MISSION

Local quality-of-life lobbies often organize around a specific crisis or individual resource. These circumstances will largely determine the group's initial mission statement; however, a visionary and ambitious mission statement can lead to broader and deeper support. Although the mission should be relatively stable over time, there is no reason why it should not evolve as circumstances and the organization itself change. If the initial mission was narrowly drawn, the board should consider restating the mission more broadly. On the other hand, the board must guard against setting an overly ambitious agenda and creating unrealistic expectations.

THE BENEFITS OF PLANNING

A nonprofit organization best identifies its mission, objectives, and strategies through organizational planning. Just as a successful community bases its actions on a comprehensive plan, and a successful businessman generally develops a business plan, so should a successful nonprofit corporation develop a focused operating plan. Effective planning can increase organizational productivity. Since local nonprofits depend upon volunteer directors and tight budgets, focus and a concern for productivity will help to lighten the burdens volunteers must bear and yield more results for the money. Moreover, planning will enhance an organization's ability to get results, increasing credibility with potential donors and local officials. A plan also provides a clear sense of mission and helps an organization evaluate its progress toward fulfilling that mission.

Planning is one of the principal responsibilities of the board of directors. If the organization has a staff, however, it should be a joint effort of board and staff, since staff plays the critical implementation role. Two types of planning should be developed: annual plans and long-range plans, perhaps with a five-year horizon. Both should be updated yearly. In planning, board members and staff should review:

- The organization's mission and objectives;
- The organization's programs;
- Last year's accomplishments and failures;
- New objectives on both the one-year and long-range horizons;
- The strategies and resources necessary to meet those objectives; and
- The division of labor among board, staff, and volunteers.

The product of this planning process should be an operating plan to guide next year's actions. Objectives should be listed in order of priority. Where possible, each objective should be quantified (e.g., "accept five conservation easements") to help in evaluating progress. Identify the strategies for accomplishing each objective to ensure that the objectives are realistic.

Organizational planning is necessary but not sufficient if the group is to succeed; effective implementation is the measure of success. At each meeting, the board should review the organization's progress toward each objective.

Making Effective Use of Volunteers

Local nonprofit organizations vary greatly in the scope of their mission, the geographic scope of their focus, the amount and sources of their financial support, and in many other ways. One constant, however, is dependence upon the creative energies of volunteers. Effective volunteer recruitment and management is, therefore, critical. Like any important resource, volunteers must be carefully cultivated, nurtured, and conserved.

Despite an instinctive commitment to volunteerism, nonprofit boards of directors (they are themselves, after all, volunteers) may hesitate to commit an organization to the extensive use of volunteers. Some of the principal reasons for hesitance include:

- Potential liability;
- Board-volunteer relations;
- Staff-volunteer relations; and
- Supervisory demands.

The liability risks associated with volunteer programs are real and potentially serious. The most basic advice is to rely on a twofold strategy of prevention and insurance. Prevention is, in part, accomplished by avoiding unduly risky assignments and by providing adequate volunteer training. Even with careful preventive measures taken, accidents do happen and, therefore, a nonprofit organization should carry adequate liability insurance.

The staff-volunteer and board-volunteer issues are also important. There are several suggestions to keep in mind in preventing poor organizational relationships: (1) ensure that staff members work effectively with, and do not feel threatened by, volunteers; (2) involve staff in volunteer training and recruitment; and (3) use retreats and other social functions to improve relationships.

The problem of volunteer supervision and oversight is one of the most important facing any nonprofit. Although the needs will depend on the specific project and task involved, adequate attention to training and supervision will vastly increase the benefits a nonprofit yields from undertaking a volunteer-oriented approach.

The following suggestions can improve volunteer supervision:

- Treat volunteer training and orientation as investments that will yield a more effective volunteer program;
- Carefully select volunteer supervisors for their knowledge, their carefulness, and their ability to work with others;
- Involve staff or volunteer supervisors in developing the volunteer program and in selecting volunteers;
- Carefully define both supervisory and volunteer roles, and encourage communication between those in each capacity;
- Designate a volunteer coordinator from among the board or volunteer cadre, and make that person a focal point for issues concerning volunteers; and
- Include a thorough evaluation of the volunteer program as part of the regular organizational evaluation process.

RECRUITING VOLUNTEERS

There are many avenues available for volunteer recruitment. Before marshaling the troops, however, bear in mind that:

- Not all program activities lend themselves to volunteer participation;
- The recruitment of volunteers should be guided by the nonprofit's overall program priorities (i.e., use the volunteers where they are most needed); and
- Volunteers should not be recruited until there is a program in place for training, using, and supervising them.

Once these concerns are satisfied, actual recruitment can proceed. The basic recruitment task of getting the word out can be done through newspaper notices; flyers placed on bulletin boards in public buildings, high school or college classroom buildings, senior citizen centers, supermarkets, and so forth; flyers mailed with local utility bills (a local utility may consider this a useful public relations avenue for

them); and public service radio or cable television spots. A nonprofit also may consider exchanging volunteer lists with other local groups with similar objectives. All of the publicity mechanisms discussed later in this chapter can be used for volunteer recruitment as well.

Screening volunteer candidates is important. Prospective candidates should be interviewed by a board member or volunteer coordinator. Ask for references if the task at hand is sensitive or difficult. While the objective is not to discourage volunteers, it is important to recognize that one "bad" volunteer can materially harm the track record and effectiveness of any nonprofit organization.

KEEPING VOLUNTEERS

Although some turnover among volunteers can be productive, too much turnover can be detrimental. Successful recruitment does not guarantee success in the task of maintaining volunteer resources. The following suggestions will, however, serve a nonprofit well as a guide to volunteer management:

- Cultivate a feeling of "belongingness," in part by helping volunteers understand the nonprofit's mission, objectives, and programs, and by making them feel part of its accomplishments;
- Assign volunteer duties on the basis of mutual accommodation, not by compulsion, and disperse or rotate the menial or otherwise undesirable assignments frequently;
- Keep good time records and avoid overworking or underworking anyone; and
- Develop a mechanism for recognizing and thanking dedicated volunteers. Even though volunteers in any nonprofit activity are generally motivated by the cause itself, a program of volunteer recognition can help meet a natural human need and inspire further volunteer contributions.

Recognizing the contributions of volunteers can make up for the lack of material benefits. Some of the means of rewarding volunteers include:

- Certificates, awards, plaques;
- Banquets, dinners, receptions, or other ceremonial and social functions in their honor;
- Reimbursements for out-of-pocket expenses;
- Recognition through local media;
- Recognition by community, civic, or political leaders, preferably in writing;

- The opportunity to lead or chair an important activity or meeting;
- "Merit badges," T-shirts, pins, caps, bumper stickers, or other products advertising their contribution (especially for young volunteers); and
- A personal word of thanks from the board chair.

Making Effective Use of Consultants

Volunteer-based nonprofit organizations may require expertise not available among the group's members or volunteers (such as to conduct a wetlands delineation or a traffic analysis). After deciding to hire a consultant, attention must be paid to proper selection and management of the appropriate consultant to avoid the potential problems that may arise in such relationships.

It often requires experience to know when to hire a consultant and when to undertake a task "in house"; however, the following tasks generally call for consultant assistance:

- Projects in which independent expertise would lend credibility to the project;
- Time-consuming projects that will not be repeated soon enough to justify hiring new staff;
- Projects requiring specialized expertise not available on a group's board, staff, or among its volunteers; and
- Specific tasks requiring sustained attention or specialized expertise.[1]

"Consultants" come in many guises and may not always advertise themselves as such. Once a decision has been made to retain a consultant, likely places to look for the most appropriate one include:

- Professional consulting firms specializing in the type of services required;
- Independent consultants providing similar services, typically at lower cost due to lower overhead expenses;
- Large nonprofit organizations such as the American Farmland Trust, Partners for Livable Places, the Land Trust Exchange, the National Trust for Historic Preservation (especially its Main Street Program), the National League of Cities, the American Planning Association, or state or local organizations;
- Government agencies such as the city planning or engineering department, the county agricultural extension office, the county or state forester, the state historic preservation office, the state department of environmental protection, the U.S. Soil Conservation Service, or the National Park Service;
- University or college faculty (either in their official capacity or as independent consultants) and/or graduate students that may assist as part of their formal educational program or informally in, for example, planning, engineering, architecture, cartography, biology, forestry, or soil science departments.

There are many ways to find the best consultant for the task. Perhaps the most effective informal approach is to get references from other, similar groups. A more formal approach, warranted by a long-term or high-cost project, is to prepare and distribute a detailed request-for-proposals (RFP). An RFP can identify consultants with a proven track record on similar projects. The RFP can also produce new approaches to the task not thought of by the group. A compromise between these two approaches is to distribute an informal RFP to a relatively small list of consultants known to be qualified to undertake the project.

Simply issuing an RFP does not solve the search problem, however. An ambiguous or poorly written RFP may create misunderstandings about the task and cause qualified consultants not to respond. The "table of contents" for an RFP might contain the following:

- Summary of the project and the consulting services being sought;
- Detailed description of the project;
- Detailed description of the services required;
- Type of contract (e.g., fixed price or time and expenses);
- Minimum qualifications sought from consultants;
- Evaluation criteria and procedures;
- Instructions for submission of proposals (including address and deadline); and
- Name of contact person in the organization to whom questions should be addressed.[2]

Written proposals should demonstrate an understanding of the nature of the work and the tasks involved. Proposals should include an estimate or bid on the project cost, preferably separate from the substantive proposal itself. This facilitates separate consideration of the two issues of proposal quality and cost.

A team within the organization should review each proposal to assess the consultant's understanding of the organization and the project, the thoughtfulness of the proposal, and the consultant's apparent ability to deliver the appropriate product. The consultants submitting the best proposals should be invited to interview. Because an individual, not a proposal or even a firm, will be hired, it is important to obtain explicit commitments that those who interview will perform or actively supervise all work.

Cost is usually inappropriate as the sole criterion for selecting a consultant. Only where the project is entirely ministerial or mechanical (in which case an RFP probably is not necessary) should cost be an overarching factor. What should be sought is value—quality services at a competitive cost.

MANAGING THE CONSULTANT'S WORK

Once a consultant has been selected and a project begins, attention shifts to ensuring project success. The point of departure for managing the consultant's work is a written contract agreed to at project commencement. Typical contract provisions include:

- Scope of services;
- Project schedule;
- Compensation, including method and timing of payments;
- Progress reporting requirements; and
- Methods of resolving cost overruns and disputes.

Potentially troublesome contingencies should be resolved at this point, rather than left for later. Beyond the management foundation provided by a carefully drawn and discussed contract, the following points will help ensure a productive relationship with the consultant:

- Establish clear lines of communication between one contact person within the organization and the consultant or the project manager for the consultant;
- Make sure that all instructions to the consultant are unambiguously articulated and consistent with the contract;
- Negotiate a work plan with the consultant, laying out all interim deadlines and reporting requirements;
- Avoid meetings when a telephone conference call will suffice; and
- Provide adequate written feedback on the quality and timeliness of the consultant's work.

Successful Publicity Strategies ─────────

Achieving a nonprofit organization's mission requires substantial financial and volunteer resources. An effective publicity program is necessary to garner the necessary public support. A successful publicity strategy requires familiarity with the various local media. With such knowledge, a local nonprofit organization can effectively target its publicity efforts.

The most important publicity avenues include:

- *Electronic Media*
  Radio/TV talk shows
  Public service spots
  Video documentaries
- *Print Media*
  Newspaper and magazine articles
  Editorials
  Letters to the editor
  Company newsletters
  Newspaper and magazine advertisements
  Transit ads
- *In-House Media*
  Newsletters
  Annual reports
  Brochures
  Flyers/handouts/fact sheets
  Logos
- *Other Mechanisms*
  News releases
  Press conferences
  Speakers' bureaus

Working successfully with the media requires sensitivity to their needs. Under severe time pressure, newspeople tend to screen out anything that does not entail a "newsworthy" event or happening. To be newsworthy, it should be concrete, out of the ordinary, and understandable to the average person. In increasing the newsworthiness of your event or story, think of the following questions:

- Is the public invited?
- Is the event or story different from other community events?
- Are the speakers or their subject of special interest?
- Is there anything particularly unusual or distinctive associated with the story?[3]

A nonprofit organization should cultivate friendly relationships with local newspeople and educate them about its purposes and methods. An important requirement for cultivating a beneficial relationship with the local media, however, is to develop a reputation (either collectively, or through individual directors or staff) as a credible source of information on local conservation and growth management topics. In this way, reporters and others may come to need you as much as you need them.

A local organization may consider creating a publicity committee to coordinate publicity efforts. This committee could direct the preparation and distribution of news releases; prepare and distribute literature; coordinate a community speakers' bureau; bring in outside speakers; and prepare and distribute newsletters and annual reports.

SELECTING THE APPROACH

Given the variety of media and ways of getting information out about an organization and its activities, it is important to tailor the publicity approach to the desired outcome.

News conferences and releases. Local nonprofit organizations may find it useful to employ press conferences as a publicity device. Press conferences are appropriate only for especially newsworthy events. A more traditional publicity tool is the news release. In preparing a news release, keep in mind the following suggestions:

- Prepare the release so it is easily usable—triple-space and use wide margins, put a contact person and phone number at the top.

- Work with local media to determine their format and timing preferences.

- Briefly present all crucial information in the release—who, what, where, why—the release itself may become the news article, with little or no editing.

- If the organization has been working with a particular reporter, send the release to him or her, in addition to the editor.

- Quote directors, prominent supporters, and/or local officials in the text of the release.

- Time a release far enough in advance of an event so there is time for follow-up questions, but not so far in advance that the event is forgotten.

Public service announcements and advertising. Public service advertising consists of time and space that is contributed to an organization free of charge as a public service. While the FCC no longer requires stations to provide time for public service announcements or advertising, most still do as a service to the community. Since competition for air time is fierce, a good rapport with local television or radio representatives is important. They must fully understand and support an organization's program before they will provide free air time. Contact the radio and television stations in your area for information on their public service programs. If necessary, meet with their public affairs representative to describe your program and get

your announcement approved for airing. Be sure to stress the benefits to the community resulting from your efforts.

Local public affairs programs. Local public affairs programs include talk shows, commentaries, political programs, and similar programs concerning local or regional public affairs. Identify such programs in your media area and contact those responsible for the show with an explanation of your organization and the topics you consider newsworthy. Supply as much background information as possible.

Editorials and letters to the editor. Nonprofit organizations can use their local newspapers to establish a credible reputation in their community. One of the best ways to do this is to have board members and prominent supporters write editorials and letters to the editor on issues of concern to the organization.

Annual reports and newsletters. Annual reports and newsletters are effective ways to communicate with members, volunteers, prospective supporters, and the press. Properly designed and written, an annual report can be both informative and inspiring, and can become a useful marketing device. An annual report should contain:

- The report of the president or executive director on the group's accomplishments and goals;

- A focus on each program element or significant accomplishment;

- A highlight on volunteer and staff contributions;

- A highlight of major benefactors—individuals, corporations, and foundations; and

- A summary of the group's audit or financial status.

A newsletter is a useful way to inform both members and nonmembers, and to involve other groups and members by encouraging contributions to each issue. Given the financial and time demands required to publish a credible newsletter, an organization should not feel obligated to publish an issue until it has something worthwhile to write.

Brochures. A nonprofit organization should consider publishing promotional brochures, including a general membership brochure and brochures describing the objectives and accomplishments of each program. These need to be updated periodically.

Nonprofit Fund-raising

Most nonprofit activists are more interested in the substantive work for which their organization was created than in raising money. While the substance is more rewarding, fund-raising makes that substance—and the organization itself—possible.

One standard description of nonprofit fund-raising is that it is "90 percent research and cultivation, only 10 percent asking." "Cultivation" means the process of contacting, educating, persuading, and cajoling potential donors to support a project or program. Systematic research and cultivation is critical for obtaining philanthropic support.

Both research and cultivation entail considerable time and attention to detail. The best way to manage this burden is to go about the task as efficiently as possible. The following steps will promote efficiency:

- Establish fund-raising goals (perhaps linked to the organization's projects);
- Establish a fund-raising strategy;
- Organize a research process;
- Develop contacts and a cultivation process for each contact; and
- Follow through with focused and well-written proposals.

Beyond using a systematic fund-raising approach, the following suggestions will ease fund-raising:

- *Obtain tax-exempt status.* While *ad hoc* groups can raise money, it is easier if the group forms a tax-exempt nonprofit corporation. This will also allow donors to deduct donations.
- *Know what you need.* Before asking for money, determine how much money you need and for what purposes—a specific project, general operations, an endowment, or land acquisition.
- *People give to people.* However meritorious your cause, money flows to those whom donors know and respect. Select a diverse board of directors and advisory committee, including at least several members with communitywide recognition and respect. Representation from the local business sector can be particularly helpful.
- *Know thy prospect.* Carefully target potential donors and tailor your request to meet their specific interests and patterns of giving.
- *Fund-raising is salesmanship.* Know your product and be prepared to sell it to a potential funder. Don't be sheepish: you are giving funders an opportunity to contribute to a vital cause and to be a partner with a successful organization.
- *Write thoughtful proposals.* Proposals should be clear, to the point, organized, and persuasive.
- *Emphasize your accomplishments.* An existing or-

ganization should stress its record of accomplishments. New groups should emphasize the qualities and experience of the board members and, if possible, obtain formal endorsements from prominent local citizens and organizations.

- *Broaden your support.* Do not limit yourself to standard private or public grants. Broaden your support base to include membership, in-kind contributions from local businesses, fund-raising events, and benefits. The broader your support, the more secure you will be.
- *Use fund-raising for publicity.* Use fund-raising to increase your group's visibility. Greater visibility in turn enhances fund-raising efforts. New grants should be announced; membership campaigns widely touted; and events publicized. You may have to spend a little to earn more.

WHERE TO GET FUND-RAISING INFORMATION

A nonprofit fund-raising campaign should involve compiling information on potential benefactors to identify those whose interests correspond with the group's mission and needs. To those new to the nonprofit world this can be a time-consuming and confusing task.

Many nonprofit organizations rely upon foundation grants to provide operating funds. The best foundations to approach are those who in the past have funded similar organizations or projects. The most comprehensive data on private foundations is available through the Foundation Center, either directly at their San Francisco office, or through their publications at your local library.[4] The center's publications identify foundations by: (1) subject interest (i.e., which causes particular foundations support); (2) type of grant, whether for operating, endowment, property acquisition, or other purposes; and (3) geographic location, both where they are headquartered and where they give. Useful Foundation Center publications include:

- *The Foundation Directory.* Includes data on the 3,363 largest U.S. foundations, focusing on their location, purpose, financial resources, grant amounts, staff or contact person, and trustee. It is indexed by field of interest, geographic location, name, donors, and trustees;
- *National Data Book.* Similar to *The Foundation Directory,* this resource provides data on 22,000 U.S. foundations.
- *COMSEARCH printouts.* Available by subject category, these identify all grants of more than $5,000 made by over 500 U.S. foundations.

Sources of information about corporate and government funding prospects are listed in the Information Resources and Organizational Resources sections at the end of the chapter.

MEMBERSHIP AND INDIVIDUAL SUPPORT

Most local nonprofit organizations rely largely upon membership and other individual support. Indeed, individual donations comprise nearly 90 percent of all charitable money received in the United States.

One of the perennial questions faced by local nonprofit corporations is whether to be a "membership" organization. The term "member" suffers from some ambiguity: in a legal sense, a "member" of a nonprofit organization has a formal role in its governance. Many nonprofits have "members" in the common sense of the term (i.e., supporters who pay annual dues) without having "members" in the legal sense. These groups simply find it easier and more meaningful to designate such contributors as "members" rather than "supporters."

Legal "members" have a role somewhat analogous to the stockholders of a publicly held for-profit corporation in that they have a policy-making voice through the ability to vote on matters of importance. Many nonprofits consider this to be an unnecessary organizational burden, preferring governance to vest solely in their board of directors, and provide for "members," but specify in the bylaws that they are nonvoting members.

Building a Membership Base
Building a membership base, particularly for local nonprofits unable to invest in an expensive direct mail campaign, can be a laborious process. The benefit is that a strong membership base provides a stable, long-term source of support that can help an organization through times when other funding sources dry up.

Many groups, both local and national, maintain more than one category of membership. By designating multiple categories, each associated with a different giving level, the nonprofit encourages giving over and above the basic dues amount. Donors above some threshold should receive special treatment and recognition, and a special plaque or print may be appropriate for these donors. In part, this is a matter of simple courtesy; more practically, it reinforces the donor's identification with the organization.

Prospect lists, mailing lists, multiple membership categories, thank you notes—all of these elements of building a membership base suggest formalizing the process. Indeed, one of the most effective ways to approach membership fund-raising is to undertake a formal membership campaign. The establishment of

explicit fund-raising goals helps to energize and motivate a group.

The task of approaching prospective members is a key element of a membership campaign. The most common approach is with an introductory letter and personal follow-up. The appeal letter should be short and direct. People are more likely to support a specific project or activity than an abstract cause; therefore, the letter should stress tangible projects. Everyone receives direct mail appeals; use the effective ones as models. An introductory letter can be greatly improved by including a brochure describing the organization and reprints of news articles highlighting the group's accomplishments. Introductory letters should include return-addressed envelopes.

Target mailings to select groups may be possible. National or regional nonprofit organizations use large direct mail campaigns to build membership rolls. Typically, these campaigns are designed and run by professionals in direct mail techniques. Small local groups, looking to build a stable, but smaller, narrower constituency, are probably best advised to stick with the more modest mailing approaches. More sophisticated and well-funded organizations will find it productive to consult periodically with a professional.

Membership Benefits
In return for their support, members expect to receive benefits. Some nonprofits use their newsletter to serve this function. Some form of recognition might also be used, such as a certificate of membership. Start with only one or a few modest membership benefits. It is easier to start small and add more, rather than to raise expectations, cut back, and disappoint people.

BEQUESTS

A promising form of individual philanthropy is the giving of bequests. The fastest-growing category of giving today, bequests can be a useful avenue for building organizational independence, particularly through the establishment of an endowment. Bequest campaigning is, however, a sophisticated and sensitive type of fund-raising. Generally, bequests come only to organizations that have built considerable visibility and a stable reputation. The best bequest campaigns are developed in close coordination with estate lawyers, bank trust officers, and others experienced in such matters.

GIFT CATALOGS

Catalogs describing items needed by the organizations to prompt potential donors are an innovative fund-raising tool that has been used effectively by many nonprofits and public agencies. Catalogs meet benefactors' preferences for giving specific, tangible gifts; put into writing the organization's major physical needs; facilitate solicitation by describing the group's needs in a single document that can be presented to potential supporters; and give donors the opportunity to select specific contributions for which they can feel personally responsible.

FUND-RAISING EVENTS

One of the most promising fund-raising techniques for small or new nonprofit organizations is a fund-raising event. The list of events that can be profitable as fundraisers is limited only by one's imagination. Some frequently used examples include:

- Dinners/barbecues;
- Auctions;
- Runs/bicycle tours/walk-a-thons;
- Bake sales or tag sales;
- Festivals/carnivals;
- Raffles;
- Concerts/dances;
- Art/photography contests; and
- Poster or T-shirt sales.

It is helpful to favor events that have some intrinsic relationship to the organization's mission. Many conservation nonprofits have developed "river festivals" or "valley days" or other appropriate celebrations to raise both money and public awareness. These events raise money directly—at the time of the event itself—as well as indirectly, by increasing organizational visibility, membership, and contributions.

The following suggestions should prove useful in planning a fund-raising event:

- *Choose a profitable event.* The best event is one yielding a large *net* return. Maximize revenue, minimize expense. This is common sense, but many groups look only at potential revenues in choosing an event and neglect to consider expenses.
- *Be creative.* Pick a unique event or unique theme. This will stimulate interest, both within the organization and in the media.
- *Plan well in advance.* This is especially true if it is a new event. Repeat events improve planning and logistical efficiency.
- *Don't reinvent the wheel.* Talk with other organizations that have done a similar event before.
- *Count on Murphy's Law.* Anything that can go

wrong, will. Have fallback plans, extra supplies and volunteers, and rain-date plans.

- *Publicize.* Without a thorough publicity strategy, all planning and logistical arrangements are wasted.
- *Pick a prominent chairman.* Find a highly visible community leader to serve as honorary chairperson for the event. Attempt to get free entertainment from a prominent local entertainer.
- *Marshal volunteers.* The best way to ensure volunteer participation is to involve people in choosing and planning the event. Successful volunteer motivation depends upon making people feel part of the overall effort and making the process fun.
- *Send invitations.* Individually invite people in addition to the usual supporters of the organization. Target the best potential supporters.
- *Say "Thank you."* Immediately after the event, publicize the success, and formally thank all donors and volunteers. A simple letter will suffice.
- *Keep good records.* Throughout planning and executing an event, keep track of money, time, and problems. This will make the next event run better.

INFORMATION RESOURCES

Connors, Tracy D., ed. *Planning for a Change: A Citizen's Guide to Creative Planning and Program Development.* Boulder, CO: VOLUNTEER: The National Center for Citizen Involvement.

Davis, Barbara H. "How and Why to Hire a Consultant." In the Grantsmanship Center: *Whole Nonprofit Catalog* (Winter 1987): 7–9.

Flanagan, Joan. *The Grassroots Fundraising Book. How to Raise Money in Your Community.* Boulder, CO: VOLUNTEER: The National Center for Citizen Involvement.

Gil, Efraim, Enid Lucchesi, Gilbert Tauber, and Dudley Onderdonk. *Working with Consultants.* Report No. 378. Chicago: American Planning Association Planning Advisory Service.

Written for local land use planners, this short report provides useful suggestions on deciding whether or not hiring a consultant is appropriate, choosing the best available consultant, and managing a consultant's work once a project is underway.

The Grantsmanship Center. *Whole Nonprofit Catalog.* Los Angeles, CA: The Grantsmanship Center.

A free quarterly catalog providing articles on subjects related to fund-raising and nonprofit management, as well as advertisements for consulting and other technical assistance services available for nonprofits.

Gurin, Maurice G. *What Volunteers Should Know for Successful Fundraising*. Boulder, CO: VOLUNTEER: The National Center for Citizen Involvement.

Hanlon, Brenda, ed. *The Best of "Voluntary Action Leadership."* Boulder, CO: VOLUNTEER: The National Center for Citizen Involvement.

Internal Revenue Service. The Internal Revenue Service publishes several publications useful for tax-exempt organizations. These publications are available at minimal or no cost from the Internal Revenue Service by calling the tax information number listed in your local telephone book under "United States Government, Internal Revenue Service." The more helpful publications include:

1. *Tax-Exempt Status for Your Organization* (Publication 557, January 1982). Every tax-exempt organization should obtain a copy of this detailed, 40-page pamphlet. It contains practical instructions and detailed explanations of various legal issues.
2. *Charitable Contributions* (Publication 526, November 1981).
3. *Tax on Unrelated Business Income of Exempt Organizations* (Publication 598, September 1981).
4. *Determining the Value of Donated Property* (Publication 561, November 1981).
5. *Sales and Other Dispositions of Assets* (Publication 544, November 1981).
6. *Basis of Assets* (Publication 551, November 1981).

Land Trust Exchange. *National Directory of Conservation Land Trusts*. Alexandria, VA: Land Trust Exchange, 1989.

This book gives useful information about each of the several hundred land trusts operating throughout the country.

————. *National Directory of Local and Regional Land Conservation Organizations*. Alexandria, VA: Land Trust Exchange.

Lists land trusts and other local and regional land conservation organizations. Information on each organization includes address, contact name, types of land they protect, and their level of activity.

————. *Why Form a Land Trust*. Alexandria, VA: Land Trust Exchange.

A short report highlighting the necessity for, and role and history of, land trusts.

Wolfe, Joan. *Making Things Happen: The Guide for Members of Volunteer Organizations*. Andover, MA: Brick House Publishing Company, 1981.

A brief discussion of key organizational concerns for effective volunteer organizing.

ORGANIZATIONAL RESOURCES

Foundation Center
312 Sutter Street, San Francisco, CA 94108
(415) 397-0903

This organization publishes a range of information about charitable foundations and their grant-making policies and practices including *The Foundation Directory*.

The Grantsmanship Center
650 South Spring Street, Suite 507, Los Angeles, CA 90014
(213) 689-9222

The Grantsmanship Center publishes *Researching Foundations: How to Identify Those That May Support Your Organization; Grantsmanship Center News*, a bimonthly publication on fund-raising techniques; and *Exploring the Elusive World of Corporate Giving*.

Land Trust Exchange
1017 Duke Street, Alexandria, VA 22314
(703) 683-7778
The Land Trust Exchange provides a broad range of technical assistance and services to local and regional land trusts and land conservation groups. It publishes *Land Trusts' Exchange*, a periodical with useful information for local land conservation groups.

CHAPTER 7

Seizing the Initiative

GET A SEAT AT THE TABLE

BE FAMILIAR WITH GROWTH MANAGEMENT TOOLS

STATEWIDE GROWTH MANAGEMENT PROGRAMS

PLANNERS CAN OFTEN BE YOUR BEST FRIENDS

DON'T BE INTIMIDATED BY LEGAL LIMITATIONS

UNDERSTAND THE REAL ESTATE MARKET
    Walk a Mile in a Developer's Shoes

NEGOTIATE FROM STRENGTH

RECOGNIZE THAT THE PROCESS IS POLITICAL

ABOVE ALL ELSE, CREATE A VISION FOR YOUR
  COMMUNITY'S FUTURE

PROFILES
    1,000 Friends of Oregon
    MSM Regional Council, New Jersey
    The Vermont Land Trust
    California Coastal Conservancy

INFORMATION RESOURCES

Development is not a job of building roads into lovely country,
but of building receptivity into the still unlovely human mind.
—ALDO LEOPOLD

ARTICLES in the mass media about land use controversies typically highlight the polarization that characterizes many conflicts. As these disputes play themselves out, often over many years, the "solution" may be described as a victory for one side, a bitter defeat for the other. The divisive forces acting on both proponents and opponents of a real estate development project can be powerful; getting beyond them requires both will and creativity.

Alternative scenarios can and have been written, however. In a growing number of communities, developers and citizens' groups have worked out creative solutions that serve the interests of both. Part of the impetus for such creativity on the part of developers is the realization that public opposition to a proposal is capable of delaying permit approval long enough to tip the economic feasibility of the project in a negative direction. Savvy developers are thus alert to public sentiment and opportunities to increase their prospects for prompt project approval. Their willingness to be flexible may be considerable, especially in the early stages of a project before substantial investments in design, marketing research, and engineering have been made.

For citizens, the impetus for seeking creative solutions is often the realization that simple opposition to every proposal can limit long-term effectiveness. As one planner has noted:

> By being so unrelentingly hostile to marks of man, the simon pures are boxing themselves out of an effective role. They can't talk alternatives. They may say they're not against growth, that all they want is to protect the particular resource that is threatened by a particular project, but the truth is that they are incapable of seeing any site as suitable for development.[1]

The interplay of residents, local officials, and sophisticated developers can lead to creative solutions to land use problems and to the forging of a shared vision for a community's future. Armed with an understanding of how developers think and a willingness to identify and pursue creative alternatives to protracted conflict—either before a local planning body or in the courts—a citizen or local group can play a critical role in the local land use decision-making process. At times, it may be appropriate to approach a developer early in the development process to ensure quality development or to find a creative solution to an undesirable proposal. At other times, it may be appropriate to initiate broad policy negotiations to create a shared vision for the future of the community. In any event, several general principles should be kept in mind to increase the effectiveness of citizen participation and the chances for achieving successful communities.

While each action requires different skills and responses, political acumen, thorough preparation, and good humor are all necessary ingredients for successful citizen involvement. Similarly, energy, ability to commit time, and persistence are common traits for effective participation in land use decisions.

Beyond these traits, knowing when and how to oppose a proposal, to negotiate over one, or to work cooperatively to forge a vision requires sensitivity to several factors. Specifically, it requires a basic familiarity with the technical and legal aspects of growth management, negotiating skills, and a willingness, at times, to search with opponents for creative solutions. An understanding of how the real estate market functions and an appreciation for how developers think and operate are also important. Above all, effective citizen action requires an awareness that politics underlies all major land use decisions and the development of an inspiring yet attainable vision for the community's future.

Get a Seat at the Table

Effective participation in local land use decision-making first requires that citizens who care about their community actively participate in local processes and that their views be considered by those with power to make decisions, such as local officials, state highway department officials, landowners, and developers. Creating a vision for the future of the community and taking actions to implement that vision will be futile unless those with power agree with—or at least consider—the expressed views. These views may be

154

expressed at a variety of different forums—or tables—including negotiations, presentations at business or civic group meetings, testimony at public hearings, lawsuits, or elections.

The degree to which citizens who care about managing local growth get a seat at the table when land use decisions are made and the extent to which their views are considered and followed depend upon several factors. Political clout, the soundness of the position, the persuasiveness with which the position is articulated, legal doctrines, organizational and financial resources, access to the media, and the ability to press legal claims are among them.

Various incentives exist within growth management processes for citizens to participate and have their views carefully considered. If not given a seat at the table, citizens can cause delays, increases in expenditures, and perhaps the undoing of decisions. Recourse to the courts and the ballot box through initiatives, binding and nonbinding referenda, and recall movements can create risks, political turmoil, and financial costs for local officials who engage in arbitrary land use actions.

Frustrated by a lack of willingness among developers and county officials to consider their views, citizens in Orange County, California, for example, put their case forward to the voters on a June 1988 land use ballot initiative. Though the measure ultimately failed in a hard-fought campaign, it caused the views of these citizens to be taken much more seriously by the other interests in the county. Similarly, local officials and builders took notice in November 1988, when voters on Cape Cod, Massachusetts, overwhelmingly approved a nonbinding referendum to impose a one-year, Cape-wide development moratorium.

While getting a seat at the table can be difficult, the more complex task involves knowing what to do once you have gained that seat. Citizens can make a critical mistake by failing to recognize the need to change tactics once they have earned a position in the decision-making process and are sitting at the table with decision-makers.

Whether in hostile or more hospitable places, impassioned advocates need to recognize when to make the transition from outsiders seeking attention to constructive partners in community land use efforts. Once an individual or organization is recognized as a legitimate player in reaching and implementing local land use decisions and has obtained a seat at the table where decisions are made, different tactics and skills will likely be more effective in getting the desired results. Skillful participants, therefore, must know when to change—and, in fact, be able to change—tactics.

Be Familiar with Growth Management Tools

The process of managing community growth involves land use planning and a host of other growth management techniques, including regulations, taxing and spending measures, and land acquisition. Numerous decision-making points and players are involved. Although the theory behind growth management tools can be very different from the realities of how they are applied, an understanding of their objectives and the processes for implementing them can increase the effectiveness of concerned citizens.

Some growth management techniques are more complicated to understand than others; some may be relatively simple to conceptualize but require tremendous staff sophistication and resources to implement effectively. There are as many kinds of plans and planning processes as there are zones and taxes, with each having direct consequences for potential land uses and ultimately the way an area looks, functions, and feels.

Involved citizens can generally rely on professionals for explaining various growth management tools—floating zones, tax credits, conservation easements, for example—and how they might be applicable in specific situations. Some familiarity with the various methods for managing growth can, however, increase citizen effectiveness and, at a minimum, allow citizens to ask the right kinds of questions about a proposed development or local government action. Appendix A contains a primer describing the most widely-used growth management tools; Appendix B looks at the federal tax benefits that can encourage local land conservation efforts.

Sometimes strong technical tools and consensus for using them at the community level can be hampered by activities outside the local jurisdiction. A county, for example, may be trying to encourage growth into a neighboring unincorporated area. This may attract commercial activity away from an established community and degrade important resources. A state might decide to build roads or facilities in ways and locations that undermine local efforts.

Statewide Growth Management Programs

Several states—including Oregon, Florida, New Jersey, Maine, Rhode Island, Vermont, and Georgia—have attempted to provide localities with a comprehensive framework for managing growth and protecting key assets. These programs have met with

varying degrees of success, but all offer promise and have proven important in building awareness and strengthening local capabilities to manage growth. Following a relatively quiet period after much activity at the state level in the 1970s, there has been a recent resurgence of interest in state growth management programs. Since the mid-1980s, several eastern states have either developed new programs or refined existing ones.

OREGON

Oregon's comprehensive statewide land use management program was established by Senate Bill 100, the Land Use Act of 1973.[2] Protection of the state's agricultural and other sensitive natural lands was a prime motivation behind the program. The act established the Land Conservation and Development Commission (LCDC), which was charged with formulating state-

wide planning goals and policies. By 1975, LCDC had established some 15 goals, including ones concerning agricultural land, open space, urban growth, forestry, and housing.

Following the adoption of state goals, cities and counties had to develop comprehensive plans and implement development regulations consistent with the state goals and policies. As part of this, local governments also delineated boundaries of areas appropriate for future urban growth and those that are to remain rural for a 20-year planning period. State agencies were also required to adopt plans consistent with state goals, subject to review by the LCDC.

The delegation of authority within the program—with local planning and zoning regulations guided by general statewide goals and objectives and subject to state approval—has become a model for programs in other states, including Maine, Georgia, New Jersey, and Maryland's Critical Area Program.

By most accounts, Oregon's program has been effective in providing a consistent framework for local growth management efforts.[3] The program has received consistent and increasing public support in a series of statewide referenda. A statewide nonprofit land use organization, 1,000 Friends of Oregon, which is profiled below, has been instrumental in improving the program's effectiveness, building a constituency for it, and bringing about consistency among various levels of government.

VERMONT

Vermont's Act 250, the Land Use and Development Law,[4] was enacted in 1972, in response to rapid growth and particularly to second-home development. It established a program of direct state development permitting to protect Vermont's environment. Under Act 250, the State Environmental Board reviews all projects that are likely to have a greater than local impact.

Act 250 had mixed results and largely focused on controlling the development of scattered second-home projects through permit review. Moreover, the program operated without a statewide planning component. Recognizing the shortcomings of enforcing state land use regulations with no planning program, Governor Madeleine Kunin established the Governor's Commission on Vermont's Future in 1987 and gave it responsibility for making recommendations on how Vermont can improve its growth management. The commission issued its report, "Guidelines for Growth," at the end of 1987, recommending changes in Act 250 as well as other state actions to improve Vermont's ability to control and direct growth. In 1988, the recommendations went through the legislative process and became the foundation for new growth management legislation.

The new legislation—called Act 200—does not require towns to develop comprehensive plans. Rather, a middle course was chosen: the state provides technical and financial assistance to local governments for planning. Access to the state's Geographic Information System (GIS) is conditioned upon local planning. Cooperating local plans must be consistent with regional plans. In turn, regional plans must be consistent with state guidelines. State agency actions must also be consistent with regional plans.

In addition to encouraging local comprehensive planning, Act 200 contained noteworthy funding inducements for a wide constituency: it allotted $20 million to the Vermont Housing and Land Conservation Trust Fund; created a milk price subsidy; and implemented a 95 percent tax relief program for working farms. The legislature also increased the state's real estate transfer tax, with the proceeds to be divided between funding local and regional planning efforts and supporting the Vermont Housing and Land Conservation Trust Fund.

FLORIDA

Florida has enacted a series of increasingly ambitious growth management statutes. In 1972, the state enacted the Environmental Land and Water Management Act, which established critical area and development of regional impact (DRI) regulatory programs. These programs apply state oversight to a limited number of development proposals or a limited geographic area.* The state experience in both programs, however, was important to the later expansion of the state role in the 1980s.[5]

In 1975, the state enacted the Local Government Comprehensive Planning Act. This statute required all cities and counties in the state to adopt comprehensive plans, but provided for little state review.

In 1984 and 1985, as a result of continuing rapid growth, increasing traffic congestion, and inadequate infrastructure, Florida passed new legislation requiring local governments to adopt comprehensive plans and development regulations. These local plans are reviewed by the state for consistency with the state plan. Communities that refuse to bring their policies into conformance with the state plan face financial sanctions. The legislation also provides great latitude for citizens to challenge plans in administrative hearings and to appeal plans to the governor and Cabinet.

Perhaps the most significant state policy requires "infrastructure concurrency": no new development will be approved until and unless the necessary public facilities are in place to serve the development. The legislation also requires the state's 11 regional planning councils to develop Comprehensive Regional Policy Plans to implement the state plan. These regional plans are the basis for review of developments of regional impact. State agencies must also adopt "functional plans" to implement the state plan.[6]

Following Oregon's experience, a new group—1,000 Friends of Florida—has been formed to ensure that the state's growth management program is enforced and that a broad constituency exists for its success.

---

* In the critical area program, a particular geographic area can be selected for special management attention, including review and approval of local land use plans and regulations within the critical area and review and modification of local development permits. The Florida Development of Regional Impact Program applies to development projects meeting certain threshold sizes and characteristics. State-established regional planning councils review local government development permits for these projects, with the review being somewhat similar to an environmental impact statement.

NEW JERSEY

New Jersey, the nation's most densely populated state, has for years grappled with the consequences of urban and suburban sprawl. In 1986, the state legislature passed the State Planning Act, creating the New Jersey State Planning Commission and its staff arm, the Office of State Planning. The Office of State Planning was placed within the Department of the Treasury, which is seen is neither pro- nor anti-development, to help demonstrate the relationship between state planning and spending. The commission has prepared a State Development and Redevelopment Plan to provide an integrated and comprehensive plan for the state's development and conservation needs. The plan establishes planning objectives for land use, housing, economic development, transportation, natural resources, conservation, agriculture, farmland retention, recreation, urban and suburban redevelopment, historic preservation, public facilities and services, and intergovernmental coordination.

An innovative aspect of New Jersey's law is a process called "cross-acceptance." Cross-acceptance is defined as a "process of comparison of planning policies among governmental levels with the purpose of attaining compatibility among local, county, and state plans." The act requires the proposed state plan and land use map to be submitted to the counties and municipalities to negotiate cross-acceptance of the plan. Consistency between state and local plans is to be achieved through these negotiations between state and local officials.

Localities are not absolutely required to prepare plans that conform to the state plan, but the commission is authorized to withhold state highway, transit, sewer, water, park, and open space spending in localities that do not bring their local policies into conformance with the state plan. The state plan also contemplates enforcement of the plan through its environmental permitting.

RHODE ISLAND

In 1988, Rhode Island adopted the Rhode Island Comprehensive Planning and Land Use Regulation Act. This statute requires each municipality to adopt a local comprehensive land use plan "which relates development to land capability, protects our natural resources, promotes a balance of housing choices, encourages economic development, preserves and protects our open space, recreational, historic, and cultural resources and provides for orderly provision of facilities and services." Within one year of plan adoption, municipalities must bring their land use regulations into conformance with the plan. Munici-

palities must also adopt a capital improvements program to ensure that adequate public facilities exist for the anticipated development. These plans must include elements for land use, housing, economic development, natural and cultural resources, services and facilities, open space and recreation, and circulation.

Local plans are reviewed by the state division of planning for consistency with the state plan. The division of planning will write a plan for a community that fails to adopt an acceptable local plan.

MAINE

Maine also adopted comprehensive statewide land use planning legislation in 1988. The Maine Comprehensive Planning and Land Use Regulation Act, based on the Oregon model, has three major components.

First, the statute creates statewide land use goals "to provide overall direction and consistency to the planning and regulatory actions of all state and municipal agencies affecting natural resource management, land use and development."

Second, the law mandates local comprehensive planning and growth management programs. Localities must submit their plans and programs to the newly created Office of Comprehensive Land Use Planning to be reviewed for consistency with state goals and policies. As in New Jersey, the penalty for a community's failure to adopt a certified local growth management program within the mandated time frame is denial of funds to the locality under various planning, open space acquisition, and community development block grant programs. Local plans must include an inventory and analysis of local and regional resources; a policy development section that relates the findings of the inventory and analysis to the state goals; and an implementation strategy that includes a timetable for implementation. The guidelines in the statute are rather specific: each municipality must establish growth areas and rural areas and policies to implement this distinction; a capital investment plan; ordinances and policies to protect water quality, natural resources, access to coastal waters, agricultural and forestry resources, historic and archaeological resources, access to outdoor recreational opportunities, and to ensure that local policies encourage the provision of affordable housing within the community.

Third, the state provides technical and financial assistance, and local training to assist localities in implementing the program. In addition, the program creates an innovative municipal legal defense fund, in which the state attorney general assists municipalities with the defense of approved local land use ordinances.

Concerned citizens need to be aware of the opportunities provided by applicable regional and state programs and help their communities capitalize on them. In places where states and regional governments are not active, citizens should work with various interests to seek support—be it legislative, administrative, financial, or technical—from these levels of government for their activities.

Planners Can Often Be Your Best Friends _____

Buried in the planning offices of most localities will often be a concerned citizen's best friend. These people may be known kindred spirits or so overwhelmed by the day-to-day tasks confronting them that they are difficult to reach. Nevertheless, local planning officials care deeply about the quality of life in their communities. They are trained in and comfortable with setting goals and objectives for the area and developing a vision for its future. It would be a serious mistake for concerned citizens to not seek them out and develop strong working relationships with them.

Beyond helping to develop a broad community vision and consensus, local planners realize that there are creative alternatives to yes/no decisions on specific applications for development approval. The increasing use of techniques such as performance standards, flexible zoning techniques, and development agreements, for example, have increased the opportunity for and importance of working with local planning staff in growth management decisions.

Don't Be Intimidated by Legal Limitations _____

In 1987, the United States Supreme Court decided two important cases that have heightened concerns over the legal limits to local efforts to regulate land use and manage growth. While the actual ramifications of these decisions are still not clear, and their impacts may be far less important than first thought, these decisions have been used by some as the basis for demanding that localities choose between approving a development proposal or having to pay a landowner millions of dollars in damages.

Understandably, such threats can be a powerful tool for getting favorable local action on a development proposal. This is especially true in smaller communities that often lack the legal resources to defend against such claims and act with confidence about the legality of their decisions.

Growth management efforts that dramatically affect the feasibility of a development proposal—and thus a parcel's value—can raise significant legal issues that require attention. There are, however, severe thresholds one must overcome to successfully challenge a local land use decision and several ways in which a locality can effectively strengthen its legal defenses.

The following are general suggestions that can help local decision-makers avoid successful legal challenges to their land use programs and decisions.

- *The best defense is a good offense: the comprehensive plan.* A comprehensive planning process that includes thorough documentation and analysis of local development trends, the local costs and impacts of development, and the adverse effects that a growth management program will address will help immensely in preventing and withstanding legal challenges. Courts are more likely to invalidate land use restrictions imposed with *post hoc* planning or *ad hoc* decision-making, rather than by even-handed implementation of comprehensive community planning.

- *Carefully document the connection between the ends (land use objectives) and the means (specific regulations).* This will minimize exposure to taking, substantive due process, and equal protection challenges. The impacts of a regulation on a specific landowner may be much more tangible and direct (and therefore more compelling to a judge) than the communitywide benefits of the regulation. For this reason, the public benefits of a regulation should be clearly and convincingly explained in the regulation. The connection between the projected impacts of a development and an exaction should be clearly documented.

- *Preserve an economically feasible land use to the extent possible.* This will help avoid or defend taking challenges. Where a regulation would prohibit all economically feasible land uses on certain property, explore means of transferring densities off-site through a transfer of development rights program. On the other hand, a locality should not be overly intimidated by the specter of a taking claim. Frequently, fear of a court challenge imposes a greater limitation on effective land use regulation than necessary. Remember that there is no constitutional right to use one's property in the most profitable manner, that there is no constitutional protection against downzoning, and that numerous decisions hold that there is no constitutional right for a landowner to degrade wetlands or to place structures within floodways. Courts are almost certain to uphold a reasonable land use regulation when the regulation does not deny a landowner all economically viable use of a parcel.

- *Carefully draft buffer zone regulations to ensure that they do not result in a regulatory "taking" by prohibiting all economically reasonable use of a parcel.* An open space buffer or a setback requirement is likely to be upheld so long as some economically reasonable use is permitted on the parcel as a whole.* For this reason, parcel size is an important consideration in drafting river or wetland protection programs or other resource conservation districts. In addition, courts are more likely to uphold restrictive buffer regulations if the buffer zone is within a floodplain.

- *Tie moratoria and other temporary restrictions to a good faith process.* A moratorium should have a

---

* At least one state—Washington—does not follow this general rule. In *Allingham v. Seattle,* 109 Wash. 2d 947 (1988), the Washington Supreme Court struck down as a taking a greenbelt ordinance requiring landowners to leave one-half of the parcel undeveloped.

limited and clearly defined duration, so that it does not prohibit, but only delays, use of property. If the moratorium is intended to buy time for a planning effort, create and follow a reasonable schedule for completion of the planning effort. Lift the moratorium as soon as the planning effort is completed. If the moratorium is based upon public infrastructure inadequacies, develop a definite schedule and budget for rectifying those problems. If a moratorium must last for an extended period, provide a "relief valve," allowing some low-intensity development to proceed.

- *Leave open the opportunity on the public record for a landowner to resubmit an improved development proposal.* The courts generally will not address a legal challenge until a landowner has obtained a "final, definitive position" from the local regulators prohibiting any economically reasonable use of the property. If a development application is denied, make sure that the public record clearly shows that the board or agency would con-

BRAIN HALVES AT WORK PLANNING A NEW DEVELOPMENT

THE DEVELOPER   THE DESIGNER   THE FINANCIER   THE PUBLIC OFFICIAL

sider a modified or more appropriate development proposal. Make sure that the reasons for denial are supported by the development regulations and the comprehensive plan.

- *Maximize the public visibility of the planning process and individual decisions.* This will help to avoid vested rights challenges, charges of collusion, and violations of procedural fairness.

- *Do not use regulatory powers to facilitate public acquisition or to reduce the price of land to be acquired.* Carefully avoid creating any inference that public acquisition is a factor, even a minor factor, in a regulatory decision.

Understand the Real Estate Market

Although changes in land use appear to occur quickly, the development process is usually fairly deliberate. The actual groundbreaking, or even the submission of development applications for the first major development in an area, signals, in most cases, the culmination rather than the commencement of the process by which an entire corridor or area is developed. Before development proposals are made public, the following actions may have occurred and created a momentum for development of an area: real estate developers have invested in appreciated property or have acquired options to buy this property, and have paid substantial consultant fees; public utilities such as sewer, water, fire protection services, and a local road network are in place; the local government has anticipated tax revenues or development fees from the projected development to finance these public investments; developers have already lined up tenants from the local business community who may have relied in their business planning on the new development; and banks may have already made land acquisition loans and be planning on construction loans.

The best opportunity to influence a community's future may be in areas where land prices are still relatively low. Yet, campaigns to influence development proposals are often galvanized after this predevelopment activity has taken place. This predevelopment activity may have already created rising expectations and a powerful momentum for a specific kind of development to go forward. For this reason, it is much more effective and efficient to create more sensitive development and preserve important resources or areas by implementing effective strategies as early as possible.

Development trends can sometimes be spotted informally through what might be termed "windshield surveys." "Land for sale" signs along the roadsides are a clear indication of transition, both in ownership and, frequently, in land use. Notices posted on property of pending zone change requests indicate that the transition in land use is even further along. A trained eye can also observe more subtle changes, such as the testing of soil conditions or the idling of formerly cultivated farmland.

Useful early indicators of impending land development include:

- *Turnover in ownership of undeveloped land.* Land ownership in rural areas traditionally is a long-term affair, with few transfers and many of these between members of the same family. Evidence of accelerating turnover, either throughout an entire area or on an individual parcel, often precedes impending changes in land use. Information about land ownership and transfers can be obtained from the local recorder's office, property tax assessor, or private real estate brokers. Likewise, acquisition of contiguous parcels by the same or affiliated entities may indicate major development plans for an area.

- *Division of large parcels.* Subdivision of large farms and other rural land into smaller parcels, even into relatively large parcels by urban or suburban standards, often indicates future development activity. The exception to this general rule is that creation of a few residential parcels, perhaps for family members, on a large farm often implies that the landowner intends to maintain agricultural use of the balance of the farm. On the other hand, for example, division of a 1,000-acre farm into ten 100-acre parcels may indicate future development.

- *Rising land prices.* As rural land is subdivided and sold to absentee owners, land prices generally climb. Because land owners with development expectations can often justify paying higher prices than farmers or passive users, they readily bid up the area's real estate market. They may also provide evidence to current owners that development is inevitable, helping to create the "impermanence syndrome" discussed in chapter 1. Information about land prices can be obtained through local real estate brokers, newspapers (which often publish real estate sales prices), and the recorder's or tax assessor's office.

- *State and local plans.* Governmental plans, and especially capital investment programs, are good indicators of future land use. In addition to local comprehensive plans (which may or may not be reliable indicators of future land use), federal and state highway and bypass construction programs, sewer or water extension programs, and public projects such as airport or reservoir construction forewarn of future growth.

WALK A MILE IN A DEVELOPER'S SHOES

At times, the focus for citizen attention must necessarily be on a specific development proposal for an individual parcel, rather than on working toward a broader vision of community land uses. Attempting to promote a particularly worthy development, seeking to increase its sensitivity to surrounding resource needs, or fighting a rearguard action to oppose it all require citizens to have some basic understanding of how a developer thinks about and analyzes a project.

Where the objective may be to raise the quality of a particular development proposal, reduce its intensity, mitigate its off-site impacts, or shift the costs of addressing the environmental or fiscal impacts of a proposal to the developer, an understanding of real estate finance and economics is required to appreciate how much the proposal can be modified without making the project too risky or too costly to go forward.

Where the objective is to convince a developer to undertake a project, it is important to know what tax incentives, financing packages, and other benefits can help to convince developers and investors to get involved. This requires an understanding of the market feasibility of the proposed use. Understanding the economics of development can also help to identify public incentives necessary to make such a project work.

The extent of project planning and analysis undertaken by a developer typically varies directly with the scale of the proposed project and the amount of investment at stake. The typical steps in analyzing the feasibility of a development proposal are:

- *Defining project goals and objectives.* Aside from seeking to maximize profits, many developers are strongly motivated to minimize "up-front" costs

and delay spending to the extent possible until they have obtained construction financing and have successfully marketed a portion of the project. Citizen groups will often find that a developer will be more forthcoming if costs can be delayed until financing has been obtained or several units have been sold or leased. Concerned citizens should bear in mind that the ultimate test of success for a developer is not necessarily local approval, but rather the closing of a construction loan, and successful marketing of the project. Negotiators should ensure that all conditions and understandings are apparent to potential lenders and investors and will bind them, should they take over the project. Moreover, a developer's assertion that a proposed condition would render a project "unbankable," and thus not viable, should often be taken seriously. In these situations, citizens may wish to consider alternative ways to reach the same objective without jeopardizing the developer's ability to finance the project.

- *Analyzing general market conditions and project feasibility.* After developing project goals and objectives, developers typically conduct a general market feasibility analysis. This is the broadest form of project analysis, encompassing both the direct forces of supply and demand, as well as indirect social, political, and environmental influences. Market studies are often required by banks and other institutional lenders or investors as a condition of receiving project financing. More often than not, market studies are based on the qualitative, professional judgment of real estate appraisers and consultants. Yet the difficulty of quantifying certain aspects of the study often limits the precision of such studies.

- *Creating a development program.* In its later stages, the market analysis leads to an initial development program. This program projects the uses and densities ("the product mix") feasible, given the identified market conditions and the site's physical capacity to withstand development and zoning controls. Preliminary sketch plans for the proposal will be developed. These sketch plans permit projection of the estimated costs and revenues of the proposal in a document called a *pro forma.* Projected revenues are based upon information obtained from the market feasibility studies. Both the *pro forma* and preliminary sketch plans provide an early indication of the costs and financial feasibility of a project before substantial engineering, site work, and other development expenses are incurred. The performance of the project will be modeled over time through a cash flow projection. This model provides a multiyear financial picture (as opposed to the "snapshot" pro-

vided by the *pro forma*). The results of this modeling also may lead to necessary revisions to the sketch plan and product mix.

- *Deciding whether and how to proceed.* Throughout the development process, the developer is constantly faced with the decision whether and how to go forward with the proposal. The basic options include: proceeding with obtaining necessary land use permits and financing for the proposal; aborting the project and selling the site or allowing the option on the site to expire; delaying the project until political or market conditions change; bringing in a partner or major investor as a joint venturer; or reformulating the development concept. Of course, if a decision is made to proceed, the developer continues to have the option—at a higher cost—of reconsidering should, for example, regulatory, financing, or market conditions change.*

Negotiate from Strength

Land use negotiations focus on a wide variety of project characteristics, including:

- Uses;
- Densities;
- Phasing of development;
- Architectural and landscape design details;
- Infrastructure requirements and financing; and
- Mitigation of environmental and fiscal impacts.

In addition to negotiations over specific development proposals, broader "policy negotiations" or consensus-building activities over growth management plans and policies increasingly occur at the local level.

Negotiation, with or without a mediator, is neither a panacea nor a guarantor of creative solutions to complex, emotion-filled land use issues. Nevertheless, if properly used, it can, at times, be an effective way for citizens to achieve important growth management objectives.

The first step in negotiating anything is to determine

---

* This section highlights the analytical process and points to sources of more detailed information in the Information Resources section. It is based largely on Barrett and Blair, *How to Conduct and Analyze Real Estate Market and Feasibility Studies.* This methodology is only prototypical. Individual developers will combine the components of this "model" approach in various ways or at various levels of detail that reflect project characteristics and their own financing needs and business methods. Moreover, although these components are logical, sequential phases, the analytical process in reality is often circular, with each component being in a constant state of revision, influencing the revision of other components.

whether negotiations are appropriate and are likely to be successful. The following are among the considerations to bear in mind in addressing these concerns:

- All parties (there may be more than two) must have a reason or incentive to bargain. They must feel they have a tangible stake in resolving the dispute at hand. They must believe that negotiations will produce a result equivalent to or better than any result achievable without negotiations. The delays and costs of litigation may provide this incentive by weighing heavily on the minds of all parties.

- The issues should be "ripe." That is, they must be well defined and recognized by the parties. In some cases, this requires development plans to be past the conceptual stage.

- There should be possible "trade-offs." There needs to be a large enough number of issues, or optional approaches to the issues, to permit the parties to trade off among them to find an acceptable solution. None of these issues can involve a party's funda-

mental values. If values are truly fundamental, trade-offs will not be acceptable. "Not in my backyard" zealots and die-hard property rights advocates are not likely to find much to negotiate.

- There must be perceived approximate equality in the power or "leverage" of the parties. The developer may have financial power and professional expertise; public officials or citizens' groups have permitting authority or the power to delay construction.

- There needs to be an expectation that an agreement will be implemented. Otherwise, everyone's time will have been wasted.

Once a determination is made that negotiations are worth pursuing, officials and community groups should spend time preparing to negotiate. At a minimum, the following "homework" should be undertaken:

- *Know your own needs.* Know what you hope to achieve; know the minimum you will accept; know your opening position and your supporting arguments; anticipate your weaknesses.

- *Know their needs.* Attempt to "walk in their moccasins"; gather as much information as you can about the developer's financial needs and circumstances; attitudes about conservation and the community; costs of carrying the land; and constraints and deadlines. Be able to anticipate the developer's opening positions and arguments.

- *Develop alternative proposals.* Armed with some knowledge of the developer's needs, develop several alternative proposals for consideration.

Once negotiations begin, there are some basic principles of good bargaining that can help maximize the prospects for a successful outcome:

- *Speak with one voice.* The appearance of dissension, or fundamental differences of opinion among citizens' group members, may provide developers with weaknesses to exploit or may convince them that the group is not in a position to negotiate or implement a negotiated agreement.

- *Separate people from problems.* Human antagonism can obscure substantive issues. Hard as it may be, the personal aspects of a dispute should be identified and minimized.

- *Focus on underlying interests, not articulated positions.* While disputes appear to be about positions, they are really about interests. For each interest, there may be several arguable positions, thereby increasing the prospects for identifying mutually agreeable positions.

- *Negotiate collaboratively.* Negotiating should be approached as a collaborative, *problem-solving* exercise. The objective is to find a mutually satisfactory resolution. Each party should be flexible, avoiding a competitive or antagonistic atmosphere. A positive feeling among all parties about both the negotiating process and outcome will increase the prospects for faithful implementation of the ultimate agreement.

- *Avoid stalemate.* If any impasse is reached on an important issue, table it and move on to a more tractable matter. By settling the relatively easy questions first, you can engender the necessary atmosphere of trust and confidence to tackle tougher concerns. Moreover, if "sticky wickets" are left to the end, you have minimized the chances that your counterparts will walk out, since they will have already invested much time and effort in the process.

- *Be professional.* A businesslike and confidential posture will help engender an atmosphere of trust.

Developers are more likely to deal with citizens and community groups if they believe them to be reasonable. Reinforcing this perception during the negotiations can only help.

- *Play it straight.* Without laying all your cards out, avoid the appearance of playing games or striking poses.

- *Avoid ultimatums.* These only alienate the other party and poison an otherwise collaborative atmosphere. If an ultimatum is necessary, save it until toward the end, when the other party has made an investment in the process.

- *Maximize your options.* The more options you have, even if they are only apparent, the more power you have. Avoid revealing your options, and possibly thereby eliminating them, until you have to. If your options are in fact limited, avoid revealing this fact.

- *If you give something, get something.* Major concessions should be matched by major concessions.

Recognize That the Process Is Political

In order to participate in growth management decisions and to help implement a vision for a community, effective participation in local, and perhaps state, political processes is absolutely critical. In the final analysis, virtually every major land use decision in a community is made by its elected officials, with political considerations uppermost in their minds.

Several talents and commonsense rules-of-thumb are required, depending on the level of involvement and the stage of the process. Perhaps the most important rule is to get articulate and energetic people who care about the future of the community elected to local political office. The job of developing and implementing a positive vision that will lead to a successful community is made much easier if the right people control land use decisions.

Other important rules for effective political action include:

- *Know the decision-making process.* Knowledge of procedural rules and timetables is critical in knowing how and when to effectively participate in the process.

- *Know the key decision-makers.* Key decision-makers include council members, planning commissioners, and staff members. Do not make the mistake of only calling or writing them when you have a complaint or negative comment; talk to them about the good things that are happening in the community as well. Convince them that you want only to improve the community, even if they do not support your specific objectives. Look for ways to increase your effectiveness by building bridges with local officials.

- *Be a credible resource for public officials.* Public officials are generally busy people and often overloaded with information and opinions from many sources. They value comments and sources of information they can trust; therefore, fulfill the commitments you make to them.

- *Build effective coalitions.* Be creative in identifying common ground with other interest groups. It may be particularly effective to build coalitions on specific issues with influential groups that are not natural allies.

- *Pick your issues strategically.* Do not wage or prolong counterproductive campaigns. Weigh the damage to your long-term efforts from alienating public officials and the public by fixating on a no-win campaign or losing sight of the big picture.

- *Staying power is critical.* Planning and growth management is an ongoing process. Specific development proposals may be in the review process for many months or even years. You will be taken more seriously when you are perceived as a permanent factor.

- *Do your homework.* Stay informed about the issues and the actors. When meeting with public officials or addressing a public hearing, there is no substitute for thorough preparation.

- *Do their homework.* Keep public officials informed about growth management and resource protection issues. Give them useful articles, studies, and sample land use ordinances from other nearby communities.

- *Clearly articulate why public officials should support your position.* Give public officials reasons that complement their interests for supporting your position. For example, demonstrate the public popularity of your position, the strength of your support, and the fiscal responsibility of good growth management.

- *Get effective public speakers for your position.* When speaking at a public hearing, make specific recommendations, support your position with accurate information, stay on the point, and be prepared to answer questions. In almost all situations, an organized but extemporaneous statement is more effective than reading from a written statement. It is usually most effective to prepare a written submission and then summarize its contents in your own words.

Above All Else, Create a Vision for Your Community's Future

Concerned citizens, local officials, planners, landowners, and developers often do not have or cannot agree on a clear vision of what the community should be. As a consequence, many communities are at a substantial disadvantage in attempting to take charge of their future, especially in the face of heavy growth pressures.

Opposing development projects and dealing with details like zone changes, site plan review, and revisions to the comprehensive plan are not sufficient by themselves to create successful communities. Effective action by concerned citizens requires going beyond merely "managing growth" to developing a vision of what the community should become and working persistently to carry forth that vision into reality.

As James Rouse, the master builder of Columbia, Maryland, Faneuil Hall in Boston, Harbor Place in Baltimore, and many other notable areas, put it:

> The most important thing we have yet to learn is that there is so much more we can do about creating successful communities and successful lives for the people of our country than we attempt to do. We continually fall short of the possible that is out there in front of us because we envisage so little as possible. We are always undershooting in what we believe it is possible to do.[7]

An influential vision sets forth a positive ideal of what makes the community distinctive and how it can channel inevitable change to enhance existing assets. Such a vision entails both protecting distinctive assets and creating quality development that builds on and enhances, rather than detracts from, such resources.

Natural and cultural assets are what make a community distinctive. A community's assets and distinctive character are what inspire people, create a sense of concern, and motivate action. Protecting local assets is also an important way to build consensus for action, even in the absence of a larger, more detailed vision of an area's future. Concerned citizens will not get very far in developing a vision (or opposing specific development proposals) without focusing their efforts on the positive assets a community has or can create.

Assets include not only those already in existence —rivers, open space, historic structures, and the like—but also ones that can be created. New development can become a new community asset: witness Baltimore's Harbor Place and Aquarium, San Antonio's Riverwalk, or the main streets being renovated in small towns across the country.

Market trends, laws, and traditions dictate continued growth and change for America's communities. The population is growing and shifting among areas. People continue to want their own homes and yards and are free to move from one part of the country to another. And the real estate market decides, in broad terms, where development goes.

Thus, development will continue to occur. Citizen action may be able to move it from one community to another or to shape its density, character, and cost. But such action cannot ultimately prevent change. The failure to accept this is what causes many people to regard all development as the enemy and make it impossible to achieve successful communities in light of the polarization and the poorly designed sprawl that often ensues.

Development comes in many forms, shapes, and designs. Depending on its location, size, design, and function, it has many kinds of impacts—both good and bad. Effective citizens recognize the distinctions among various development proposals and judge them on their individual merits. They factor appropriate development into their vision for their community's future. Recognizing the benefits that certain kinds of development can bring to a community—jobs, a needed mix of housing types and prices, a balanced tax base, good design, and so forth—the involved citizen, in fact, works to foster the right type of development in locations where it best meets local needs, in addition to working to protect community resources.

Concerned citizens work with other residents, groups, and local officials to ensure that good development is encouraged and rewarded. This is a sometimes difficult task that may anger important constituencies for preservation and threaten to undo valuable coalitions—ones that enabled you to get a seat at the table in the first place. Yet the skillful citizen helps create an environment where not all development is regarded as pollution. Such an environment is essential to being taken seriously by both those who have the resources to help build successful communities and those who have the power to determine permissible land uses in the area. Moreover, it is essential to achieving a realistic vision for the community's future.

GROUPS MAKING A DIFFERENCE

Profiled below are some key groups working in various parts of the country and at various levels of government to make a difference.

1,000 Friends of Oregon: A Watchdog for Land Use

1,000 Friends of Oregon is a statewide, public interest nonprofit organization formed in 1975 to give the public a direct voice in ensuring that Oregon's statewide land use planning law is faithfully implemented. The law requires local governments to adopt comprehensive land use plans and zoning regulations consistent with state planning goals. The Land Conservation and Development Commission (LCDC) has responsibility for overseeing the process at the state level.

Public participation is at the heart of Oregon's land use planning process. Oregonians can appeal city, county, state, or special district land use decisions and challenge whether those decisions meet statewide planning goals. As an organization of professional lawyers and planners, 1,000 Friends has the resources to overcome financial and political barriers that often preclude individuals from challenging local land use decisions. The staff provides no-cost legal assistance to citizens in addition to conducting planning research and public education.

Success Stories _____

One of the keys to the success of 1,000 Friends is the variety of mechanisms it has used to ensure that local governments abide by state planning laws. These have included:

- Appealing local decisions and plans before the state Land Conservation and Development Commission and the courts;
- Preparing studies and background papers on important land use issues;
- Testifying before the state legislature;
- Forging broad-based coalitions among diverse interest groups;
- Working with governors and executive staffs; and
- Assisting local governments in preparing their local comprehensive plans.

The organization has focused principally on ensuring the effectiveness of exclusive farm use zones to protect agricultural lands and on ensuring that affected localities draw workable urban growth boundaries to provide for needed development, affordable housing, and protection of valuable resources. One of 1,000 Friends' most important accomplishments was in obtaining interpretations of state land use policy that allows the program to support both affordable housing and land conservation objectives.

Throughout its first 14 years, 1,000 Friends worked primarily to ensure that the provisions of the statutes and statewide planning goals, created in 1973 and 1974, were met. The organization concentrated its efforts at both the local level and at the state level in hearings and litigation before the LCDC. On a jurisdiction-by-jurisdiction basis, the organization questioned whether the state's policies had been implemented in specific local plans and on certain parcels of land. In this way, 1,000 Friends played an active role in many of the major, formative land use rulings by the LCDC and the courts.

The organization chose its battles carefully, selecting cases that had the potential to set a precedent for interpreting the legislative intent of the state land use law. The primary intent of its early lawsuits was to elicit key court decisions on the meaning of Oregon's planning law and enable individuals to challenge local interpretation of these laws. At the same time, 1,000 Friends galvanized citizen support to deter three different ballot measures to repeal the state's land use planning program.

Due in part to 1,000 Friends' efforts, Oregon's land use law has been largely successful. By August of 1986, the comprehensive plans and zoning of 36 counties and 241 cities had been revised to comply with state goals. The result has been the rezoning of approximately 30 million acres, nearly all of Oregon's private land. Urban areas now have more incentives for affordable housing. Rural areas have some 16 million acres of farm land and 9 million acres of forest land zoned for conservation purposes. All 241 cities have established urban growth boundaries.

With the initial step of Oregon's program successfully taken, 1,000 Friends is taking on new challenges that fall roughly into four areas:

- Ensuring successful implementation of the "periodic review statutes." To make certain that city and county plans remain consistent with state planning goals, they must be reevaluated within four years of their initial acknowledgment by the LCDC and subsequently every four to seven years. The plans are reviewed for (1) changes in circumstances on which the plan is based; (2) consistency of new goals or administrative rules adopted since the plan was acknowledged; (3) progress of unfinished planning work; and (4) coordination with state agency plans. The organization assists citizens in making sure that no changes occur in plans during the periodic review process that threaten natural resources or efficient growth.

- Establishing county-level land use organizations, independent of 1,000 Friends, to which it will provide technical assistance. The county organizations are patterned after the county branches of Britain's Council for the Protection of Rural England. A coalition of private industry trade associations in the state, the Oregon Business Council, has formed to inject industry's concerns into the local planning process.

- Exploring options with landowners, foresters, county officials, and financial institutions by which feasible timber production and financial goals can be met on western Oregon's 2.2 million acres of nonindustrial timberlands. This project is an example of 1,000 Friends' initiative to create market-oriented financial and management mechanisms to make conservation policies feasible.

- Assisting land use policy development in other states. 1,000 Friends of Oregon has played a significant role in the enactment of growth management legislation and in the establishment of citizen organizations to support this legislation in several states. For example, 1,000 Friends of Florida is a strong statewide organization recently formed with assistance from 1,000 Friends of Oregon to monitor that state's growth management legislation.

Organizational Structure

1,000 Friends of Oregon has a staff of 13 including attorneys and land use planners; it has a membership of about 6,000. The 13-member board of directors and 10-member advisory board include local officials and business, industrial, agricultural, and environmental interests.

The organization's budget is about $550,000 and is expected to increase to $750,000 in 1989. Funding is derived almost equally from three sources: membership payments, gifts from individuals beyond membership payments, and grants from foundations.

CONTACT

1,000 Friends of Oregon.
3000 Willemette Building
534 Southwest Avenue
Portland, OR 97204

MSM Regional Council, New Jersey: Comprehensive Planning Efforts

MSM is a nonprofit organization that works to improve growth management in central New Jersey. MSM stands for Middlesex, Somerset, Mercer, which are the three New Jersey counties surrounding Princeton, constituting the 500-square-mile geographic scope of the council. Thirty-two local governments—townships, boroughs, cities, and special districts—make up the governmental patchwork of the region. MSM's mission is to plan for the long-term regional growth of the area, which has experienced heavy development pressure since the late 1970s.

The city of New Brunswick lies at the northern tip of the three counties, at the edge of what used to be considered the outermost reach of the New York City metropolitan area. The state capital, Trenton (in Mercer County), lies 20 miles south down U.S. Route 1. Massive development of the Route 1 corridor between New Brunswick and Trenton has blurred the boundary between metropolitan Philadelphia and New York.

Over the past decade, numerous "footloose" high-technology corporations have moved in along the highway. They have transformed much of the landscape from agrarian open space to office complexes and shopping malls. The tri-county population is now well over 600,000.

MSM is attempting to promote regional cooperation, long-range planning, and growth management. MSM is an influential research and advocacy organization promoting consensus between developers, governments, public constituencies, and other independent groups in the region.

Success Stories

Established in 1968, MSM has acted as an adviser to state agencies and, as such, has been instrumental in the establishment and direction of New Jersey's state planning program.

MSM has recognized that a "regional plan must be forged with the active participation of those affected." Thus, MSM provided the impetus for a "Regional Forum," a public/private initiative that convened some 250 representatives from public agencies, business, the real estate industry, and nonprofit groups to create the necessary environment for the adoption of a regional comprehensive plan.

In December 1987, the Forum issued a report entitled *An Action Agenda for Managing Regional Growth*, which recommends planning actions for the region in five issue areas: transportation, economic development, land use, growth management, and environment/infrastructure. In this last area, the Forum advocates retaining 40 percent of the region in open space, by according permanent protection for contiguous areas of open space called "greenways," and by requiring very low-density development in locally designated "conservation areas." The Forum also recommends higher-density development in centers of varying size and scale that can provide efficient transportation services and encourage walking and bicycling. The Forum concluded that regional growth and preservation of open space are not necessarily incompatible.

MSM is now engaged in several programs to make the Action Agenda happen. For example, the council has published a *Growth Management Handbook* that will describe effective tools for managing growth in

New Jersey. The council is conducting an educational and outreach program for local municipalities. The council is also pursuing a legislative program to improve land use administration and growth management in New Jersey.

Organizational Structure

MSM is a nonprofit organization, whose board members include managers from local corporations like Squibb, Mobil, and Merrill Lynch; presidents and vice-presidents from large local banks; representatives from small local businesses; senior officers of local institutions, including Rutgers and Princeton universities; developers; and citizens. No members are elected officials or planning officers. It has four full-time staff, three of whom are professionals.

Its membership is more than 700, and like the board of directors, comprises a representative cross-section of interests. Some 110 companies, 20 municipalities, 600-plus individuals from the three counties, but primarily the Princeton area, where MSM is headquartered, make up the membership.

MSM's annual budget is approximately $350,000 with funds coming in roughly equal proportions from state government contracts, private foundations, and members. Among revenues from members, two-thirds comes from corporations and businesses, with the balance from individuals.

CONTACT

MSM Regional Council
621 Alexander Road
Princeton, NJ 08540

The Vermont Land Trust: Protecting a State's Heritage

The Vermont Land Trust is a private nonprofit land trust established in 1977. Originally known as the Ottauquechee Land Trust, the organization enlarged its scope to encompass all of Vermont in 1987.

The trust was founded to preserve Vermont's settlement pattern of small villages and hamlets surrounded by farms and managed woodlands. The trust believes that Vermont's strong natural and historic qualities, fostered by the state's traditional settlement pattern, are being overlooked as rapid increases in property values make farming and woodland management economically infeasible. With people willing to pay far more for a parcel of land than its productive capability warrants, new housing development will inevitably replace established farms. The cumulative impact of this activity threatens Vermont's rural character and environmental assets.

To address these issues, the Vermont Land Trust works with private landowners to acquire and protect agricultural and forest lands. Through conservation easements, shared equity arrangements, and development restrictions, the trust creates opportunities for farmers and woodland managers to purchase and lease land at prices that more closely reflect the land's agricultural and silvicultural value.

The trust solicits donations of land, development rights, and conservation easements. When critical acreage cannot be preserved in this fashion, the trust seeks the assistance of local residents to purchase the property. A community steering committee is then created to oversee the project. To recover the property's purchase price, the trust often uses limited development, selling or developing a portion of the parcel with strict development controls, enabling the remaining acreage to be sold with conservation restrictions that prevent development but allow farming and forestry.

Vermont towns frequently call upon the trust for technical assistance with innovative growth management strategies or land conservation plans. Usually, the trust assists only those towns that can provide funding.

Successes

In its two years as a statewide organization, the Vermont Land Trust has achieved major successes in several areas:

VERMONT HOUSING AND CONSERVATION TRUST FUND

In 1985, the Vermont Land Trust proposed the creation of a public trust fund to encourage the acquisition of development rights on farmland. Due to the proposal's limited constituency and a severe state deficit, no legislative action was taken. Realizing that creating a trust fund requires a broader base of political support, the Land Trust put together a coalition of conservation and affordable housing advocates. The coalition was a marriage of environmental preservation, farming, and low-income housing interests, that developed in response to market forces that were responsible for both the loss of farm and forest land, and the rapid increase in housing prices.

The Housing and Conservation Coalition, as the association is officially known, lobbied the Vermont general assembly to establish a housing and conservation trust to fund one-time grants and low- and no-interest loans to innovative projects that protect farmland, preserve natural areas and historic sites, acquire public recreation resources, and provide affordable housing.

The Coalition succeeded, and in 1987, the Vermont legislature appropriated $3 million to establish the Vermont Housing and Conservation Trust Fund. With less than one year of activity and strong public support, the legislature appropriated an additional $20 million to the fund in 1988. In addition, the legislature created a permanent revenue base for the trust fund by raising the state's real estate transfer tax.

FARMLAND PRESERVATION AND AFFORDABLE HOUSING

In 1987, the Vermont Land Trust prevented the auction and subdivision of the 772-acre Brassknocker Farm, located in East Craftsbury. The trust partially financed the purchase through 65 charitable creditors, who cosigned for $200,000 of the purchase loan.

In order to repay the loan, the trust divided the farm into four parcels of 422, 248, 49, and 30 acres. The 30-acre parcel is reserved for low-income housing. An additional 24 acres were sold to a local landowner for permanent conservation. The trust sold three smaller parcels, with deed restrictions, allowing no more than nine houses to be built on the parcels. The trust divided the remaining acreage into 11 zones, ranging in size from 3 to 84 acres, each containing one carefully selected house site. The proceeds from the sales are expected to repay the entire loan, leaving the 772 acres with 20 homes and restrictions protecting the remaining undeveloped land for open space, farming, and maple syrup production.

HISTORIC PRESERVATION

In 1988, the Vermont Land Trust received a one-year $150,000 low-interest loan from the Vermont Housing and Conservation Trust Fund to acquire the Theron Boyd House located in Quechee. The loan enables the trust to hold the eighteenth-century house until 1989, when the Vermont Division of Historic Preservation intends to purchase the site.

METTOWEE VALLEY CONSERVATION PROJECT

The trust began the Mettowee Valley Conservation Project (MVCP) in 1986. MVCP seeks to coordinate the growth management and resource conservation activities of the towns of Dorset, Rupert, and Pawlet. The project was financed with foundation grants and matching funds from local fund-raising. Initially, a project steering committee was organized to work with the municipalities, and, in 1988, a full-time project coordinator was hired to aid the towns in planning and farmland preservation.

Organizational Structure

The Vermont Land Trust has a staff of ten that includes attorneys and land use planners. Along with individual memberships, the trust offers an affiliated program that gives small local and regional land trusts technical and legal advice. The trust currently has four regional offices: Woodstock, Montpelier, Brattleboro, and Mettowee Valley. In 1989, a fifth office is scheduled to open in the Champlain Valley. The King Farm in Woodstock also doubles as the trust's central office.

The trust receives the largest share of its funds from contributions and grants for individual projects. The membership also accounts for a sizable share of the budget. The trust's other sources of income derive from paid consulting work on open space design and land use planning, leasing fees from trust-owned land, and sales of conservation lands where appropriate. Its annual budget is about $450,000.

CONTACT

Vermont Land Trust
King Farm
Woodstock, VT 05091

California Coastal Conservancy: An Effective Complement to Regulations

The California Coastal Conservancy was created by the California legislature in 1976 with the mission to preserve, enhance, and restore California's coastal resources through nonregulatory means. The conservancy was formed as a sister agency to the California Coastal Commission, which regulates development in the coastal zone and works with coastal localities to prepare and implement their plans for resource conservation and development. The conservancy, on the other hand—usually in response to requests from local governments, citizens, public agencies, or the legislature—assists coastal communities to resolve conflicts between the rights of private landowners and the desires for resource conservation and public access.

The conservancy is successful in large part because it is complemented by a powerful regulatory program. The conservancy's effectiveness also illustrates how public entities can effectively foster private sector efforts.

The California Coastal Conservancy's jurisdiction extends throughout the California coastal zone, which runs 1,100 miles from Oregon to Mexico, and up to five miles inland.

The conservancy uses a variety of strategies to protect coastal resources. It acquires land and funds or directly undertakes a wide variety of projects that further the purposes of the state's coastal act. Its projects are grouped under the following programs:

- Public access;
- Urban waterfront restoration;
- Resource enhancement;
- Coastal restoration;
- Agricultural land preservation;
- Site reservation;
- Donations and dedications; and
- Nonprofit organization assistance.

Success Stories

In the ten years since its inception, the California Coastal Conservancy has carried out hundreds of projects in cooperation with local governments, other public agencies, landowners, nonprofit organizations, and citizen groups. It has protected or helped local agencies and nonprofits protect over 13,000 acres of sensitive coastal wetland, open space, agricultural, or other land. A few examples of the conservancy's projects follow.

- The conservancy provides financial and technical assistance to communities to increase public access to California's coast. For example, in August of 1986, the conservancy made a grant of $576,000 to the city of Long Beach to develop the first phase of a three-mile bicycle and pedestrian trail along its downtown beach. The citizens of Long Beach helped to plan and design this trail, which runs along a beach that hosts many community events. The trail is expected to serve 2 million people annually and alleviate bicycle and pedestrian traffic on congested downtown streets.

- The conservancy seeks to balance new development in small city waterfronts with the preservation of historic waterfront activities. To this end, the conservancy approved four grants of $50,000 each in 1986 for the restoration of waterfronts in small cities.

- The conservancy lent San Diego County $1 million to purchase 15 acres of coastal sage scrub and mixed chaparral—two habitats of which few remain in California—which were slated for residential development.

- The conservancy led several efforts to protect the Los Penasquitos Lagoon, located in the city of San Diego and designated by the California Department of Fish and Game as one of the 19 coastal wetlands most in need of protection. Although 1,326 acres of the land were preserved in a state reserve, another 250 acres were owned by industry. Encroachment of industrial development threatened the lagoon, which provides rare habitat for wildlife, including several endangered species. The conservancy negotiated a sale of 226 acres by the San Diego Gas and Electric Company to the State Department of Parks and Recreation for $2.85 million. The conservancy also acquired the other major property that was in private hands. The conservancy developed a plan for the lagoon in 1985, which includes enhancement and monitoring activities, access development, sediment control measures, and park and open space expansion. The plan is being carried out, in part, by the Los Penasquitos Lagoon Foundation, a local organization established with the assistance of the conservancy, and funded through watershed developers' fees.

- The conservancy conducts stream restoration and comprehensive watershed activities, recognizing the link between upstream areas and downstream marshes, lagoons, and estuaries. For example, to reverse the degradation of the Tomales Bay watershed in Marin County, caused primarily by sedimentation, the conservancy has employed erosion controls—such as revegetation, streambank stabilization, and sediment traps—and encouraged local ranchers to do the same.

Organizational Structure

The conservancy has a seven-member board of directors consisting of California state officials—the secretary of resources, director of finance, and chairman of the California Coastal Commission—and four public members, two each appointed by the president pro tem of the Senate and the speaker of the Assembly.

In addition, three members from the Senate and three from the Assembly act as ex-officio members. Board members serve four-year terms and the chairman is appointed by the secretary of resources. The conservancy has a staff of over 50.

The Coastal Conservancy authorized nearly $32 million of funding in 1986. The conservancy is funded by three state general obligation bonds passed by the voters in 1976, 1980, and 1984. The conservancy also receives periodic grants from other sources such as the state's Environmental License Plate Fund and Energy and Resources Fund, and from the federal government.

CONTACT

California Coastal Conservancy
1330 Broadway
Suite 1100
Oakland, CA 94610

INFORMATION RESOURCES

Land Use Law

Godschalk, David R., David J. Brower, Larry D. McBennett, and Barbara A. Vestal. *Constitutional Issues of Growth Management*. Chicago: American Society of Planning Officials Press, 1979.

Analysis of the legal aspects of growth management. Discusses the rationale for growth management; the constitutional bases of growth management; the variety of types of legal challenges to growth management programs; hypothetical cases illustrating legal issues; and policy considerations.

Hagman, Donald G., and Julian Conrad Juergensmeyer. *Urban Planning and Land Development Control Law*. St. Paul: West Publishing Company, 1986.

An excellent legal textbook.

Mandelker, Daniel R. *Land Use Law*. Charlottesville, VA: The Michie Company, 1982.

Provides a thorough and well-organized discussion of land use law.

Meck, Stuart, and Edith M. Netter, eds. *A Planner's Guide to Land Use Law*. Chicago: American Planning Association Planners Press, 1983.

A collection of articles by leading authorities on land use law topics, including the relationship of the planning process to land use controls, procedural constraints on land use decision-making, alternatives to zoning, constitutional limits on regulations, municipal liability, performance controls, and ordinance drafting.

Morgan, Terry D. "Municipal Responses to the Supreme Court's Non-Regulatory Taking Opinions." *Land Use Law* (November 1987): 3–8.

This brief article summarizes recent Supreme Court decisions, including *First English* and *Nollan* and suggests strategies municipalities might use to ensure their regulations avoid problems raised in these cases.

Netter, Edith M., ed. *Land Use Law: Issues for the Eighties*. Part 2. Chicago: American Planning Association Planners Press, 1984.

A collection of articles dealing with legal aspects of various land use topics, including vested rights, developer exactions, regulations of signs and billboards, design controls and historic preservation, antitrust and land use, and procedural and substantive due process.

Siemon, Charles L., Wendy V. Larsen, and Douglas R. Porter. *Vested Rights: Balancing Public and Private Development Expectations*. Washington, D.C.: Urban Land Institute, 1982.

Detailed examination of vested rights issue. Looks at the existing legal framework, suggests alternative means by which local governments and developers can avoid vested rights problems.

Wright, Robert R., and Susan Webber. *Land Use in a Nutshell*. 2d ed. St. Paul: West Publishing Company, 1985.

Provides a concise and readable overview of land use law.

Growth Management

DeGrove, John M. *Land, Growth & Politics*. Chicago: American Planning Association, 1984.

Discusses the development and implementation of growth management programs in California, Colorado, Florida, Hawaii, North Carolina, Oregon, and Vermont.

Healy, Robert G., and John S. Rosenberg. *Land Use and the States*. Washington, D.C.: Resources for the Future, 1979.

Analyzes the history and effectiveness of state land use initiatives in Vermont, California, and Florida, and examines alternative approaches and issues associated with such programs.

Kusler, Jon A. *Regulating Sensitive Lands*. Washington, D.C.: Environmental Law Institute, 1980.

This guidebook discusses techniques to protect flood plains, lake and river shores, coastal zones, wetlands, and similar sensitive lands. It includes a comprehensive discussion of state resource protection programs and resources protection legal decisions.

Leonard, H. Jeffrey. *Managing Oregon's Growth: The Politics of Development Planning*. Washington, D.C.: The Conservation Foundation, 1983.

Provides an in-depth description of Oregon's growth management program.

Popper, Frank J. *The Politics of Land-Use Reform*. Madison: University of Wisconsin Press, 1981.

Assesses the land use reform movement and several state land use regulatory programs. Describes the history of land use regulation as a public policy issue, evaluates the economic and environmental effects of the programs, and suggests how to make land use programs work better.

Impact Review and Development Feasibility

American Farmland Trust. *Density-Related Public Costs*. Washington, D.C.: American Farmland Trust, 1986.

Useful source demonstrating that in the case study community of Loudoun County, Virginia, large lot residential zoning is a fiscal drain on the community.

Barrett, G. Vincent, and John P. Blair. *How to Conduct and Analyze Real Estate Market and Feasibility Studies*. New York: Von Nostrand Reinhold Co, 1987.

Provides a detailed overview of the preparation and use of real estate market and financial feasibility analyses. Includes several case studies illustrating the use of these analytic techniques.

Burchell, Robert W., David Listokin, and William R. Dolphin. *The New Practitioners Guide to Fiscal Impact Analysis.* New Brunswick, N.J.: Center for Urban Policy Research, 1985.

Summarizes fiscal impact analysis methodologies, including techniques for projecting the costs and revenues associated with residential and non-residential development.

Canter, L.W., S.F. Atkinson, and F. L. Leistritz. *Impact of Growth: A Guide to Socio-Economic Impact Assessment and Planning.* Lewis Publishers, 1985. (Available from the American Planning Association).

A comprehensive step-by-step guide to assessing the social and economic impacts of development.

Dowell, David E. "Reducing the Cost Effects of Local Land Use Controls." In *Growth Management: Keeping on-Target?* edited by Douglas R. Porter. Washington, D.C.: Urban Land Institute and Lincoln Institute of Land Policy, 1986.

Provides useful suggestions on how to identify and ensure an adequate supply of land for housing to mitigate the housing price effects of growth control measures.

Greenberg, Froda, and Jim Hecimovich. *Traffic Impact Analysis.* Planning Advisory Service Report No. 387. Chicago: American Planning Association, 1984.

An accessible introduction to techniques assessing the traffic impacts of large-scale development.

Miami Valley Regional Planning Commission (MVRPC). *The Large-Scale Development Impact Review Manual.* Dayton, OH: 1981.

Developed by a regional planning agency to assist local officials, planners, and citizens in determining the short- and long-term physical, social, fiscal, environmental, and economic effects posed by land developments of state, regional, or multijurisdictional significance. (Available from MVRPC at 117 South Main Street, Suite 200, Dayton, OH 45402.)

National Recreation and Park Association. *Recreation, Park, and Open Space Standards and Guidelines.* Washington, D.C.: National Recreation and Park Association, 1983.

Provides authoritative guidelines on recreational facilities requirements and space requirements for recreational lands and facilities.

People for Open Space. *A Resource Manual on Assessing Residential Land Availability.* San Francisco, CA: People for Open Space, 1982. (Available from POS at [415] 543-4291.)

POS is a long-standing Bay Area conservation group that has developed a Housing/Greenbelt Program aimed at promoting more efficient use of urbanized land to relieve development pressure on greenbelt open space. This manual provides practical guidance on how to identify underutilized land that might provide new housing development opportunities.

Porter, Douglas R. *Streamlining Your Local Development Process.* Managing Design and Development Technical Bulletin Number 10. Washington, D.C.: National League of Cities, 1981.

Summarizes how communities can streamline their development review and permitting process to improve the timeliness and quality of review decisions.

Roddewig, Richard J. "Preservation Law and Economics." In *A Handbook on Historic Preservation Law,* edited Christopher J. Duerkson. Washington, D.C.: The Conservation Foundation and the National Center for Preservation Law, 1983.

Explains how developers and planners analyze an historic preservation project.

Roddewig, Richard J., and Jared Shlaes. *Analyzing the Economic Feasibility of a Development Project: A Guide for Planners.* Planning Advisory Service Report No. 380. Chicago, IL: American Planning Association, 1983.

Explains how planners can analyze the economic feasibility of a project from the developer's perspective in order to identify the most effective public incentives to ensure project success.

Schneider, Devon M., David R. Godschalk, and Norman Axler. *The Carrying Capacity Concept as a Planning Tool.* Chicago: American Planning Association, 1979.

Introduces the carrying capacity concept as a planning tool. Provides specific examples of carrying capacity analysis.

Stryker, Perrin. *How to Judge Environmental Planning for Subdivisions: A Citizen's Guide.* Chicago: American Planning Association, 1981.

This short book explains how to evaluate land and water resource impacts of subdivision proposals. Discusses the 18 important questions.

Planning and Politics

Creighton, James L. *The Public Involvement Manual.* Cambridge, MA.: Abt Books, 1981.

Written primarily as a handbook for public officials, it is also helpful to citizens interested in increasing public participation in the land use planning process.

Healy, Robert G., and James L. Short. *The Market for Rural Land: Trends, Issues, Policies.* Washington, D.C.: The Conservation Foundation, 1981.

Examines the economic forces that are changing the rural land market, principally including the demand for resource land. Provides six case studies of changing markets, addresses land use policy and planning issues that are suggested by market trends.

Preservation Action. *Blueprint for Lobbying: A Citizens Guide to the Politics of Preservation.* Washington, D.C.: Preservation Action, 1984.

Focuses on historic preservation, provides basic suggestions on how to lobby at the federal, state, and local levels.

Smith, Herbert H. *Citizens Guide to Planning.* Chicago, IL: American Planning Association, 1979.

A general lay person's introduction to planning written in accessible language by a veteran planner.

Negotiations

Bacow, Lawrence S., and Michael Wheeler. *Environmental Dispute Resolution.* New York: Plenum Publishing Corporation, 1984.

Bingham, Gail. *Resolving Environmental Disputes: A Decade of Experience.* Washington, D.C.: The Conservation Foundation, 1986.

Provides a description and analysis of the effectiveness of alternative dispute resolution techniques, particularly negotiation and mediation.

Cohen, Herb. *You Can Negotiate Anything.* Toronto: Bantam Books, 1980.

Provides practical strategic advice on negotiating successfully, with emphasis on finding win/win solutions.

Fisher, Roger, and William Ury. *Getting to Yes: Negotiating Agreement Without Giving In.* New York: Penguin Books, 1983.

A classic guide to the techniques of creative negotiation. Provides concrete suggestions for dealing with common negotiating roadblocks.

Levitt, Richelle L., and John J. Kirlin. *Managing Development Through Public/Private Negotiations.* Washington, D.C.: Urban Land Institute, 1986.

McCarthy, Jane, and Alice Shoret. *Negotiating Settlements: A Guide to Environmental Mediation.* Washington, D.C.: American Arbitration Association, 1984.

Provides an overview of the use of mediation in resolving environmental disputes. Walks the reader through the various stages of the mediation process, from feasibility assessment to implementation.

Sullivan, Timothy J. *Resolving Development Disputes Through Negotiations.* New York: Plenum Publishing Corporation, 1984.

APPENDIX A

A Primer on Growth Management Tools and Techniques

Traditional elements in the growth management process include:

- Planning, such as preparing a comprehensive plan, which may include specific small area plans such as a downtown plan or a commercial corridor plan, and specific functional elements or plans such as housing, open space, historic preservation, recreation, and transportation elements;

- Implementing regulations and strategies, such as zoning regulations, subdivision ordinances, and land acquisition programs; and

- Capital improvements planning and budgeting, and scheduling future investments in public facilities such as streets, sewer collection and transmission lines, and parks.

The growth management process can involve the following:

1. Determination of community goals, objectives, and policies;

2. Analysis of the community's existing or *de facto* growth policies;

3. Inventory of available growth management tools and techniques;

4. Adaptation of appropriate tools and techniques for the community;

5. Synthesis of selected tools into a system for managing growth; and

6. Continued monitoring of and refinements to the system over time.[1]

The effect of implementing growth management tools and changing market conditions creates the need to reevaluate and modify the land use plan, which in turn leads to further refinements to the various growth management tools. This process varies considerably from place to place and rarely proceeds in the orderly manner intended: growth management tools are often implemented long before plans are adopted; permit decisions are made that undermine local plans.

Planning

"Land use planning" is a broad term. According to the American Planning Association:

Planning is a comprehensive, coordinated and continuing process, the purpose of which is to help public and private decision makers arrive at decisions which promote the common good of society. This process includes:
(1) Identification of problems or issues;
(2) Research and analysis to provide definitive understanding of such problems or issues;
(3) Formulation of goals and objectives to be attained in alleviating problems or resolving issues;
(4) Development and evaluation of alternative methods (plans and programs) to attain agreed upon goals and objectives;
(5) Recommendation of appropriate courses of action from among the alternatives;

(6) Assistance in implementation of approved plans and programs;

(7) Evaluation of actions taken to implement approved plans and programs in terms of progress towards agreed upon goals and objectives; and

(8) A continuing process of adjusting plans and programs in light of the results of such evaluation or to take into account changed circumstances.[2]

Ideally, a local comprehensive plan is a product of this planning process. Additionally, a comprehensive plan is not static, but must be updated regularly in response to the effect of growth management strategies and changing community conditions.

A comprehensive plan should embody a community's vision of what it wants to become and how it intends to get there.[*] This vision should serve as an overall policy guide for public and private decisions that affect community development, including the implementation of land use regulations and other growth management strategies.

In fact, however, this process rarely proceeds as rationally as intended. Zoning ordinances and other growth management strategies are often revised or implemented without the benefit of prior revision to a comprehensive plan. Permit decisions that undermine community plans and goals are common. However, the degree of inconsistency between plans and other growth management techniques varies considerably from state to state and community to community.

A representative table of contents for a plan for a small community might include the following elements:

- Description of the planning process;

- Statement of community goals, objectives, and policies;

- Inventory of the community's natural and cultural assets, and assessment of possible threats to these assets;

- Description of existing community conditions, with special focus on the downtown, principal commercial corridors, and other key areas of the community;

- Description of existing and projected:

  Land use patterns;
  Transportation and traffic circulation conditions;
  Public safety conditions and facilities;
  Housing supply, mix, and future housing demand;
  Utility service conditions and facilities (water, sewer, solid waste, and energy);
  Open space and natural resource conditions;
  Recreation conditions and facilities;
  Economic conditions and assets, and economic development and redevelopment prospects;
  Historic preservation efforts;

- Projections of how development at permitted densities will affect the community's appearance, character, natural resources, cultural assets, economic development, fiscal conditions, and public services;

- Description of environmental constraints to development; and

- Description of future capital facilities planning and budgeting.

In many states, the minimum contents of local plans are mandated by state statute. While qualitative measures of the adequacy of local plans are difficult to legislate, evaluation of the adequacy of a comprehensive plan should focus on such questions as:

- Are planning goals, objectives, and policies clearly articulated with priorities set forth?

- Are the goals, objectives, and policies internally consistent? Is there coordination between the various elements?

- Is the plan based upon the results of a broad and meaningful public participation process?

- If maps are included, do they clearly identify land uses and the other geographic aspects of the plan? Do the maps accurately capture local geography and existing physical conditions?

- Are the economic, environmental, and public service assumptions underlying the plan clearly identified? Are they realistic?

Specific Growth Management Techniques

Planning is but one of the numerous local tools available to manage growth. The preparation and adoption of a comprehensive plan is, in fact, only the beginning of the growth management process.[3] Plans are not self-executing, they can be implemented only through land use regulations, capital facilities spending, land

---

   [*] "Comprehensive plans" are referred to by various terms including "plan of development," "master plan," and "community plan." Traditional comprehensive plans are of the "physical" variety, i.e., they specifically identify appropriate land uses for individual parcels of land. Alternatively, some communities have adopted so-called "policy plans," which enumerate long-range objectives intended to guide future community development and serve as broad guidelines for specific land use regulations. A common approach is to merge the physical and policy approaches into a hybrid overall plan.

acquisition, and other strategies. These growth management techniques can be grouped into four basic categories:

- Land use regulations;
- Public spending and taxing policies;
- Land acquisition; and
- Private voluntary preservation and development techniques.

Although the techniques commonly appear as discrete options, most successful growth management programs, in fact, combine several separate techniques. Successful communities continually experiment with adapting various complementary strategies and techniques to meet their particular needs, which are constantly evolving.

LAND USE REGULATIONS

The authority for local land use planning and regulation is derived from the "police power" that authorizes states to enact laws to protect the public health, safety, and general welfare. States have delegated substantial portions of this broad regulatory authority to local governments. The most important and promising regulatory techniques for managing growth include zoning (in its numerous permutations); height limits; cluster zoning and planned unit development; subdivision regulations; exactions; adequate public facilities ordinances; transfer of development rights; and moratoria.

Zoning

Zoning is the most commonly used local device for regulating the use of land. Initially developed in the early part of this century basically to insulate residential neighborhoods from the negative impacts of industrial development, the essence of the traditional "Euclidian" zoning ordinance remains the physical separation of potentially incompatible land uses.*

Zoning regulates the use of land and structures—for example, commercial versus residential—and the dimensional characteristics of permitted uses, such as minimum lot sizes, the placement of structures on lots (i.e., minimum setbacks from street or property lines), the density of development, and the maximum height of buildings. In addition, zoning ordinances increas-

ingly regulate nondimensional aspects of development such as landscaping, architectural design and features, signage, traffic circulation, and storm-water management.

Zoning ordinances consist of a text and a zoning map. The text describes permitted uses in the various districts, establishes standards for uses within these districts, and provides for administration and enforcement. The map divides the jurisdiction into districts. Changes to a zoning ordinance text or map occur through an amendment process that is initiated either by the local government, a landowner, or, in some cases, by local residents.

Conventional zoning promotes strict segregation of uses and predictable dimensional and density regulations. From this orderly and static pattern, land use regulation has evolved into a system of numerous techniques designed to balance the predictability of conventional zoning with administrative flexibility, discretionary review of individual developments, and specialized techniques to meet particular local needs.

Special Permits. Special permits (also referred to as conditional uses or special exceptions) are the most widely used device allowing individual review and approval of proposed developments that require individual scrutiny to avoid or alleviate particular problems. In most zoning ordinances, uses are permitted within a district either "by right," with no individual discretionary review of the proposed development, or by special permit, in which case a zoning board reviews individual proposals in accordance with standards set forth in the ordinance. The special permit is available if the proposal adequately complies with the provisions in the ordinance, which typically deal with traffic and other impacts of the proposal.

A special permit should be distinguished from a variance, which is an individual exemption from zoning requirements. Variances typically are allowed when the impact of a zoning requirement would impose an undue hardship on a landowner due to unique conditions of the individual parcel. In many cases, variances may be granted from dimensional standards, but not use limitations.

Floating Zones. Floating zones serve the same purpose as special permits, but provide the locality with more discretion. The standards for a floating zone are set forth in the text of a zoning ordinance, but the district is not mapped; rather the district "floats" above the community until a second, later ordinance amendment brings the zone to the ground. The second ordinance affixes the floating zone to a particular par-

* So named because the zoning ordinance of the Village of Euclid, Ohio, was the subject of an early landmark decision from the U.S. Supreme Court that upheld the validity of zoning. *City of Euclid v. Ambler Realty Company,* 272 U.S. 365 (1926).

cel that meets the standards set forth in the zoning text for the district.

The floating zone technique gives a locality greater discretion over a proposed use than does a special permit. A decision on a proposed rezoning to apply the floating zone is a legislative function in most states and is rarely overturned by the courts; while a special permit application is an administrative function and must be granted if the proposed use is shown to meet the stated criteria.

Conditional Zoning and Development Agreements. Sometimes a landowner may seek a rezoning, but the locality is unwilling to permit the whole range of uses or densities that the proposed zoning classification would allow. Instead of denying the rezoning, the local government may wish to impose conditions on the prospective rezoning. With conditional zoning, a local government may make rezoning conditional on an applicant's acceptance of concessions or conditions that are not otherwise imposed in the proposed zoning district. The applicant makes a unilateral commitment to these concessions in exchange for the rezoning; however, the local government makes no reciprocal obligation to rezone the property. Many states have upheld the use of conditional zoning, while several others have rejected its use.

Contract zoning also permits a locality to impose individual conditions on a rezoning, but—unlike conditional zoning—the municipality, in exchange, enters into an enforceable agreement to grant the desired zone change. In many states, contract zoning has been held invalid, because the locality bargains away its police power without state enabling legislation to do so.

A growing number of states (including California, Maine, Hawaii and others) have enacted legislation authorizing contract zoning or "development agreements" to regulate large-scale development. Development agreements typically are enforceable agreements between a developer and a local government, which lay out precisely the land uses and densities a developer may place on a large parcel and the public benefits the developer must provide as a condition of approval. The use of development agreements allows a single "master" approval for a large-scale, phased development. This approach provides developers and lending institutions the certainty of knowing early in the development process the amount and type of development authorized. Development agreements often also provide that the developer's right to complete all phases of a project vests earlier than it would in the absence of the agreement, which benefits developers when arranging financing. In exchange for this regulatory certainty, the local government may negotiate with the developer for a better package of public benefits than it could otherwise obtain.

Bonus or Incentive Zoning. Bonus or incentive zoning allows a developer to exceed a zoning ordinance's dimensional limitations if the developer agrees to fulfill conditions specified in the ordinance. The classic example is when an ordinance authorizes a developer to exceed height limits by a specified amount in exchange for providing open spaces or plazas adjacent to the building.

Overlay Zones. This zoning technique differs from conventional mapped zoning districts. An overlay zone applies a common set of regulations and standards to a designated area that may cut across several different preexisting conventional zoning districts. These regulations and standards apply in addition to those of the underlying zoning district. Two common examples of overlay zones are the flood zones created under the National Flood Insurance Program and many historic districts.

Flood zones often are described in local zoning ordinances, but are not initially mapped on the zoning map. Rather, the ordinance provides that the flood district regulations apply to areas within the 100-year floodplain, as designated in federal Flood Insurance Rate Maps. An overlay flood zone may allow the uses and densities permitted in the underlying zone, but impose additional construction and flood-proofing requirements.

Overlay historic districts often permit the uses and densities permitted in the underlying zone, but require that structures within the historic district be built or maintained in conformance with regulations to ensure historic compatibility.

Large Lot Zoning. Large lot zoning or minimum lot size zoning—requiring that lots in a residential zone be at least, for example, 5 acres and in some cases as much as or more than 40 acres—is often used to reduce the density of residential development. The environmental and economic effects of large lot zoning vary with the specific situation. When used judiciously in areas with significant development constraints, large minimum lot size zoning can effectively reduce the negative impacts of development on sensitive landscapes or natural resources. To work effectively, large lot zoning must usually be used in combination with regulations that accommodate market demand in other more suitable areas. Overreliance on large lot zoning, however, often encourages land consuming and inefficient low-density sprawl.

Agricultural Zoning. Agricultural zoning establishes minimum parcel sizes large enough to ensure that each parcel can sustain a viable agricultural operation. Some districts require minimum lot sizes of as much as 160 acres. Agricultural districts often also prohibit land uses that are incompatible with agriculture. (This technique is discussed in chapter 1, Agricultural Land.)

Zoning Based on Performance Standards. Zoning regulations often use performance standards to regulate development based on the permissible effects or impacts of a proposed use rather than simply the proposed dimensions. The complexity and sophistication of these standards vary widely, depending on the objectives of the program and the capacity of the locality to administer a complex program. Performance zoning may supplement or replace traditional zoning districts and dimensional standards. Under performance zoning, proposed uses whose impacts would exceed specified standards are prohibited.

Performance standards are widely used to regulate noise, dust, vibration, and other impacts of industrial zones, and are increasingly used to regulate environmental impacts, such as the limiting of storm-water runoff resulting from development.

Point Systems. Some communities use performance standards in combination with point systems. A proposed project must amass a minimum number of points in order to receive a permit. As opposed to the self-executing nature of conventional zoning, where a landowner can determine if a project is permissible by reading the zoning map and text, point systems require case-by-case review to determine if a specific land use is permissible. Permissible uses and densities of a parcel are determined at the time of permit application, with the applicant providing documentation that the proposal will comply with the various standards. Breckenridge, Colorado, has implemented a well-known development point system.

Height Limits
Localities limit building heights either townwide or by zoning district. In addition, height restrictions are sometimes used in conjunction with site-specific standards to prohibit structures that would be visible from scenic points or would block scenic views. (This technique is discussed in chapter 4.)

Cluster Zoning and Planned Unit Development
"Cluster zoning" (also known as "open space zoning") and the "planned unit development" (PUD) describe land use control devices that allow flexible design and clustering of development in higher densities on the most appropriate portion of a parcel in order to provide increased open space elsewhere on the parcel. These techniques, which exist in many forms, have become increasingly popular as more communities realize that conventional zoning and subdivision regulations often result in unsightly low-density sprawl with no intervening open space. These alternative clustering techniques can offer several benefits relative to conventional zoning, including:

- Limiting encroachment of development in and adjacent to environmentally sensitive areas;
- Reducing the amount of open land disturbed by development, thereby encouraging the preservation of agricultural lands, woodlands, and open landscapes;
- Reducing the amount of roads and utility lines needed for new development, which can reduce the cost of housing and public services.

Cluster development techniques typically do not allow increased overall development density, but simply rearrange development to preserve open land and improve site design. The concept can be demonstrated by a simple example of cluster development: a developer has 100 acres in an area zoned for one-half-acre residential lots, which could be developed into around 200 buildable lots, using up the entire 100 acres. Under a cluster zoning program, the developer could cluster the 200 units on 50 acres, for example, and permanently dedicate 50 acres of open space for public use.

A recent publication of the Center for Rural Massachusetts, *Dealing with Change in the Connecticut River Valley: A Design Manual for Conservation and Development* (cited at the end of this appendix), provides excellent demonstrations of clustering techniques and shows with aerial graphics how cluster development improves the landscape relative to development under conventional zoning regulations.

Subdivision Regulations
Subdivision regulations are widely used to regulate the conversion of land into building lots. In rural communities, they are often the principal or only means by which a community regulates residential development.

Subdivision regulations were originally enacted primarily to facilitate land transfer by providing a method for landowners to file a subdivision plat with numbered lots, rather than with the traditional metes and bounds lot descriptions. In the 1920s and 1930s, cities began to use these regulations to manage the quality of streets, storm drainage systems, lot layout, and the adequacy of utility services. Typically, subdivision ordinances articulate design standards and materials for streets and utility systems, site topography, sidewalks, curbs and gutters, storm-water management, landscaping, open space, and recreational facilities. More recently, subdivision regulations have been widely used not only to improve the engineering and physical design of on-site public improvements, but also to require the provision of dedicated recreational lands, off-site road improvements, and other public services.

Development Exactions and Impact Fees

"Development exaction" is a generic term that describes a variety of mechanisms by which communities require dedication of land or facilities or payment of a fee in lieu of land or facilities. Exactions are referred to by many names, including "dedications," "linkage requirements," "mandatory tithing," and "mitigation requirements." Exactions are either explicitly mandated in development regulations or imposed informally on a case-by-case basis in rezoning or special permit negotiations. Impact fees require a developer to pay an amount of money determined by a uniform formula rather than by negotiation or tradition.

Traditionally, exactions have required subdivision developers to provide on-site infrastructure such as roads, parks, sewer lines, and drainage facilities. Realizing that to require certain on-site improvements such as parks might be inefficient or inequitable, many communities began to require developers to pay fees in lieu of improvements in certain situations. These fees are then earmarked for providing those facilities to serve the development.

Recently, municipalities have begun imposing impact fees to finance an expanding variety of public facilities and services in virtually all regulatory contexts. Martin County, Florida, for example, has enacted a Beach Impact Fee Ordinance, which requires developers to contribute to a fund, based upon the projected recreational demand resulting from the proposed development, to purchase and maintain public beachfront property.

Financially strapped large cities have been most aggressive in imposing development exactions, requiring developers of large projects to pay impact or linkage fees for numerous public services. San Francisco, for example, requires developers of large-scale downtown projects to pay impact fees for affordable housing, transit, public parks, and child care. Boston imposes fees for both housing and job training. In Honolulu, developers of large projects commonly must pay for off-site sewer improvements, park land and facilities, on-site and off-site road and transportation system improvements, police and fire protection

facilities, school sites and buildings, on-site or off-site affordable housing, water supply infrastructure (perhaps including reservoirs), and employment programs for area residents. San Diego finances capital facilities for suburban development through "flexible benefits assessments," which combine impact fees and special assessments. These fees finance parks, roads, libraries, schools, utilities, drainage systems, transit service, and police and fire protection. (The legal limitations on the use of exactions and impact fees are discussed in chapter 2.)

Adequate Public Facilities Ordinances

This type of ordinance conditions development approval upon a finding that adequate public facilities are available to serve proposed development. The ordinance sets quantitative standards for required public service levels and links development approval to the ability of public services that serve the proposed development to comply with these standards. The public services that have the most significant impact on development decisions are water, sewer, and the traffic circulation network. Other public services sometimes linked to development approval are storm-water management facilities, parks and recreational lands, emergency response time, and mass transit. Florida requires all local governments to adopt adequate public facilities standards. After the state approves a local plan and development regulations, the local government cannot issue development permits unless public services can be provided for the development at the established level of service.

Transfer of Development Rights

Transfer of development rights (TDR) is an innovative growth management technique based on the concept that ownership of land gives the owner many rights, each of which may be separated from the rest and transferred to someone else. One of these separable rights is the right to develop land. With a TDR system, landowners are able to retain their land, but sell the right to develop the land for use on other property.

Under a typical TDR program, a local government awards development rights to each parcel of developable land in the community or in selected districts, based on the land's acreage or value. Persons can then sell their development rights on the open market if they do not want to develop their property or are prohibited by regulation from developing the property at a desired density. Land from which development rights have been sold cannot be developed.

There are many possible variations on TDR, but a system can work in the following way. Suppose A owns four acres of land that has been allocated two development rights. If local regulations require A to have one right per acre in order to fully develop the land, A has three choices. A can develop just two acres and expend all the development potential for the parcel; A can buy two development rights on the market and develop the entire four acres; or A can sell the two rights at a market-determined price and preclude any development of the property. If the land is in an agricultural or historic district, regulations may restrict development of the parcel, in which case A can only develop the parcel at a low density and sell the balance of the development rights for use on another site.

TDR can reduce substantially the value shifts and economic inequities of restrictive zoning. For example, it can allow the market to compensate owners whose land cannot be developed because of its environmental, scenic, or historic significance. By selling development rights, a landowner can receive profit from property appreciation without developing the parcel.

TDR requires a high level of staff expertise to design and administer. The novelty of the TDR concept and the sophistication required to make it work properly reduces its attractiveness and political acceptance in many communities.*

Moratoria and Interim Development Regulations
Moratoria and interim regulations are designed to substantially restrict development for a limited period. They can impose a complete temporary moratorium on all development or on specific types of intensive development. A moratorium can apply to zoning approvals, subdivision approvals, and building permits.

Restrictive interim regulations must generally relate to one of two permissible goals. Either they must relate to planning—used to restrain development until a plan can be developed or a permanent growth management program implemented—or necessary to protect public safety, health, or the environment by preventing potentially hazardous overburdening of community facilities (such as a sewage treatment facility). The duration of a moratorium should be specified when enacted, and should be tied to the time period necessary to develop a plan, implement a growth management program, or upgrade public facilities related to the relevant safety or environmental problem.

LOCAL SPENDING AND TAXING POLICIES

Although not traditionally viewed as methods of managing development, local expenditure and property taxation policies may have significant impacts on land use. Public facilities such as roads, water systems, sewers, and public transit can especially influence the level and characteristics of development in a community. A local growth management strategy is incomplete unless it accounts for these influences.

Capital Improvements Programming
The provision of municipal services is an important local tool for managing development. A municipal decision whether to extend or expand public utilities or facilities strongly influences the economic feasibility of most large private development projects. The extension of municipal services is generally governed by a city's capital improvements program (CIP), a timetable by which a city indicates the timing and level of municipal services it intends to provide over a specified duration. Generally, the CIP covers a five- to ten-year period, although it may be shorter or longer depending upon the municipality's confidence in its ability to predict future conditions.

Capital programming, by itself, influences land development decisions. By committing itself to a timetable for expansion of municipal services, a locality influences development decisions to some extent, especially in areas where on-site sewage disposal or water supply is unusually expensive or infeasible. A capital program may also be used effectively as part of a more comprehensive program to manage development. By properly coordinating its utility extension policy with its planning and growth management program, a community can control the direction and pace of development. Using a comprehensive plan to delineate the location and type of development desired and a capital program to schedule the provision of services, a locality can inform developers when development of a particular parcel will be encouraged and the type of development that will be allowed. In addition, a municipality can regulate the pace of development to coincide with the availability of adequate public services.

Preferential Assessment
Most states have enacted preferential or use-value property tax assessment programs for farmland and open space land. With use-value assessment, property taxes for a parcel are based upon the value of the parcel only considering its current use, rather than its value based upon the property's development potential. Use-value assessment can reduce the property tax assessments for lands whose value for development purposes exceeds its value for agricultural or forestry uses. Reduced property tax assessments can lessen the need to sell or develop sometimes caused by high property taxes. (These programs as they relate to agricultural resources are discussed in chapter 3.)

_____
* Montgomery County, Maryland, has implemented perhaps the most successful TDR program with approximately 20,000 acres preserved for farmland due to the program. The program is described in a profile in chapter 1.

Special Assessments

The special assessment is the local taxation technique that has the greatest potential impact on growth management policy. A special assessment, while not technically a tax, is a method of raising revenue in which all or part of the cost of a facility is charged to a landowner who derives a special benefit from the facility. Special assessments are often used for road improvements, street lighting, off-street parking, sewers, and water systems. The fee is usually proportionate to the distance the facility abuts a parcel, the area of the land served by the facility or improvement, or the value added to the land served.

Improvement Districts

Special improvement districts have been created in many forms to raise revenue for traffic circulation improvements, aesthetic improvements, or other public improvements within a limited area. Landowners within a specified district are levied a special tax or assessment (sometimes through tax increment financing), which is used to make public improvements that benefit that district.

LAND ACQUISITION

Local governments enjoy broad authority under state enabling legislation to acquire real property interests, either through voluntary sale or condemnation, for any legitimate public purpose. Land acquisition is an important supplement to land use regulations as a means of managing growth and protecting critical resources. Although localities generally use land acquisition to directly control the use of the specific parcel acquired, several communities have used land acquisition to influence the community's general growth policies. For example, Boulder, Colorado, has used the proceeds of local bond issues and a local sales tax to acquire a large amount of land in the foothills and farming districts surrounding the city to prevent environmentally destructive and fiscally unsound development of these areas. (This program is discussed in chapter 1.)

Local land acquisition programs are generally funded either by local property taxes, sales taxes, or real estate transfer taxes. Bond issues backed by one of these taxes are commonly used. Nantucket, Massachusetts, and Block Island, Rhode Island, for example, impose a 2 percent conveyance tax on most transfers of real estate to fund local open space acquisition programs. (The federal Land and Water Conservation Fund and, more recently, state land acquisition programs have also been important revenue sources for recreational land acquisition and improvement programs.)

Fee Simple Acquisition

The ownership of land is often analogized to ownership of a "bundle of rights," including, for example, the right to control access to the land, the right to develop property, the right to mine coal from beneath the land, the right to hunt on the land, and so forth. (Each of these are subject to reasonable police power regulations.) When one person owns all the rights associated with a parcel (the entire bundle), this person is said to own the land "in fee simple"; however, these rights can be owned separately, in which case an owner is said to own a "less-than-fee interest."

Local governments generally acquire fee simple ownership for parks and other property needed for municipal uses, such as for schools or landfills. Fee simple acquisition provides the greatest level of control over the use of a parcel; however, it is also usually the most expensive method of land acquisition. In addition to the substantial acquisition costs, fee simple acquisition removes property entirely from local tax rolls and can result in significant maintenance costs. For these reasons, localities and land trusts often prefer alternative land protection techniques to full ownership in fee.

Acquisition of Easements

The acquisition of easements constitutes a particularly useful tool for many local governments and land trusts. Easements are effective devices for preserving sensitive lands, providing public access along rivers or greenways, and allowing landowners to obtain income, estate, and property tax benefits for land stewardship while they continue to live on their land.

Easements are among the distinct property rights that may be sold separately from the other rights (in other words, "separated from the fee"). Easements can be divided into two categories: affirmative or negative. The owner of an affirmative easement has the right to do something with or on property belonging to someone else. An affirmative easement, for example, may authorize a utility company to place electric lines across someone's property or may authorize the public to pass over property to a riverside fishing spot.

The owner of a negative easement has the right to prohibit certain activities on property belonging to someone else. A negative easement may prohibit a landowner from constructing a building that would interfere with a scenic view from a neighboring parcel. A negative easement—for instance, an easement that prohibits development but allows a landowner to continue to farm and live on a parcel—may provide many of the same public open space benefits as full fee acquisition, but can generally be acquired at a substantially lower cost than a fee interest. In addition, management costs are usually assumed to a large degree by the private landowner, rather than by the public agency or land trust that holds the easement. Another fiscal advantage of easements is that the land remains on the tax rolls, albeit at a reduced value. Negative easements, however, may create long-term administrative, enforcement, and maintenance costs.

Easements may also be characterized as "appurtenant to the land" or "in gross." An appurtenant easement benefits one parcel of land (the "dominant estate") at the expense of another parcel (the "servient estate"). Usually these parcels are adjacent. For example, an appurtenant easement may grant the owner of the dominant estate access over an adjoining parcel to a county road. An easement in gross exists for the benefit of the person who owns the easement, regardless of whether that person owns any nearby land that is benefited. There is a strong presumption that if an easement is not clearly in gross, it is appurtenant.

The rules governing conveyance of appurtenant easements often differ from those governing easements in gross. When a parcel benefited by an appurtenant easement is sold, the benefits of the easement pass with the land to the new owner, even if the deed does not mention the easement. The benefits created by an easement in gross do not, by comparison, pass automatically to a new owner when the property is transferred. In some states, easements in gross are not recognized or are not transferrable to another person. Under traditional legal doctrines in many states, easements, and especially easements in gross, were difficult to enforce for various reasons. Because of these difficulties, almost all states have passed specific statutes authorizing conservation easements.

Conservation Easement Statutes.   Conservation easement statutes clarify the ambiguities and remove the barriers to enforcement of certain easements. These statutes set forth rules governing the definition, creation, transfer, and enforcement of easements created to conserve land or buildings. Although conservation easement statutes vary from state to state, some of the more important provisions typically found in conservation easement statutes include the following:

- *Definitions.* Most states define conservation easements to include a broad spectrum of property interests that restrict the development, management, or use of land. Typically, easements may be created to retain land in its natural condition, to provide recreational access, or to preserve and maintain the land's historic or architectural character.

- *Creation and Transfer.* Conservation easements must be created in writing. Some states require that conservation easements must be held by govern-

mental agencies or be approved by a central authority (for example, the secretary of environmental affairs in Massachusetts) and that conservation easements held by nonprofit corporations or trusts be approved by the relevant local government.

- *Permitted Holders.* Many states authorize only certain types of entities to hold conservation easements. These entities usually include governmental agencies, land trusts, corporations, and other entities whose purposes include conservation or preservation.

- *Enforcement.* The most important benefits of conservation easement statutes involve granting clear validity to conservation easements and eliminating most of the technical barriers to enforcement of conservation easements.

- *Relation to Nonstatutory (Common Law) Easements.* Some statutes are more comprehensive than others. If a state statute does not address a common law defense to enforcement, a conservation easement would still be subject to the defense, such as the defense that an easement in gross cannot be transferred.

PRIVATE VOLUNTARY LAND PROTECTION TECHNIQUES

Land acquisition and conservation techniques available to local governments or private nonprofit organizations can provide an important complement to local regulatory and public spending measures. A public or private land trust can use a range of land acquisition and conservation techniques, singly or in combination, to meet local conservation and growth management objectives. In towns such as Nantucket, Massachusetts, Block Island, Rhode Island, and Davis, California, municipalities have established local land trusts as municipal or quasi-municipal entities. These land trusts participate in the private real estate market as representatives of the public interest and use the range of voluntary land conservation techniques available to private land trusts.

The two most important private land protection techniques used by land trusts to protect land or historic buildings are fee simple acquisition and acquisition of easements.

Although land or easement acquisition are the conservation techniques most commonly employed by land trusts, there are many other private voluntary land protection tools to consider.*

---

* This section is comprised, in part, of material reprinted by permission of the California State Coastal Conservancy, from Stephen F. Harper, *The Nonprofit Primer: A Guidebook for Land Trusts* (Oakland, CA: California State Coastal Conservancy, 1984).

A common factor in these tools is that they provide land trusts a method to control or influence the use of valuable parcels with limited expenditures of money.

Other than acquisition at full market value, the principal private tools available to preserve land include:

- Donation or bargain sale of fee simple interests, conservation easements or other less-than-fee interests in land;
- Options to buy;
- Rights of first refusal;
- Leases and management agreements;
- Preacquisition;
- Limited or controlled development; and
- Conservation investment.*

Donation or Bargain Sale

In addition to purchasing land for conservation purposes at its full fair market value, land trusts often acquire property, whether fee or less-than-fee interests, through donation or bargain sale. Full-value purchase is rarely the approach of first preference because of the expense of acquisition and management.

Donation, when available, is the option of choice for obvious reasons. Donation also offers the conservation-minded landowner the greatest potential tax benefits.

In between full-value purchase and donation lies the bargain sale approach. A bargain sale involves a combination of donation and purchase, in which a landowner transfers property at a price below fair market value. The landowner may thus obtain tax benefits as well as a direct cash payment.

Options

An option is a widely used real estate contract device that provides a party with a temporary right—but not obligation—to purchase property. An option is the exclusive right to purchase a property at a specified price within a specified time. The party is not obligated to purchase the land; however, the landowner is prevented from accepting offers from other potential purchasers during the term of the option. Options can generally be acquired at a fraction of the ultimate purchase price, or they may be donated by the landowner. The deadline imposed by an option may be useful to a land trust in marshaling the funds necessary to purchase a parcel or finding a suitable private purchaser.

* Many land trusts have compiled descriptions of these alternatives in a succinct brochure to be used in building landowner interest and confidence. This type of brochure can introduce landowners to conservation techniques, and to the income and estate tax benefits accruing from donations and bargain sales. The Land Trust Exchange in Alexandria, Virginia, can provide sample brochures.

The land trust can purchase the property during the option period; if not, the option interest expires.

Rights-of-First-Refusal

A right-of-first-refusal is an agreement between a landowner and a second party in which the landowner agrees that if he receives a legitimate offer from a third party to buy the property, he will notify the second party and give the second party a specified period of time in which to match the third party offer under similar terms, before the landowner will accept the offer from the third party. Land trusts can acquire such rights, by purchase or donation, in order to tie up a parcel without having to buy it immediately. If a potential purchaser with conservation objectives makes an offer on the property, the land trust may decide not to exercise the right-of-first-refusal. Although both an option and a right-of-first-refusal can be donated, the land trust's legal position will be improved if the interest is created in a written contract, a minimal amount is paid for the contract interest, and the contract is recorded in proper form in the appropriate land records office.

Leases and Management Agreements

These tools provide a land trust with temporary control or influence over a parcel without the expense of acquisition. Leases and management agreements are flexible instruments that can be drafted to implement any number of desired relationships between a landowner and a land trust. Leases generally give a land trust the right to manage and occupy property for a certain time, while management agreements specify the terms and restrictions under which the landowner continues to manage the property. Generally, both devices are recorded in the land records and remain in force for their full term even if the land changes hands.

Preacquisition

Land trusts may acquire property to hold and manage in perpetuity. In other cases, land trusts serve as an intermediary for a public land management agency. A public agency may wish to work with a private land trust for preacquisition because a private organization can often negotiate and undertake other necessary steps for acquisition faster and more adeptly than the public agency. After land is acquired by a land trust and turned over, public land management agencies can often manage additional adjacent land more economically than could a private trust. Ownership by a public agency also confers more protection against condemnation by other public agencies, such as a state highway department, than does private land trust ownership.

Even when a land trust intends to retain ownership

of a parcel, it may be wise for its deeds and other title documents to provide for transfer of the title to a public agency or to a larger local, regional, or national land trust if the trust itself ceases to exist or is unable to manage its holdings.

Limited or Controlled Development

Increasingly employed by innovative land trusts, this technique typically entails clustered development or other limited development of a portion of a parcel in order to finance acquisition and preservation of the balance of the parcel. Development is generally limited to nonsensitive or previously disturbed portions of a parcel. Limited development (also called "controlled development" or "creative partial development") can permit land stewardship and substantial resource protection in situations when donation is not possible and acquisition for full preservation is not financially feasible. Limited development is often feasible because building lots or houses adjacent to restricted open space are frequently more valuable than otherwise.

This tool often lends itself to the formation of a partnership for joint development between the trust and a landowner. In such partnerships, the latter provides the land and the land trust provides planning and land protection expertise, community goodwill, assurance that the open space portions of the property will be permanently protected from development, and development capital. (See the profile of the Housatonic Valley Association in chapter 2 for an example of successful limited development.)

When considering limited development, a land trust should obtain professional assistance from bankers, builders, real estate agents, and other development professionals to determine whether development at the density necessary to finance the acquisition is feasible from a financial perspective. This tool is only appropriate for parcels of sufficient size and with appropriate conditions to allow creative partial development without endangering the resources that are worthy of protection. Finally, before undertaking limited development, a land trust should ensure that its proposed actions will not endanger its mission and public reputation as a conservation organization. The public that volunteers time and donates money may not readily accept the limited development concept, especially without an educational effort by the land trust.

Conservation Investment

Many real estate development ventures are financed through syndications, in which numerous individuals or entities join together to finance a project. In return, the investors receive some combination of periodic income, capital gain upon resale, and, perhaps, significant tax benefits. This technique can be adapted for land conservation. Although the Tax Reform Act of 1986 reduced the income tax advantages of most types of real estate investments, creative tax-saving arrangements are still possible.

In some cases, a land trust may sell property subject to appropriate deed restrictions or conservation easements to a buyer looking for an aesthetically pleasing place to live or own a vacation home. In other cases, "charitable investors" may be persuaded to invest in a working farm, fishing preserve, or ranch with deed restrictions to allow only agriculture, forestry, or other open space uses. Investors would receive a percentage of the operation's income and tax benefits (for example, through depreciation of capital assets, deductions for business expenses, or deductions for mortgage interest payments) as well as the satisfaction of knowing they have helped conserve open land.

INFORMATION RESOURCES

Babcock, Richard F., and Charles L. Siemon. *The Zoning Game Revisited*. Boston: Lincoln Institute of Land Policy, 1985.

Updated version of a classic book on zoning and the land use regulation process. Provides case studies of 11 local and regional land use programs, their origins, development, legal aspects, and political history.

Brower, David J., Candace Carraway, Thomas Pollard, and C. Luther Propst. *Managing Development in Small Towns*. Chicago: American Planning Association Press, 1984.

Provides a comprehensive overview of the use of growth management measures in small towns, including techniques based upon local land acquisition, public spending, taxation, and regulatory powers. Provides tangible guidance in assessing the need for growth management and in implementing specific techniques.

Chapin, F. Stuart, and Edward J. Kaiser. *Urban Land Use Planning*. 3d ed. Urbana: University of Illinois Press, 1979.

A leading land use planning textbook.

Clark, John. *The Sanibel Report: Formulation of a Comprehensive Plan Based on Natural Systems*. Washington, D.C.: The Conservation Foundation, 1976.

Explains the process leading to the development of a performance-based comprehensive planning process and overlay zoning program for Sanibel Island, Florida. The basis for the program is mitigating the impacts of development on vegetation, wildlife, coastal process, geology, or hydrology of the barrier island.

Conservation Foundation. *Groundwater Protection*. Washington, D.C.: The Conservation Foundation, 1987.

This book contains the final report of the National Groundwater Policy Forum and a guide to problems, causes, and government responses to groundwater pollution.

Diehl, Janet, and Thomas S. Barrett. *The Conservation Easement Handbook: Managing Land Conservation and Historic Preservation Easement Programs*. Trust for Public Land and Land Trust Exchange, 1988. Available from Land Trust Exchange, 1017 Duke Street, Alexandria, VA 22314.

Authoritative and well-written book that provides solid information about establishing and managing easements programs.

Hoose, Phillip M. *Building an Ark: Tools for the Preservation of Natural Diversity Through Land Protection*. Covelo, CA: Island Press, 1981.

Provides an overview of private techniques to preserve open space and important wildlife and plant resources. Includes chapters on conducting natural heritage inventories, private land protection techniques, and lobbying state government to protect our natural heritage.

Kusler, Jon A. *Regulating Sensitive Lands*. Washington, D.C.: Environmental Law Institute, 1980.

This thorough book discusses regulatory programs to protect floodplains, lake and stream shores, coastal zones, wetlands, rivers, areas of scientific interest, and similar sensitive areas. It discusses state resource protection programs and cases.

Land Trust Exchange. *Organizing a Land Trust: Starting a Land Conservation Organization in Your Community*. Available from Land Trust Exchange, 1017 Duke Street, Alexandria, VA 22314.

The Land Trust Exchange publishes this handout and others about land trusts.

McHarg, Ian. *Design With Nature*. Garden City, N.Y.: The Natural History Press, 1969.

A pioneering introduction to regional land use planning based upon the development constraints and opportunities presented by natural systems. Contains case studies showing how environmental and scenic inventories can be combined to indicate where development should be directed.

Meshenberg, Michael J. *The Administration of Flexible Zoning Techniques*. Planning Advisory Service Report No. 318. Chicago: American Society of Planning Officials, 1976.

Provides an introduction to and analysis of flexible zoning techniques, including PUDs, special permits, floating zones, overlay zoning, tract zoning, incentive zoning, exactions, and TDR.

Sanders, Welford. *The Cluster Subdivision: A Cost-Effective Approach*. Planning Advisory Service Report No. 356. Chicago: American Planning Association, 1980.

Provides detailed guidance on the design of cluster subdivision ordinances. Includes legal guidance and excerpts from several local zoning ordinances.

Smith, Herbert H. *The Citizen's Guide to Planning*. Chicago: American Planning Association, 1979.

A lay person's general introduction to planning written by a veteran planner. Provides overviews of the planning process; the role of the local planning commission; the relationship between plans and regulations; and the connection between capital improvements and planning.

Smith, Herbert H. *The Citizen's Guide to Zoning*. Chicago: American Planning Association, 1983.

Provides a basic primer on all aspects of zoning and zoning administration, the citizens' role in zoning hearings, frequent problems with zoning, and emerging zoning techniques.

Thurow, Charles, William Jones, and Duncan Erley. *Performance Controls for Sensitive Lands: A Practical Guide for Local Administrators*. Planning Advisory Service Report Nos. 307, 308. Chicago: American Society of Planning Officials, 1975.

An early, comprehensive discussion of the use of performance standard regulations to protect environmental resources, including streams and lakes, aquifers, wetlands, woodlands, and hillsides. Includes excerpts of illustrative performance control ordinances.

Whyte, William H. *The Last Landscape*. Garden City, New York: Doubleday and Company, 1970.

An early, but still valuable look at both the politics of planning and land use regulation and how specific techniques can be employed to protect specific resources.

Yaro, Robert D., et al. *Dealing with Change in the Connecticut River Valley: A Design Manual for Conservation and Development*. Amherst, MA: Center for Rural Massachusetts, University of Massachusetts, 1988.

This valuable publication discusses the advantages of clustered development, provides practical planning standards for preserving distinctive lo-cal character while accommodating economic development, includes sample ordinance language for clustered development, and includes excellent aerial graphics showing various landscapes before development, after conventional development, and after creative site-sensitive development. This book builds a convincing argument for clustered development regulations.

APPENDIX B

Tax Benefits of Private Land Conservation

Tax policies can be major determinants of whether and how land is conserved or developed. In fact, an important factor motivating landowners to donate property to land trusts or other conservation organizations has been the tax benefits available under federal income and estate tax laws.

Although the Tax Reform Act of 1986 significantly changed the federal taxation of real estate transactions and reduced the income tax advantages of donating property for conservation purposes, the potential federal income and estate tax advantages of conservation donations remain an important tool for land trusts and local governments. Under the changes made by the 1986 tax reforms, income tax benefits will rarely, if ever, be the primary reason for a conservation donation. Federal income tax savings, however, coupled with estate tax benefits, can still provide important incentives for a conservation-oriented landowner.

The federal income tax laws also provide significant tax incentives for rehabilitation of old and historic buildings. Local planners, decision-makers, conservation organizations, and land trusts should understand these tax incentives in order to counsel landowners about the significant tax savings for contributing to a community's quality of life by rehabilitating old or historic structures. Moreover, these federal tax incentives may be an important factor in a local decision to designate an historic district.

This chapter contains three sections:

- A basic description of the income tax benefits of charitable gifts of land or interests in land for conservation purposes and the eligibility requirements for these benefits;

- A reprint of an article describing the effects of the Tax Reform Act on charitable giving of land, and explaining the important estate tax benefits of conservation contributions; and

- A reprint of a handbook describing federal historic rehabilitation tax incentives.

Key Questions on the Tax Benefits of Land Donations

A number of questions need to be addressed in considering the income tax benefits of private land donations: When are donations eligible for income tax deductions? What tax benefits are available? How are conservation contributions valued? When might a bargain sale (part sale and part donation) or a tax-exempt land swap be appropriate? And how can the individual tax benefits of a conservation donation best be explained?

WHEN ARE DONATIONS OF LAND ELIGIBLE FOR INCOME TAX DEDUCTIONS?

Tax benefits for donations of land for conservation purposes have been available for some time. Section

170(f) of the Internal Revenue Code establishes the general parameters within which income tax deductions for contributing property for conservation purposes can be taken. While the rules in this area were changed substantially in 1980 and 1984, the Tax Reform Act of 1986 enacted no changes. A taxpayer may claim a deduction for contributing a full interest in real estate or a partial interest that qualifies in one of the following categories:

1. An undivided portion of a fee interest;
2. A remainder interest in a residence or farm (for example, a landowner might retain the exclusive right to use a farm for the landowner's life, with the ownership transferred to a land trust upon the landowner's death);
3. Certain gifts in trust;
4. A qualified conservation contribution.

The definition of a "qualified conservation contribution" is important for landowners who may be interested in donating a conservation easement (where the landowner retains ownership of the property but gives up the right to develop it) or an easement to allow public access. The definition has two elements: one concerning the nature of the organization receiving the contribution, and the other concerning the purpose of the contribution. The donation must be made to a tax-exempt publicly supported charity—such as a land trust—a government agency, or a charity controlled by a government agency.* The purpose of the donation must be "exclusively for conservation purposes." The tax law defines "conservation purposes" as:

1. The preservation of land areas for outdoor recreation by, or the education of, the general public;
2. The protection of a relatively natural habitat of fish, wildlife, or plants, or similar ecosystem;
3. The preservation of open space (including farmland and forest land) where such preservation is
   a. For the scenic enjoyment of the general public; or
   b. Pursuant to a clearly delineated federal, state, or local governmental conservation policy, and will yield a significant public benefit; or
4. The preservation of an historically importtant land area or a certified historic structure.

In addition, a qualified conservation contribution must be granted in perpetuity; it cannot have a limited duration.†

IF A DONATION IS ELIGIBLE, WHAT TAX BENEFITS ARE AVAILABLE?

Assuming that both the recipient and the donation qualify for income tax deductions, what specific income tax benefits are available to a landowner for a "qualified conservation contribution"? One of the best summaries of these benefits is provided by a brochure, The Tax Benefits of Contributing Farmland and Farmland Easements, produced and made available by the American Farmland Trust (AFT):

The fair market value of your contribution will constitute the amount available for deduction. The portion of this amount which you may actually deduct, however, depends upon your particular tax situation, including the amount of other charitable contributions you made during the taxable year. In every case of a charitable contribution of farmland or a conservation easement or restriction, you should consult with your personal tax advisors.

Charitable deductions of the type available for conservation contributions are generally deductible up to 30 percent (50 percent under certain conditions) of your income for the year of your contribution. If the value of your conservation contribution exceeds 30 percent of your income, then the excess may be carried over and deducted (subject to the same 30 percent limitation) in each of five succeeding taxable years.

[Land given outright] is deductible in the amount of its fair market value at the time of the contribution. The fair market value should be determined by an independent appraiser. The value of remainder interests contributed for conservation should take into account any depreciation (computed on the straightline method) and depletion taken with respect to the property, and that value should be discounted at a rate of six percent per annum for the length of the period, actually determined, until the remainder becomes a promissory interest. Conservation easements and restrictive covenants are typically, although not always, valued as the difference between the fair market value of the property involved before and after the grant of the easement or restrictive covenant.

In essence, the annual percentage limitation on the amount that a taxpayer can deduct works as follows: an individual taxpayer can deduct up to 30 percent of adjusted gross income in any one year. The taxpayer can then carry over and deduct from income in future years any unused portion of the contribution, for the next five years, subject each year to the 30 percent limitation.

An example may help to explain these rules (called carry-over rules): Suppose a taxpayer with taxable income of $200,000 wished to donate property worth

---

* See chapter 6 for a discussion of organizing and managing a land trust or other nonprofit entity to ensure that it qualifies as a publicly supported charity.

† These requirements are set forth in Section 170(g) of the Internal Revenue Code. A less-exacting standard applies for estate tax purposes.

$75,000. The donation would exceed the $60,000 annual limit by $15,000 (30% × $200,000 = $60,000). The taxpayer could therefore claim a $60,000 deduction in the year of the donation, and claim the remaining $15,000 the next tax year.

The annual percentage limitation for corporate gifts is 10 percent of income, with the same five-year carryover period as for individual deductions. For a corporation, the donation in the example would exceed its $20,000 limitation by $55,000 (10% × $200,000 = $20,000). The corporation could claim a $20,000 deduction in the year of the donation and claim $20,000 for each of the next two years and the final $15,000 deduction in the third year.

In addition to these income tax deductions, conservation donations are not subject to capital gains taxation.*

HOW ARE CONSERVATION CONTRIBUTIONS VALUED?

The value of an easement or other conservation restriction depends upon the degree of land use limitation it imposes. On the other hand, the value of the property interest that the landowner retains depends upon what land uses remain permissible under the restriction, and the value of the property limited to those uses. The amount of the available charitable deduction is the difference between the fair market value of the property based upon its most profitable use (i.e., "its highest and best use") without the conservation restriction and its fair market value at its most profitable use subject to the restriction. Therefore, a conservation easement on tidal wetlands or other land with slight development potential would have a low value, while the value of a conservation easement on buildable oceanfront land would likely constitute a very substantial portion of the total value of the parcel.

Although the valuation process is beyond the purview of a land trust or other nonprofit corporation that will receive donations of conservation lands or easements, land trust officials should be wary of inflated appraisals that could cause the IRS to question the specific deduction and bring increased scrutiny to the land trust's activities.

IF A LANDOWNER IS UNABLE OR UNWILLING TO MAKE AN OUTRIGHT DONATION, WOULD A BARGAIN SALE BE APPROPRIATE?

One of the principal questions in structuring a conservation transaction is whether the donor's situation and objectives suggest an outright donation or a bargain

sale. The concept of a land donation is straightforward: a landowner gives land or an interest in land to a land trust free of any payment or consideration. The landowner then takes a tax deduction (within the limits of the law) in the amount of the fair market value of the donated property.

On the other hand, a bargain sale is a combination of charitable donation and real estate sale. It involves the sale of property at a price below the property's fair market value. Within the usual limitations, a taxpayer can claim a charitable deduction equal to the difference between the fair market value of the property and the sale price paid by the conservation charity. With the tax benefits of a partial donation and the cash proceeds from the sale price, a bargain sale may provide the landowner with a yield close to that of a sale at full market price. Moreover, by dealing with a land trust, a landowner may avoid broker's commissions and other closing costs and the difficulties and uncertainties resulting from a commercial buyer's need to finance the acquisition.

When a landowner sells appreciated property, the capital gain realized from the sale is subject to income taxation.† A donation would avoid this tax altogether, while a bargain sale provides partial escape—in an amount proportional to the percentage of the property's total value that the landowner donates. (In other words, the more donated, the more saved on taxes.)

WOULD A LAND SWAP ENABLE A LANDOWNER TO FULFILL CONSERVATION OBJECTIVES?

In light of increased capital gains rates as a result of the Tax Reform Act of 1986, land trusts will likely encounter more situations in which exchanges of land can be used creatively to further conservation objectives.[1] Prior to the Tax Reform Act, the maximum effective tax rate on certain (i.e., long-term) capital gains was 20 percent, compared with 50 percent for other types of income. The Tax Reform Act implemented a uniform rate for capital gains income and ordinary income, resulting in an increased capital gains tax.

Land trust officials should recognize when a likekind exchange may allow a conservation-minded landowner to exchange a parcel with no significant natural resource values (but that produces rental income, for example) for another parcel that is worthy of protection (for example, an undeveloped parcel with high development potential and little income-

---

* The potentially significant estate tax savings are discussed later in this appendix.

† The capital gain realized equals the proceeds from the disposition of the property in excess of the seller's "basis" in the property. The basis is generally the original purchase price paid by the seller for the property plus the seller's investment in the property, minus any depreciation that the seller has taken.

producing potential unless it is developed). If both parcels have appreciated considerably since they were acquired, a swap may allow a person who owns income-producing property to invest in sensitive undeveloped property and allow a person who is "land rich, but cash poor" to obtain income-producing property. This swap may enable both parties to avoid capital gains taxes, while putting sensitive undeveloped property in the hands of a conservation-minded landowner.

WHY IS IT LESS DESIRABLE NOW FOR LANDOWNERS TO DONATE APPRECIATED PROPERTY THAN IT WAS BEFORE THE TAX REFORM ACT?

The Tax Reform Act of 1986 introduced the alternative minimum tax, which has the effect of discouraging substantial gifts of appreciated property. The act now requires taxpayers to compute their taxable income in two ways and to pay the greater of the two figures. First, taxable income is computed in the customary manner, with the taxpayer taking the usual deductions, credits, and exclusions. Second, the taxpayer computes the alternative minimum tax, which requires that taxable income *include* certain deductions, credits, and nontaxed income that are excluded in computing the regular tax. The items that must be included when computing the alternative minimum tax are called "preference items" and include, most importantly for land conservation purposes, the difference between the basis and the fair market value of the donated property at the time of the gift (i.e., the taxpayer's unrealized appreciation in the property). The alternative minimum tax rate is currently 21 percent of taxable income.

If a taxpayer is subject to the alternative minimum tax, the deduction available for conservation contributions is limited to the basis in the property. The taxpayer cannot deduct the amount that the property appreciated.

This provision not only discourages significant gifts of appreciated property, but also makes the job of explaining to landowners the tax consequences of a significant land donation more difficult. The new tax act therefore increases the need for land protection advocates to be able to explain clearly to a potential donor the specific tax consequences of a major gift of land.

HOW DOES A LAND PROTECTION ADVOCATE EXPLAIN THE TAX BENEFITS OF CONSERVATION DONATIONS OF LAND TO A POTENTIAL DONOR?

The motivations of potential conservation donors are frequently complex and not always apparent. Without doubt, a desire to preserve natural and scenic values is important, since landowners are seldom, if ever, fully compensated through tax benefits for their acts of stewardship. This is even more true in light of the reduced income tax rates, increased capital gains exclusion, and the new alternative minimum tax enacted in the Tax Reform Act of 1986. Landowners looking for the maximum financial return from a parcel are not likely to be interested in conservation contributions. Nevertheless, the income and estate tax benefits of making conservation contributions are an important marketing point for land trusts.*

Discussions of conservation tax benefits can easily become complex and abstruse. Land trust officials should become familiar enough with tax benefit analysis comfortably to work with landowners, tax lawyers, and accountants in structuring conservation transactions. It is particularly helpful if a land trust has a relationship, through its board or otherwise, with a tax attorney or accountant who can lend expertise to this important part of a land trust's business.

The tax consequences of a conservation donation depend upon the specific circumstances of the landowner. In order to analyze the income and estate tax consequences of a conservation transaction, a land trust must obtain factual information concerning both the value of the property involved and the financial circumstances and objectives of the landowner. This information can often be obtained from the landowner directly or, in the case of property value, from public land records, title insurance reports, and other sources. In the absence of such knowledge, a land trust may form educated estimates from public land records, local appraisers, and real estate brokers.

The estimated tax consequences of a conservation transaction can be summarized and arranged in a clear and presentable format and presented to a landowner to explain the consequences of making a donation or entering into a bargain sale. Because many potential donors are not familiar with the federal tax consequences of conservation contributions, the analysis should be as readily understandable as possible.

Table 1 is a sample format for such an analysis.† This example supposes that a landowner sells a parcel worth $225,000 to a land trust for $100,000. Although

---

* This point is discussed in detail later in this appendix.

† The federal and state tax codes are complex and the financial circumstances of each landowner vary. The analyses presented here have been simplified for illustrative purposes. Land trust officials should familiarize themselves with the basics of tax benefit analysis and, wherever possible, use expert assistance before adapting the formats used in this guidebook. The objective is to illustrate the basic format, not to provide a formula for all situations. As with any tax matter, the reader should consult competent counsel to determine the effect of the tax laws in specific situations before taking action.

Table 1

Federal Tax Consequences of a Bargain Sale (1988)
(Computing Taxable Income by the Regular Method)

(Status: Married Filing Jointly)

Facts/Assumptions		*Options*	
		Bargain Sale at $100,000	Sale at Fair Market Value
1. Land Value Computations			
	Fair market value	$ 225,000	$ 225,000
(less)	Part contributed	− (125,000)	− 0
	Part sold	$ 100,000	$ 225,000[a]
(less)	Basis (purchase price)	− (13,320)	− (30,000)
	Capital gain	$ 86,680	$ 195,000
2. Income Computations			
	Salary and interest income	$ 300,000	$ 300,000
(plus)	Capital gain	+ 86,680	+ 195,000
	Gross income	$ 386,680	$ 495,000
(less)	Itemized deductions and exemptions	− (100,000)[b]	− (100,000)
(less)	Charitable deduction	− (100,000)	0
	Taxable income	$ 186,680	$ 395,000
3. Tax Computations			
	Federal income tax (from 1987 tables)	$ 61,812	$ 142,015
4. After-Tax Income			
	Gross income	$ 386,680	$ 495,000
(plus)	Basis (recouped through sale)	+ 13,320	+ 30,000
(less)	Taxes	− 61,812	− 142,015
	Net after-tax income	$ 338,188	$ 382,985
5. Cost to Landowner of Bargain Sale		$ 44,797	

Note: This analysis does not include state income tax provisions.

[a] The basis is $30,000, which is reduced pro rata in the case of a bargain sale, so that the taxpayer deducts the portion of the basis that he sells at market values, but not the portion that he contributes.

[b] The deductibility of contributions in any one year is, in most cases, limited to 30 percent of adjusted gross income. The difference between the total value donated ($125,000) and the deduction claimed this year in this example ($100,000) is not lost; rather it can be carried over to the succeeding tax year.

the specific numbers used are only an example, the format can readily be adapted for other circumstances to demonstrate the after-tax consequences of a bargain sale. In this case, a land trust could demonstrate to a landowner that, after considering tax savings, the cost of a $125,000 contribution (the difference between the property's fair market value and its sale price to the land trust) is only $44,796. The tax benefits do not completely compensate the landowner; they do, however, greatly reduce the cost of charity.

Table 2

Federal Tax Consequences of a Bargain Sale (1988)
(Computing Alternative Minimum Tax)

(Status: Married Filing Jointly)

Facts/Assumptions		Options	
		Bargain Sale at $100,000	Sale at Fair Market Value
1. Land Value Computations			
	Fair market value	$ 225,000	$ 225,000
(less)	Part contributed	− (125,000)	− 0
	Part sold	$ 100,000	$ 225,000
(less)	Basis	− (13,320)	− (30,000)
	Capital gain	$ 86,680	$ 195,000
2. Income Computations			
	Salary and interest income	$ 300,000	$ 300,000
(plus)	Capital gain	+ 86,680	+ 195,000
	Gross income	$ 386,680	$ 495,000
(less)	Itemized deductions and exemptions	− (100,000)	− (100,000)
(less)	Charitable contribution	(− 0 −)[a]	− 0 −
	Taxable income	$ 286,680	$ 395,000
3. Tax Computations			
	Federal income tax (Taxable income × 21%)	$ 60,203	N.A.[b]
4. After-Tax Income			
	Gross income	$ 386,680	$ 495,000
(plus)	Basis (from sale)	+ 13,320	+ 30,000
(less)	Taxes	− 60,203	− N.A.
	Net after-tax income	$ 339,797	N.A.
5. Cost to Landowner of Bargain Sale		Determined by regular tax	

Note: This analysis does not include state income tax provisions.

[a] In this example, the value of the gift is not deductible because in computing the minimum tax, it is a preference item.

[b] In this example, the taxpayer's federal income tax if he sold the property at fair market value would be figured by the regular method and would be $142,015.

TAX ANALYSIS OF A BARGAIN SALE COMPUTING ALTERNATIVE MINIMUM TAX

Analyzing the same bargain sale, table 2 computes taxable income using the alternative minimum tax. In this particular example, the donor's tax is greater when figured by the regular method, so the alternative minimum tax is not a factor.

TAX ANALYSIS OF OUTRIGHT DONATION

The previous figures assume that the landowner would sell the land, whether in an arm's length transaction at its fair market value or to a land trust at a reduced value. In other cases, however, a landowner may have no immediate desire to sell the property, but wants to make an outright donation to a conservation charity.

Using the same assumptions regarding land value and landowner income, table 3 illustrates the immediate gain in after-tax income from such a donation. In this example, the easement donation would allow the landowner's tax obligations to be reduced by $34,650, if taxes were figured only by the regular method. Taxes must also be computed by the alternative minimum tax method, as shown in table 4.

Table 4 demonstrates that the alternative mini-

mum tax would increase landowner tax liability with the donation from $34,650 (based upon the regular method to figure taxes) to $42,000. This compares with landowner tax liability of $66,940 if no donation was made.

These examples are presented as single-year transactions. That is, the bargain sale or donation is consummated in a single year, as are most tax deductions. Sometimes, however, transactions are more drawn out,

Table 3

Federal Tax Consequences of an Outright Donation (1988)
(Computing Taxable Income by the Regular Method)

(Status: Married Filing Jointly)

Facts/Assumptions		Options	
		Without Donation[a]	With Donation
1. Easement Value Computations			
	Fair market value (before easement)	$ 225,000	$ 225,000
(less)	Fair market value (after easement)	− (225,000)	− 100,000
	Value of easement	$ 0	$ 125,000
2. Income Computations			
	Adjusted gross income	$ 300,000	$ 300,000
(less)	Itemized deductions and exemptions	− (100,000)	− (100,000)
(less)	Charitable deduction	− 0	− (90,000)[b]
	Taxable income	$ 200,000	$ 110,000
3. Tax Computations			
	Federal income tax (from tax tables)	$ 66,940	$ 32,290
4. After-Tax Income Computations			
	Gross income	$ 300,000	$ 300,000
(less)	Taxes	− 66,940	− 32,290
	Net after-tax income	$ 233,060	$ 267,710
5. Net Value of Donation (Tax Savings from Donation)		Determined by Alternative Minimum Tax	

Note: This analysis does not include state income tax provisions.

[a] This assumes that the landowner retains all interest in the land.

[b] Due to the 30 percent limitation, excess contribution value ($125,000 − $90,000 = $35,000) can be carried over to reduce tax liability in the following year.

when landowners realize much larger deductions than they can take in a given tax year. In other situations, land trusts proposing a donation or bargain sale find themselves competing with another prospective buyer who wishes to purchase on installment or seller-financed terms. In these circumstances, the above format must be altered to show the effects of alternative transactions over a multiyear period. Then, in order to account for the time value of money, each year's net, after-tax result must be discounted back to the present in order to yield meaningful comparative values. For some people, a given amount of money is worth more today than next year; therefore, a land trust may be able to offer a landowner a better deal from a bargain sale in which the seller may receive more cash immediately than the landowner could realize from an

Table 4

Federal Tax Consequences of an Outright Donation (1988)
(Computing Alternative Minimum Tax)

(Status: Married Filing Jointly)

Facts/Assumptions		Options	
		Without Donation[a]	With Donation
1. Easement Value Computations			
	Fair market value (before easement)	$ 225,000	$ 225,000
(less)	Fair market value (after easement)	− (225,000)	− (100,000)
	Value of easement	$ 0	$ 125,000
2. Income Computations			
	Adjusted gross income	$ 300,000	$ 300,000
(less)	Itemized deductions and exemptions	− (100,000)	− (100,000)
(less)	Charitable deduction	− 0	− 0 [b]
	Taxable income	$ 200,000	$ 200,000
3. Tax Computations			
	Federal income tax (200,000 × 21%)	$ N.A.	$ 42,000
4. After-Tax Income Computations			
	Gross income	$ 300,000	$ 300,000
(less)	Taxes	− N.A.	− 42,000
	Net after-tax income	$ N.A.	$ 258,000
5. Net Value of Donation			
	(Tax savings)	$ 24,940	

Note: This analysis does not include state income tax provisions.

[a] This assumes that the landowner retains all interest in the land.

[b] The contribution is a preference item, therefore there is no deduction when computing the alternative minimum tax.

installment sale or a sale with seller financing in which payment is spread over several years.

ESTATE TAX CONSEQUENCES OF CONSERVATION DONATIONS

Donations of conservation lands can provide important estate tax benefits by lowering the taxable value of an estate. Even though recent tax law changes, particularly the Economic Recovery Tax Act of 1981, have substantially reduced estate tax liability for most estates, there are still many "land rich" taxpayers whose estates are highly exposed to tax liability. For these landowners, the estate tax benefits of a substantial land donation may far exceed the potential income tax advantages. The Tax Reform Act of 1986, in its final form, made essentially no changes that will affect planned giving. Thus, conservation contributions are still available as estate planning tools. Table 5 provides one sample format for analysis of the estate tax benefits of a conservation transaction. In this case, the value of a 30-acre estate is reduced from $25,000 per acre to $1,000 per acre by means of an easement donation.

Impacts of Recent Tax Changes on Gifts of Land*

INCOME TAX CHANGES IN 1986

Income tax advantages of gifts of land to conservation charities and units of government were diminished by the 1986 Tax Reform Act. The value of a charitable contributions deduction for income tax purposes was reduced. My concern is that analyses that look purely at the income tax picture may overlook a less obvious but important tax aspect of land contributions, the savings in estate or other types of taxes payable at the death of an owner that a gift or devise of land can generate. Both landowners and land-saving charities should be mindful of estate tax saving benefits and not assume that merely because a lifetime gift is marginally unattractive the owner may not be able to achieve important benefits from a gift through his or

* The following material is reprinted with permission from an article entitled "Gifts of Land: Diminished Income Tax Benefits Do Not Mean That Landowners Should Forego Land Gifts," by Russell L. Brenneman, which first appeared in *Connecticut Woodlands* (Spring 1988).

Table 5

Estate Tax Consequences of Easement Donation (1988)

Facts/Assumptions		Without Donation	With Donation[a]
Fair market value of land		$ 25,000/ac	$ 1,000/ac
Value of gross estate (assuming 30 acres)		$ 750,000	$ 30,000
(less)	Debts and expenses	− (20,000)	− (20,000)
	Adjusted gross estate	$ 730,000	$ 10,000
(less)	Marital deduction	− 0	− 0
	Taxable estate	$ 730,000	$ 10,000
Federal estate tax liability[b]		$ 28,660	0
Net Value of Donation (Tax Savings)			$ 28,660

The donation of an easement would, in this example, save the succeeding generation from paying $28,660 in federal estate taxes.

Note: The projected figure assumes that the landowner retains all interest in the land.

[a] When computing the alternative minimum tax, the donation is a preference item and cannot be deducted.

[b] After Federal Unified Credit—from tax table.

her will. It is important to remember as well that some income tax benefits remain and that the value of property given during life will not be included in the owner's estate. It is also true that recent changes in the Internal Revenue Code may make it easier to secure an estate tax charitable contributions deduction for a devise of a conservation easement than to secure such a deduction for income tax purposes.

Two particular provisions of the Tax Reform Act of 1986 affect the value of charitable contributions. The reduction of the highest effective tax rate from 50 percent to 33 percent made all charitable contributions less beneficial to the giver. The amount of otherwise taxable income that could be "sheltered" by charitable gifts was reduced across the board.

The other provision has special meaning for landowners, as well as for owners of objects that have always been attractive for charitable gifts, such as paintings and the like. Before the 1986 change, the amount of the donor's income tax deduction was the value of the donated property at the time of the gift, regardless of what it might have cost. If Greenacre cost the taxpayer $50,000 and at the time of the gift it was worth $600,000, the taxpayer was entitled to deduct $600,000. There were some limitations on the amount of such "capital gain" property that could be deducted in any year, and special "carryovers" for that kind of property. But essentially the taxpayer could shelter otherwise taxable income up to the full value of the property, and that was that.

The 1986 act materially changed the picture. Now the difference between the taxpayer's cost or "basis" and the value of the donated property at the time of the gift must be treated as a "preference" item for purposes of determining the "alternative minimum tax." The idea of the alternative minimum tax is that no taxpayer should escape the income tax scot-free; at least in theory, everyone with income above a certain level should have to pay at least some tax. Unless this issue is addressed, taxpayers could shelter most or all of their income through deductions, credits, and other devises sprinkled throughout the Internal Revenue Code for those clever enough to find them. The way the Congress has dealt with this is to require taxpayers to figure their taxable income in two ways: first, with all their deductions, exclusions from income and the like as has been customary; and then, in a second way, *without* reducing taxable income by certain deductions and credits (called "preferences"). The appropriate tax rate is applied to the taxpayer's income figured in the first way, and then a so-called alternative minimum tax rate of 21 percent is applied to the taxable income figured in the second way. The taxpayer pays the greater of the two taxes.

The Tax Reform Act of 1986 added to the list of "preferences" many items that had not been considered preferences prior to that time. One of the new additions was the amount of the difference between the taxpayer's basis, or cost, of property given to charity and its value at the time of the gift. In the example given above, the $550,000 difference between cost and value would be a preference. A tax at the rate of 21 percent may have to be paid on this increase in value, depending upon the circumstances, which are likely to be quite peculiar to each taxpayer. One can easily see how the effect of that provision on tax motivated owners of land whose value has appreciated considerably.

While I have not been able to discover a reliable and comprehensive collection of information about the actual behavior of landowners in the presence of the changes, both logic and the smattering of empirical information that I do have suggest that the effect of 1986 act on gifts of land has been dampening at best. It is easy to point to the truth that historically many conservation gifts have been made without any reference whatsoever to tax benefits and also to point out that many donors of land are primarily motivated by noneconomic concerns. However, all of these things are relative, and it is difficult for me not to conclude that the 1986 act has had an extremely negative effect on land gifts when the two aspects that I have pointed out are coupled; that is, the reduction in the tax rates (and thus the marginal benefit of all contributions) and the inclusion of appreciation as a preference item. My operating assumption, then, is that many landowners and conservation charities have turned away from land-saving transactions because the income tax benefits just haven't been there.

ESTATE TAX REDUCTION

The thesis of this article is that neither landowner nor organization should turn away without closely examining another aspect of the landowner's tax picture. That aspect is the situation the landowner's heirs will find themselves in if the landowner should die owning Greenacre. When we die, another type of tax becomes payable; an estate or succession tax, however named, payable to the United States and to the state in which the property is located. The point that I have to make can be made solely by reference to the federal estate tax.

Several things have happened in recent years that perhaps have desensitized us to the impact of the federal estate tax. In a very substantial revamping of this area of the Internal Revenue Code, the Congress in 1981 liberalized prior rules so that the value of property that is left to one's surviving spouse passes to him or her tax free (that is, there is an unlimited "marital deduction"); and, through provisions more complicated than I care to get into, no tax is payable at the time of our death (unless we have made certain kinds of gifts in our lifetimes) unless the net taxable value of the property in our estate exceeds $600,000. These provisions so eased prior rules that many taxpayers and their advisers concluded that tax-oriented estate planning (and estate tax saving charitable contributions) no longer were as critical as before. After all, a great many of us are married, and $600,000 does seem like an awful lot of money. However, we should not feel so secure; in many situations the conclusion that we need not be concerned about estate taxes may be unwarranted and may do a disservice to our families.

My claim is that many of us who may have relatively modest incomes and who certainly do not think of ourselves as wealthy may be much richer than we think we are. Or at least Uncle Sam will think so when we pass away. For one thing, virtually everything we own will be included in figuring up the value of our taxable estate. Without particularly noticing it and not considering it any more "upscale" than the life patterns of our economic peers, we may have acquired second homes here or there and the furnishings needed to make them comfortable. We have accumulated collections, ostensibly for personal enjoyment but often with an eye cocked toward the marketplace. We have interests in insurance policies and retirement plans that may be included in our taxable estates. Recent events notwithstanding, even our investments may have done rather well. All of it does add up. And we have our real estate, some of which we bought years ago at a price some of us may barely remember.

Since I am fond of making generalizations, allow me to make a few: First, the rate of increase in the value of open land in much of the country over the last ten years has exceeded the wildest expectations of 99.9 percent of the owners of that land. Even today, many owners do not have a clear idea of the present worth of their property, which very often was acquired with little thought of it as an "investment." Second, the rate of appreciation of any land that is related to water—on it, along it, or within sight of it—has exceeded the rate of appreciation for virtually all other land. Third, land as a component of the total property holdings of most landowners has appreciated at a rate disproportionately high to the rate of appreciation of virtually all of the other categories of holdings that the landowner may own. Fourth, the rate of depreciation of the value of land (if any depreciation there has been) has been disproportionately low compared with the rate of depreciation of many of the other assets of owners in the present time of disruption in the capital markets (to use the kindest phrase that comes to mind).

Assuming that an appreciable number of those generalizations in fact is true, if a lot of us were to put pencil to paper, we might find that we are a lot richer than we have thought of ourselves as being. The fact that our incomes have remained relatively modest is irrelevant. In many cases, a disproportionate amount of our "riches" may be represented by the present value of our land. At least, that is the way Uncle Sam will look at it when the time comes for paying the estate tax. While we ponder this as landowners, we should also bear in mind several things about the federal estate tax. First, it is a capital levy; that is, the amount of the tax has little to do with any income that we might or might not be deriving from our estate, but instead the tax is based upon the aggregate value of our property at the time we die. Second, once an estate rises in net value above that $600,000 threshold the tax rates are substantial, and they are graduated. The rates begin at 33 percent but they accelerate rapidly, and the top rate is 55 percent. Third, the tax has to be paid in cash nine months after death. If the executor doesn't have the cash, property must be sold to provide the necessary money. Owning a lot of very valuable land at the time of death thus results not only in a higher tax to start with but also a "liquidity" burden on the estate. If we do not wish our executor to sell the land, the executor must sell something else, and the "something else" may well be investments priced at depressed values.

CONSERVATION EASEMENTS

Landowners and land-saving charities should also bear in mind that recent legislation means that in many circumstances it will be easier to get an estate tax deduction for a gift of a conservation easement than it would be for the owner to get an income tax deduction were he to make the gift while alive. The rules are different for the estate tax deduction in one important respect. In both cases, the deduction is available only if the easement is for "conservation purposes." "Conservation purposes" have been exclusively, and some would say narrowly, defined by the Internal Revenue Code since 1980. However, beginning in 1987, the narrow definition of this term for income tax purposes does not apply for purposes of the estate tax. While in the absence of any particular estate tax definition it is unclear exactly what the term "conservation purposes" means in the estate tax law, quite evidently the intention of Congress was to liberalize the estate tax definition. Therefore, a landowner who wishes to make a transfer of an easement and finds that his proposal does not meet the "conservation purposes" test for income tax purposes should not give up. He still may be able to reap the substantial rewards of an estate tax deduction if he makes the transfer during his lifetime (recognizing that he will not achieve the income tax deduction) or if he makes a testamentary transfer of the easement through his will.*

Because the foregoing summary may be somewhat cryptic to some, a little history of the development of the income tax deduction is in order. Prior to 1969, the value of charitably donated "easements" and similar restrictions on property was deductible under the general rules pertaining to charitable contributions. In 1969, Congress chose to deny the deduction for a gift of a "partial interest" in property. Seemingly, a conservation easement would be such a partial interest, but Congress specified in the conference report on the legislation that the new law did not intend to disallow a deduction for an "open space easement in gross" if the easement were granted "in perpetuity." Deductions accordingly were allowed for gifts of easements after 1969. In 1980, the law was again changed to allow a deduction, in the case of an easement, only if it is "exclusively for conservation purposes." The code defines "conservation purposes" as:

1. The preservation of land areas for outdoor recreation by, or for the education of, the general public;

2. The protection of a relatively natural habitat of fish, wildlife, plants, or similar ecosystem;

3. The preservation of open space (including farmland and forest land) for scenic enjoyment of the general public or pursuant to a governmental conservation policy and such preservation will yield a significant public benefit; or

4. The preservation of an historically important land area or a certified historic structure.

These provisions apply to contributions of easements for income tax purposes. While they may seem to be relatively clear, in fact the language in many instances is ambiguous. For example, what is meant by a "relatively natural" habitat? What expression must there be of a "governmental conservation policy" and what is meant by "significant public benefit"? It would be reassuring to be able to say that the regulations that have been adopted to interpret these terms resolve the ambiguity in all cases, but in fact this is not the case; there are many gray areas. While this uncertainty may be troubling enough to the taxpayer hoping for an income tax deduction, until the recent legislation, the uncertainty had an even more disconcerting effect: because the same standards applied under the estate and gift tax provisions of the code, a taxpayer whose transaction fell on the wrong side of the line could find

---

* Section 1422 of the Tax Reform Act of 1986 "decoupled" both the gift and estate tax provisions from the "conservation purposes" test of Section 170(h)(4)(A).

himself in a situation in which not only was he denied an income tax deduction, but his unqualifying transfer could make him liable to pay a federal gift tax as well! (Before leaving income tax matters, it should be noted that the strictness of the "conservation purposes" requirements that remain must be added to the disincentives noted above for taxpayers seeking income tax deductions for contributions of conservation easements.)

Fortunately, the Tax Reform Act of 1986 provided that the strict definition of "conservation purposes" for income tax purposes shall not henceforth apply for estate and gift tax purposes. What this means in the example given above is that the taxpayer could fall short of meeting one of the specific criteria of the income tax definition and yet not be liable for any federal gift tax if his donation fell within a more general definition of "conservation purposes." And, if the taxpayer should choose to devise the easement in his will, an estate tax charitable contributions deduction would be allowed if the devise meets the general test of "conservation purposes." Unfortunately, a degree of ambiguity remains because, in the absence of a statutory definition of "conservation purposes" for the estate and gift taxes, the taxpayer, the land-saving charity, and their advisers are left with the same problem that they had between 1969 and 1980; that is, just what does "conservation purposes" mean under the estate and gift taxes?

This much can be said: whatever the exact meaning may be, a more liberal rule of "conservation purposes" applies for the estate and gift taxes than for the income tax. Landowners and land-savers looking at such approaches should not abandon them merely because the income tax "purposes" are not present. They should remember, too, that in many situations, without the owner's surrender of title to any property, a grant of an easement by him, whether or not an income tax deduction is available, can effectively reduce the value of his estate and thus aid his family both by reducing the gross amount of the estate tax and by ameliorating liquidity problems associated with payment of that tax.

WHAT TO DO

If you are a landowner: If you own land that may have significance as open space, or wildlife habitat, for its natural beauty or geologic uniqueness, because it has agricultural soils or wetlands, or may have importance as protection for adjacent fragile areas, you may wish to consider whether a gift of this land, or a portion of it or some interest in it (such as an easement), makes sense for you from your overall tax standpoint giving particular consideration to the estate tax consequences of your owning the land at the time of your death. You may have rejected the idea of a gift because the marginal income tax benefits were not there for you after the Tax Reform Act of 1986. You may want to revisit that decision in light of the estate tax. You may have rejected the idea of a conservation easement in light of the rigid income tax tests of "conservation purposes" in effect since 1980. You may want to rethink that issue in light of the changes in the estate tax rules for conservation easements. You should remember that property that may not have particular distinction in terms of the conservation programs of national or state organizations may have enormous meaning for your local community. And you should remember as well that not only do land-saving charities protect land but that state and local governments do as well.

If you are a land-saving charity: If you are involved with a land conservation charity, such as a land trust, incorporate into your acquisition strategy a program to attract gifts of land that have primary emphasis on estate tax benefits to donors. You should be particularly mindful of this, in my view, if you are concerned with land adjacent to water or if you are operating in an area that has experienced significant real estate appreciation. Don't give up on a prospect merely because an analysis of his situation suggests that income tax benefits are not substantial enough to be attractive. Revisit the situation with attention to the landowner's estate tax situation. A small personalized brochure would help, and some of your active members should be trained so that they are comfortable talking about this subject with potential donors, without becoming tax experts. If you have abandoned the idea of a conservation easement because the "conservation purposes" test does not seem to be met, you may wish to look at this situation again in the light of possible estate tax benefits. Remember that an owner who, for quite understandable reasons, may find it difficult to reach the "closure" on a lifetime gift represented by signing a deed to a cherished piece of real estate may find it easier to put you in his will because he knows that the decision is not irrevocable; once that step has been taken, at a later time the owner may be more comfortable in making a lifetime transfer. In the meantime, Greenacre is safeguarded, assuming that the owner does not transfer it to someone else before his death.

A Guide to Tax-Advantaged Rehabilitation

The following section is reprinted with permission from *A Guide to Tax-Advantaged Rehabilitation* by Sally G. Oldham, Jayne F. Boyle, and Stuart M. Gins-

berg and published by the National Trust for Historic Preservation. This handbook uses a question and answer format to provide a clear explanation of the federal historic rehabilitation tax incentives.

WHAT IS THE REHABILITATION TAX CREDIT?

Federal tax law offers a unique incentive to taxpayers who contribute to the preservation of this nation's old and historic buildings. By rehabilitating directly or investing in the rehabilitation of eligible buildings, taxpayers can take advantage of a two-tier tax credit.

The federal income tax credit is equal to 20 percent of the cost of rehabilitating historic buildings or 10 percent of the cost of rehabilitating nonhistoric buildings constructed before 1936. These credits provide a dollar-for-dollar reduction of income tax owed. While the 20 percent credit is available for rental residential buildings, neither credit is available for homes or apartments occupied by their owners.

Rehabilitation investment gives old and historic buildings a place in the contemporary real estate market, thereby guaranteeing their continued use and contribution to an area's economic vitality. In some cases, rehabilitation involves relatively small expenditures to renew a building's structural or mechanical systems. In others, rehabilitation may involve a complete reconstruction of a building's interior spaces.

In the case of historic buildings, the goal of the rehabilitation credit is not to preserve a building as a museum, but to put it back to use to meet current housing, retail, commercial, and industrial needs. However, these needs must be met through construction that is appropriate to a building's historic character.

During its recent consideration of tax reform legislation, Congress heard witness after witness testify that the rehabilitation tax credit has been responsible for the dramatic revitalization of cities and towns throughout the country. Representative Lindy Boggs (D—La.) testified that

> the rehabilitation tax credit has worked as has no other tool to encourage and facilitate the preservation of historically or architecturally significant structures and has contributed to reversing the downward trend in the older sections of our nation's cities. It has worked by making projects not otherwise economically feasible into reasonable, cost-effective investments. It has worked by creating jobs for people in construction, by putting derelict and abandoned houses and buildings back into commerce.

The retention of the rehabilitation tax credit, at a time when Congress eliminated many tax incentives that proliferated throughout our tax laws, reflects Congress's continued recognition of the social and economic benefits this country derives from such rehabilitation projects. The Senate Finance Committee, in articulating its reasons for retaining the credit in its tax reform legislation, stated that the credit was necessary because "the social and aesthetic values of rehabilitating and preserving older structures are not necessarily taken into account in investors' profit projections."

From 1982 through 1985, the historic rehabilitation credit alone has stimulated an estimated $8.8 billion of investment in more than 11,700 historic buildings. This investment not only has been made in large projects, such as Union Station in St. Louis, the Willard Hotel in Washington, D.C., and the Pullman Factory in Chicago, but in smaller projects as well. Almost 80 percent of historic commercial projects incur expenditures of less than $1 million, and nearly 40 percent involve expenditures of less than $150,000.

This range in the size and type of projects, and the similar diversity of nonhistoric rehabilitations, such as the renovation of corner stores, brownstones, restaurants and schools, demonstrate the breadth of opportunity that still exists for people to participate in this program. Some of the basic requirements for obtaining these incentives are described below.

WHAT BUILDINGS QUALIFY?

The rehabilitation credit is available for historic and nonhistoric buildings, but only if they are used in a trade or business or held for the production of income. Buildings eligible for the 20 percent rehabilitation credit include those used for rental residential as well as nonresidential purposes, while buildings eligible for the 10 percent rehabilitation credit must be nonresidential, commercial and industrial buildings.

Certified Historic Structures
To qualify for the 20 percent rehabilitation credit, a building must be a "certified historic structure." A certified historic structure is one that is:

- Listed individually in the National Register of Historic Places; or
- Located in a "registered historic district" and certified by the secretary of the interior as being of historic significance to the district.

A registered historic district is any district that is:

- Listed in the National Register of Historic Places; or
- Designated under a state or local statute certified by the secretary of the interior as containing criteria that will substantially achieve the purpose of pre-

serving and rehabilitating buildings of significance to the district and that is certified as substantially meeting all of the requirements for the listing of districts in the National Register.

The National Register of Historic Places is maintained by the U.S. Department of the Interior. It includes approximately 45,000 listings, 12 percent of which are historic districts. It is estimated that National Register listings encompass some 500,000 buildings. Properties qualifying for National Register listing must meet one or more of four broad criteria (see page 204).

To nominate an individual property or historic district for listing, a nomination form is submitted for review to the state historic preservation officer (SHPO) appointed by the governor of each state. After review and approval at the state level, the nomination is forwarded to the National Park Service in the Department of the Interior for review and listing.

A building within a listed historic district is accorded certified historic structure designation through the submission of Part I of the Historic Preservation Certification Application (OMB Form No. 1024-0009). This form is available from SHPOs and the National Park Service. After review by the SHPO, the application is forwarded to the National Park Service for final approval.

If a property is individually listed in the National Register, it is already a certified historic structure and it is not necessary to complete Part I of the Historic Preservation Certification Application.

If the certification request is for a building not yet listed in the National Register or for a building in a potential historic district, the Part I form will be reviewed to make a preliminary determination as to whether the building may qualify for certified historic status when and if the property is listed in the National Register. Such determinations are not binding and become final as of the date of listing in the National Register.

The SHPO's recommendation for approval or denial of certified historic structure status is given significant weight; the final determination, however, is made by the National Park Service, which notifies the owner of the decision.

Old Nonhistoric Buildings
A 10 percent rehabilitation credit is available for nonresidential, nonhistoric buildings built before 1936. No certification is required for these buildings.

The 10 percent rehabilitation credit is not available for certified historic structures. A building located within a registered historic district is not eligible for the 10 percent credit unless it is certified by the Department of the Interior as not contributing to the historical significance of the district. A request for certification of nonsignificance also is made through Part I of the Historic Preservation Certification Application. Review of such a request follows the general procedures outlined above.

National Register Criteria for Evaluation

The quality of significance in American history, architecture, archaeology, engineering, and culture is present in districts, sites, buildings, structures, and objects that possess integrity of location, design, setting, materials, workmanship, feeling, and association and

a. That are associated with events that have made a significant contribution to the broad patterns of our history; or

b. That are associated with the lives of persons significant in our past; or

c. That embody the distinctive characteristics of a type, period, or method of construction, or that represent the work of a master, or that possess high artistic values, or that represent a significant and distinguishable entity whose components may lack individual distinction; or

d. That have yielded, or may be likely to yield, information important in prehistory or history.

The Secretary of the Interior's Standards for Rehabilitation

1. Every reasonable effort shall be made to provide a compatible use for a property which requires minimal alteration of the building, structure, or site and its environment or to use a property for its originally intended purpose.

2. The distinguishing original qualities or character of a building, structure, or site and its environment shall not be destroyed. The removal or alteration of any historic material or distinctive architectural features should be avoided when possible.

3. All buildings, structures, and sites shall be recognized as products of their own time. Alterations which have no historical basis and which seek to create an earlier appearance shall be discouraged.

4. Changes which may have taken place in the course of time are evidence of the history and development of a building, structure, or site and its environ-

ment. These changes may have acquired significance in their own right, and this significance shall be recognized and respected.

5. Distinctive stylistic features or examples of skilled craftsmanship which characterize a building, structure, or site shall be treated with sensitivity.

6. Deteriorated architectural features shall be repaired rather than replaced, wherever possible. In the event replacement is necessary, the new material should match the material being replaced in composition, design, color, texture, and other visual qualities. Repair or replacement of missing architectural features should be based on accurate duplications of features, substantiated by historical, physical, or pictorial evidence rather than on conjectural designs or the availability of different architectural elements from other buildings or structures.

7. The surface cleaning of structures shall be undertaken with the gentlest means possible. Sandblasting and other cleaning methods that will damage the historic building materials shall not be undertaken.

8. Every reasonable effort shall be made to protect and preserve archaeological resources affected by or adjacent to any project.

9. Contemporary design for alterations and additions to existing properties shall not be discouraged when such alterations and additions do not destroy significant historic, architectural, or cultural material and such design is compatible with the size, scale, color, material, and character of the property, neighborhood, or environment.

10. Wherever possible, new additions or alterations to structures shall be done in such a manner that if such additions or alterations were to be removed in the future, the essential form and integrity of the structure would be unimpaired.

WHAT REHABILITATIONS QUALIFY?

To receive a rehabilitation credit, a taxpayer must substantially rehabilitate a qualifying historic or old building.

Substantial Rehabilitations

A substantial rehabilitation means a taxpayer's expenditures must exceed the greater of the "adjusted basis" of the building, or $5,000, during any 24-month period (or 60-month period in the case of "phased rehabilitations," defined below) selected by the taxpayer. The period must end with or within the taxable year in which the credit is claimed.

The adjusted basis in a building is its purchase price plus the amount of any previous capital improvements. This sum is reduced by depreciation deductions already taken. The basis does not include that part of the cost of the property allocable to the land value.

Thus, for example, if a taxpayer's basis in a building is $100,000, the taxpayer generally would have to incur more than $100,000 of rehabilitation expenditures during a 24-month period to have a substantially rehabilitated building.

A phased rehabilitation is a rehabilitation consisting of two or more distinct stages of development. These stages must be set forth in written architectural plans and specifications that are completed before the physical work on the rehabilitation begins.

Certified Historic Rehabilitations

For a rehabilitation to qualify for a 20 percent credit, the Department of the Interior must certify that the rehabilitation is consistent with the historic character of the building and, where applicable, with the district in which the building is located. Application for this determination is made through Part 2 of the Historic Preservation Certification Application. Following review by the SHPO, the application is forwarded to the National Park Service for a decision. This application may be submitted to the SHPO and the National Park Service at any time during the course of rehabilitation. The National Park Service, however, strongly urges taxpayers to file applications before commencement of work so that modifications may be made more easily, if necessary.

Notice of approval of proposed work or certification of completed work is sent to the taxpayer by the National Park Service. If modifications are proposed during the course of construction, the National Park Service requests that it have the opportunity to review and approve changes that might affect the historic qualities of the structure.

However, a rehabilitation receives final certification only after all work has been completed. A taxpayer whose proposed work has been approved must submit a Request for Certification of Completed Work with photographs documenting the completed project in order to receive final certification.

All elements of a rehabilitation project must meet the Secretary of the Interior's Standards for Rehabilitation (see page 204). In evaluating rehabilitation work, state and federal officials review all aspects of the work, including any new construction. While the rehabilitation process may involve some repair or alteration of an historic building to provide for an efficient contemporary use, it must not destroy or damage the material and features, both interior and exterior, that are important in defining the building's historic character.

Nonhistoric Rehabilitations

No certification of rehabilitation work is necessary to obtain the 10 percent credit for nonhistoric rehabilitation. However, certain existing building elements must be retained to qualify for this credit. Specifically: (1) 50 percent or more of the existing external walls must be retained in place as external walls; (2) 75 percent or more of the existing external walls must be retained in place as internal or external walls; and (3) 75 percent or more of the existing internal structural framework must be retained in place.

No similar requirements apply to certified historic structures.

WHAT EXPENDITURES QUALIFY?

Rehabilitation expenditures must be capital in nature and depreciable as real property to qualify for a credit. Routine maintenance costs such as painting and repairs are not eligible unless they are part of an overall rehabilitation. Acquisition and building enlargement costs do not qualify.

Rehabilitation expenditures allocable to that portion of a building that is, or is reasonably expected to be, "tax-exempt use property" also do not qualify.

Rehabilitations Involving Tax-Exempt Entities

The use of the rehabilitation credit to preserve property used by governments or nonprofit organizations is limited because the credit cannot be claimed on "tax-exempt use property." In the case of real estate, tax-exempt use property generally means that portion of the property that is leased to a tax-exempt entity in a "disqualified lease." Property leased to a tax-exempt entity would be considered leased under a disqualified lease if:

- The lease term exceeded 20 years;
- The lease occurred after the sale of the property by, or the property was leased from, the tax-exempt entity (sale-leaseback situation);
- The lease included an option to purchase or sell the property; or
- Part or all of the property was financed, directly or indirectly, by a tax-exempt obligation, and the tax-exempt entity (or a related entity) participated in the financing.

Even if property is leased to a tax-exempt entity in a disqualified lease, such property is not subject to the tax-exempt entity leasing limitations if the portion determined to be tax-exempt use property is less than

35 percent of the "net rentable floor space" of the property. The net rentable floor space of a building does not include the common areas.

WHEN CAN THE CREDIT BE CLAIMED?

Generally, the credit is claimed for the taxable year in which the rehabilitation is completed.

For historic rehabilitations, an approved Request for Certification of Completed Work must be submitted to the Internal Revenue Service within 30 months of claiming a credit. The credit may be claimed before completion if construction is planned for two or more years and a taxpayer elects to claim the credit on the basis of "qualified progress expenditures."

WHO CAN TAKE THE CREDIT?

The credit is available to the owners and, in certain situations, renters of a qualified rehabilitated building. Renters may obtain the credit for rehabilitation expenditures that they have incurred, provided that the lease term remaining on the date the rehabilitation is completed is at least 27.5 years for a residential building or 31.5 years for a nonresidential building. Purchasers of a rehabilitated building before the completion of its rehabilitation are eligible to receive the credit.

HOW IS DEPRECIATION COMPUTED?

A taxpayer may deduct annually a portion of the adjusted basis of a rehabilitated building. The deduction generally is computed using the straight-line method over a period of 31.5 years for nonresidential real estate and over a period of 27.5 years for residential rental real estate. The depreciable basis of a rehabilitated building must be reduced by the amount of rehabilitation credit claimed.

WHAT OTHER RESTRICTIONS APPLY?

Many factors other than the benefits described above must be taken into account before considering undertaking or investing in a rehabilitation project. The rehabilitation incentives operate within the context of a building's local real estate market, its economic profile, and project investors' individual tax situations. Numerous federal corporate and individual tax provisions affect the ability of investors to make full use of the tax benefits. Taxpayers should seek the advice of a professional adviser before initiating or investing in a rehabilitation project.

WHAT OTHER TAX BENEFITS ARE AVAILABLE?

Other tax provisions may contribute to the preservation and rehabilitation of historic buildings. They include the deduction for donating a historic preservation easement and the new low-income housing credit.

Historic Preservation Easements

A charitable contribution deduction is allowed for the donation of an historic preservation easement to a preservation organization. This deduction applies to both commercial property and owner-occupied housing. An easement is an agreement by owners of property to relinquish their right to alter or demolish property and to abide by other preservation conditions that are enforced by the donee preservation organization or governmental body. These restrictions must be permanent to qualify for a federal charitable deduction and must apply to all future purchasers of the property. A typical agreement protects the facades of a building but may also restrict the development of adjoining lands and interior features or require maintenance of property elements. In addition, the public must have some visual access to the donated property.

The value of the contribution of an historic easement is the difference between the fair market value of the property before the granting of the restriction and the fair market value of the property after the granting of the restriction. The basis of the structure must be reduced by the value of the easement. This basis reduction must be allocated between the building itself and the underlying land.

For taxpayers subject to the alternative minimum tax, the untaxed appreciation on charitable contributions of appreciated property is considered a preference item.

Low-Income Rental Housing Credit

Owners of residential rental property providing low-income housing may claim separate tax credits for new construction and rehabilitation of low-income housing and for certain costs of acquisition of existing housing to serve low-income individuals if such credits are issued by the state.

FOR MORE INFORMATION

The National Trust for Historic Preservation publishes for its members *Preservation News* 12 times a year and *Historic Preservation* magazine 6 times a year. Both contain up-to-date information and articles on the rehabilitation incentives and historic preservation. For information on membership, write National Trust for Historic Preservation, 1785 Massachusetts Avenue, N.W., Washington, D.C. 20036, Attn: Membership Division. Dues start at $15.

Historic Preservation Tax Incentives Certification of Rehabilitation Workbook is the only complete compilation of all legal, technical, and administrative documents related to the historic rehabilitation incentives. This looseleaf binder, prepared by the National Park Service for its review staff, contains all certification precedents, guidance, and regulatory materials. For information on this publication, write Tax, National Trust for Historic Preservation, 1785 Massachusetts Avenue, N.W., Washington, D.C. 20036.

Preservation Law Reporter is published quarterly by the National Trust. This looseleaf service contains articles on tax issues, updates on legislative and regulatory activities, litigation summaries, and a comprehensive reference volume. A one-year subscription costs $195. To order, write the National Trust or call (202) 673–4035.

A Directory of Historic Preservation Lawyers is published by the National Trust. Preservation attorneys are listed by state with a brief description of their areas of practice. For a copy of the directory, send $3 to General Counsel, National Trust for Historic Preservation. For listing information, write the trust or call (202) 673–4035.

The Member Organization Program of the National Trust provides firms, organizations, and agencies with regular publications containing comprehensive information on preservation issues, programs, and practices. To become a member organization, write the National Trust. Dues start at $50.

Notes

Chapter 1

1. William Toner, *Saving Farms and Farmland: A Community Guide*, Planning Advisory Report No. 333 (Chicago, IL: American Society of Planning Officials, 1978), 14.

2. Agricultural economics are an important factor in the early stages of the farmland conversion process. Farmers cannot continue to work their land very long unless the prices they receive for their products allow them to make a living. Recent hard times, particularly in the Midwest, have driven this commonsense proposition home.

3. William Toner, *Saving Farms and Farmland . . .* , op. cit., p. 14.

4. National Agricultural Lands Study, *The Protection of Farmland: A Reference Guidebook for State and Local Government*, 1981, Washington, D.C.: U.S. Gov't Printing Office.

5. William Toner, *Saving Farms and Farmland . . .* , op. cit., p. 9.

6. Telephone conversation, Arthur Kunz, Suffolk County Department of Planning, December 20, 1988.

7. Daniel S. Carol, "New Jersey Pinelands Commission," in *Managing Land-Use Conflicts: Case Studies in Special Area Management*, ed. David Brower and Daniel S. Cato (Durham, NC: Duke University Press, 1987).

8. David Brower et al., *Managing Development in Small Towns*. (Chicago, IL: American Planning Association, 1984), 72.

9. California Government Code, Sections 51200-51295.

10. National Agricultural Lands Study, op. cit., p. 59.

11. Wisc. Stat. Ann., Ch. 91.

12. National Agricultural Lands Study, op. cit., p. 61.

13. See New York Agriculture and Markets Law, Sections 300 to 307; Virginia Code, Sections 15.1–1506 to 1513.

Chapter 2

1. Ann Breen and Dick Rigby, "Sons of Riverwalk," *Planning* (March 1988): 26–31.

2. See *Nollan v. California Coastal Commission*, 107 S.Ct. 3141 (1987), for an example of circumstances under which public access cannot be mandated as a condition of building permit approval. Public access dedication requirements are valid in many situations.

3. Portions of this discussion appear in Rolf Diamont, J. Glenn Eugster, and Christopher J. Duerksen, *A Citizen's Guide to River Conservation* (Washington, D.C.: The Conservation Foundation, 1984), 57–58.

4. This discussion of the Oregon program appears in Diamont et al., op. cit., pp. 58–60.

5. PL 90-542; 16 U.S.C. Sections 1271–87. American Rivers is a nationwide nonprofit river protection organization working to improve local river protection programs through state and federal Wild and Scenic River designation.

6. *American Rivers*, vol. 16, no. 3 (September 1988) p. 2. (Newsletter of American Rivers).

7. PL 90–448; 42 U.S.C. Sections 4001 et seq.

8. Jon Kusler and Hazel Groman, "Wetlands Hydrology: An Introduction," *National Wetlands Newsletter* (March–April 1987): 2.

9. The Conservation Foundation, op. cit., p. 290.

10. Id.

11. The potential role of wetlands in flood protection is becoming better understood. In assessing flood protection alternatives along the Charles River near Boston, the U.S. Army Corps of Engineers concluded that wetlands protection was the most cost-effective approach. It estimated that destruction of the surrounding wetlands would cause flood damage averaging $17 million a year. U.S. Fish and Wildlife Service, *Wetlands of the United States*, p. 21.

12. The Conservation Foundation, op. cit., p. 291; United States Fish and Wildlife Service, op. cit., p. 29.

13. The definition of wetlands used in the federal wetland protection program is as follows: "The term 'wetlands' means those areas that are inundated or saturated by surface or ground water at a frequency and duration sufficient to support, and that under normal circumstances do support, a prevalence of vegetation typically adapted for life in saturated soil conditions. Wetlands generally include swamps, marshes, bogs, and similar areas" (33 C.F.R. 323.2[c]). Connecticut is one of the few states to regulate wetlands based solely upon soil type rather than largely upon prevalent vegetation. The statutory definition of wetlands in Connecticut is "land, including submerged land, [not including tidal wetlands] which consists of any of the soil types designated as poorly drained, very poorly drained, alluvial, and flood plain by the National Cooperative Soils Survey, as may be amended from time to time, of the Soil Conservation Service of the United States Department of Agriculture."

(CGS Section 22a–38-15). See also Charles Thurow et al., *Performance Controls for Sensitive Lands: A Practical Guide for Local Administrators*, Planners Advisory Service Report Number 307 (Chicago: American Planning Association, 1975), 38.

14. Dr. Jon A. Kusler, *Our National Wetland Heritage: A Protection Guidebook* (Washington, D.C.: Environmental Law Institute, 1983), 23.

15. Thurow, op. cit. p. 46.

16. 43 Fed. Reg. 55975–56907 (1978). See also Margaret S. Race and D. R. Christie. "Coastal Zone Development: Mitigation, Marsh Creation, and Decision-Making." *Environmental Management*. 6:317–328 (1982).

17. U.S.C. Sections 1451–1464 (1988).

18. Connecticut, Florida, Maine, Maryland, Massachusetts, Michigan, Minnesota, New Hampshire, New Jersey, New York, North Dakota, Oregon, Pennsylvania, Rhode Island, Vermont, and Wisconsin have state programs to protect inland wetlands.

19. See Connecticut GS Sec. 22a–36; Massachusetts GLC 131 Section 40, 40A; New Hampshire RSA 483–A: 1 et seq.; and Rhode Island GL 2-1-18 et seq. New York's Freshwater Wetlands Act, at NY Envtl. Conserv. Law Art. 24, is also a leading state wetlands protection program.

20. In each state, the courts have approved the wetlands protection programs, limited to typical "takings" requirement that the regulations not deprive a landowner of all beneficial use of a parcel. See, for example, *Manor Development Corporation v. Conservation Commission of the Town of Simsbury*, 180 Conn. 692 (1980); *Lovequist v. Conservation Commission of the Town of Dennis*, 393 N.E.2d 858 (1979); *Sibson v. State*, 336 A.2d 239 (1975); and *State v. Capuano Brothers*, 384 A.2d 610 (1978).

21. *Laws of North Dakota*, 1987, Chapter 642 (Senate Bill 2035). See Jay A. Leitch, David M. Saxowsky, and Michael G. McKenna, "North Dakota Wetlands Protection Law," *National Wetlands Newsletter* (September–October 1987): 13–15.

22. Section 301, 33 USC 1311.

23. 33 USC 1344.

Chapter 3

1. See Institute for Urban Design, Project Monograph No. 2, "Lowell, Massachusetts: Preservation Key to Revitalization," March 1985.

2. See Butte-Anaconda Historical Park System Master Plan, Executive Summary, 1985; and the Beaumont Plan, "Where Oil Became an Industry." Each is available from the town government.

3. Brandywine Conservancy, *Protecting Historic Properties: A Guide to Research and Preservation* (Chadds Ford, PA: Brandywine Conservancy, 1984), 76.

4. See Richard J. Roddewig, "Preservation Law and Economics," in *A Handbook on Historic Preservation Law*, ed. Christopher Duerksen (Washington, D.C.: The Conservation Foundation and The National Center for Preservation Law, 1983), 427.

5. David Doheny, General Counsel, National Trust for Historic Preservation, personal communication, 1988.

6. For detailed guidance on drafting a local preservation ordinance and model provisions selected from ordinances from cities and towns around the country, see Duerksen, ed., *A Handbook on Historic Preservation Law*, op. cit., Appendix A, "Recommended Model Provisions for a Preservation Ordinance with Annotations," p. A5. The National Trust for Historic Preservation does not publish a model ordinance, but published this annotated collection of sample provisions. The National Trust also provides consulting services for drafting and administering local historic preservation ordinances. See also Richard J. Roddewig, *Preparing a Historic Preservation Ordinance*, American Planning Association Planners Advisory Service Report No. 374 (Chicago Il: American Planning Association, 1983), 7.

7. Christopher Duerksen, ed., *A Handbook on Historic Preservation Law*, op. cit., p. 70.

8. Id., p. 72.

9. Id., p. 74.

10. Id.

11. Id., p. 75.

12. Richard J. Roddewig, *Preparing a Historic Preservation Ordinance*, op. cit., p. 15.

13. See, for example, *A-S-P Associates v. City of Raleigh*, 258 S.E.2d 444 (N.C. 1979).

14. D.C. Code Ann. Sec. 5-1010(b).

15. Easements are discussed in Appendix A.

16. *Penn Central Transportation Company v. New York City*, 438 U.S. 104 (1978).

17. For a more in-depth discussion, see Duerksen, ed., *A Handbook on Historic Preservation Law*, op. cit., pp. 53–56.

18. Roddewig, op. cit., p. 448.

19. "Trust Joins Suit to Save Jobbers Canyon," *Preservation News* (June 1988): 1.

20. Hawaii Rev. Stat. Section 6E-8 to 10 (1976).

21. Ill. Ann. Stat. Ch. 127, Section 133d1-d14.

22. Kansas State Ann. Sec. 75-2724.

23. New Mexico Stat. Ann. Sec. 18-6-12. See also James P. Bieg, *The Power to Preserve: New Mexico Historic Preservation Laws and Techniques* (Santa Fe: New Mexico Municipal League, 1980).

24. Michael Mantell, "State Preservation Law," in Christopher J. Duerksen, ed., op. cit. p. 170.

25. Christopher J. Duerksen, and Michael Mantell, *Beyond the Sesquicentennial: New Directions for Texas Preservation Laws and Programs* (Washington, D.C.: The Conservation Foundation, 1986), 22.

26. Id.

27. Paula Huntley and Hisashi B. Sugaya, *Heritage and Tourism in California*, Sacramento, CA: California Task Force, 1984.

28. Duerksen and Mantell, op. cit., p. 22.

29. N.C. Gen. Stat. Section 105-278(a) (Supp. 1977).

30. Or. Rev. Stat. Section 358.475-.565 (Supp. 1977) and 1975 Or. Laws 514, Section 15.

31. 16 USC 470.

32. Brandywine Conservancy, op. cit., p. 57.

33. 49 USC 1651-59 (1976).

34. 12 USC 1703 (1976).

35. 42 USC 4321-61 (1976).

Chapter 4

1. Christopher J. Duerksen, *Aesthetics and Land-Use Controls: Beyond Ecology and Economics*, Planners Advisory Service Report No. 399, (Chicago, Il: American Planning Association, 1986), 3.

2. *Berman v. Parker*, 348 U.S. 26 (1954). The most far-reaching passage is quoted at the introduction to this chapter.

3. *Penn Central Transportation Company v. New York City*, 438 U.S. 104, 129 (1978)—upholding the city's efforts to preserve Grand Central Station.

4. Duerksen, op. cit., p. 1.

5. Roger W. Schmenner, *Making Business Location Decisions* (Englewood Cliffs, N.J.: Prentice-Hall, 1982); and Roger W. Schmenner, "Location Decisions of Large Firms: Implications for Public Policy," *Economic Development Comment* 5 (January 1981): 5, quoted in Todd K. Buchta, "Will We Live in Accidental Cities or Successful Communities," *Conservation Foundation Letter* 6 (1987): 2.

6. Aesthetic resources and techniques to protect and enhance them are closely interrelated; therefore, these three sections should be viewed as complementary rather than exclusive methods for improving a community's appearance. Moreover, this discussion should be considered in connection with the Historical and Cultural Resources chapter, which together provide a complete overview of the means of protecting and enhancing the built environment.

7. 23 USC 131.

8. Ruth Norris, "Billboard Blight," *Outdoor America* (Summer 1986): 24.

9. Off-premise signs are frequently referred to as "billboards," even though a billboard may actually be an on-premise sign. For simplicity, we use the term "billboard" to mean off-premise advertising sign.

10. Sign control statistics in this section are from Coalition for Scenic Beauty, *Sign Control News* 4, nos. 3 and 4 (1987).

11. See *Donrey Communications Co. v. City of Fayetteville*, 660 S.W. 2d 900 (Ark 1983); *R.O. Givens, Inc. v. Town of Nags Head*, 58 N.C. App 697 (1982); *Major Media of the Southeast, Inv. v. City of Raleigh*, 792 F.2d 1269 (1986).

12. Duerksen, op. cit., p. 31.

13. Memorandum of Federal Highway Administration from Edward V. A. Kussy, Assistant Chief Counsel, to G. B. Saunders, Chief of Real Estate Division, dated May 12, 1987, re Colorado Outdoor Advertising Control, Denver sign ordinance and 23 USC 131(g); memorandum of Federal Highway Administration from Joseph M. O'Connor, Associate Administrator for Right-of-Way and Environment, to Louis N. MacDonald, Regional Federal Highway Administrator, dated July 6, 1987, re Colorado Outdoor Advertising Control, Denver Sign Ordinance and 23 USC 131(g); letter from Anthony J. McMahon, Chief Counsel, Federal Highway Administration, to Gilbert D. Douglas, Assistant City Attorney, City of Houston, dated April 15, 1986; and letter from Secretary of Transportation Jim Burnley to the Honorable James J. Howard, Chairman, House Committee on Public Works and Transportation, dated November 13, 1987. These correspondence are on file at The Conservation Foundation or are available from the Federal Highway Administration; (202) 366–2026.

14. *State of South Dakota v. Volpe*, 353 F. Supp. 335 (D.S.D. 1973).

15. Ruth Norris, op. cit., p. 24.

16. See Southern Environmental Law Center, *Visual Pollution and Sign Control: A Legend Handbook on Billboard Reform*, p. 21; Coalition for Scenic Beauty: Fact Sheet on Model Ordinance Provisions. Both organizations are referred to at the end of the chapter.

17. Charles F. Floyd, "Requiem for the Highway Beautification Act," *Journal of the American Planning Association* 48, no. 4 (Autumn 1982): 441.

18. Hawaii's action dates back to 1911, when a citizens' organization—Outdoor Circle—organized both a campaign to ban billboards and a boycott of billboard-advertised products. Outdoor Circle was successful in its war of attrition and acquired the only remaining billboard company in 1927.

19. Vt. Stat. Ann. Sections 481-505 (1985).

20. Southern Environmental Law Center, op. cit., p. 9.

21. Wash. Rev. Code Ann. Section 47.42 (1986).

22. Southern Environmental Law Center, op. cit., p. 10.

23. Oregon Stat., Sections 377.700–377.844, 377.992 (1983).

24. Southern Environmental Law Center, op. cit., p. 10.

25. Southern Environmental Law Center, op. cit., p. 11.

26. Duerksen, op. cit., pp. 27–28.

27. See *City of Lake Wales v. Lamar Advertising*, 414 So.2d 1030 (Fla. 1982).

28. Duerksen, op. cit., p. 32.

29. Jerry Jones, "Scottsdale's Five-Foot Height Limit," *Planning* (July 1985): 26–27.

30. R. Bruce Laidlaw, "Ann Arbor's 20-Year-Old Ordinance," *Planning* (July 1985): 28.

31. *American Outdoors: The Report of the President's Commission* (Washington, D.C.: Island Press, 1987), 163.

32. *Scenic Byways 88*, published by the Federal Highway Administration, contains state-by-state program descriptions. California, Tennessee, and Virginia have leading state scenic highway designation programs.

33. Connecticut General Statutes, Section 7-149a.

34. President's Commission, op. cit., p. 165.

35. Conservation easements are discussed in Appendix A.

36. This tool is discussed in chapter 3. For an excellent exposition of creative clustered development options, see Robert D. Yarro et al., *Dealing with Change in the Connecticut River Valley: A Design Manual for Conservation and Development* (Amherst, MA: Center for Rural Massachusetts, University of Massachusetts, 1988).

37. See John E. Rahenkamp, and William G. Hengst, "Road Corridor Overlay Zoning for Roadside Enhancement," *Urban Land* (May 1988): 11–15.

38. Duerksen, op. cit., pp. 21–22.

39. Personal communication, Steve Maki, Monterey County Planning Department, Coastal Planning Team, December 22, 1988.

40. Duerksen, op. cit., pp. 19–21.

41. Sherry Kafka Wagner, "Creating Your City's Image," Design and Development Technical Bulletin No. 4 (Washington, D.C.: National League of Cities, 1982).

42. Quoted in James E. Betran, and James D. Mertes, "Urban Design Process, Goals, Implementation—The Lubbock Experience," paper presented at 1982 annual meeting of the American Planning Association in Dallas, Texas, May 9, 1982, p. 6.

43. Robert Campbell, quoted in Zotti, Edward: "Design by Committee," *Planning* (May 1987): 23.

44. Duerksen, op. cit., pp. 6–7, quoting Norman Williams, *American Land Planning Law*, 3.31 Sec. A.07.

45. See Peggy Glassford, *Appearance Codes for Small Com*

munities. Planners Advisory Service Report No. 379 (Chicago: American Planning Association, 1983).

46. Duerksen, op. cit., p. 14.

47. "Making Cities Beautiful Again," *Southern Living* (May 1985): 160.

48. Duerksen, op. cit., p. 25. See also Robert Coughlin et al., *Private Trees and Public Interest Programs for Protecting and Planting Trees in Metropolitan Areas.* Research Report 10. (Philadelphia: University of Pennsylvania, Department of City and Regional Planning, 1984).

49. Duerksen, op. cit.

50. Coalition for Scenic Beauty, *Sign Control News* (June–July 1987): 1.

51. *Landmark Land Company, Inc. v. City and County of Denver,* 728 P.2d 1281 (1986); but for the more restrictive, minority approach see *Corrigan v. City of Scottsdale,* 720 P.2d 528 (Ariz. App. 1986), *affirmed in part, reversed in part,* 720 P.2d 513 (Ariz. 1986) (striking down hillside protection ordinance).

52. See *Village of Hudson v. Albrecht, Inc.,* 458 N.E. 2d, 852 (1984) and *Morristown Road Assoc. v. Bernardsville,* 103 N.J. Super. 58, 394 A. 2d 157 (1978).

53. *Major Media of the Southeast, Inc. v. City of Raleigh,* 621 F. Supp. 1446, 1451 (E.D.N.C. 1985), *affirmed* 792 F.2d 1269 (1986). See also *Ghaster Properties, Inc. v. Preston,* 200 N.E. 2d 328 (Ohio 1964).

54. Federal Highway Administration, *Safety and Environmental Design Considerations in the Use of Commercial Electronic Variable Message Signing,* FHWA/RD 80/51, June 1980.

55. Many communities have found that local businesses do not rely significantly on outdoor advertising. A recent survey reported that over one-half of the billboard industry's revenue in 1983 came from advertisements for tobacco (37 percent) and alcoholic beverages (15 percent). James Peters, "Signs of Success" *Planning* (July 1985): 25.

56. Bill Robinson, "Group Posts Guidelines on Billboards," *The State.* Columbia, South Carolina, July 23, 1988.

57. *City Council of the City of Los Angeles v. Taxpayers for Vincent,* 466 U.S. 789, 104 S.Ct. 2188 (1984).

58. Id., at 2130.

59. This was the specific holding in *City Council of the City of Los Angeles v. Taxpayers for Vincent,* 466 U.S. 789, 104 S.Ct 2188 (1984), discussed earlier in this chapter.

60. See, for example, *Metromedia, Inc. v. City of San Diego,* 453 U.S. 490 (1981).

61. *Major Media of the Southeast, Inc. v. City of Raleigh,* 792 F.2d 1269 (1986).

62. Southern Environmental Law Center, op. cit., p. 25.

63. These factors are discussed earlier in this chapter.

64. See, for example, *Matthews v. Town of Needham,* 764 F.2d 58 (1st Cir. 1985); *Meros v. City of Euclid,* 594 F.Supp. 259 (N.D. Ohio 1984); *State v. Miller,* 416 A.2d 821 (N.J. 1980).

Chapter 5

1. *The Open Space Imperative: Greenspaces and Greenways* (New York: Regional Plan Association, 1987), p. 3.

2. *The Report of the President's Commission on Americans Outdoors: The Legacy, The Challenge* (Washington, D.C.: Island Press, 1987), 133.

3. Id., p. 142.

4. *Nollan v. California Coastal Commission,* 107 S.Ct. 3141 (1987), a recent U.S. Supreme Court decision limiting the local ability to require dedications in certain circumstances.

5. *Converting Rails to Trails* (Washington, D.C.: Rails-to-Trails Conservancy, 1987), iii.

6. Charles Thurow, et al., *Performance Controls for Sensitive Lands: A Practical Guide for Local Administrators,* Planning Advisory Service Report Nos. 307, 308 (Chicago, IL: American Society of Planning Officials, 1975), 59.

7. The National Arbor Day Foundation, 100 Arbor Avenue, Nebraska City, NE 68410, administers a program called Tree City USA that assists localities in developing woodland protection programs.

8. Carol E. Youell, "Municipal Regulation of Timber Harvesting—The Connecticut Experience." Paper presented at the New England Society of American Foresters, 64th Annual Winter Meeting, March 8, 1984, Worcester, Massachusetts.

9. Thurow et al., op. cit., p. 63.

10. Lawrence S. Earley, "Before the Bulldozers," *Wildlife in North Carolina* (April 1988): 12–15.

11. Thurow et al., op. cit., p. 73.

12. *Sellon v. City of Manitou Springs,* 745 P.2d 229 (Colo. 1987).

13. Thurow et al., op. cit., p. 73.

14. Ibid., p. 75.

15. Andree Brooks, "Soil-Based Zoning Is Taking Hold," *The New York Times*, December 12, 1982.

16. See Paul Danish, "Boulder's Self-Examination," in *Growth Management: Keeping on Target?* ed. Douglas R. Porter (Washington, D.C.: Urban Land Institute/Lincoln Institute of Land Policy, 1986), 26.

17. Exceptions to this rule are that courts frequently uphold regulations that prohibit any development of wetlands and floodways, or that permit only agricultural uses so long as agriculture is feasible on the parcel. Courts also generally uphold regulations requiring undeveloped buffer strips along, for example, streams or scenic roadways, so long as the buffer does not prevent development of entire parcels.

18. *Nollan v. California Coastal Commission*, 107 S.Ct. 3141 (1987).

19. These statutes vary from state to state. For more information, see James C. Kozlowski, "A 'Cut and Paste' of Model Rec. Use Law to Include Public," *Parks and Recreation* (March 1987); and "President's Commission Examines Public Recreation on Private Lands," *Parks and Recreation* (June 1986).

Chapter 6

1. See Barbara H. Davis, "How and Why to Hire a Consultant," in the Grantsmanship Center: *Whole Nonprofit Catalog* (Winter 1987–88): 7–9.

2. See Gil Efraim et al., *Working with Consultants*, Report No. 378, (Chicago, IL: American Planning Association Planning Advisory Service): 10–12.

3. Joan Wolfe, *Making Things Happen: The Guide for Members of Volunteer Organizations* (Andover, MA: Brick House Publishing Company, 1981).

4. Information about this organization and other sources of information on foundations are listed in the Information Resources section of this chapter.

Chapter 7

1. Herbert H. Smith, *Citizens Guide to Planning* (Chicago: American Planning Association, 1979), 11.

2. Oregon Revised Statutes Section 197.225.

3. Jeffrey H. Leonard, *Managing Oregon's Growth: The Politics of Development Planning* (Washington, D.C.: The Conservation Foundation, 1983).

4. 10 V.S.A., Chapter 151.

5. John M. DeGrove, and Nancy E. Stroud, "State Land Planning and Regulation: Innovative Roles in the 1980s and Beyond," *Land Use Law and Zoning Digest* (March 1987): 3.

6. *Id.*, p. 7. For a thorough description and analysis of Florida's 1985 growth management legislation, see Hopping, Boyd, Green and Sams, *Florida's 1985 Growth Management Legislation—A Summary and Analysis.* Available from Hopping, Boyd, Green and Sams, Suite 420, Lewis State Bank Building, Tallahassee, Florida 32314.

7. "Successful Communities," June 1988 conference.

Appendix A

1. Brower, David J., Candace Carraway, Thomas Pollard, and Luther C. Propst. *Managing Development in Small Towns.* Chicago: American Planning Association Press, 1984: 1–2.

2. American Planning Association, Planning Policies, APA Action Agenda, APA News (in *Planning*), 24B (July 1979); quoted in Donald G. Hagman, and Julian C. Juergensmeyer. *Urban Planning and Land Development Control Law*, 2d ed. (St. Paul: West Publishing Company, 1986): 25.

3. Although professional planners define "planning" to include steps to implement plans, the means by which local governments can manage growth are broader than what many people think of as planning. Therefore, the term "growth management" is used to describe the process and techniques available to influence the characteristics of community growth.

Appendix B

1. Section 1031 of the tax code provides that in certain situations, a landowner may defer taxation "on the exchange of property held for productive use in a trade or business or for investment if such property is exchanged solely for property of like kind which is to be held either for productive use in a trade or business or for investment."

Index

About the Authors

Michael A. Mantell is the general counsel of World Wildlife Fund and The Conservation Foundation, where he oversees legal and congressional affairs for the two affiliated organizations. He directed the Successful Communities Program and the Land, Heritage and Wildlife Program of the foundation in Washington, D.C., and managed its State of the Environment and National Parks Projects. A principal author of *National Parks for a New Generation* and *A Handbook on Historic Preservation Law*, he has also been involved in foundation work on wetland and floodplain protection, industrial siting, and environmental dispute resolution. Before joining the foundation in 1979, he was with the city attorney's office in Los Angeles, where he worked on various environmental matters. Michael Mantell is a graduate of the University of California at Berkeley and Lewis and Clark College Law School, and serves as chairman of an American Bar Association Subcommittee on Federal Land-Use Policy.

Stephen F. Harper is a Washington-based environmental policy and planning consultant and writer. He formerly directed the Nonprofit Organization Assistance Program of the California State Coastal Conservancy and served as assistant director of the American Farmland Trust. He has also served in staff capacities with the U.S. Environmental Protection Agency, the Colorado State Legislative Council, and in several state agencies in New Jersey. He authored *The Nonprofit Primer*, a guidebook to management of citizen conservation organizations, published by the California State Coastal Conservancy. Stephen F. Harper has a master's in public affairs from Princeton University's Woodrow Wilson School of Public and International Affairs, a B.A. from the University of Colorado, and has completed additional graduate planning studies at the University of Pennsylvania.

Luther Propst is the field director for The Conservation Foundation's Successful Communities Program in Washington, D.C., where he oversees the delivery of technical assistance in land use matters to communities nationwide. Before joining The Conservation Foundation, he was an attorney in the Land Use Group with the Hartford, Connecticut, law firm of Robinson & Cole, where he represented governments, developers, and local environmental organizations in land use matters. Luther Propst received his law degree and master's of regional planning from the University of North Carolina at Chapel Hill. He co-authored *Managing Development in Small Towns*, published in 1984 by the American Planning Association, and has taught land use law as an adjunct professor at the Western New England College School of Law.

Henry R. Richmond
1,000 Friends of Oregon
Portland, Oregon

Richard J. Roddewig
Clarion Associates
Chicago, Illinois

James W. Rouse
The Enterprise Foundation
Columbia, Maryland

Joseph L. Sax
University of California
Berkeley, California

Susan E. Sechler
The Aspen Institute
Washington, D.C.

William H. Whyte
Street Life Project
New York, New York

Also Available from Island Press

Americans Outdoors: The Report of the President's Commission: The Legacy, The Challenge, with case studies
Foreword by William K. Reilly
1987, 426 pp., appendixes, case studies, charts
Paper: $24.95 ISBN 0-933280-36-X

The Challenge of Global Warming
Introduction by Dean Edwin Abrahamson
Introduction by Senator Timothy E. Wirth
In cooperation with the Natural Resources Defense Council
1989, 350 pp., tables, graphs, bibliography, index
Cloth: $34.95 ISBN: 0-933280-87-4
Paper: $19.95 ISBN: 0-933280-86-6

The Complete Guide to Environmental Careers
By The CEIP Fund
1989, 300 pp., photographs, case studies, bibliography, index
Cloth: $24.95 ISBN: 0-933280-85-8
Paper: $14.95 ISBN: 0-933280-84-X

Crossroads: Environmental Priorities for the Future
Edited by Peter Borrelli
1988, 352 pp., index
Cloth: $29.95 ISBN: 0-933280-68-8
Paper: $17.95 ISBN: 0-933280-67-X

Natural Resources for the 21st Century
Edited by R. Neil Sampson and Dwight Hair
In cooperation with the American Forestry Association
1989, 350 pp., index, illustrations
Cloth: $34.95 ISBN: 1-55963-003-5
Paper: $24.95 ISBN: 1-55963-002-7

The Poisoned Well: New Strategies for Groundwater Protection
By the Sierra Club Legal Defense Fund

1989, 400 pp., glossary, charts, appendixes, bibliography, index
Cloth: $31.95 ISBN: 0-933280-56-4
Paper: $19.95 ISBN: 0-933280-55-6

Reopening the Western Frontier
Edited by Ed Marston
From *High Country News*
1989, 350 pp., illustrations, photographs, maps, index
Cloth: $24.95 ISBN: 1-55963-011-6
Paper: $15.95 ISBN: 1-55963-010-8

Resource Guide for Creating Successful Communities
By Michael A. Mantell, Stephen F. Harper, and Luther Propst
In cooperation with The Conservation Foundation
1989, approximately 300 pp., charts, graphs, illustrations
Paper: $19.95 ISBN: 1-55963-015-9
Cloth: $34.95 ISBN: 1-55963-031-0

Rush to Burn
From *Newsday*
Winner of the Worth Bingham Award
1989, 276 pp., illustrations, photographs, graphs, index
Cloth: $29.95 ISBN: 1-55963-001-9
Paper: $14.95 ISBN: 1-55963-000-0

Shading Our Cities: Resource Guide for Urban and Community Forests
Edited by Gary Moll and Sara Ebenreck
In cooperation with the American Forestry Association
1989, 350 pp. illustrations, photographs, appendixes, index
Cloth: $34.95 ISBN 0-933280-96-3
Paper: $19.95 ISBN: 0-933280-95-5

War on Waste: Can America Win Its Battle with Garbage?
By Louis Blumberg and Robert Gottlieb
1989, 325 pp., charts, graphs, index
Cloth: $34.95 ISBN: 0-933280-92-0
Paper: $19.95 ISBN: 0-933280-91-2

Wildlife of the Florida Keys: A Natural History
By James D. Lazell, Jr.
1989, 254 pp., illustrations, photographs, line drawings, maps, index
Cloth: $31.95 ISBN: 0-933280-98-X
Paper: $19.95 ISBN: 0-933280-97-1

These titles are available from Island Press, Box 7, Covelo, CA 95428. Please enclose $2.00 shipping and handling for the first book and $1.00 for each additional book. California and Washington, D.C., residents add 6% sales tax. A catalog of current and forthcoming titles is available free of charge.